Very truly yours
D. Schenck

North Carolina 1780-81

Being a History of the Invasion of the Carolinas by the British Army under Lord Cornwallis in 1780-81

David Schenck, LL.D.

HERITAGE BOOKS
2007

HERITAGE BOOKS
AN IMPRINT OF HERITAGE BOOKS, INC.

Books, CDs, and more—Worldwide

For our listing of thousands of titles see our website
at
www.HeritageBooks.com

A Facsimile Reprint
Published 2007 by
HERITAGE BOOKS, INC.
Publishing Division
65 East Main Street
Westminster, Maryland 21157-5026

Copyright © 1889 David Schenck, LL.D.

— Publisher's Notice —
In reprints such as this, it is often not possible to remove blemishes from the original. We feel the contents of this book warrant its reissue despite these blemishes and hope you will agree and read it with pleasure.

International Standard Book Number: 978-0-7884-1441-1

TO THE MEMORY

OF

BRIGADIER GENERAL JETHRO SUMNER,

THE HERO OF EUTAW SPRINGS,

WHOSE LOFTY COURAGE, WHOSE UNDAUNTED SPIRIT AND
UNSWERVING PATRIOTISM DESERVE THE ADMIRA-
TION OF MANKIND, THIS BOOK IS DEDICATED,
AS THE ONLY MONUMENT WHICH THE
AUTHOR IS ABLE TO RAISE IN
HONOR OF THAT EMI-
NENT SOLDIER.

INTRODUCTION.

The author, who has been, since 1882, a citizen of Greensboro, North Carolina, has frequently visited the spot, where, on Thursday, the 15th day of March, 1781, the battle of Guilford Court-House was fought. It is located five miles north of the city, on the Cape Fear and Yadkin Valley Railroad.

A visit to the battle-field, in the Autumn of 1886, suggested the idea of the formation of "The Guilford Battle Ground Company," which was incorporated by the Legislature of North Carolina, March the 7th, 1887.

The author was elected President of that Company, and in the examination of the different histories of the battle of Guilford Court-House, by Lee, Johnson and some other writers of less reputation, he became convinced that great injustice had been done to the militia of North Carolina, in regard to their conduct on that occasion. Further research confirmed this opinion and led to the conviction that the injustice done to North Carolina was not confined to the events occurring in this battle, but that the State had been robbed of the honor due her for repelling the British invasion in 1780-'81; that the credit of her noble deeds had been ascribed to others; that the citizenship of her heroes had been claimed by other States, and that the truth, in regard to these stirring events, had, either intentionally or by gross negligence, been greatly and wrongfully perverted to the injury of her good name.

The author, therefore, as a dutiful son of North Carolina, determined to write this book in defence of his native State, and in vindication of the honor and patriotism of her people. His work is now submitted to the judgment of public opinion.

In the preparation of this History, the author desires to acknowledge his obligation for assistance to the Honorable William L. Saunders, Secretary of State for North Carolina; to David Hutcheson, Esq., Assistant Librarian of Congress, and J. C. Birdsong, Esq., State Librarian of North Carolina. He is particularly indebted to Colonel Saunders for the very valuable correspondence of Brigadier General Jethro Sumner, which has hitherto been unpublished and inaccessible to the public.

GREENSBORO, N. C., September 20th, 1889.

TABLE OF CONTENTS.

CHAPTER I.

Invasion of Georgia, South and North Carolina, 1780-'81—Its Cruel and Desperate Character—Organization of North Carolina Regulars and Minute Men, 1775-'76—Their Movements—Death of Gen. James Moore—Death of Gen. Francis Nash—Reorganization of the Six Regular Regiments—The North Carolina Militia in South Carolina, 1779—Mr. Pinckney's Complimentary Letter in regard to North Carolina Troops............Page 17.

CHAPTER II.

Condition of the States of Georgia, South and North Carolina in 1779-'80—Siege of Charleston—All the North Carolina Regulars of the Continental Line captured—Patriotism and Public Spirit unabated—Massacre of Buford's Command by Tarleton—Battle of Ramsour's Mill, the 20th June, 1780—Col. William R. Davie—Affair at Hanging Rock—Campaign of McDowell and Shelby, August, 1780—The Deckhard Rifle—Generals Rutherford, Gregory and Butler—Battle near Camden—Gates' Defeat—Splendid Courage of Colonel Dixon's North Carolinians in the Battle—Flight of Gates to Charlotte ....Page 37.

CHAPTER III.

The Scattered Troops and Militia assemble at Charlotte—Colonel W. L. Davidson—General Sumner in Command of the Militia—Letter from Governor Nash—Patriotism of the People—Cornwallis leaves, September 7th, 1780, for North Carolina—Defence of Charlotte by Davie and Graham—Hostile Spirit of the People—Colonel Patrick Ferguson—Movements of the Whig Leaders—Battle of King's Mountain ....Page 99.

CHAPTER IV.

Cornwallis Retreats from Charlotte to Winnsboro—General Morgan joins Gates at Hillsboro—Gates moves from Hillsboro to Charlotte—General Nathanael Greene supersedes Gates December 4th, 1780, at Charlotte—Personal Sketches of Greene and Cornwallis—Greene Moves to "Camp Repose" on the Pee Dee—Morgan sent to the Western Part of the State December 16th—Sketch of General Morgan—Lee's Legion joins Greene—Character of Lee—The North Carolina Riflemen join Morgan 310 Strong—The Fight at Hammonds' Store—Maneuvering of Tarleton and Morgan—Their respective Strength—Tarleton's Character—Battle of Cowpens January the 17th, 1781 __ Page 178.

CHAPTER V.

Morgan's Retreat from Cowpens to the Catawba River—Sends his Prisoners by Island Ford to Virginia—He Crosses the Catawba with his Main Army at Sherrill's Ford January 23d, 1781—Cornwallis reaches Ramsour's Mill the 25th—Destroys all his Heavy Baggage—Greene meets Morgan the 30th at the Catawba; Orders the Army from "Camp Repose" to join Morgan on the Yadkin—Battle at Cowan's Ford February 1st—Death of General William Lee Davidson—Frederick Hager, the Tory, Fires the Fatal Shot—Morgan Crosses the Yadkin at Trading Ford—The two Armies Unite Finally at Guilford Court-House February 10th—General Morgan Disabled by Rheumatism—Greene's Great Confidence in Him—Retreat of Greene into Virginia—Crosses the Dan, February 14th .... Page 226.

CHAPTER VI.

Greene on the Dan—Cornwallis at Hillsboro—General Andrew Pickens, of South Carolina, selected by a Brigade of North Carolina Militia at Shallow Ford, to lead Them—Movements of General Richard Caswell with the Militia in the East—"Council Extraordinary," its Acts—General John Butler's Movements—Major Craig, of the British Army, enters Wilmington January the 29th, 1781—Letter of Governor Abner Nash—Greene Recrosses the Dan February 23d, 1781—Graham's Dash at Hart's Mill—Pyle's Defeat, 25th February, 1781—Affair at Whitsill's Mill, March 6th—Lieutenant Colonel Webster's Marvelous Escape from Death—Reinforcements Reach General Greene at High Rock Ford, on Haw River, Sunday, March the 11th, 1781 ....Page 260.

CHAPTER VII.

North Carolinians with Greene at the Battle of "Guilford Court-House"—Virginians with Him—The Troops constituting His Regular Army—The Number and Character of the Troops under Cornwallis—Description of the Battle-Ground—Description of the Battle—Defence of the North Carolina Militia—Incidents and Anecdotes of the Battle—Results of the Battle in its Effect on the Military History of the Country—Mr. Benton's Review of the Importance of this Battle—The Precursor of Yorktown—The Lesser the Father of the Greater Event.
Page 293.

CHAPTER VIII.

The Retreat of Cornwallis from Guilford Court-House—Pursued by General Greene—Disbandment of the Militia—Colonel James Read's Command from North Carolina Remains with Greene—The Militia who Fled from Guilford Court-House Reorganized as Part of the Continental Line under Major Pinketham Eaton—Battle of Hobkirk's Hill—Fall of the British Outposts—Splendid Courage and Dash of the North Carolinians at Augusta, June 5th, 1781—Death of Major Eaton—Greene Retires to the High Hills of Santee, 16th July, 1781 .. Page 388.

CHAPTER IX.

General Jethro Sumner Raises a Brigade of Continental Troops in 1781—His Correspondence in Regard Thereto—Marches, in July, 1781, to Join General Greene—Colonel John B. Ashe, Major John Armstrong and Major Reading Blount, his Lieutenants—Brigade Numbers 800 Men—North Carolina Militia Join Greene—General Sumter, of South Carolina, Recruits his Brigade in Rowan and Mecklenburg Counties........Page 426.

CHAPTER X.

Battle of Eutaw Springs, Fought the 8th day of September, 1781—The Noble Part borne by North Carolinians in this Battle—Greene Retires to the High Hills of the Santee—Hears of the Fall of Yorktown—The War Virtually Ends .... Page 444.

CHAPTER XI.

Sketches of Charles and Joseph McDowell—Joseph Graham—Major "Hal." Dixon—General Rutherford—General Butler—Brigadier General Jethro Sumner—The End............ Page 463.

ILLUSTRATIONS.

David Schenck	Frontispiece
Major Joseph Graham	opposite page 112
Major Joseph McDowell	opposite page 176
Battle field of Guilford Court-House	386

MAPS.

North and South Carolina	16
Battle of Camden	88
Battle of King's Mountain	164
Battle of Cowpens	210
Battle of Guilford Court-House	320
Battle of Hobkirk's Hill	402
Battle of Eutaw Springs	446

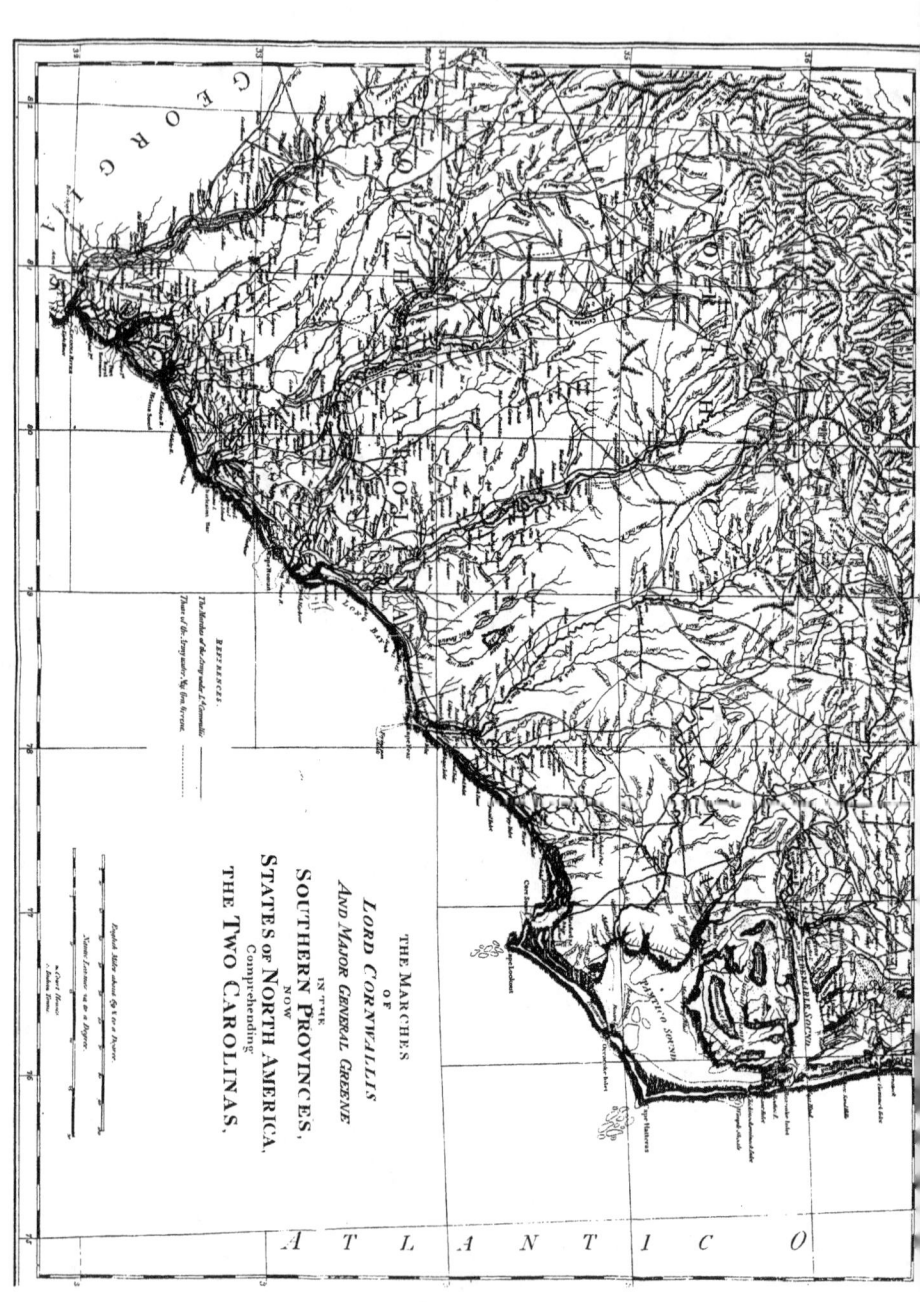

NORTH CAROLINA, 1780-'81.

CHAPTER I.

Invasion of Georgia, South and North Carolina, 1780-'81 – Its Cruel and Desperate Character—Organization of North Carolina Regulars and Minute Men, 1775-'76—Their Movements—Death of Gen. James Moore—Death of Gen. Francis Nash—Reorganization of the Six Regular Regiments—The North Carolina Militia in South Carolina, 1779—Mr. Pinkney's Complimentary Letter in regard to North Carolina Troops.

THE student of history who reads carefully the incidents connected with the invasion of the three Southern States, Georgia, South Carolina and North Carolina, in 1780-'81, will be impressed with the desperation of this last attempt of the British Government to subdue the American colonies.

No respect for morality or humanity was allowed to thwart the purposes of conquest; no rights of property were to be recognized among rebels; no appeals for mercy from the helpless were to be heeded, if destruction could injure the American cause; executions, cruel and remorseless, were to be inflicted on prisoners who dared to love or fight for liberty; the savage Indian was to be incited by English emissaries to lay waste the frontiers and murder its citizens; the brutal slave was offered freedom and licentious indulgence as a reward for treachery to his master and service in the English camp; the rules of civilized warfare were to be disregarded; solemn pledges to the citizens were broken, paroles of prisoners ignored, and every oppression that devilish ingenuity could suggest was to be exercised in order to crush the spirit of the patriots and suppress the so-called rebellion. The marauding bands of the invaders committed acts of vindictiveness that would have made the Duke of Alba blush with shame.

Lord Cornwallis, who affected "amiability" and was bred a soldier, shut his eyes to these atrocities and, by proclamations in violation of his faith, breathed out terror and threats and dismay in advance of his coming; there was to be neither safety for life nor property nor virtue, unless the citizen was an active loyalist, or became an apostate to his principles. The butcheries of Tarleton were lauded as victories, and he was addressed in affectionate terms by his commander and congratulated for his conduct. Cornwallis never assumed to do justice until retaliation convinced him that such deeds as he encouraged could not be practiced with impunity, and that an unrelenting vengeance would dog his advance. It was necessity and apprehension, not justice or mercy, that compelled him to respect human beings whom the fate of war placed in his power.

This bloody and cruel invasion aroused the indignation and stirred the eloquent spirit of the younger Pitt, and, in excited language and with vehement manner, he cried out in the British Commons:

"The noble Lord has called the American war a holy war; I affirm that it is a most accursed war; wicked, barbarous, cruel and unnatural; conceived in injustice, it was brought forth and nurtured in folly; its footsteps are marked with slaughter and devastation, while it meditates destruction to the miserable people who are the devoted objects of the resentments which produced it."

The American army, under Major-General Lincoln, which had been besieged at Charleston, surrendered to Sir Henry Clinton on the 12th day of April, 1780. By the terms of the capitulation the Continental troops and sailors became prisoners of war until exchanged; the militia from the country were to return home on parole and to be secure in their property so long as their parole should be observed. But these terms were set at naught. The Continental troops were confined in the filthy, crowded prison ships, or forced to reside in the most malarious spots on the coast, so that in a few months they were reduced by deaths one-third of their number, and many of those who survived returned, at last, to their homes with their physical constitutions broken down by disease and their health forever gone.

1780. By the proclamation of Lord Cornwallis, issued in June, the prisoners on parole were required to take active part in securing the royal government. "Should they neglect to return to their allegiance," so the proclamation read, "they were to be treated as rebels to the government."

We shall see in the sequel with what sanguinary results this proclamation was enforced; but the blood of the patriots, to use a paraphrase, was the seed of the American cause, and the " burnt houses of its citizens made patriots of them all."

The military strength of North Carolina was greatly reduced by the surrender of General Lincoln's army at Charleston, and but for the unflinching patriotism and devotion to independence which pervaded her people, she too, would soon have become a prostrate State. It will be with a feeling of pride that we shall endeavor to trace the history of her military forces during this eventful period, from the siege of Charleston, its darkest day, to the victory at Eutaw Springs, where her troops constituted so large a portion of the army of General Greene and won for themselves imperishable laurels of victory.

The Legislature of North Carolina, which met at Hillsboro the 21st day of August, 1775, in the dawn of the revolution, passed an act to raise two regiments of Continental troops which had been asked for by Congress.

The following were the officers of these regiments:

First Regiment.

*James Moore, Colonel.
*Francis Nash, Lieutenant Colonel.
Thomas Clark, Major.
William Williams, Adjutant.

*Afterwards Brigadier General.

CAPTAINS.

William Daves,
William Packett,
*Henry Dickson,
Thomas Allen,
Robert Rowan,

George Daudson,
Alfred Moore,
John Walker,
William Greene,
Caleb Grainger.

LIEUTENANTS.

John Lillington,
Hesekiah Rice,
Joshua Bowman,
Hector McNeil,
William Brandon,

William Berryhill,
Lawrence Thompson,
Abraham Tatum,
William Hill,
Thomas Hogg.

SECOND REGIMENT.

†Robert Howe, Colonel.
Alexander Martin, Lieutenant Colonel.
John Patton, Major.
Dr. John White, Captain and Adjutant.

CAPTAINS.

James Blount,
‡John Armstrong,
Charles Crawford,
Hardy Murfree,
Henry Irwin Toole,

Nathan Keais,
Simon Bright,
Michael Payne,
John Walker.

*Known as "Hal" Dickson, afterwards Colonel. General Joseph Graham's Sketches.
†Afterwards Major-General.
‡Afterwards Major and commanding battalion at Eutaw Springs.

LIEUTENANTS.

John Grainger,   Joseph Tate,
Robert Smith,   William Fenner,
John Herritage,   John Williams,
Clement Hall,   James Gee,
Edward Vail, Jr.,   Benjamin Williams.

The Legislature met again the 4th day of April, 1776, at Halifax, when four additional regiments were raised, James Moore and Robert Howe having been made Brigadier Generals. The field officers were as follows:

1st Regiment—Colonel, Francis Nash; Lieutenant Colonel, Thos. Clarke; Major, Wm. Davis.

2d Regiment—Colonel, Alex. Martin; Lieutenant Colonel, John Patton; Major, John White.

3d Regiment—Colonel, Jethro Sumner; Lieutenant Colonel, William Alston; Major, Samuel Lockhart.

4th Regiment—Colonel, Thomas Polk; Lieutenant Colonel, James Thackston; Major, William Davidson.*

5th Regiment—Colonel, Edward Buncombe; Lieutenant Colonel, Henry Irwin; Major, Levi Dawson.

6th Regiment—Colonel, Alexander Lillington; Lieutenant Colonel, William Taylor; Major, Gideon Lamb.

These regiments were known as Regulars. They

*Afterwards Brigadier General and killed at Cowan's Ford.

were enlisted under an act of Congress for the war and were under the control of the general government. The Legislature also raised six battalions known as "Minute Men."

I attach a list of the officers of these troops for reference, as many of them rose to distinction during the revolution.

Officers of the battalions, ordered to be raised, appointed by the House:

EDENTON DISTRICT.—Peter Simon and John Pugh Williams, Captains; Andrew Duke and Thos. Whitmel Pugh, 1st Lieutenants; Nehemiah Long and Joseph Clayton, 2d Lieutenants; Benjamin Baily and Elisha Rhodes, Ensigns; Jerome McLaine, Thomas Grandbury and Kedar Ballard, Captains; Jacob Pollock and John Grandbury, 1st Lieutenants; Whitmel Blount and Zephaniah Burgess, 2d Lieutenants; Wm. Knott, Ensign; Roger Moore, Captain; William Goodman, 1st Lieutenant; Benijah Turner, 2d Lieutenant; Abel Mosslander, Ensign.

HALIFAX DISTRICT.—William Brinkley and *Pinketham Eaton*,* Captains; Isaac Prevat and Jas. Bradley, 1st Lieutenants; Christopher Luckey and Robert Washington, 2d Lieutenants; William Etheridge and Joseph Montford, Ensigns; John Gray and Jacob Turner, Captains; Joseph Clinch and Daniel Jones, 1st Lieutenants; Matthew Wood and Alsop High, 2d Lieutenants; William Linton and Benjamin Morgan, Ensigns.

*Afterwards Major and killed at Augusta, June, 1781.

HILLSBORO DISTRICT.—Philip Taylor and Archibald Lytle,* Captains; John Kenon and Thomas Donoho, 1st Lieutenants; Dempsey Moore and William Thompson, 2d Lieutenants; Solomon Walker and William Lyttle, Ensigns; Jas. Emmet, Captain; William Clements, 1st Lieutenant.

WILMINGTON DISTRICT.—John Ashe, Jr., and John James, Captains; Charles Hollingsworth and Daniel Williams, 1st Lieutenants; Mark McLainy and John McCan, 2d Lieutenants; David Jones and Edward Outlaw, Ensigns; Griffith John McKee, Captain; Francis Child, 1st Lieutenant.

NEWBERN DISTRICT.—Simon Alderson and John Enloe, Captains; William Groves and Geo. Suggs, 1st Lieutenants; John Custin and Henry Cannon, 2d Lieutenants; James McKenny and Shadrack Wooten, Ensigns; William Cassel and *Reading Blount*,† Captains; Henry Darnell and Benjamin Coleman, 1st Lieutenants; John Sitgreaves and John Allen, 2d Lieutenants; John Bush and Thomas Blount, Ensigns; Benjamin Stedman, Captain; Robert Turner, 1st Lieutenant; John Eborn, 2d Lieutenant; Charles Stewart, Ensign.

SALISBURY DISTRICT—Robert Smith and William Temple Cole, Captains; William Brownfield and James Carr, 1st Lieutenants; William Caldwell and David Craig, 2d Lieutenants; Thomas McLure and Joseph Patton, Ensigns; Thomas Haines and Jesse Saunders, Captains; Thomas Pickett and William Clover, 1st Lieutenants; John

---

*Afterwards Colonel in the Continental line.
†Commanded battalion of Regulars at Eutaw Springs.

Madaris and Pleasant Henderson, 2d Lieutenants; John Morpis and Thomas Grant, Ensigns; William Ward, Captain; Christopher Gooding, 2d Lieutenant; John Whitley, 1st Lieutenant; Richard Singletary, Ensign; Willis Pope, 2d Lieutenant; John Hopson, Ensign; George Mitchell and Austin Council, Captains; Amos Love and Thomas White, 1st Lieutenants; Benjamin Pike and Thomas Armstrong, 2d Lieutenants; Reuben Grant and Denny Poterfeild, Ensigns; James Farr, 2d Lieutenant; James Coots, Ensign; Joseph Phillips and John Nelson, Captains; James Shepperd and William Dent, Jr., 1st Lieutenants; Micajah Lewis and James Starrat, 2d Lieutenants; William Meredith and Alex. Nelson, Ensigns; *John Baptiste Ashe,*[*] Captain; George Dougherty, 1st Lieutenant; Andrew Armstrong, 2d Lieutenant; Joshua Hadley, Ensign; James Cook, Captain; Adam Hampton, 1st Lieutenant; John Walker, 2d Lieutenant; Adam McFadden, Ensign.

LIGHT HORSE.

1st Company—John Dickerson, Captain; Samuel Ashe, Jr., Lieutenant; Abraham Childers, Cornet.

2d Company—Martin Pfifer, Captain; James Sumner, Lieutenant; Valentine Beard, Cornet.

3d Company—James Jones, Captain; Cosimo Madacy, Lieutenant; James Armstrong, Cornet.

The first two regiments of Regulars seem to have

[*] Commanded battalion of Regulars at Eutaw Springs.

been hurried off to South Carolina to repel the first attack on Charleston in 1776, for in the Life of Iredell, vol. 1, p. 325, we read that the "two battalions of Continental troops from North Carolina, under Cols. James Moore and Alexander Martin, are spoken of as numbering fifteen hundred men." The gallantry of the officers and men is sufficiently attested by Gen. Charles Lee, in a letter to Edmund Pendleton, to whom he writes on the 29th June, 1776, in these words:

"I know not which corps I have the greatest reason to be pleased with, Mughlenbergh's Virginians or the North Carolina troops. They are both equally alert, zealous and spirited."*

Col. James Moore had been promoted, while at Charleston, to the rank of Brigadier General, on account of his gallant and meritorious conduct, but while in that vicinity he contracted some malarial disease which so prostrated him that he returned to the mansion of his brother, Judge Maurice Moore, near Wilmington, to recruit his health. He found his brother also declining rapidly, and in a few days both of these distinguished men were in the pale hands of death, in the same house, and were buried at the same time.

General Moore had given brighter promise of future greatness than any of his cotemporaries in the military service, and his death was grievously and universally lamented.

*Life of Iredell, vol. 1, Appendix.

Col. Francis Nash, of Hillsboro, was promoted to the vacancy caused by General Moore's death, and succeeded immediately to the command of the brigade.

It further appears that in July and August, 1776, the whole six regiments of North Carolina Regulars were concentrated at Wilmington, North Carolina, where they were drilled twice a day and subjected to rigid military discipline until November, when they received orders to march North. They numbered about 4,000 men at that time. On reaching Halifax, North Carolina, they were countermarched to Charleston, South Carolina, to meet the British, who were near St. Augustine, and threatening Georgia. Here they remained until March, 1777.*

On the 15th day of that month, these six regiments were ordered to join General Washington, whose losses in the retreat from New York City, across the State of New Jersey, had reduced his army to 7,000 effective men. The North Carolinians reached his camp, at Middlebrook, New Jersey, in June. Such substantial increase of the army enabled Washington to assume the aggressive once more, and on the 11th day of September, these troops participated in the battle of Brandywine; October the 4th, they were engaged at Germantown; at Monmouth June 20th, 1778, and at Stony Point July 16th, 1779. They were also with

*University Magazine, May, 1855, p. 158.

their commander in the winter of 1777–'78 at Valley Forge.

Brigadier-General Francis Nash, their gallant and patriotic leader, was killed at Germantown. Wheeler, in his Reminiscences, says, "his thigh was shattered by a spent cannon-ball, and the same shot killed his aid, Major Witherspoon, son of Rev. Dr. Witherspoon, President of Princeton College. He was buried at Kulpsville, Montgomery county, Pennsylvania, twenty-six miles from Philadelphia. John F. Watson, Esq., a patriotic citizen, has placed a handsome monument over his grave.*

I find, however, in Moore's History, vol. 1, p. 243, the following account of his death:

"I am assured by my excellent and most sensible friend, Dr. Richard B. Haywood, that he had it from the lips of Col. William Polk, that he (Polk) was also injured in the same battle, and was with General Nash when he died ; they were both shot down by a volley which came from their left and raked their line with terrible effect. This deadly round was the work of the Queen's Yagers. General Nash was shot through the face in such a manner that he lost both his eyes, while Colonel Polk was wounded in the tongue and was unable to speak. He used to repeat a remark of General Nash, that both were thus unfitted for future service and would be useful to each other in the trip home. General Nash

---

NOTE.—This account of Wheeler is very nearly the same as that of Hugh McDonald in University Magazine, vol. 5, 208. McDonald was an illiterate man, a private soldier.

*Wheeler's Reminiscences, p. 332.

died a few days after the battle, but Polk recovered to enjoy future military laurels and the multiplied honors of a long and useful life."

Governor Graham, in his lecture on General Greene, says: "Through the remainder of this year (1777) other troops followed from the State and the nine regiments called for by Congress appear to have all gone forward to this department of the army" under Washington.

McDonald speaks of Hogun's and Ingram's regiments, which he calls the 8th and 9th, reaching camp, and says Colonel Armstrong joined them a few days before the battle of Germantown, fought in June, 1777. The roster,* however, puts Hogun as Colonel of the 7th and Armstrong of the 8th. Ingram was only Lieutenant Colonel of the 8th.

The roster puts John P. Williams as Colonel of the 9th, with William Polk as Major.

As the sources of information in regard to the history of our regular troops, while under Washington, are so extremely meagre, I draw from the McDonald record, as suggestive merely, for I do not give credence to all the stories he relates, and especially do I discredit the very base statement made by him in regard to Colonel Alexander Martin. It is to be regretted that General Wheeler, in his Reminiscences, should quote it without naming the author. The gentleman who furnishes the McDonald journal to the University Magazine has

*See Appendix A.

taken the precaution to state that McDonald was ignorant and uneducated and "had to employ another hand some years afterwards to write down what he related." It seems to have been an effort to relate from memory the events of the war, without having any written data before him, and while it may be correct in the main, its details are hardly to be relied upon.*

It is from this journal we learn of the reorganization of the North Carolina Regulars, and his account seems to be confirmed by subsequent and cotemporaneous events transpiring in regard to those regiments. He informs us that—

"On the 1st of May, 1778, our brigade from North Carolina was inspected and the seven regiments which had been two years in service were discovered to be too small for their officers. The 7th Regiment, commanded by Colonel Armstrong, having joined us a few days before

---

*The statement of McDonald, published in the University Magazine, October, 1856, was, that Colonel Alexander Martin was cashiered for cowardice at the battle of Germantown, and sent home to Hillsboro with a wooden sword.

This is not true. In a letter from Thos. Burke to Cornelius Harnett, dated Philadelphia, November 20th, 1777, he says:

"Colonel Martin has been tried by a court-martial or court of inquiry, I don't know which, on his behavior at Germantown, and *acquitted*."

On the 8th November, he writes again:

"Colonel Martin has been tried and *acquitted* and has since resigned." (See University Magazine, February, 1861.)

The many honorable positions, including that of Governor and Senator, subsequently conferred by the State on Colonel Alexander Martin, shows the confidence and esteem in which he continued to be held by his fellow-citizens in North Carolina.

the battle of Germantown, in which it lost some of its men, all except the two last that joined us* were reduced to three regiments and the surplus officers were discharged and sent home to North Carolina."

The 6th regiment (formerly Lillington's) was put into the 1st (formerly Moore's), under the command of Colonel Thomas Clark, of New Hanover County.

The 4th (formerly Thomas Polk's) was put into the 2d (formerly Robert Howe's), under the command of Colonel John Patton.

The 5th regiment (formerly Edward Buncombe's, who was killed at Germantown) was put into the 3d (formerly Jethro Sumner's), under Colonel Jethro Sumner.

The oldest captain of each regiment that was broken up, was retained in the regiments to which they were attached, with the privilege of selecting the men who should compose their companies from the regiment to which they first belonged.†

Colonel James Hogun was promoted to be the Brigadier General of this brigade.

Governor Graham states that —

"In a letter from Governor Burke, then a delegate in Congress, to Governor Caswell, in January, 1779, he (Burke) justifies his support of Hogun for the appointment of Brigadier General over Colonel Thomas Clark, whom the Legislature recommended, upon the ground of

---

*He seems to allude to Hogun's and Ingram's regiments that he speaks of as the 8th and 9th.
†University Magazine, vol. 5, p. 362.

priority of commission and also that Colonel Hogun had, at Germantown, behaved with distinguished intrepidity and that Colonel Clark had been restrained by superior command which denied him the opportunity to obtain the like distinction."

In the autumn of 1779, the movements of Sir Henry Clinton, who had succeeded Sir William Howe in the command of the British Army, indicated his intention to transfer the seat of war to the South, and General Washington determined to detach the Southern troops under his command to that section of the country for its defence.

The North Carolina Regulars were then under the command of Brigadier General James Hogun, who had been promoted January 9, 1779.[*] In November, 1779, these troops began their tedious march for Charleston, South Carolina, encountering great severity in the weather on their way. When they passed through Philadelphia, as we learn from Governor Graham's lecture, they numbered about 700 men. Recruits had been gathered at Halifax, North Carolina, to reinforce them, but they were never sent forward.

General Hogun reached Charleston the 13th day of March, 1780.

Leaving the North Carolina Regulars at Charleston, it will be necessary to see what the other forces from this State had been doing for the protection and safety of South Carolina.

[*] University Magazine, March, 1878, p. 9, by Gov. Graham.

Major General Lincoln succeeded Major General Howe, of North Carolina, in the command of the Southern forces in December, 1778. General Howe had incurred the displeasure of the Governors of Georgia and South Carolina, whom he had reproached for failing to give him a proper support, and Mr. Christopher Gadsden, of South Carolina, had been impulsive enough to use opprobrious language about General Howe. This provoked a challenge, and on the 13th day of August, 1778, near Charleston, a duel was fought, in which General Howe's bullet grazed Mr. Gadsden's ear. Explanations and a reconciliation followed. Mr. Gadsden fired his pistol in the air.

Early in 1779 the British General Prevost marched to Savannah, and Colonel Campbell took possession of Augusta.

An earnest appeal was made to Governor Caswell, of North Carolina, for assistance, and he was offered a major general's commission in the Continental line and a position as second in command to General Lincoln. Governor Lowndes, of South Carolina, seconded this appeal in frequent letters, but Governor Caswell, after deliberation, thought proper to decline the honor. He, however, called out three thousand militia and conferred the command on Major General John Ashe, of New Hanover. The troops were from Wilmington, Newbern, Edenton and Halifax districts. The State had no arms, and sent the militia forward to South Carolina on the promise of that State to equip them; but so scarce were arms that only the most inferior patterns could be furnished. The danger was imminent, and the militia were hurried forward without discipline or training, against the remonstrances of General Ashe, and a large body of them were surprised and defeated at Briar Creek, in Georgia, March 3d, 1779, and, as their "tour" of three months was nearly at an end, most of them returned home.

General Ashe demanded an investigation, and, though the court-martial "acquitted him of any imputation on his personal honor or courage, he received censure for want of sufficient vigilance," which saddened the evening of this good man's life. His patriotic and brave spirit, which had in all times of trial and danger defied the enemies of his country, could not endure the unmerited censure of his friends; the wound rankled in his heart, and he retired from military service to seek the solace of his home. He was, however, compelled to live in seclusion, as the British were then in possession of Wilmington. Shortly after his return his place of retreat was divulged by his body servant, a negro, and a force of the enemy were detailed for his capture. In the attempt to escape General Ashe was wounded in the leg and taken prisoner. He was then thrust into prison where he contracted small-pox and on this account was paroled. But in October, 1781, he sank under his accumulated sufferings, and died at the house of a friend in Sampson County. No braver, better or purer man ever served his

State, and his sad fate only endeared his memory the more to those who knew and loved him.

1779. "A second contingent of militia, under General Rutherford, of the Salisbury District, and General John Butler, of the Guilford District, accompanied by the recent levies of North Carolina troops of Lytle's and Armstrong's regiments, entered South Carolina in the early spring, and participated in the battle of Stono in June, and the militia returned after their tour of five months expired."*

On the 24th day of February, 1779, Charles Pinckney writes to his aunt, Mrs. Pinckney:

"As to further aid from North Carolina, they have agreed to send us 2,000 more troops immediately. We now have upwards of 3,000 of their men with us, and I esteem this last augmentation as the highest possible mark of their affection for us and as the most convincing proof of their zeal for the glorious cause in which they are engaged. They have been so willing and ready on all occasions to afford us all the assistance in their power that I shall ever love a North Carolinian, and join with General Moultrie in confessing that they have been the salvation of this country."†

As late as the 6th of April, 1780, Colonel Harrington, of North Carolina, with Colonel Woodford's Virginia troops, entered the city of Charleston.

*Documentary History of the American Revolution, p. 106.
†Governor Graham's Lecture, University Magazine, April, 1878.

It is almost impossible, among the shifting scenes of that day, when the militia were going and coming every few months, to locate the commanders and their troops, and trace their services in the camp; we can only catch glimpses of these gallant men now and then through the shadowy lights of history, and leave conjecture to fill the spaces in their career.

CHAPTER II.

Condition of the States of Georgia, South and North Carolina in 1779-'80—Siege of Charleston—All the North Carolina Regulars of the Continental Line captured—Patriotism and Public Spirit unabated—Massacre of Buford's Command by Tarleton—Battle of Ramsour's Mill, the 20th June, 1780—Col. William R. Davie—Affair at Hanging Rock—Campaign of McDowell and Shelby, August, 1780—The Deckhard Rifle—Generals Rutherford, Gregory and Butler—Battle near Camden—Gates' Defeat—Splendid Courage of Colonel Dixon's North Carolinians in the Battle—Flight of Gates to Charlotte.

THE lamentable condition of the States of Georgia and South Carolina in the winter of 1779-'80 is thus graphically described by Bancroft:

"Before the end of three months after the capture of Savannah, all the property, real and personal, of the rebels in Georgia was disposed of. For further gains, Indians were encouraged to bring in slaves wherever they could find them. All families in South Carolina were subjected to the visits of successive sets of banditti, who received commissions, as volunteers, with no pay or emolument but that derived from rapine, and who, roaming about at pleasure, robbed the plantations alike of patriots and loyalists.

"The property of the greatest part of the inhabitants of South Carolina was confiscated, families were divided, patriots outlawed and savagely assassinated, houses burned, and women and children driven shelterless into the forest; districts so desolated that they seemed the abode only of orphans and widows."

Major General Lincoln, with less than two thousand effective men, occupied the city of Charleston, and determined to defend it to the last. He took no counsel from his officers, and learned no wisdom from past experience. The only army of the Continental Government in the South was to be annihilated at one fell blow, when it should have retreated, and, by maneuvering in front of the superior enemy, at least have maintained a show of resistance and afforded a nucleus around which the numerous partisan bands of Whigs might have rallied, and, when opportunity offered, strike a blow for freedom.

Sir Henry Clinton, who was then in command of the royal army, resolved to renew the attack on Charleston, and, to prevent a repetition of the disaster of 1776, he determined to command the expedition in person. On the 26th day of December, 1779, he sailed with a numerous fleet from New York, on which was embarked eight thousand five hundred soldiers. They encountered severe storms on the way, nearly all the horses perished, vessels laden with ordnance went down, others were separated entirely from the fleet, and many of the transports were captured by American privateers. It was nearly the end of January, 1780, before most of the ships reached Tybee, the place of rendezvous in Georgia. The expedition was so crippled that Clinton immediately ordered Lord Rawdon's brigade of three thousand men, then in New York, to join him.

Charleston was at that time a city of fifteen thousand inhabitants all told, but was wealthy, and among its leaders were representatives of large British interests. The country around the city was flat and three sides of the city lay upon the water. An enemy who commanded the sea could easily invest it by throwing up its works across the narrow entrance of land which lay between the Ashley and Cooper rivers. There were no forts nor ramparts for its defence, and General Lincoln could rely only on the temporary field works which he was able to construct.

This was the situation, when on the 26th day of February, 1780, the British forces first came in sight of the city. On the 27th, the officers of the Continental squadron reported to General Lincoln that they were unable to prevent the entrance of the British fleet. "It was then that the attempt to defend the city should have been abandoned," said Washington. Clinton moved with caution to the attack, leaving nothing to chance, and it was not until the 9th day of April that "Arbuthnot, taking advantage of a gentle east wind, brought his ships into the harbor without suffering from Fort Moultrie or returning the fire."*

On the 10th, the city was summoned to surrender, but Lincoln replied, "From duty and inclination, I shall support the town to the last extremity."

There was yet time for the American army to escape, but Lincoln procrastinated from day to day

*Bancroft, vol. 5, p. 377.

until the British had completed the investment of the city, and nothing was left but to fight "to the last extremity" or to surrender on humiliating terms to the enemy.

"On the 13th of April, Lincoln for the first time called a council of war and suggested an evacuation. The officers replied, 'We should not lose an hour in getting the Continental troops over Cooper river, for on their safety depends the salvation of the State.'"

Lincoln, however, dismissed the council without action, and this procrastination and "slowness of perception and will" cost the Colonies the army which they had, with so many sacrifices, collected to oppose this formidable invasion. The usual steps of progress in the siege took place, the British continued to advance their works, and Lincoln made but a feeble resistance.

There was only one sortie made by the besieged. This was on the 24th day of April, and was conducted by Lieutenant Colonel Henderson.* He led out three hundred men and attacked the advanced working party of the British, killed several and captured eleven prisoners. In this affair Capt. Moultrie, of the South Carolina line, was

---

*This attacking party numbered 300 men, and was composed of detachments from Hogun's North Carolinians, Woodford's Virginians, and Scott's brigade, and 21 South Carolina Continentals. *Gibbs Doc. His.* (*1857*), *p. 133*. The leader was Colonel William Henderson, of the South Carolina Continental troops, who afterwards commanded Sumter's brigade at Eutaw. He was formerly from Granville County, N. C., brother of Major Pleasant Henderson. *See Pleasant Henderson's petition for pension under act of 1832.*

killed.* On the 26th of April the British flag was seen floating over Fort Moultrie, and the garrison became disheartened. A council of war was called and negotiations opened between Clinton and Lincoln, but the terms of surrender offered by the former were rejected. On the 11th of May, however, the " British had crossed the wet ditch by sap and advanced within twenty-five yards of the lines of the besieged." Lincoln was now pressed on all sides by his friends to surrender and save the unnecessary effusion of blood, and under the circumstances he assented to the terms of Clinton without conference or explanation. Mr. Bancroft says, " This was the first instance in the American war of an attempt to defend a town, and the unsuccessful event, with its consequences, makes it probable that if this method had been generally adopted the independence of America could not have been so easily supported."†

The defence of Charleston was disapproved by General Washington, who urged that the army should keep the open country where it could be free to attack or retreat as circumstances dictated and he pointed out the danger of risking both the army and the city on the result of a siege where the Americans could be greatly outnumbered by concentrating the British forces on that point.

The British commander, in order to magnify his victory, claimed to have captured five thousand prisoners, swelling the number by the civilians

*Ramsay's South Carolina, p. 186.   †Bancroft, vol. 5, p, 187.

whom he put on the list; but the real number of Continental soldiers who surrendered was only 1,977, and 500 of these were, at that time, lying in the hospitals prostrated by the dreadful malaria of the coast.* More than 1,000 of these Continental soldiers were the North Carolina regulars, who were detached from the army of Washington, and their recruits. They were composed of the three regiments "compressed" from the original six which marched from Wilmington, North Carolina, and the two other regiments who joined Washington later. General Hogun commanded these troops—all veterans. In addition to the regulars, there were over 1,000 North Carolina militia at the fall of Charleston; so that, by this great blunder of General Lincoln, North Carolina lost her whole force of Continental soldiers, leaving not even one regiment in which the stragglers might be collected. Colonel Clarke, of New Hanover, and Colonel Patton, commanded two of these regiments of regulars.

    I regret that my most diligent inquiry has failed to discover any future record of General Hogun. That he was a brave and skillful officer his rapid promotion proves, and to this is added the positive testimony of Governor Burke who effected his promotion over his seniors in office. His family name exists now in Alabama and these persons trace their genealogy to North Carolina. It is more than probable, if not certain, that General Hogun died in captivity, as did hundreds of others of these brave men.

*Ramsey's History of South Carolina, p. 188.

The loss of these troops was a terrible blow to North Carolina, but it did not destroy her spirit nor lessen her determination to be free. She called on her militia to rally to her standard and put forth every effort to stay the progress of the invader. We shall see how nobly and courageously the people responded to the call.

By the terms of the capitulation, the militia from the country were to return home as prisoners of war, on parole, and to be secure in their property so long as their parole was observed. Many of the officers and troops were confined in prison ships reeking with filth and the germs of disease while others were sent to unhealthy locations on the coast during the sickly summer of 1780. One-third of their number perished from disease while others were so prostrated as to be unfitted for military duty. Following the trace of these gallant men, we find that on the 11th day of March, 1781, in the midst of the most thrilling events in North Carolina, General Greene renewed negotiations with Lord Cornwallis for the exchange of prisoners.

"The negotiation was first commenced whilst the American army lay at Halifax Old Court House (Virginia), but was then broken off because the British commissioner insisted on considering paroled privates as prisoners of war, to favor their practice of exacting paroles of all the militia in the country. The negotiation was renewed and finally adjusted by Colonel Carrington, on the American side, and Captain Frederick

Cornwallis, on that of the British, at a subsequent meeting, held on the Pee Dee on the 8th May, 1781."*

The American prisoners were shipped to Jamestown, Virginia, where they were exchanged, June 22d, 1781,† and soon thereafter history records their services again in various military capacities in the South.

What followed the fall of Charleston is so graphically described by Mr. Bancroft, that I quote it entire :

"For six weeks all opposition ceased in South Carolina. One expedition was sent by Clinton up the Savannah to encourage the loyal and reduce the disaffected in the neighborhood of Augusta; another proceeded for the like purpose to the district of Ninety-Six, where Williamson surrendered his post and accepted British protection. Pickens was reduced to inactivity. Alone of the leaders of the patriot militia, Colonel James Williams‡ escaped pursuit and preserved his freedom of action. A third and large party under Cornwallis moved across the Santee towards Camden.

"The rear of the old Virginia line, commanded by Colonel Buford, arriving too late to reinforce the garrison of Charleston, had retreated toward the northeast of the State.

"They were pursued, and on the twenty-ninth of May were overtaken by Tarleton with seven hundred calvary

---

*Johnson's Life of Greene, vol. 1, p. 470.
†Wheeler's Reminiscences, p. 399, and Wheeler's History, vol. 2, p. 281.
‡Formerly of Granville County, North Carolina, and afterwards killed at King's Mountain.

and mounted infantry. Buford himself, and a few who were mounted, and about a hundred of the infantry, saved themselves by flight. The rest, making no resistance, vainly sued for quarter. None was granted.*

" A hundred and thirteen were killed on the spot ; a hundred and fifty were too badly hacked to be moved ; fifty-three only could be brought into Camden as prisoners. The tidings of this massacre, borne through the Southern forests, excited horror and anger, but Tarleton received from Cornwallis the highest encomiums.

" The capture of Charleston suspended all resistance to the British army.

" The men of Beaufort, of Ninety-Six, and of Camden, capitulated under the promise of security, believing that they were to be treated as neutrals, or as prisoners on parole. The attempt was now made to force the men of Carolina into active service in the British army, and so to become the instrument of their own subjection.

1780. "On the 22d of May, confiscation of property and other punishments were denounced against all who should thereafter oppose the King in arms, or hinder any one from joining his forces.

" On the first of June a proclamation by the commissioners, Clinton and Arbuthnot, offered pardon to the penitent on their immediate return to allegiance; to the loyal, the promise of their former political immunities,

---

*"In this bloody encounter Captain John Stokes, of Guilford County, North Carolina, participated with his company and was horribly mutilated by the brutal troopers of Tarleton. One of his hands was cut off and he was besides badly wounded in many places on his body. He was the brother of Governor Montford Stokes and Judge of the U. S. District Court in North Carolina." Moore's History, vol. 1, p. 264.

including freedom from taxation, except by their own legislature.

"On the 3d of June, Clinton, by a proclamation which he alone signed, cut up British authority in Carolina by the roots. He required all the inhabitants of the province, even those outside of Charleston, 'who were now prisoners on parole,' to take an active part in securing the royal government.

"Should they neglect to return to their allegiance,' so ran the proclamation, 'they will be treated as rebels to the government of the King.' He never reflected that many, who accepted protection from fear or convenience, did so in the expectation of living in a state of neutrality, and that they might say: 'If we must fight, let us fight on the side of our friends, of our countrymen, of America.'

"On the eve of his departure for New York, he reported to Germain: 'The inhabitants from every quarter declare their allegiance to the King, and offer their services in arms. There are few men in South Carolina who are not either our prisoners or in the army with us.'"

So complete was the subjugation of South Carolina, and so hopeless appeared to them the future of that State, that "many fainted at the hard option between submission and ruin." Charles Pinckney, lately President of the South Carolina Senate, classing himself among those who, from the hurry and confusion of the times, had been misled, desired to show every mark of allegiance. Rawlins Lowndes, who but a few months before had been President of the State of South Carolina, excused himself for having reluctantly given way to necessity, and accepted any test to prove that, with the unrestrained dictates of his own mind, he now attached himself to the royal government. Henry Middleton, President of the first American Congress, though still partial to a cause for which he had been so long engaged, promised to do nothing to keep up the spirit of independence, and to demean himself as a faithful subject."*

At the end of June, 1780, Cornwallis reported that all resistance in Georgia and South Carolina had ceased, and that as soon as the harvest was gathered he would march into North Carolina and subdue that State. He little suspected that those who appeared so submissive under duress were then meditating revenge for his indignities, and that common suffering was bringing exiles and patriots into concert of action and that they only waited the magnetic names of such leaders as Marion and Sumter and Clarke to form them into a combined force of relentless foes.

Clinton, on the 5th of June, had sailed for New York, and left Lord Cornwallis in command of his victorious army.

Cornwallis had 5,000 troops in South Carolina and 2,000 in Georgia, and expected to supplement this force with regiments he determined to organize among the loyalists of those States. The inhabitants in the districts were enrolled; the men above forty years were to be held responsible for order and the younger men were held liable to military service.

*Bancroft, vol. 5, pp. 393-'4.

Major Patrick Ferguson was sent into the districts to see that these organizations were made and the lists furnished to the commander. Any one found thereafter in arms against the King was to be sentenced to death for desertion and treason. "Commissions were put into the hands of men void of honor and compassion, and who gathered about them profligate ruffians and roamed through the State indulging in rapine and ready to put patriots to death as outlaws. Cornwallis never regarded a deserter, or any one whom a court-martial sentenced to death, as a subject of mercy. A quartermaster of Tarleton's Legion entered the house of Samuel Wyley, near Camden, and, because he had served as a volunteer in the defence of Charleston, cut him in pieces."

The recitation of the wrongs and oppressions inflicted by this heartless commander upon the people of these prostrate States might be lengthened into a volume of itself. Lord Rawdon, the next in command to Lord Cornwallis, vied with his chief in the burthens and exactions which he put upon the unfortunate and wretched citizens, and boasted of his shame and inhumanity.

Cornwallis established military posts at Georgetown, Beaufort, Charleston and Savannah, on the coast, and at Augusta, Ninety-Six and Camden, in the interior. Camden was the key between the North and the South.

We shall now leave Cornwallis indulging the delusive idea that he had conquered a lasting peace by breaking the strength and spirit of his seemingly helpless victims, and only waiting for the harvest to be gathered that he might find subsistence for the sanguinary hordes which he expected to lead in triumph through the devoted province of North Carolina. He knew her history: that in 1771 her citizens had made armed resistance to extortion and tyranny at the bloody field of Alamance; that the men of Mecklenburg had been the first to hurl defiance at British authority, and he was impatient to visit upon them the power of his wrath.

Mr. Houston, a member of Congress from Georgia, hearing of the oppressive measures inflicted on his people, wrote to Mr. Jay in prophetic language:

"Our misfortunes are, under God, the source of our safety. When they have wrought up the spirit of the people to fury and desperation, they will be driven from the country."

The perilous condition of Charleston had aroused apprehensions over the whole country for the safety of that city and the army which was hemmed in its narrow limits. Washington, understanding the importance of prompt and decisive measures for the rescue of Lincoln, detached from his small army of only ten thousand five hundred men, the Maryland division of 2,000 men, and the Delaware regiment, and put them under marching orders for the Carolinas.

The Baron DeKalb was given the command, but he met with many obstructions in his way. Charleston fell before he had passed through the State of Virginia. He entered North Carolina the 20th June, 1780, and halted at Hillsboro to rest his weary troops.

North Carolina was at this time in poor condition to resist invasion or repel her aggressive enemy. All of her regulars were languishing in British prisons on the sea-coasts; such of her militia as had learned to make war in the recent campaigns of Georgia and South Carolina, and their veteran officers, were fettered with paroles and many of those who returned before Charleston was invested came to their homes with shattered constitutions and enfeebled by the malaria of that unhealthy region.

She had only her militia and a part of her "minute men" to whom she could appeal for aid; and yet, so patriotic was the response to her call, that more men offered their services than could be armed. The State was almost destitute of military equipments.

The Legislature called for 8,000 militia to repel the invasion, and Caswell in the east and Rutherford in the west were soon actively engaged in organizing these forces. "North Carolina made a requisition for arms on Virginia and received them. With a magnanimity which knew nothing of fear, Virginia laid herself bare for the protection of the Carolinas."[*]

[*]Bancroft, vol. 5, p. 384.

In the western part of the State, General Griffith Rutherford, of Rowan County, on the approach of Tarleton, after the massacre at the Waxhaws, put himself at the head of 900 militia from the surrounding country and advanced to meet him, but on Tarleton's retreat they were temporarily disbanded.

The subsequent actions of this command are so lucidly and accurately related by General Joseph Graham, of Lincoln County, that we prefer to incorporate it in this work, rather than attempt to condense or enlarge it:

"Battle of Ramsour's Mill,
"Fought the 20th day of June, 1780.

"On the 3d of June, General Rutherford was informed of the advance of a part of the troops, under Lord Rawdon, to Waxhaw Creek, thirty miles south of Charlotte, and issued orders for the militia to rendezvous on the 10th, at Rees' plantation, eighteen miles northeast of Charlotte. The militia, to the number of eight hundred, promptly assembled on the 12th. Having heard that Lord Rawdon had retired to Hanging Rock, General Rutherford advanced ten miles to Mallard Creek.

"On the 14th the troops under his command were organized. The cavalry, sixty-five in number, under Major Davie, were equipped as dragoons, and formed in two troops under Captains Simmons and Martin. A battalion of three hundred light infantry was placed under the command of Colonel Wm. L. Davidson, a regular officer, who could not join his regiment in

Charleston, after that place was invested, and now joined the militia.

"Five hundred men remained under the immediate command of General Rutherford. On the evening of the 14th he received intelligence that the Tories were embodying in arms beyond the Catawba River, in Tryon County, about forty miles northwest of his (then) position. He issued orders to Colonel Francis Locke, of Rowan, Major David Wilson, of Mecklenburg, to Captains Falls and Brandon, also to other officers, to make every effort to raise men to disperse the Tories, it being deemed impolitic by General Rutherford to weaken his own force until the object of Lord Rawdon's expedition was better ascertained

"On the 15th, General Rutherford advanced two miles to the south of Charlotte. On the 17th he was informed that Lord Rawdon had retired toward Camden, and the Tories were assembled in force at Ramsour's Mill, near the south fork of the Catawba. A man by the name of John Moore, whose father and family resided about six miles from Ramsour's Mill, had joined the British army the preceding winter, and leaving the detachment under Cornwallis on the march from Charleston to Camden, he arrived at his father's on the 7th of June, wearing a sword and an old tattered suit of regimentals. He announced himself as a lieutenant colonel of the regiment of North Carolina loyalists commanded by Colonel John Hamilton, of Halifax County. He gave to the people of the neighborhood the first particular account they had received of the siege and capture of Charleston and the advance of the British troops to Camden. He appointed the 10th of June for an assembling of the people in the woods on Indian Creek, seven miles from

Ramsour's. Forty men assembled, and Moore told them it was not the wish of Lord Cornwallis that they should embody at that time, but that they and all other loyal subjects should hold themselves in readiness, and in the meantime get in their harvest; that before the getting in of the harvest it would be difficult to procure provisions for the British army; and that as soon as the country could furnish subsistence to the army, it would advance into North Carolina and support the royalists.

" Before this meeting broke up an express arrived to inform them that Major Joseph McDowell, of Burke County, with twenty men, was within eight miles of them, in search of some of the principal persons of their party. Confident of their strength, they resolved to attack McDowell, but some preparation being necessary, they could not march until next morning, when, finding he had retired, they pursued him to the ledge of the mountains which separate the counties of Lincoln and Burke, and not being able to overtake him, Moore directed them to return home and meet him on the 13th at Ramsour's Mill. On that day two hundred men met Moore, and they were joined on the next day by many others, among whom was Nicholas Welch, a major in the regiment commanded by Colonel Hamilton. He had lived in that neighborhood and had joined the British army eighteen months before. He was directly from the army of Lord Cornwallis, and gave information of Colonel Buford's defeat. He wore a rich suit of regimentals, and exhibited a considerable number of guineas, by which he sought to allure some, while he endeavored to intimidate others by an account of the success of the British army in all operations of the South and the total inability of the Whigs to make further opposition.' His conduct had the desired effect, and much more confidence was placed in him than in Colonel Moore. They remained in camp until the 20th, during which time a detachment, commanded by Colonel Moore, made an unsuccessful attempt to capture Colonel Hugh Brevard and Major Joseph McDowell, each of whom came into the neighborhood with a number of Whigs to harass the Tories, who were assembling.

"By the 20th nearly thirteen hundred men had assembled at Ramsour's, one-fourth of whom were without arms. General Rutherford resolved to concentrate his force and attack them as soon as he learned that Lord Rawdon had retired to Camden. With this view, he marched, on Sunday, the 18th, from his camp, south of Charlotte, to the Tuckaseege Ford, on the Catawba River, twelve miles nearer to Ramsour's. In the evening of that day he dispatched an express to Colonel Locke, advising him of his movement, and of the enemy's strength, and ordering Locke to join him on the 19th in the evening, or on the 20th in the morning, a few miles in advance of the Tuckaseege Ford. The express was neglected and did not reach Colonel Locke. The morning of the 19th was wet, and the arms of General Rutherford's men were out of order. At midday the weather cleared up and orders were given to the men to discharge their guns. This discharge produced an alarm in the neighborhood, and the people, thinking that the Tories were attempting to cross the river, many of them came in with arms and joined Rutherford. In the evening he crossed the river and encamped sixteen miles from Ramsour's.

"When Rutherford crossed the river, it was believed he would march in the night and attack the Tories next

morning; but, expecting that his express had reached
Colonel Locke, he awaited for Locke's arrival, that he
might, on the next day, march in full to the attack.

"At ten o'clock at night, Colonel James Johnston,*
of Tryon County, reached Rutherford's camp. He had
been dispatched by Colonel Locke to give notice of his
intention to attack the Tories at sunrise the next morning, and requesting Rutherford's co-operation. Rutherford, in confident expectation that his express had reached
Colonel Locke, shortly after Colonel Johnston had left,
made no movement.

"In pursuance of the orders given to Colonel Locke,
and the other officers at Mallard, on the 14th, they
severally collected as many men as they could, and, on
the morning of the 18th, Major Wilson, with sixty-five
men, passed the Catawba at Tool's Ford and joined
Major McDowell with twenty-five men. They passed
up the river at right angles with the position of the
Tories, to join the detachment of friends who were
assembling at the upper fords.

"At McEwen's Ford, being joined by Captain Falls,
with forty men under his command, they continued
their march up the east side of Mountain Creek, and
on Monday, the 19th, they joined Colonel Locke, Captain
Brandon and other officers, with two hundred and seventy
men. The whole force united amounted to four hundred men. They encamped on Mountain Creek, sixteen
miles from Ramsour's.

"'The officers met in council and they were unanimous
in the opinion that it would be unsafe to remain in that
position, as the Tories could attack them after a march
of a few hours, and, from the inferiority of their force,

---

*Father of Robert Johnston, Esq., of Lincoln county.

they had no doubt the Tories would march on them as soon as they learned where they were.

"It was first proposed that they should recross the Catawba at Sherrill's Ford, six miles in their rear, and wait for reinforcements, believing that they could prevent the Tories from crossing. To this, it was objected that a retrograde movement would embolden the Tories, whose numbers were increasing as fast as, probably, their own numbers would increase, after they had recrossed the River, and no additional security could therefore be obtained by such a movement.

"It was next proposed that they should march directly down the river and join General Rutherford, who was then distant from them about thirty-five miles.

"It was said this movement could be made without risk, as, in making it, they would not be nearer Ramsour's than they were. To this prudent proposition it was objected that nearly all the effective Whigs of that section were from home either with them or General Rutherford, and such a movement would leave their families exposed and their houses unprotected from pillage; that it would also be a dangerous movement for themselves and they might encounter them in their march. It was insinuated that these propositions proceeded, if not from fear, at least from an unwillingness to meet the Tories, and therefore another proposition was made, which was, notwithstanding their disparity of force, they should march during the night and attack the Tories in their camp early next morning.

"It was said that, the Tories being ignorant of their force and suddenly attacked, would be easily routed. The more prudent members of the council could not brook the insinuation of cowardice, and, trusting to that fortune which sometimes crowns even rashness with success, it was unanimously resolved immediately to march and at daybreak to attack the Tories. Colonel Johnston, being well acquainted with the country, was immediately dispatched to apprise General Rutherford of this resolution.

"Late in the evening they commenced their march from Mountain Creek, and passing down the south side of the mountain they halted at the west end of it for an hour in the night, and the officers convened to determine on the plan of attack. It was determined that the companies commanded by Captains Falls, McDowell and Brandon should act on horseback and march in front. No other arrangements were made and it was left to the officers to be governed by circumstances after they should reach the enemy. They resumed their march and arrived within a mile of the enemy's camp at daylight.

"The Tories were encamped on a hill three hundred yards east of Ramsour's Mill and a half mile north of the present flourishing village of Lincolnton. The ridge stretched nearly to the east on the south side of the millpond, and the road leading to the Tuckaseege Ford, by the mill, crosses the point of the ridge in a northwestern direction. The Tories occupied an excellent position on a summit of the ridge, their right on the road fronting the south. The ridge has a very gentle slope, and was then interspersed with only a few trees, and the fire of the Tories had full rake in front for more than two hundred yards. The foot of the hill was bounded by a glade, the side of which was covered with bushes. The road passed the western end of the glade at right angles; opposite the centre of the line and on the road a fence extended from the glade to a point opposite the right of the line. The picket guard, twelve in number, were stationed on the road, two hundred and fifty yards south of the glade, and six hundred yards from the encampment.

"The companies of Captains Falls, McDowell and Brandon, being mounted, the other troops under Colonel Locke were arranged in the road, two deep behind them, and, without any other organization or orders, they were marched to battle. When the horsemen came within sight of the picket, they perceived that their approach had not been anticipated.

"The picket fired and fled to their camp. The horsemen pursued, and turning to the right, out of the road, they rode up within thirty steps of the line and fired at the Tories, who, being in confusion, had not time to form their line; but seeing only a few men assailing them, they quickly recovered from their panic, and poured in a destructive fire, which obliged the horsemen to retreat. They retreated in disorder, passing through the infantry, who were advancing; several of the infantry joined them and never came into action. At a convenient distance the greater part of the horsemen rallied, and returning to the fight, exerted themselves with spirit during its continuance. The infantry hurried to keep near the horsemen in pursuit of the picket, and their movements being very irregular, their files were opened six or eight steps, and when the front approached the Tories, the rear was eighty poles back.

"The Tories seeing the effect of their fire, came down the hill a little distance and were in fair view. The infantry of the Whigs kept the road to the point between the glade and the corner of the fence opposite the centre of the Tories.

"Here the action was renewed; the front fired several times before the rear came up. The Tories being on their left they deployed to the right in front of the glade and came into action without order or system. In some places they were crowded together in each others' way; in other places there were none. As the rear came up, they occupied those places, and the line gradually extending, the action became general and obstinate on both sides. In a few minutes the Tories began to retire to their position on the top of the ridge, and soon fell back a little behind the ridge, to shelter part of their bodies from the fire of the Whigs, who were fairly exposed to their fire. In this situation their fire became very destructive, so that the Whigs fell back to the bushes near the glade, and the Tories, leaving their safe position, pursued half way down the ridge. At this moment Captain Harden led a party of Whigs into the field and under cover of the fence, kept up a galling fire on the right flank of the Tories; and some of the Whigs discovering that the ground on the right was more favorable to protect them from the fire of the Tories, obliqued in that direction towards the east end of the glade. This movement gave their lines the proper extension. They continued to oblique in this direction until they turned the left flank of the Tories; and the contest being well maintained in the centre, the Tories began to retreat up the ridge. They found part of their position occupied by the Whigs. In that quarter the action became close, and the parties mixed together in two instances; and, having no bayonets, they struck at each other with the butts of their guns. In this strange contest, several of the Tories were taken prisoners, and others, divesting themselves of their mark of distinction (a twig of green pine-top stuck in their hats), intermixed with the Whigs, and all being in their common dress, escaped unnoticed.

"The Tories finding the left of their position in possession of the Whigs, and their centre being closely pressed, retreated down the ridge towards the pond, exposed to the fire of the centre and of Captain Harden's company behind the fences. The Whigs pursued until they got entire possession of the ridge, when they discovered, to their astonishment, that the Tories had collected in force on the other side of the creek beyond the mill. They expected the fight would be renewed, and attempted to form a line, but only eighty-six men could be paraded. Some were scattered during the action, others were attending to their wounded friends, and, after repeated efforts, not more than one hundred and ten men could be collected.

"In this situation of things, it was resolved that Major Wilson and Captain Wm. Alexander, of Rowan, should hasten to General Rutherford and urge him to press forward to their assistance. Rutherford had marched early in the morning, and at a distance of six or seven miles from Ramsour's, was met by Wilson and Alexander. Major Davie's cavalry was started at full gallop, and Colonel Davidson's infantry were ordered to hasten on with all possible speed. At the end of two miles they were met by others from the battle, who informed them that the Tories had retreated. The march was continued, and troops arrived on the ground two hours after the battle had closed. The dead and most of the wounded were still lying where they fell.

"As soon as the action begun, those of the Tories who had no arms, and several who had, returned across the creek. They were joined by others when they were first beaten up the ridge, and by two hundred well armed, who had arrived two days before from Lower Creek, in Burke County, under Captains Whiston and Murray. Colonel Moore and Major Welch soon joined them. Those of the Tories who continued the fight to the last crossed the creek and joined as soon as the Whigs got possession of the ridge. Believing that they were completely beaten, they formed a stratagem to secure their retreat. About the time that Wilson and Alexander were dispatched to General Rutherford, they sent a flag, under a pretence of proposing a suspension of hostilities, to make arrangements for taking care of the wounded and burying the dead. To prevent the flag officer from perceiving their small number, Major James Rutherford and another officer were ordered to meet him a short distance from the line. The proposition being made, Major Rutherford demanded that the Tories should surrender in ten minutes, and then the arrangements should be made that were requested.

"In the meantime, Moore and Welch gave orders that such of their men as were on foot, or had inferior horses, should move off singly as fast as they could, and when the flag returned not more than fifty remained. They immediately fled. Moore, with thirty men, reached the British army at Camden, where he was threatened with a trial by a court-martial for disobedience of orders in attempting to embody the royalists before the time appointed by the commander-in-chief. He was treated with disrespect by the British officers, and held in a state of disagreeable suspense; but it was at length deemed impolitic to order him before a court-martial.

"As there was no organization of either party, nor regular returns made after the action, the loss could not be ascertained with correctness. Fifty-six lay dead on the side of the ridge where the heat of the action prevailed. Many lay scattered on the flanks and over the ridge toward the mill. It is believed that seventy were killed, and that the loss on each side was equal. About one hundred men on each side were wounded, and fifty Tories were taken prisoners. The men had no uniform, and it could not be told to which party many of the dead belonged. Most of the Whigs wore a piece of white paper on their hats in front, and many of the men on each side being excellent riflemen, this paper was a mark at which the Tories often fired, and several of the Whigs were shot in the head. The trees, behind which both Whigs and Tories occasionally took shelter, were grazed by the balls; and one tree on the left of the Tory line, at the root of which two brothers lay dead, was grazed by three balls on one side and two on the other.

"In this battle neighbors, near relations and personal friends fought against each other, and as the smoke from time to time would blow off, they would recognize each other. In the evening, and on the next day, the relations and friends of the dead and wounded came in, and a scene was witnessed truly afflicting to the feelings of humanity.

"After the action commenced, scarcely any orders were given by the officers. They fought like common soldiers, and animated their men by their example, and they suffered severely. Captains Falls, Dobson, Smith, Bowman and Armstrong were killed; and Captains Houston and McKissick wounded."

The battle of Ramsour's Mill was fought the very day the Baron DeKalb arrived at Hillsboro, North Carolina.

Its effect was to completely crush out the Tory element in that portion of the State, and they never attempted to organize again during the war. The men who assembled at Ramsour's Mill to resume their allegiance to the British Government were not marauders in search of plunder, nor violent men seeking revenge for injuries inflicted in border warfare; they were nearly all simple-minded, artless Germans, industrious, frugal and honest citizens, who had never been in arms before, nor suffered persecutions from the Whigs. They believed the representatives of the army of Cornwallis, who informed them that the royal authority had been re-established in the South, and they were confirmed in this by the accounts of the absolute subjection of South Carolina and Georgia, and the example of leading citizens of those States who had "taken British protection." They came to renew their citizenship and allegiance, as they thought duty and conscience required. Only a few hundred were armed, they were undisciplined and unorganized, and yet, when contending for what they believed to be right, they evinced a courage and resolution worthy of a better cause.

Though Cornwallis encamped on this very ground, in the January following, and urged them to join the royal standard again, none of them were afterwards found among the British forces. They went back to their peaceful and plentiful homes "wiser and better men."

Captain Dobson, of the Whigs, was buried upon the battle-field and several of his family have been laid beside him. His grave, surrounded by a neat brick wall, is near the highway leading north from Lincolnton to Newton, Catawba County. The next day after the battle the friends and neighbors of both parties assembled and decently interred the dead. A long trench or grave was dug, running northeast and southwest, and into this were placed Whig and Tory alike, while those who performed this sad rite were representatives of both sides. A large pine tree on the summit of the hill, in the field, marks the line of this burial place.

The McDowell mentioned in General Graham's narrative was Joseph McDowell, of Burke County, known as "Quaker Meadows Joe" to distinguish him from his cousin "Pleasant Garden Joe." McDowell was afterwards a leader at King's Mountain and Cowpens, a member of Congress, and brigadier general of militia, and was called General Joseph McDowell. We shall have occasion to speak more fully in regard to him hereafter.

After the battle of Ramsour's Mill, Major Davie took position on the north side of Waxhaw Creek, south of Charlotte. Here he was reinforced by Major Crawford with some South Carolina troops, and 35 Catawba Indians under their chief "New River," and the Mecklenburg County militia under Colonel Higgins:

"Davie was one of the most splendid and knightly figures on the American continent. He was then fresh from his law books and only 25 years old. Tall, graceful and strikingly handsome, he had those graces of person which would have made him the favorite in the clanging lists of feudal days. To this he added elegant culture, thrilling eloquence, and a graciousness of manner which was to charm in after days the *salons* of Paris. He had won high honors and had been dangerously wounded at Stono, on the 20th June, 1779. Since then he had expended the whole of his estate in equipping, at his own cost, the only organized body of troops now left to do battle in behalf of the cause he loved."*

"General Davie was not only distinguished as an intelligent but an intrepid soldier. His delight was to lead a charge; and, possessing great bodily strength, is said to have overcome more men, in personal conflict, than any individual in the service."†

Such was the soldier and hero who was now, in this dark and depressing hour of our history, about to strike the British outposts and restore confidence and hope to the people. He was on familiar ground, among the scenes of his early childhood and maturer years. He was inspired by a fervid ambition to deeds of valor and patriotism, and his friends and associates were to be witnesses of his achievements. Their hopes of deliverance from the sword and the prison, or perhaps the gallows, were centred on him, and with noble daring he entered the lists determined with his little band of patriots and soldiers to strike the foe before "the harvest

*Moore's History, vol. 1, p. 265.
†Garden's Anecdotes of the Revolution, p. 39.

5

was gathered." He was now in four and a half miles of Hanging Rock, one of the British outposts, and on the 20th July, he intercepted at Flat Rock a convoy of provisions and clothing intended for that garrison. The dragoons and volunteer loyalists who guarded the convoy were captured and brought to camp. The wagons and provisions were destroyed, but the horses, which were much needed, and the arms more so, were brought off in safety.

This seemingly small affair aroused the spirit of his troops and they were ready for adventurous deeds. Davie resolved to gratify this spirit, and planned a strike at Hanging Rock. "With forty mounted riflemen and the same number of dragoons he approached the outpost. It was garrisoned by a strong force. While he was reconnoitering the ground to begin the attack, he received the information that three companies of mounted infantry, returning from an excursion, had halted at a house near the post. This house was in full view of Hanging Rock. It was a point of a right angle made by a lane, one end of which led to the enemy's camp, the other end to the woods. Davie advanced cautiously from the end near the woods, while he detached his riflemen, whose dress was similar to the Tories, with orders to rush forward and charge. The riflemen passed the enemy's sentinels without suspicion or challenge, dismounted in the lane, and gave the enemy, before the house, a well-directed fire; the surprised loyalists fled to the other end, where they were received by the dragoons in full gallop, who charged boldly on them and gave them another destructive volley. They retreated in confusion to the angle of the lane, where they were received by the infantry and charged with impetuosity, which closed up all retreat. The dragoons surrounded them and they were cut to pieces in the very face of the British camp at Hanging Rock."* One hundred good muskets, recently issued to these recreant Tories, and sixty horses, so much in demand for the mounted riflemen, were secured by this second adventure. There was joy in the American camp, confidence was restored and the troops were eager to follow their dashing leader wherever his vigilance discovered a place to strike. They had arms and ammunition and horses now, furnished by Lord Cornwallis through his recent converts to loyalty, and they felt the impulse to use them.

Colonel Sumter, of South Carolina, and Colonel Irwin, of North Carolina, had made an attempt on Flat Rock, the day that Davie cut the loyalists to pieces at Hanging Rock, but had been repulsed with severe loss.

Davie had not, to this time, lost a single man. Colonels Sumter and Davie now met at Lansford, on the Catawba River, and agreed to unite their forces and make a combined attack on Hanging Rock. This was on the 5th day of August, 1780.

When Major Davie advanced to the Waxhaws, General Rutherford moved up the Yadkin River,

*Wheeler's History, vol. 2, p. 192.

hoping to overtake or intercept Colonel Samuel Bryan, a Tory leader, from the upper Yadkin, who had embodied the loyalists of that section and was on his way to join the swelling numbers of Lord Cornwallis.

These Tories presumed, too, that the struggle was over, and, like vultures, were flocking together to share the prey. Bryan was too fleet for Rutherford. The news of Ramsour's Mill had put expedition into the feet of these renegades, and they marched with great celerity until they reached Hanging Rock. There were about 100 of them.

The garrison of Hanging Rock had in it now these North Carolina Tories, and about the same number of Tarleton's troops, who had taken part in the dreadful massacre of Buford's men, near where Davie lay in camp.

Goaded by the tales of horror which the witnesses of that wretched butchery daily poured into his ears, and mortified beyond measure that North Carolina Tories were now in front of him, in the ranks of the oppressors, and remembering that his own fellow-citizen, Captain Stokes, had been slashed and dismembered of his good right arm by the men who were in the garrison of Hanging Rock, Davie was impatient to avenge himself and his State upon this miscreant band. "Tarleton's Quarters," meaning the black flag of revenge, had become a familiar by-word in the American camp, and the soldiers of Tarleton had little hope or reason to expect mercy when the day of reckoning should come. The

Whigs of that day seldom had time to take Tory prisoners, and no place to put them if captured.

I shall now incorporate the account of the

Battle of Hanging Rock

as related by Major Davie himself. It is taken from Wheeler's History:

"On the 5th day of August, the detachments met again at Lansford, on the Catawba. Their strength was little diminished; Major Davie had lost not one man. The North Carolina militia under Colonel Irwin and Major Davie numbered about five hundred men, officers and privates, and about three hundred South Carolinians under Colonels Sumter, Lacy and Hill.

"It became a matter of great importance to remove the enemy from their posts, and it was supposed, if one of them was taken, the other would be evacuated. Upon a meeting of the officers, it was determined to attack the Hanging Rock on the following day. As this was an open camp, they expected to be on a more equal footing with the enemy, and the men whose approbation in those times was absolutely requisite, on being informed of the determination of the officers, entered into the project with spirit and cheerfulness. The troops marched in the evening and halted about midnight within two miles of the enemy's camp, and a council was now called to settle the mode of attack.

"Accurate information had been obtained of the enemy's situation, who were pretty strongly posted in three divisions.

"The garrison of Hanging Rock consisted of five

hundred men; one hundred and sixty infantry of Tarleton's Legion, a part of Colonel Brown's regiment, and Bryan's North Carolina Tory regiment. The whole commanded by Major Carden.

"The regulars were posted on the right; a part of the British legion and Hamilton's regiment were at some houses in the centre, and Bryan's regiment and other loyalists some distance on the left, and separated from the centre by a skirt of woods; the situation of the regular troops could not be approached without an entire exposure of the assailants, and a deep ravine and creek covered the whole of the Tory camp.

"Colonel Sumter proposed that the detachments should approach in three divisions, march directly to the centre encampments, then dismount, and each division attack its camp. This plan was approved by all the officers but Major Davie, who insisted on leaving the horses at this place and marching to the attack on foot, urging the confusion always consequent on dismounting under a fire, and the certainty of losing the effect of a sudden and vigorous attack. This objection was, however, overruled. The divisions were soon made, and as the day broke the march recommenced. The general command was conferred on Colonel Sumter, as the senior officer; Major Davie led the column on the right, consisting of his own corps, some volunteers under Major Bryan, and some detached companies of South Carolina refugees; Colonel Hill commanded the left, composed of South Carolina refugees, and Colonel Irwin the centre, formed entirely of the Mecklenburg militia. They turned to the left of the road to avoid the enemy's picket and patrol, with an intention to return to it under cover of a defile near the camp; but the guides, either from ignorance or timidity, led them so far to the left that the right centre and left divisions all fell on the Tory encampment. These devoted people were soon attacked in front and flank and routed with great slaughter, as the Americans pressed in pursuit of the Tories who fled toward the centre encampment. Here the Americans received a fire from one hundred and sixty of the Legion infantry, and some companies of Hamilton's regiment posted behind a fence; but their impetuosity was not one moment checked by this unexpected discharge; they pressed on, and the Legion infantry broke and joined in the flight of the loyalists, yielding their camp, without a second effort, to the militia.

"At this moment a part of Colonel Brown's regiment had nearly changed the fate of the day. They, by a bold and skillful maneuvre, passed into a wood between the Tory and centre encampments, drew up unperceived, and poured in a heavy fire on the militia forming from the disorder of the pursuit on the flank of the encampment. These brave men took instinctively to the trees and brush-heaps, and returned the fire with deadly effect; in a few minutes there was not a British officer standing, and many of the regiment had fallen, and the balance, on being offered quarters, threw down their arms.

"The remainder of the British line, who had also made a movement, retreated hastily towards their former position and formed a hollow square in the centre of the cleared ground.

"The rout and pursuit of these various corps by a part of one detachment, and plunder of the camp by others, had thrown the Americans into great confusion.

"The utmost exertions were made by Colonel Sumter and the other officers to carry the men on to attack the

British square; about two hundred men and Davie's dragoons were collected and formed on the margin of the roads, and a heavy but ineffectual fire was commenced on the British troops. A large body of the enemy, consisting of the Legion infantry, Hamilton's regiment, and Tories, were observed rallying, and formed on the opposite side of the British camp, near the wood; and lest they might be induced to take the Americans in flank, Major Davie passed around the camp under cover of the trees, and charged them with his company of dragoons. The troops, under the impressions of defeat, were routed and dispersed by a handful of men.

"The distance of the square from the woods, and the fire of the two pieces of field artillery, prevented the militia from making any considerable impression on the British troops, so that, on Major Davie's return, it was agreed to plunder the encampment and retire. As this party were returning towards the centre, some of the Legion cavalry appeared and advanced up in the Camden road with a countenance as if they meant to keep their position, but on being charged by Davie's dragoons, they took the woods in flight, and only one was outdone.

"A retreat was now become absolutely necessary; the British commissary's stores were taken in the centre encampment, and a number of the men were already intoxicated; the greatest part were loaded with plunder, and those in a condition to fight had exhausted their ammunition. About an hour had been employed in plundering the camp, taking the paroles of the British officers, and preparing litters for the wounded.

"All this was done in full view of the British army, who consoled themselves with some military music, and an interlude of three cheers for King George, which was immediately answered by three cheers for the hero of America. The militia at length got into the line of march, Davie and his dragoons covering the retreat; but as the troops were loaded with plunder, and encumbered with their wounded friends, and many of them intoxicated, this retreat was not performed in the best military style. However, under all these disadvantages, they filed off unmolested, along the front of the enemy, about one o'clock.

"The loss of the Americans was never correctly ascertained, for want of regular returns, and many of the wounded being carried immediately home from action. Captain Read, of North Carolina, and Captain McClure, of South Carolina, were killed. Colonel Hill, South Carolina, Major Wynn, South Carolina, Captain Craighead, Lieutenant Fleucher, Ensign McLinn, wounded.

"The British loss greatly exceeded ours. The loss of Bryan's regiment was severe. Sixty-two of Tarleton's Legion were killed and wounded.

"Major Davie's corps suffered much while tying their horses and forming under a heavy fire from the Tories, a measure which he had reprobated in the council which had decided on the mode of attack.

"It is an evincible trait in the character of militia, that they will only obey their own officers in time of action, and this battle would have been more decisive had the troops not fallen into confusion in pursuit of the loyalists and the Legion infantry, by which circumstances the different regiments became mixed and confounded; or, had the divisions of this army left their horses where it was proposed they should, and marched in such a manner as to have assailed each encampment at the same time, a vigorous and sudden attack might have prevented the British from availing themselves of their superior discipline; the other encampments must have been soon carried, and the corps remaining distinct, would have been in a situation to push any advantages that Davie's column might have gained over the British line.

"This account is nearly *verbatim* from the manuscript left by Mr. Davie.

"After the affair at Hanging Rock, Major Davie conveyed his wounded to a hospital, which his foresight had provided at Charlotte, then hastened to the general rendezvous for the army under General Gates at Rugely's Mills.

"On the 16th of August, 1780, about ten miles from Camden, Major Davie, on his way to unite his forces with General Gates, met a soldier. He was an American, and was in full speed. He arrested him as a deserter, but soon learned from him that on that fatal day, the whole American army, under General Gates, and the whole British force, under Cornwallis, had met, and that the British were triumphant. This unexpected information was too soon confirmed by the appearance of General Gates himself, in full flight.

"General Gates desired Major Davie to fall back on Charlotte, or the dragoons would soon be on him. He replied, 'His men were accustomed to Tarleton, and did not fear him.' Gates had no time to argue, but passed on.

"Of General Huger, who then rode up, Major Davie asked how far the directions of Gates ought to be obeyed, who answered, 'Just as far as you please, for you will never see him again.' He again sent a gentleman who overtook General Gates, to say, that if he wished, he would return and bury his dead. The answer of Gates was, 'I say retreat! Let the dead bury the dead.'"

The massacre of Buford's men was partially avenged. Bryan's Tories ended their weary march to fall before the sabres of Davie's dragoons, and learned that treachery was as dangerous as it was dishonorable.

The Americans had now crossed bayonets with British infantry, flushed with victory and pride, and led them away captive. The spell of invincibility which had surrounded them was broken, their prestige was gone, and they were no longer dreaded nor feared by the Americans. Major Davie retreated to Charlotte sullen and irritated, and was rejoiced when a leader came in whom he confided. Leaving him at Charlotte, I will follow another band of patriots, who had gathered on the right of Davie and under leaders as impetuous and bold, if not as accomplished, as he, and whose track was marked by victory and vengeance keen and severe.

In 1780, before the formation of the State of Tennessee, the counties of Washington and Sullivan, the homes of Colonel Isaac Shelby and Colonel John Sevier—"Nollichucky Jack" as his soldiers and neighbors familiarly and lovingly called him—were in North Carolina, and both of these military heroes held civil and military offices in this State.

Both of these men were the friends and fellow-soldiers of Colonel Charles McDowell, of Burke, and their lives ran parallel even to the storming of King's Mountain and the death of Patrick Ferguson. Governor Swain, in the University Magazine of

March, 1861, says that the most correct account of the expeditions, in the summer of 1780, of McDowell and Shelby, is found in the "National Portrait Gallery" (now before me), and that it was known to have been written substantially by Shelby himself; and I shall offer no apology for transferring it to these pages. My object in this work is to give as nearly as possible the exact truth of history, and I can imagine no safer guide to such a result than to let those who made the history, if they be honest and true, tell the tale. Many authors, in endeavoring to extract truth from cotemporary narratives, give the gloss of their own feelings or judgment to the acts they record and seize only upon such facts as seem essential to establish their own opinion of these deeds:

Colonel Isaac Shelby and Colonel Charles McDowell's Campaign in 1780.

"In the summer of 1780, Colonel Shelby was in Kentucky locating and securing those lands which he had five years previously marked out and improved for himself, when the intelligence of the surrender of Charleston, and the loss of the army, reached that country. He returned home in July of that year, determined to enter the service of his country, and remain in it until her independence should be secured. He could not continue to be a cool spectator of a contest in which the dearest rights and interests of his country were involved.

"On his arrival in Sullivan, he found a requisition from Colonel Charles McDowell, requesting him to furnish all the aid in his power to check the enemy, who had overrun the two Southern States, and were on the borders of North Carolina. Colonel Shelby assembled the militia of his county, and called upon them to volunteer their services for a short time on that interesting occasion, and marched, in a few days, with three hundred mounted riflemen, across the Alleghany Mountains.

"In a short time after his arrival at McDowell's camp, near the Cherokee Ford of Broad River, Colonel Shelby, Lieutenant Colonels Sevier and Clarke, the latter a refugee officer from Georgia, were detached, with six hundred men, to surprise a post of the enemy in front, on the waters of the Pacolet River. It was a strong fort, surrounded by abattis, built in the Cherokee war, and commanded by that distinguished loyalist, Captain Patrick Moore. On the second summons to surrender, after the Americans had surrounded the post within musket shot, Captain Moore surrendered the garrison, with one British sergeant major, ninety-three loyalists, and two hundred and fifty stand of arms, loaded with ball and buckshot, and so arranged at the portholes as to have repulsed double the number of the American detachment.

"Shortly after this affair, Colonels Shelby and Clarke were detached, with six hundred mounted men, to watch the movements of the enemy, and, if possible, to cut up his foraging parties.

"Ferguson, who commanded the enemy, about twenty-five hundred strong, composed of British and Tories, with a small squadron of British horse, was an officer of great enterprise, and, although only a major in the British line, was a brigadier general in the royal militia establishment, made by the enemy after he had overrun

South Carolina, and was esteemed the most distinguished partisan officer in the British army.

"He made several attempts to surprise Colonel Shelby, but his designs were baffled. On the first of August, however, his advance, about six or seven hundred strong, came up with the American commander at a place he had chosen for battle, called Cedar Spring, where a sharp conflict ensued for half an hour, when Ferguson approached with his whole force.

"The Americans then retreated, carrying off the field fifty prisoners, mostly British, including two officers.

"The enemy made great efforts for five miles to regain the prisoners; but the American commander, by forming frequently on the most advantageous ground to give battle, so retarded the pursuit that the prisoners were placed beyond their reach. The American loss was ten or twelve killed and wounded. It was in the severest part of this action, that Colonel Shelby's attention was arrested by the heroic conduct of Colonel Clarke. He often mentioned the circumstance of ceasing in the midst of battle, to look with astonishment and admiration at Clarke fighting.

"General McDowell having received information that five or six hundred Tories were encamped at Musgrove's Mill, on the south side of the Enoree, about forty miles distant, again detached Colonels Shelby, Clarke and Williams, of South Carolina, with about seven hundred horsemen, to surprise and disperse them. Major Ferguson, with his whole force, occupied a position immediately on the route.

"The American commanders took up their line of march from Smith's Ford of Broad River, just before sundown, on the evening of the 18th of August, 1780, continued through the woods until dark, and then pursued a road, leaving Ferguson's camp about three miles to the left. They rode very hard all night, frequently in a gallop, and just at the dawn of day, about a half a mile from the enemy's camp, met a strong patrol party. A short skirmish ensued, and several of them were killed. At that juncture, a countryman, living just at hand, came up and informed them that the enemy had been reinforced the evening before with six hundred regular troops (the Queen's American regiment from New York, under Colonel Innes, destined to reinforce Ferguson's army.) The circumstances attending the information were so minute that no doubt was entertained of its truth. To march on and attack the enemy then seemed to be improper; fatigued and exhausted as were the Americans and their horses, to attempt an escape was impossible. They instantly determined to form a breastwork of old logs and brush, and make the best defence in their power. Captain Inman was sent out with twenty-five men to meet the enemy, and skirmish with them as soon as they crossed the Enoree River.

"The sound of their drum and bugle horns soon announced their movements. Captain Inman was ordered to fire upon them and retreat, according to his own discretion. This stratagem (which was the suggestion of the Captain himself) drew the enemy out in disorder, supposing they had forced the whole party; and when they came up within seventy yards, a most destructive fire commenced from the American riflemen, who were concealed behind the breastwork of logs. It was an hour before the enemy could force the riflemen from their slender breastwork; and just as they began to give away in some parts, Colonel Innes was wounded, and all the

British officers, except a subaltern, being previously killed or wounded, and Captain Hawsey, a noted leader among the Tories being shot down, the whole of the enemy's line commenced a retreat. The Americans pursued them closely, and beat them across the river.

"In this pursuit Captain Inman was killed, bravely fighting the enemy hand to hand. Colonel Shelby commanded the right wing, Colonel Clarke the left, and Colonel Williams the centre. According to McCall's History of Georgia, the only work in which this battle is noticed, the British loss is stated to be sixty-three killed and one hundred and sixty wounded and taken; the American loss to be four killed and nine wounded. Amongst the former, Captain Inman and amongst the latter, Colonel Clarke and Captain Clarke. The Americans returned to their horses, and mounted with a determination to be, before night, at Ninety-Six, at that time a weak British post, distant only thirty miles. At that moment an express came up from General McDowell in great haste, with a short letter in his hand from Governor Caswell, dated on the battle ground, apprising McDowell of the defeat of the American grand army under General Gates, on the 16th, near Camden, and advising him to get out of the way, as the enemy would, no doubt, endeavor to improve their victory, to the greatest advantage, by destroying all the small corps of the American army.

"It was a fortunate circumstance that Colonel Shelby knew Governor Caswell's handwriting, and what reliance to place upon it; but it was a difficult task to avoid the enemy in his rear, his troops and their horses being fatigued, and encumbered with a large number of British prisoners. These, however, were immediately distributed amongst the companies, so as to make one to every three men, who carried them alternately on horseback, directly towards the mountains. The Americans continued their march all that day and night, and the next day until late in the evening, without even halting to refresh. This long and rapid march saved them; as they were pursued, until late in the afternoon of the second day after the action, by a strong detachment from Ferguson's army. Colonel Shelby, after seeing the party and prisoners out of danger, retreated to the western waters with his followers, and left the prisoners in charge of Colonels Clarke and Williams, to convey them to some point of security in Virginia; for at that moment there was not the appearance of a corps of Americans south of that State.

"The panic which followed the defeat of Gates and Sumter induced the corps of McDowell's army to disperse, some to the west and some to the north. The brilliancy of this affair was obscured, as indeed were all the minor incidents of the previous war, by the deep gloom which overspread the public mind after the disastrous defeat of General Gates."

This was the foretaste that Ferguson had of these "dare-devils," "over-mountain men;" these hardy hunters and Indian fighters of the mountain wilderness; these children of nature, whose experience and common sense were their only guides, and whose sleepless vigilance was their protection from danger. They all carried the Deckhard rifle, called for the maker, who lived in Lancaster, Pennsylvania. It was generally three feet six inches long, weighed about seven pounds, and ran seventy bullets to the pound of lead. This rifle was remarkable for the precision and the distance of its shot.*

Ferguson himself was one of the finest rifle shots in the world, and was the inventor of a breech-loading rifle used at that date in the British army. It could be fired seven times a minute. He, therefore, knew how effective the rifle was in the hands of a steady and determined soldier, and he dreaded the encounter with these men which was, in the near future, before him.†

There was still a third partisan corps of North Carolinians that gathered to the left of Davie on the Pee Dee.

A considerable number of North Carolina militia assembled on the 20th of July at Anson Court House. Observing this movement Major McArthur, who commanded the British forces on the Pee Dee, called in his detachments and marched to join the royal army at Camden. On the day that he left, the inhabitants, distressed by McArthur's depredations upon them, generally took up arms. Lord Nairne and one hundred and six invalids, descending the river, were made prisoners by a party of the Americans commanded by Major Thomas, who had lately been received as loyal subjects. A large boat, well filled with supplies for McArthur, was also seized. All the new-made

---

*Ramsay's Annals of Tennessee, p. 228.
†Ramsay's Annals of Tennessee, p. 224.

British militia officers, excepting Colonel Mills,* were made prisoners by their own men.†

While these partisan leaders in Western North Carolina, volunteers without wages or rations, were threatening and attacking the British outposts and intercepting and destroying their convoys, the militia of the State was assembling at Cheraw Hill, in South Carolina, where they arrived about the 1st day of August, 1780. This point is just across the State line, sixty-five miles from Charlotte and one hundred and six miles from Wilmington. The men of the west were under Brigadier General Rutherford of Rowan, those of the east under General Isaac Gregory of Camden County, and those from the centre under General John Butler of Orange. This last was an old Regulator, for whose head Tryon had offered a high reward in 1771. Butler had never ceased to hope and to struggle for freedom. The militia, to use a familiar term, were "raw" and undisciplined and not accustomed to be organized into large bodies. Their mode of fighting was in small bands, under chosen leaders individually known to every soldier in the ranks, and they followed their leader because they confided in him personally. Personal faith gave them steadiness and energy. The rifle was their weapon and a tree their protection from the cavalry and the bayonet. In this mode of warfare they excelled; they knew but little of any other.

*Captured at King's Mountain and hung.
†Ramsay's History of South Carolina, p. 202.

These generals were all sincere patriots and brave men. "General Rutherford was an Irishman by birth, uncultivated in mind and manners, but brave, ardent and patriotic,"* and, no doubt, as impulsive in his nature as any son of the Emerald Isle and as heartily opposed to British tyranny as any of his race. He resided west of Salisbury, in the Locke settlement. He was an Indian fighter and had commanded 2,400 men in 1776 in a successful invasion of the Cherokee nation. Of General Gregory we know but little, but that little is honorable alike to his courage and his patriotism. He shed his blood for the cause.

General Horatio Gates, the captor of Burgoyne's army, the accidental victor of one battle, had, on the 13th day of June, been appointed by Congress commander-in-chief of the Southern army and about the 25th of July he reached the camp of DeKalb, on Deep River, in North Carolina, seventy-five miles northeast of Caswell's camp at Cheraw, and superseded him. Sad day for American history when vanity and arrogance were promoted over unselfish courage and conservative judgment; when the martinet ranked the soldier, and the adventurer took command of the patriot.

General Washington greatly desired to have General Nathanael Greene appointed to this command, but popular enthusiasm had become so much aroused by the capture of Burgoyne that the people and their representatives in Congress were deaf to

*Wheeler, vol. 2, p. 382.

every remonstrance and impatient of any suggestion which questioned the greatness and invincibility of General Gates. It was said that Washington "had slain his thousands, but Gates had slain his tens of thousands." The opposition of Washington was attributed to jealousy and envy and he was compelled to yield reluctantly to the popular clamor. It was a repetition of the old story of republics in which the people sing hosannas one day to the conquering hero and cry "crucify him" the next; but the people are much like children or "foolish virgins"—they seldom learn wisdom except in the suffering school of experience. Like children they often need to be restrained or forced, as occasion may require, by a master's hand. A little tyranny might have been wholesome in 1780, but Washington had no element of this character in his nature. He preferred sacrifice with the people rather than glory or success through the exercise of arbitrary power. He not only yielded to Congress but gave to Gates more than one-fourth of his best troops, regulars and veterans from Maryland and Delaware.

A strange infatuation took possession of General Gates; he contemned cavalry and heard with indifference the suggestion of their necessity in an open country where they could move with celerity and obtain the information so absolutely necessary to the success of military operations. Cavalry are figuratively called the eyes and ears of an army, and these Gates closed and went forward like the blind leading the blind, and the ditch of disaster was not far removed. Caswell has been accused of "disregarding orders from the vanity of acting separately,"* but Gates was equally foolish in making no attempt to reconcile these differences and secure unity and harmony of action. DeKalb, wise, prudent and cautious, advised that Camden should be approached from the direction of Mecklenburg and Rowan, where stores could be procured for the army and a line of retreat be prepared in the event of disaster; but Gates was imperious and obstinate and would listen to no plan except marching directly through a barren wilderness to attack Rawdon, without inquiring what was his force or the strength of his situation.

"Orders were immediately issued to the troops to hold themselves in readiness to move at a moment's warning, and on the 27th July, 1780, the army was marching in the direct route across the barrens to Mark's Ferry on the Pee Dee. He had not at this time one day's provision to serve out for his army."† On the 7th day of August Gates formed a junction with Caswell and on the 13th the combined forces encamped at Rugely's Mills near Camden. The next day General Stevens of Virginia came up with a brigade of militia. In the meantime Lord Cornwallis, having been apprised of the advance of the American army, left Charleston with a large reinforcement and reached Lord Rawdon at Camden before dawn of the 14th, and at ten

---

*Bancroft, vol. 5, p. 384.
†Johnson's Life of Greene, vol. 1, p. 294.

o'clock on the night of the 15th set his troops in motion in the hope of attacking the Americans at the break of day.

General Gates was wholly ignorant that Cornwallis had reinforced Rawdon, and supposing that he could obtain an easy victory over the latter, who was inferior in numbers, he put the American army in motion on the night of the 15th of August also, with the view of surprising Lord Rawdon.

"The unhappy fate which awaited him is that which must ever attend the commander who neglects the means of intelligence. His laurels were strewn in the dust, his venerable head bowed down with humiliation, an army destroyed and the Southern States brought to the verge of ruin."*

Both armies unexpectedly met in the night. The British fired into Colonel Armand's cavalry which became disordered and fled, but the infantry under Porterfeild and Armstrong, of North Carolina, checked the advance. Both armies were surprised and apprehensive, and by mutual consent, as it were, withdrew to await the attack of the other. When the long night of weary suspense had passed the lines of battle were formed, which Bancroft thus describes: "The position of Lord Cornwallis was most favorable. A swamp on each side secured his flanks against the superior numbers of the Americans. At daybreak his last dispositions were made. The front line, to which was attached two six-pounders and two three-pounders, was commanded on the right by Lieutenant Colonel Webster, on

---

*Johnson's Life of Greene, vol. 1, p. 297.

the left by Lord Rawdon; a battalion with a six-pounder was posted behind each wing as a reserve; the cavalry were in the rear ready to charge or to pursue.

"On the American side the second Maryland brigade with Gist for its brigadier, and the men of Delaware occupied the right under DeKalb; the North Carolina division, with Caswell, the centre, and Stevens with the newly arrived Virginia militia, the left; the best troops on the side strongest by nature, the worst on the weakest.

"The first Maryland brigade, at the head of which Smallwood should have appeared, formed a second line about two hundred yards in the rear of the first. The artillery was divided between the two brigades."*

This corresponds with the account given by Steadman.†

The opposite armies being thus arranged in order of battle, Lieutenant Colonel Webster was ordered by Lord Cornwallis to advance and charge the enemy. They met Stevens on the left, who was also advancing. The Virginia militia were untrained and undisciplined and soon gave way, the retreat became a rout and they fled in every direction, throwing away their arms and knapsacks and intent only on escaping from the cavalry, which they dreaded, in their rear. The left flank of the North Carolina militia being thus exposed to a raking fire from the advancing British line and having no

---

*Bancroft, vol. 5, pp. 387–'8.
†History American War, vol. 2, p. 208.

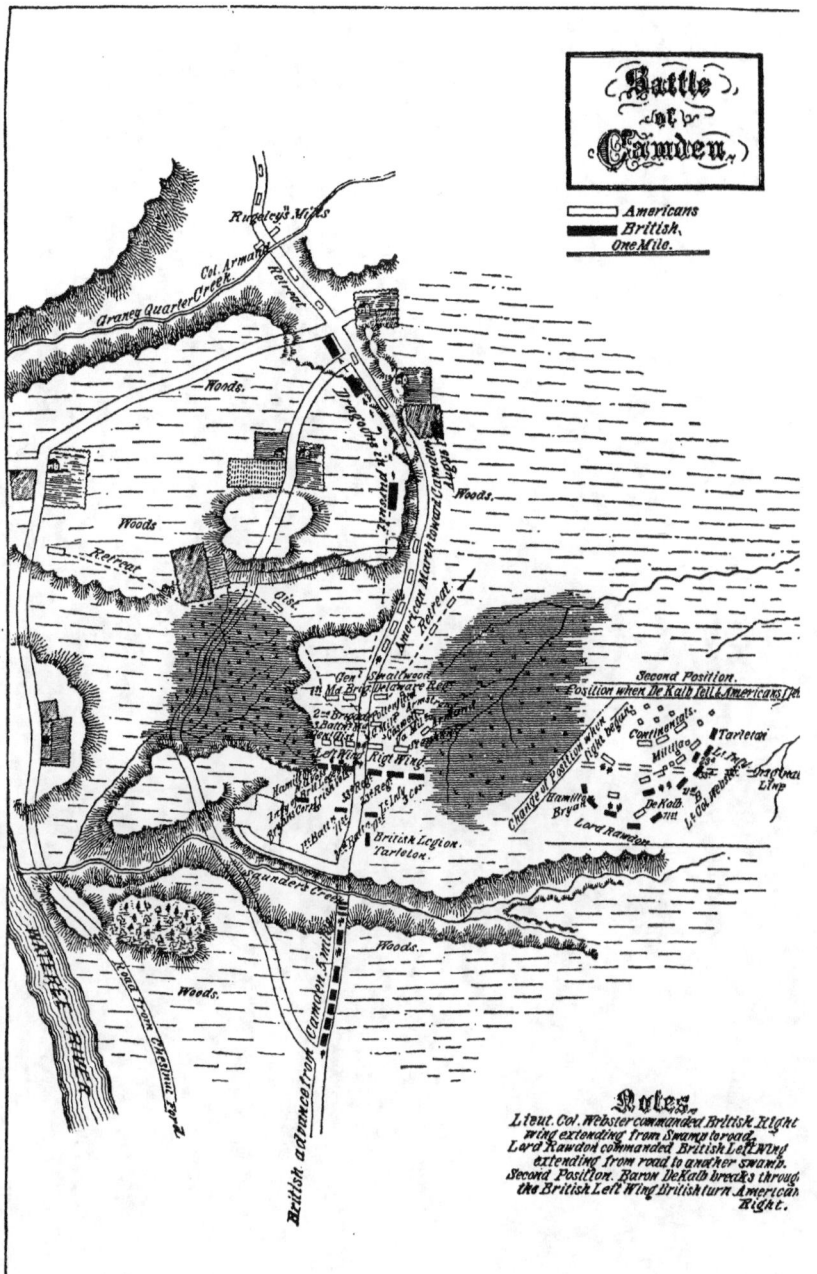

cavalry to protect them, began also to give way. General Rutherford acted with distinguished gallantry, until he received a musket ball through his thigh, which disabled him and he was captured. General Butler vainly endeavored to keep the centre of the North Carolina line in position, but it and a part of the line under General Gregory, who was on the left, fled also. General Gregory, too, was wounded during the thickest of the fight, but by his courageous example a part of his brigade stoutly maintained its position and adhered to the Maryland line.

Lee, in his "Memoirs" of the war, thus narrates the noble conduct of this part of the North Carolina militia:

" None without violence to the claims of honor and justice can withhold applause from Colonel Dixon and his North Carolina regiment of militia. Having their flank exposed by the flight of the other militia, they turned with disdain from the ignoble example; and fixing their eyes on the Marylanders, whose left they became, determined to vie in deeds of courage with their veteran comrades. Nor did they shrink from this daring resolve. In every vicissitude of the battle this regiment maintained its ground, and when the reserve, under Smallwood, covering our left, relieved its naked flank, *forced the enemy to fall back.* Colonel Dixon had seen service, having commanded a Continental regiment under Washington. By his precepts and example he infused his own spirit into the breast of his troops, who, emulating the noble ardor of their leader, demonstrated the wisdom of selecting experienced officers to command raw soldiers.

"The American war presents examples of first-rate courage occasionally exhibited by corps of militia, and often with the highest success. Here was a splendid instance of self-possession by a single regiment out of two brigades. Dixon had commanded a Continental regiment, and of course to his example and knowledge much is to be ascribed, yet praise is nevertheless due to the troops.

"While I record with delight facts which maintain our native and national courage, I feel a horror lest demagogues, who flourish in a representative system of government [the best when virtue rules, the wit of man can devise] shall avail themselves of the occasional testimony to produce a general result.

"Convinced, as I am, that a government is the murderer of its citizens which sends them to the field, uninformed and untaught, where they are to meet men of the same age and strength mechanized by education and disciplined for battle, I cannot withhold my denunciation of its wickedness and folly, much as I applaud, and must ever applaud those instances like the one before us, of armed citizens vieing with our best soldiers in the first duty of man to his country."*

The English historian Lamb, an officer in the British army, says:†

"The Continental troops behaved well, but some of the militia was soon broken. In justice to the North Carolina militia, it should be remarked, that part of the

---
*Lee's Memoirs, pp. 186–'7.
†Lamb's History, p. 304.

brigade commanded by General Gregory acquitted themselves well. They were formed immediately on the left of the Continentals, and kept the field *while they had a cartridge to fire;* Gregory himself was twice wounded by a bayonet in bringing off his men. Several of his regiment and many of his brigade, who were made prisoners, had no wound except from bayonets."

There can be no doubt that if the North Carolina militia had been supported on their left by the Virginians, that the event of this battle would have been far different from the unfortunate result which followed their stampede.

The stubborn courage of Dixon's regiment, which formed the left of the Maryland line, is the more conspicuous when we consider that it was not only attacked in front by Rawdon, but bore the brunt of the charge from the light infantry and twenty-third regiment, which had wheeled from the pursuit of Stevens and Rutherford and concentrated its fire on the North Carolinians who had stood their ground. Steadman relates that "Lord Rawdon began the action on the British left with no less vigor and spirit than Webster had done on the right; but here and in the centre, against a part of Webster's division, the contest was more obstinately maintained by the Americans, whose artillery did considerable execution. Their left flank was, however, exposed by the flight of part of the militia; and the light infantry and twenty-third regiment, who had been opposed to the fugitives, instead of pursuing them, wheeled to the left and came upon the left of the American Continentals, who after a brave resistance for near three-quarters of an hour were thrown into total confusion."*

The Marylanders and Delawares under DeKalb, with Dixon's regiment of North Carolinians, maintained their position until, outflanked and outnumbered, they were compelled to give ground. DeKalb's horse was killed under him and he himself severely wounded, but he continued the fight on foot. "At last," says Bancroft, "he led a charge, drove the division under Rawdon, took fifty prisoners and would not believe that he was not about to gain the day when Cornwallis poured against him a party of dragoons and infantry. Even then he did not yield until disabled by many wounds."

Ramsay gives the following account of the capture of DeKalb and General Rutherford:

"Major General Baron DeKalb, an illustrious German in the service of France, who had generously engaged in the support of American independence, and who exerted himself with great bravery to prevent the defeat of the day, received eleven wounds, of which, though he received the most particular assistance from the British, he in a short time expired. Lieutenant Colonel DuBuysson, aid-de-camp of Baron DeKalb, embraced his wounded General, announced his rank and nation to the surrounding foe, and begged that they would spare his life. While he generously exposed himself to save his friend, he received sundry dangerous wounds and was

*Steadman, vol. 2, p. 209.

taken prisoner.* Brigadier General Rutherford, a valuable officer of the most extensive influence over the North Carolina militia, surrendered to a party of the British Legion, one of whom, after his submission, cut him in several places."

With the fall of DeKalb all was lost. Tarleton's cavalry had now returned from the pursuit of the militia, and the only escape for the remaining Americans was to wade through the morass on their right. In this effort many of the officers made their way out singly or in groups, but Major Anderson, of the 2d Maryland, who afterwards died a glorious death at Guilford, was the only officer who succeeded in keeping any organization. About one hundred of his men clung together with him, and came safely through to Charlotte, North Carolina. "Colonel Howard and others collected some men in their train, and the whole proceeded in a state of utter dissolution to Charlotte. Scarcely any of the wagons escaped, for the horses were used to carry the wounded officers. The artillery, baggage, everything became a prize to the victor, and to the utter astonishment, but infinite relief of the scattered Americans, Lord Cornwallis, satisfied with his triumph, returned to celebrate it in Camden, by offering the lives of his prisoners to the manes of his soldiers or the demon of revenge."†

The bayonet wounds received by General Gregory, of North Carolina, and the men of his brigade

*Ramsay's South Carolina, p. 207.
†Johnson's Life of Greene, vol. 1, pp. 298-'9.

attest the fact that the militia of North Carolina stood before this terrible weapon in the hands of the disciplined regulars of the British army, and grappled with their adversaries in deadly conflict. But few instances in military history occur where the cross of bayonets is recorded; but when it is, the weapons were in the hands of veterans who had been "mechanized" into unflinching soldiers. I venture to assert that history does not record another instance where native courage and a sense of duty enabled untrained militia to engage regular troops with the bayonet and "force them back." This peculiar glory belongs to North Carolina, by the concurrent testimony of friend and foe.

Colonel Dixon, who won such immortal renown on this battlefield, was one of the officers who lost his position as major when the seven regular regiments were compressed into three in May, 1778.

He was familiarly known among his troops as "Hal. Dixon," a pet name of the soldiers who seem to have been familiar with him, and to have borne him great affection. He came to North Carolina, and as soon as the call for the militia to join Caswell was made, he volunteered, and as colonel of militia performed heroic deeds at Camden. He survived the battle, and in 1781, as we shall see, was acting as Inspector General of militia, for want of a regular command. He never sulked in his tent, and was never idle when he could find any military duty to perform. I do not know his native county. He speaks in his letters in 1781 of returning to Caswell County. The roster of regular troops has this entry opposite his name, "Dec'd July 17, 1782."

Colonel Otho Williams, who wrote a defence of General Gates, and who is said to have advised Gates to march direct to Camden, says:

"If in this affair the militia fled too soon the regulars may be thought as blameable for remaining too long on the field, especially after all hope of victory was despaired of."*

It is not within the scope of this work to discuss the merits of the question, but only to deal with facts and results.

No place of rendezvous had been appointed by General Gates in case of defeat; no order was given by him after the battle began, and every soldier who fled followed his own judgment and instinct of safety. Gates fled day and night until he reached Charlotte. He outstripped all his troops in this race.

Rivington in his Gazette of September 13th, 1780, says in regard to his continued flight, "that it was effected on a celebrated horse, the son of Colonel Baylor's Fearnaught, own brother to His Grace, of Kingston's famous 'Careles,' purchased of a general officer of the first distinction."†

It was in this Gilpin race that Gates met Colonel Wm. R. Davie, who was marching to his assistance,

*Carrington Battles of the Am. Rev., p. 517.
†Moore's Diary of Revolution, vol. 2, p. 312.

and Davie urged that at least some one should be sent to look after the dead and wounded, and Gates replied: "Let the dead bury the dead." This was the only text of Scripture that occurred to the General that day, and in its literal application he seems to have found some justification and comfort. His usual reply, when reproached, was "I know how to pit a cock but I don't know how to make it fight," but in this apology there was little reason.

Cornwallis reports the British army at two thousand two hundred and thirty-nine, and his casualties sixty-eight killed and two hundred and fifty-six wounded, but it was undoubtedly more.

General Gates subsequently reported the loss of General DeKalb and five officers killed and thirty-four officers wounded, including Lieutenant Colonels Woodford, Vaughn, Porterfeild and DeBuysson, who were captured, and that by the 29th of August seven hundred non-commissioned officers and soldiers of the Maryland division had rejoined the army.* The Delaware regiment was almost destroyed. "Lieutenant Colonel Vaughn and Major Patton being taken, its remnant, less than two companies, was afterwards placed under Kirkwood, Senior Captain.

The North Carolina militia also suffered greatly; more than three hundred were taken prisoners and a large number killed and wounded. "Contrary to the usual course of events, and the general wish, the Virginia militia who set the infamous example

---

*Carrington's Battles, pp. 517-'18.

which produced the destruction of the army, escaped entirely."*

Well did the noble Delawares maintain the name of the "Blue Hen's Chickens" on that fatal day. They were "pitted" and their dead bodies were strewn all over that bloody field, while he who "pitted" them was cutting the wind on the "son of Fearnaught."

This sobriquet of the "Blue Hen's Chickens" is said to have had its origin in the fondness of a certain Captain Caldwell for cock-fighting. He was an officer of this regiment distinguished for his daring and undaunted spirit. When officers were sent home for recruits they were admonished to get "game cocks," and as Caldwell insisted that no cock could be truly game whose mother was not a "blue hen," the expression "blue hen's chickens" was substituted for game cocks. This sport of cock-fighting was so popular in that day that General Sumter was called the "game cock" for his fighting qualities, while Marion, for his caution and cunning, was called the "swamp fox." We shall record the deeds of this gallant remnant of "blue hen's chickens" on other fields where glory and renown were won.

By this victory the British came into possession of seven pieces of artillery, two thousand muskets, the entire baggage train and prisoners to the num-

*Lee's Memoirs, p. 185.

ber of one thousand, including Generals DeKalb, Rutherford and Gregory.*

It was an appalling misfortune and carried consternation and dismay over the whole country; and had Cornwallis followed up his victory by marching at once into North Carolina the last of the Southern States in his district might have been overrun, but in the exuberance of his joy over the defeat of the conqueror of Burgoyne and the recapture of the English cannon and the subjection of South Carolina, he lost his energy and judgment and sat down to secure and organize the territory he had won, rather than add to his conquests. Tardiness was the weakness of Cornwallis. His extreme caution often taught him the danger of procrastination. It was owing to this fault that Morgan escaped with his men from the Cowpens later in the year.

*Carrington's Battles.

CHAPTER III.

The Scattered Troops and Militia assemble at Charlotte—Colonel W. L. Davidson—General Sumner in Command of the Militia—Letter from Governor Nash—Patriotism of the People—Cornwallis leaves, September 7th, 1780, for North Carolina—Defence of Charlotte by Davie and Graham—Hostile Spirit of the People—Colonel Patrick Ferguson—Movements of the Whig Leaders—Battle of King's Mountain.

ALL opposition in South Carolina seemed to be at an end.

Late on the night of the 16th of August General Gates and General Caswell reached Charlotte together in their ignoble flight. Gates, leaving Caswell to collect the scattered troops at Charlotte, pressed onward to Hillsboro, riding altogether more than two hundred miles in three and a half days. Caswell, after remaining one day, followed Gates.

Before leaving Charlotte General Caswell issued a proclamation calling on the scattered troops of the army to repair to Charlotte and for the militia to assemble there also. The militia of Mecklenburg assembled, and the fugitives from Camden came in daily, but in a deplorable condition, hungry, fatigued, and almost naked, and many had thrown away their arms.* The regular troops mostly passed on to Hillsboro, where General Gates finally established his headquarters. William L. Davidson, lieutenant colonel of regulars, who was just recovering from a wound received at Colson's

---
*General Joseph Graham in University Magazine, vol. 5, p. 97.

in July, was appointed brigadier general of the militia, in the Salisbury district, in the place of General Rutherford who was then a prisoner. General Davidson formed a brigade and encamped on McAlpine's Creek, about eight miles below Charlotte, and in the course of a few weeks was reinforced by General Sumner, who, having no regulars to command, took the command of the militia from the counties of Guilford, Caswell and Orange.*

On the 10th September, 1780, Governor Abner Nash writes to Willie Jones, that "General Smallwood, with the whole of the Maryland line left, is here (Hillsboro) by the order of General Gates. They amount to upwards of 700, which, with above 200 regulars (arrived here yesterday) from Virginia, make the whole of our Continental force. And how long they are to remain here I know not, for the general says that they must be completely refitted with clothes, tents and blankets before he will move them. The Virginia militia are mostly gone home. By the last accounts from Stevens, in Guilford, he had only about 120 men; 1200 of our militia of the *second draft*, under General Sumner, are gone to Salisbury; about 1,000 militia of the upper counties are assembled there and at Charlotte, and in about five days hence 1200 fresh men will march from this district for the westward. In short, sir, we are, for the present, left pretty much to ourselves for the defence of this State, in want of wagons, horses, magazines of provisions,

*University Magazine, vol. 5, p. 54.

arms, ammunition, tents and blankets, and a great portion of the interior part of the country against us. At the same time, I have the pleasure to assure you that *our zeal and spirit rises with our difficulties*, drafts are nearly at an end, our men yield to the necessity of the times and turn out to service with willing hearts. We are blessed with *plentiful crops*, and, with proper laws, resources may easily be drawn forth for the defence of the country."

This letter, so full of hope and courage, in a day when all seemed to be lost, and suffering and distress and confusion were on every hand, reflects honor on the history of the State, and the Governor who then wielded her executive power. Her citizens "turned out to service with willing hearts," and their "zeal and spirit rose with their difficulties."

Major Wm. R. Davie, who was hastening to join Gates, and met him in retreat, now fell back with his small force and took post at Charlotte.

A letter published in 1856 from Major Davie to General Caswell, dated August 29th, 1780, at Charlotte, presents a vivid view of the state of affairs at that crisis. He says: "Last Saturday, with some difficulty, a command of 100 horse was made up. I proceeded with them down the country as far as three miles below Hanging Rock. The Tory militia have returned to their plantations, and threaten to plunder the country, and are murdering the Whiggist inhabitants. The counties of Rowan and Mecklenburg are rich in provision and strong in men, staunch, numerous and spirited, if they were only encouraged to take the field by timely assistance. A small body of regulars, with a few militia from these counties, would still keep the enemy at bay. Our poor wounded in Camden are in a most wretched situation. Colonel Wilson told me General Rutherford had no surgeon but himself, and that many of them had never been dressed. Something should be done for them—it is cruel."*

During this uncertain state of affairs, the Legislature of North Carolina, from an exaggerated estimation of General Smallwood's services, created him a major general, and requested him, though a citizen of Maryland, to take command of our State militia. This very justly offended the pride and sensibilities of a number of State officers, and so mortified General Sumner that for a short time he retired from the service and refused to serve under Smallwood. Bancroft does not conceal his disgust at Smallwood's absence from the scene at Camden, when the reserve was ordered to support the Marylanders, Delawares, and North Carolinians, who were so sorely pressed in front and on the flanks, and Smallwood's claim to have saved them from rout is very questionable.

1780. The suspense in regard to the future movements of Lord Cornwallis was broken on the 7th day of September, when he moved out of Camden and marched by the way of the Waxhaws to

*University Magazine, vol. 5, p. 184.

Charlotte. At the same time he dispatched Colonel Patrick Ferguson in the direction of Ninety-Six, with a corps of one hundred picked regulars, where he soon attached to him about 1200 of the hardy natives in that region. His camp became the rendezvous of the desperate, the idle and the vindictive, as well as the youth of the loyalists.* Colonel Tarleton, with the cavalry and light legion of infantry, was to pursue an intermediate course and move up the western banks of the Wateree. Steadman says that "the reduction of the province of North Carolina was undoubtedly, at this time, confidently looked for. But to confound human wisdom and set at naught the arrogance and presumption of man, unexpected incidents daily arise in the affairs of human life, which, conducted by an invisible hand, derange the best concerted schemes, as will be exemplified in the event of the present expedition." An expansion of the aphorism that "man proposes but God disposes," and never was the truth so strikingly beautiful as in this historical instance. "Darkness and clouds were round about the throne of God" and his mercy seemed to have forsaken the American cause, but "justice and judgment were still the habitation of that throne." The "invisible hand" was moving in the transmontane regions among the pioneers of American civilization and they were soon to descend as a destroying angel on the invading hosts.

*Johnson's Greene, vol. 1, p. 305.

1780. On the 6th of September Major William R. Davie was appointed by Governor Nash colonel commandant of cavalry, and directed to raise a regiment; but he succeeded in raising only part of it, and with two small companies of riflemen under Major George Davidson, he took post at Providence. With fearless resolution he attacked a party of the enemy at Wahab's plantation, killed fifteen or twenty and wounded forty, and came off with ninety-six horses and one hundred and twenty-six stands of arms—a precious acquisition at that juncture, when patriots were more numerous than rifles.

On the advance of the British, Generals Sumner and Davidson retreated by Phifer's, the nearest route to Salisbury, ordering Colonel Davie, with 150 men and some volunteers under Major Joseph Graham, to watch and annoy the foe. Obeying these orders Colonel Davie entered the town of Charlotte on the night of the 20th day of September. At the same time the British were lying within a few miles of the town.*

General Graham relates that at this time the people met to talk over the situation, and "several aged and respectable citizens insinuated that further resistance would under such circumstances be temerity, and only produce more certain destruction to themselves and families, which by some other course might be averted. But this was indignantly repelled by a great majority and especially by those who had been in action at Hanging Rock. Several

---

*Wheeler's History, p. 195, from Life of Davie.

of them stated that they had seen the British soldiers run like sheep, and many of them bite the dust; that they were by no means invincible; that under suitable commanders and proper arrangements they would at any time risk a conflict with them man to man; that their cause was just and they confided that Providence would ultimately give them success, notwithstanding the present unfavorable appearances. As to endeavoring to obtain terms of the enemy, that was out of the question. That their sister State, South Carolina, had tried the experiment and found that no faith was to be placed in British promises, justice, generosity, or honor. Several of them declared that while there was any part of the North American continent to which the British authority did not extend they would endeavor to occupy that. This was one of the times which emphatically 'tried men's souls' rather than, when the enemy was at a distance, sitting in deliberative bodies and passing abstract resolves, to which it is generally applied."*

The general result of the meeting was to make resistance to the last extremity, which accorded with the spirit and judgment of Major Graham.

This accomplished writer, as well as soldier, has given us a most minute account of the daring defence of the handful of men under him and Colonel Davie. As this account has reached comparatively few through the pages of the University Magazine, I am persuaded it will prove most inter-

*General Graham in University Magazine, vol. 5, p. 53.

esting to the general reader, and therefore I copy it entire. The young "hornets" of the old nest will appreciate it, I know.

1780. "Before sunrise on the 26th day of September, Graham's party discovered the front of the enemy advancing, and two of his men, who had been sent down their left flank, reported that the whole army was in motion; that they had seen their artillery, baggage, &c., coming on. They were immediately sent to give Colonel Davie notice, and Graham's troops receded slowly before them. After going a short distance the party were covered from the view of the British by a swell in the ground. They halted and fired on their front as they approached, which the enemy returned briskly, and began to deploy. Graham's party moved on, expecting the British cavalry to pursue, but could see none. (It turned out that they were gone with Tarleton after General Sumter.)

"Within two miles of Charlotte, where the road from the ferry comes in, Tarleton joined them. In five minutes after he arrived, being indisposed after his night's march, Major Hanger took command of the cavalry, and coming in front, compelled Graham to keep at a more respectful distance. He was pursued by the front troops in a brisk canter for a mile; after that they went at a common travel until they came in sight of the village, when they halted that the rear might close up, and some of their officers endeavored to reconnoiter.

"Colonel Davie had nearly completed his disposition for their reception, and during the night and morning had the hospital and military stores removed. Charlotte stands on an eminence of small elevation above the adjacent ground; two wide streets crossing each other at right angles (Tryon and Trade streets), the court-house was in the center, a frame building raised on eight brick pillars, ten feet from the ground, which was the most elevated in the place. Between the pillars was erected a wall of rock three and a half feet high, and the open basement answered as a market for the town. Suitable gaps were made in the lots and other enclosures on the east side of the village for the troops to retire with facility, when compelled to do so. The main body was drawn up in three lines across the street leading to Salisbury, about fifty yards apart, the front line twenty steps from the court-house. Owing to the swell in the ground, and the stone wall aforesaid, the whole was nearly masked from the view of the advancing foe until he came near. One troop was drawn up on each side of the court-house in the cross street, at the distance of eighty yards from it. That on the left was masked by a brick house, that on the right by a log house. Major Dickson of Lincoln (since General Joseph Dickson), with a party of twenty men, was placed behind McComb's house about twenty-nine poles in advance of the court-house on the left of the street. Graham's command (just arrived before the enemy), with Captain John Brandon's troops from Rowan, were placed as a reserve in one line at right angles with the street where the jail now stands. In about thirty minutes after the enemy made his appearance, he had condensed his forces from the loose order of march, by sections, and increased the front of his columns—his cavalry arranged in subdivisions, his infantry in platoons (except the Legion which followed the cavalry). There appeared an interval of about one hundred yards between the columns; the cavalry advanced at a slow pace until fired on by Major Dickson's party; they then came on at a brisk trot until within fifty yards of the court-house, when our first line moved up to the stone wall and fired, then wheeled outwards and passed down the flanks of the second line, which was advancing. The enemy supposing that we were retreating, rushed up to the court-house and received a full fire on each side from the companies placed on the cross street (Trade street); upon which they immediately wheeled and retreated down the street to their infantry, halted and fronted. Their infantry passed out through the lots on each flank and advanced. Our second line, when it reached the court-house, fired at the column of cavalry in retreat, but at rather too great a distance for much execution. Their cavalry now began to move forward again, but the Legion infantry were near one hundred yards in advance on each flank. When they came in view in rear of the lots, they opened a cross-fire on each flank of Davie's men, which, for a short time, was handsomely returned from behind the buildings, but their numbers and firing increasing as they deployed, and the cavalry advancing along the street in a menacing attitude, Colonel Davie ordered a retreat. As soon as the troops who had been engaged passed the reserve, they had to sustain the whole fire of the Legion, which kept advancing parallel with the street, about eighty yards from it. The reserve held their position until they fired two rounds, and moved off in order through the *woods* on the left of the road. The British cavalry kept in thirty poles until Graham's party passed the first Muddy Branch, about three-quarters of a mile from the court-house, and one hundred yards from the road, where they wheeled and fronted (the Muddy Branch being between them and the enemy, one hundred yards beyond), and gave them one fire. They halted, waiting for their infantry, which in a short time came running down their flank and began to fire. Graham ordered his men to disperse, as the woods were thick and they all knew the country. At the distance of two or three miles the most of them collected, where the road crosses Kennedy's Creek (where Frew's farm now is), and as the woods were here thick and deemed suitable to rally in, the men were drawn up fronting the ford, and two men sent over to see whether the horse or foot were marching in front, it being decided that if the former, the troops should fire from their saddles. The men sent over had not gone one hundred yards from their party before they discovered the front of the cavalry at a small distance, and came back and gave information. The party sat on horseback waiting the approach, when the first thing that presented itself to their view, in the edge of the bottom beyond the creek, at the distance of ninety steps, was the front of a full platoon of infantry on each side of the road, on whom they instantly fired and retreated. The enemy fired nearly at the same time, and their balls passing directly through the woods where our line was formed, and skinning saplings and making bark and twigs fly, produced more of a panic in the militia than any disaster which occurred on that day. All the firing in Charlotte and beyond had generally passed over their heads, but here it appeared to be horizontal. The parties commanded by Brandon and Graham passed on in disorder by Sugar Creek Church until they ascended the hill near the cross-roads, where they formed and fronted. The enemy's infantry, which came before, and at a distance of two hundred and fifty yards halted and took to trees and fences, and commenced an irregular fire for near a half hour at long shot. Many of our men dismounted and fired in the same manner, but owing to the distance and shelter of each, it is believed no damage was done on either side. Colonel Davie, with his main force, heard the firing distinctly, and knowing the enemy were coming on, sent an officer to apprise General Davidson, who drew up his men near the ford on Mallard's Creek, where the woods and deep ravines would protect him from the cavalry. Colonel Davie himself formed a mile and a half in his front, at a place called Sassafras Fields; from thence to the cross-roads, near three miles, was an open ridge and large timber (at that time scarcely an undergrowth being upon it) which was quite favorable to the action of cavalry. During the time the enemy had halted and kept up a desultory fire, he was making his arrangements near a small creek in his rear, by placing his best horses in front and sending about one hundred cavalry through the woods to his right, in order that they might come into and up the cross-road, so as to surround the party in front. Their conduct indicated some such movement would be attempted, and the reserve and others who joined them moved on. When they passed the cross-roads, that part of the enemy which debouched were discovered coming up the road on their right within thirty poles distance, and Major Hanger, with the remainder, the same distance in their rear, the whole about three hundred and fifty in number. When the two parties joined at the cross-roads, they came on at a brisk trot, and from that to a canter, as fast as they could preserve order, until they discovered the party before them was, by their pursuit, pressed out of order. Then they charged at full speed. When the pursuit became close, near one-half took to the woods on each side of the road. The front troop of the enemy (commanded by Captain Stewart) pursued them, but the main body, commanded by Major Hanger, kept the road until they came in view of the place where Colonel Davie had formed at Sassafras Fields. Being much out of order by the pursuit, they collected their scattered troopers and returned to their Legion infantry, and one other battalion, about eight hundred men in all, which accompanied the cavalry as far as the cross-roads, and remained there drawn up in position until their return. The main body had halted in Charlotte, whither the whole repaired about sunset.

"On this day we lost Lieutenant George Locke (son of General Matthew Locke) who was literally cut to pieces in a most barbarous manner. The barrel of his rifle with which he endeavored to shelter himself from their sabres was cut in many places. He and two privates were killed, and Colonel Lindsay, of Georgia, who served as a volunteer without any command, and Adjutant Graham* and ten others were wounded. The loss of the enemy could not be ascertained, but was believed to exceed ours. Afterwards two of their dead were found, near where Locke was killed and Graham wounded, one of whom was known to have been shot by Robert Ramsay of Rowan at the time they charged. But they must have sustained the greatest damage in Charlotte. The enemy seemed to understand this Parthian kind of warfare, and maneuvered with great skill—the cavalry and infantry supporting each other alternately as the nature of the ground or opposition seemed to require.

---

*Joseph Graham received nine wounds, three with ball and six with sabre, and was left on the ground.

They taught us a lesson of the kind, which in several instances was practiced against them before the end of the war. During the whole day they committed nothing to hazard, except when the cavalry first charged up to the court-house, and received a heavy fire in front and both flanks at the same time, which compelled them to retreat before their infantry were thrown forward on their flanks. Had we omitted fighting on this day, kept our men and horses fresh (except a few to reconnoiter and give intelligence of the enemy's movements) and been in readiness to strike the foraging parties which his new position would have compelled him to send out, and thus endeavored to take him by detail, it would have been better policy than, with three or four hundred mounted militia men, of whom not one-fourth were equipped as cavalry, attacking a regular army, completely organized, of ten times their number, in an open field, when every person was sure we would be beaten. The small damage sustained in proportion to the risk appeared providential.

"Several of the British officers stated afterwards, if Colonel Tarleton had commanded their van instead of Major Hanger it would have been worse for us. General Davidson retired in the night to Phifer's plantation, twenty miles from Charlotte, and Colonel Davie behind Rocky River, sixteen miles from Charlotte, and four miles in front of Davidson."

This chivalrous defence of their homes and firesides by the men of Mecklenburg and Lincoln and Rowan, reckless as it may seem in the light of future events, is to be commended for the noble and patriotic impulses which prompted it. The lesson of experience in Parthian warfare which the

MAJOR JOSEPH GRAHAM,
MOUNTED INFANTRY 1780-81.
Afterward General of Militia, Historian, Manufacturer &c.
LINCOLN CO. N.C.

British taught them that day more than compensated for the loss they suffered in learning the lesson.

It also taught the militia that the British troops were not so dreadful in attack or destructive in the charge as they may have anticipated. It was well that they were led by so experienced and intrepid a soldier as Major Joseph Graham, whose heroic courage was so conspicuous in the fight. His soldiers were deprived of his example for two months while tender hands dressed his wounds and tender hearts sympathized with his suffering.

"He fell with nine sabre wounds and three from lead. His life was narrowly and mercifully preserved by a large stock-buckle which broke the violence of a stroke which, to human view, must have proved fatal. He received four deep gashes of the sabre over his head and one on his side, and three balls were afterwards removed from his body. After being much exhausted by loss of blood he reached the house of Mrs. Susannah Alexander, where he was kindly nursed and watched during the night."*

It was these wounds which prevented Major Graham from sharing in the glory of King's Mountain a month afterward. He was only twenty-one years old when he received this baptism of blood; but he lived to avenge it all and to see his country independent among the nations of the earth.

*Wheeler's History, vol. 2, p. 234.

Tarleton says "the King's troops did not come out of this skirmish unhurt. Major Hanger, who was in command of the Legion" (Tarleton being sick of a violent fever) "and Captains Campbell and McDonald were wounded and twelve non-commissioned officers and men killed and wounded."

Tarleton was evidently not impressed very favorably with what he discovered in this new region into which, for the first time, the King's army had penetrated, and his disparagement of the people is so honorable to their manhood and patriotism that I cannot forbear to give a few extracts from his narrative. He petulantly says:

"The town and environs abounded with inveterate enemies; the roads were narrow and crossed in every direction and the woods were close and thick. It was evident, as had been frequently mentioned to the King's officers, that the counties of Mecklenburg and Rowan were more *hostile to England than any others in America.* No British commander could obtain any information in that position which would facilitate his designs or guide his future conduct. The foraging parties were every day harassed by the inhabitants, who did not remain at home to receive payment for the produce of their farms, but generally fired from covert places to annoy the British detachments. Notwithstanding the different checks and losses sustained by the militia of the district, they continued their hostilities with unwearied perseverance, and the British troops were so effectually blockaded in their present position that very few out of a great number of messengers could reach Charlottetown in the beginning of October to give intelligence of Ferguson's situation."

Tarleton had discovered a wonderful difference in the temper and disposition of the people of the two Carolinas. The leading men of North Carolina did not hasten to express their penitence for rebellion, but met the foe with arms in their hands and when their regulars were captured, they organized the militia for defence; when these were scattered by British troopers the inhabitants fired upon them, singly and in squads, from the coverts, and scorned the British gold that was offered for the produce of their plantations. Our enemies being our judges, the men of North Carolina "were more hostile to England than any others in America." These splenetic utterances of disappointment and rage have become the pride and boast of those who provoked them. They can well respond in the old Hebrew idiom, "Thou sayest it."

The "amiable Cornwallis" seems to have become as impatient and irascible as his lieutenant, and in his cooler moments even, when writing to Colonel Balfour, of the British army, he could not find decent language sufficiently strong to express his indignation and descended to profane epithet to relieve his chafed spirit.

"Charlotte is an agreeable village," says his lordship, "but in a d—d rebellious country."

The British army which entered Charlotte the 26th September, 1780, consisted of three brigades besides the Legion infantry and cavalry and some Tories who accompanied them. The brigade on the right, commanded by Colonel Webster, encamped on the southeast of the court-house, forty poles from it. The brigade of lord Rawdon encamped across the street leading to Salisbury, thirty poles from the court-house; O'Hara's brigade on the southwest of the court-house; the cavalry, infantry and Tories encamped across the street by which they came (South Tryon).*

Cornwallis immediately took possession of Colonel Thomas Polk's mill, where he found 28,000 pounds of flour and a quantity of wheat, and killed, on an average, 100 cattle per day. The army could only be supported by Webster moving one day and Rawdon the next as covering parties to protect the foragers.†

The vicinity was aptly characterized by lord Cornwallis as a "Hornet's Nest," and this appellation clings to it until this day as the highest encomium which British malignity could unwillingly bestow upon the county.

We can imagine with what suspense and anxiety the British commander was harassed during his short stay, with his sources of information cut off, his messengers intercepted and an enemy concealed along every pathway. Here we shall leave him to contemplate the difficult task of conquering North Carolina, while we follow Ferguson to his fate at King's Mountain.

We have seen that when Cornwallis advanced towards Charlotte that orders were issued to Lieu-

*General Joseph Graham.
†Steadman.

tenant Colonel Patrick Ferguson to advance towards Ninety-Six,* in what is now Abbeville County, South Carolina, on the upper waters of the Saluda River and about sixty or seventy miles directly south of King's Mountain. The purpose of this expedition was to blend the loyalists into military organizations, overawe the Whigs, and to exercise such civil power as might be necessary to place that region of South Carolina completely under the British yoke. He was jocularly said to have had power plenary enough to justify him in celebrating the marriage ceremony. Ferguson was an intrepid soldier and had the entire confidence of his commander. His career had been bold, dangerous and brilliant.

He was the second son of James Ferguson, lord Pitfour, an eminent advocate and for twelve years a Scotch judge. When only fifteen years of age a commission was purchased for him, and on the 12th day of July, 1759, he entered the British army as cornet. He had a varied fortune on the Continent in many battles and when the war of the revolution began he found his way to America as a captain. He had heard much of the superiority of the Americans in the use of the rifle, and this inspired his genius to the invention of a weapon which would counteract the effect of this arm. Ferguson invented a new species of rifle which could be loaded at the breech, without a ramrod, and could be fired seven times in a minute.

---

*Took its name from being 96 miles from Keowee, principal town of the Cherokees.

He was at that time the best rifle shot of the British army, and in adroitness in loading and firing is said to have excelled the best American frontiersman or even the expert Indian of the forest. He was also famous as a pistol shot. While riding he would check his horse, draw a pistol from his holster, toss it aloft, catch it as it fell, aim, and shoot off a bird's head on an adjacent fence.*

In 1777 Sir Henry Clinton placed him at the head of a corps of riflemen picked from the different regiments, and he participated in the battle of Brandywine. Here he was made to experience the accuracy of American aim and the excellence of the American rifle. A rifle-ball shattered his right arm and disabled it for life; but Ferguson, with undaunted resolution, practiced sword exercise with his left until he was a formidable and skilled antagonist with that weapon.

It was at this battle, he relates, that General Washington came in the range of his rifle, but he scorned to shoot so illustrious a man in the back or allow his men to do so. There is doubt, however, as to the identity of the person and many reasons to believe that it was Pulaski and not Washington. It is, however, creditable to Ferguson as a soldier that he spared either of them from assassination.

In 1779, when Sir Henry Clinton fitted out his expedition to Charleston for the subjugation of the Southern provinces, Ferguson was assigned to command a corps of three hundred men and was

*Draper's Heroes of King's Mountain, pp. 50–51.

allowed to choose both his men and officers. He was given the rank of lieutenant colonel commandant. Early in March, 1780, Ferguson and Major Cochrane, with Tarleton's Legion infantry, were sent in pursuit of some American force and the Americans having been advised of their approach abandoned their camp, which Ferguson occupied.

Cochrane subsequently arriving in the vicinity, and supposing the persons in the camp to be Americans, charged them furiously, and a dreadful conflict took place in the night between these English detachments, until at last Cochrane recognized Ferguson's voice and stopped the carnage. Ferguson defended himself gallantly, wielding his sword in his left hand against three assailants until one of them thrust his bayonet through Ferguson's left arm. It was at this moment that Cochrane recognized Ferguson's voice and rescued him.

Ferguson was also at the surprise and defeat of Huger at Monk's Corner. Three of Tarleton's dragoons committed violence on some ladies near the village and were apprehended in the diabolical act. "Ferguson was for putting them to instant death, but Tarleton rescued them." Tarleton it was who afterwards had the "effrontery to boast that he had killed more men and ravished more women than any man in America."[*]

Ferguson is described as of "middle stature, slender make and possessing a serious countenance,

[*] Draper, p. 67.

yet it was his peculiar characteristic to gain the affections of the men under his command."

Irving says "Ferguson was a fit associate for Tarleton in hardy, scrambling partisan enterprise; equally intrepid and determined, but cooler and more open to impulses of humanity."

This was the man who was to lead the left wing of the army of Cornwallis into North Carolina and humiliate the "over-mountain men" and reduce them to subjection and obedience.

Mr. Lyman C. Draper spent twenty years of an industrious and energetic life in writing his splendid work "King's Mountain and its Heroes"—a book perfect in all its parts, evincing a research unsurpassed by any American writer, and so just to North Carolina and her soldiers in the King's Mountain campaign that I hope I will be pardoned for drawing almost entirely upon it for the facts connected with that battle. Mr. Draper has exhausted the sources of information on this portion of history, and nothing can be added to it, and, as far as my examination goes, nothing can be taken from it, without marring the truth.

The meagreness of the account by Tarleton and Steadman is astonishing. It seems to have been a historical bog to them, out of which they floundered with all haste and energy; but to the American student it is the first ebbing of the long tide of misfortune which had swept over the States of Georgia and South Carolina and submerged them in its billows. It was the first ray of hope that gleamed through the darkness and desolation of that period of conquest and wretchedness which followed the advance of a victorious invader.

It was the pivot upon which the steady line of defeat and disaster first deviated from its course and swung from the American arms.

It was the appalling defeat which brought terror to the heart of Cornwallis and drove him sick and faint from the confines of North Carolina and forced him to plunge through the mud of the Waxhaws to the rear line of his defences at Winnsboro.

Mr. Draper has therefore wisely selected this battle as one of the central events of the war for independence, and while many who were conversant with the circumstances attending it were still living, has gathered the rich stores of information and woven them into the most charming narrative of American history.

The camp of Ferguson was on Little River, which is the northern prong of the Saluda. He had come to this place with "from one hundred and fifty to two hundred of the Provincial corps," and was here joined by "the desperate, the idle, the vindictive, who sought plunder or revenge, as well as the youthful loyalists whose zeal or ambition prompted them to take up arms; all found a warm reception at the British camp, and their progress through the country was marked with blood and lighted with conflagration."*

*Draper, p. 72.

The young men of this multifarious collection were thoroughly drilled and disciplined by Ferguson in military tactics, and transformed into a body of formidable soldiers.

It was here that David Fanning, the Tory leader of Orange and Chatham counties, in North Carolina, visited Ferguson and obtained commissions for his followers who were expected to organize when Cornwallis took possession of the State; but this dream was never realized. It was Fanning, too, who forced Andrew Pickens to take British protection. It was this that so embittered General Pickens and gave impetus to his subsequent military career.

In order to train his little army and embody the Tories, Ferguson continued to move about the country and send detachments in every direction. He marched into Union district on the Tyger River and thence northward, through Spartanburg district, South Carolina, to the "Quaker Meadows," in Burke County, North Carolina, the home of Colonel Charles McDowell. The Tories plundered the citizens as they went, of cattle, horses, beds, wearing apparel, even wresting rings from the fingers of ladies, until they were heartily despised by the British officers as well as their countrymen who were contending for liberty.

1780. In July Colonel Elijah Clarke, the noted partisan leader of Georgia, formerly a Virginian, and well known to all the Whigs in upper South Carolina and western North Carolina, attempted to pass through from the Savannah River to join

Colonel Charles McDowell, but was so pressed that most of his followers retraced their steps and dispersed for a while. Colonel John Jones, of Burke County, however, proposed to lead those who would follow to North Carolina. Jones was chosen the leader of this little band and John Freeman as second in command. Passing through a Tory settlement they assumed the disguise of loyalists and hearing of a Tory gathering near by, they attacked and captured them and with them a lot of good arms and stout horses. Next day at Earle's Ford on the Pacolet, in what is now Polk County, they formed a junction with Colonel Charles McDowell.

About twenty miles south of McDowell's camp was Princes' Fort, on the north bank of the Tyger River, occupied by a British and Tory force under Colonel Innes. Unapprised of Colonel McDowell's approach Colonel Innes sent out Colonel Ambrose Mills, a Tory leader of Rutherford County, N. C., in pursuit of Jones. Mills surprised McDowell's camp, supposing the troops of Jones were alone there, and killed and wounded about thirty of them. Among the latter was Jones, who received eight cuts from the sabre. Young Noah Hampton, a son of Colonel Andrew Hampton, was roused from his slumbers and asked his name. He responded "Hampton." This was enough for the "Mills" party. They thrust him through with a bayonet while he was begging for mercy and Colonel Mills paid the penalty for this act under a limb at Gilbert town.*

Colonel McDowell was censured by Hampton for not placing videttes further from his camp, across the river.

Before sunrise the next morning Captain Edward Hampton, with fifty-two active men, including Freeman, began the pursuit of Colonel Mills, and overtaking him routed his party, killing eight at the first fire, and continued the pursuit to the very entrance of Fort Prince.

At 2 o'clock Hampton returned with thirty-five good horses and much baggage, without the loss of a man. Noah Hampton was avenged. It was more than "an eye for an eye."†

I have related in previous pages the campaign of Colonels Charles McDowell, Shelby, Clarke and Williams and the affair at Musgrove's Mill, which it is not necessary to repeat.

1780. On the 29th August Lord Cornwallis writes Sir Henry Clinton, "Ferguson is to move into Tryon County (since Lincoln) with some militia whom he says he can depend upon for doing their duty and fighting well; but I am sorry to say that his own experience, as well as that of every other officer, is against him." As McDowell,

---

*Mills was also accused of hanging Adam Cusack on the Pee Dee. Gordon, vol. 4, p. 29.

†Captain Edward Hampton was a brother of Colonel Wade Hampton of Sumter's command. He was killed by Colonel Cunningham's "Bloody Scouts" in October, on Fair Forest Creek.

Shelby, Clarke and Williams had now retired to the back parts of North Carolina and many across the mountains to their homes in Sullivan and Washington counties, Ferguson followed in that direction, and for awhile encamped at Gilberttown, three miles north of the present village of Rutherfordton. Here he issued his proclamation calling on the citizens to renew their allegiance and join the King's army. Some were overawed by this bold display of royal power in their very midst, and hearing of the rout and flight of the only Continental army then in the South, they were induced to take protection; and a few from premeditation, and by advice of the Whig leaders, took the oath in order that they might save the cattle and property of that region, as much as possible, for the use of the Whig forces and their families.*

---

*NOTE.—While in this mountain region Ferguson found he had a case of small-pox developing itself. It was one of his officers, who was left at a deserted house, taking his favorite charger with him, and there this poor fellow died in this lonely situation. It is said his horse lingered there till he died. It was long before any one would venture to this pest-house.

"There lay the rider, distorted and pale,
With the dew on his brow and the rust on his mail."

Finally some one ventured there and carried off the sword, holsters and pistols, selling them to John Ramsour of Lincoln, who gave them thirty years after to Michael Reinhardt.—*Draper's King's Mountain*, p. 147.

This sword was given by W. M. Reinhardt, son of Michael Reinhardt, to Dr. D. R. Schenck, by whom it was presented to the Guilford Battle-Ground Company in 1887, and it now hangs, at that battleground, among the Revolutionary relics collected by that company.

But Ferguson was not allowed to ravage the country with impunity. He marched, with a detachment, in search of Colonel Charles McDowell. He found him, but not where he expected or wished to find him. McDowell laid an ambuscade for him at Bedford Hill, three miles southwest of Brindletown, near a crossing of Cane Creek, called Cowan's Ford. While the British were crossing the Whigs fired upon them, severely wounding Major Dunlap, one of the favorite and most energetic officers of Ferguson's corps, in the leg, and killing others. Ferguson was forced to retire to Gilberttown to escape with his own life.

McDowell being unable to resist the large British force now in North Carolina, retreated across the Blue Ridge to the "Watauga Settlements," as the region where Shelby and Sevier lived was then called. He related to Sevier and Shelby the desolation which marked the advance of Ferguson, and urged them to join the mountain men on the other side and resist his approach.

1780. Colonel Shelby, with the approbation of Major Robertson, then proposed that an army of volunteers be raised on both sides of the mountain, in sufficient numbers to cope with Ferguson.* All the officers and some of the privates were consulted and all cordially coincided with the proposition. It was agreed that the over-mountain men should recruit and strengthen their numbers, while Colonel Charles McDowell should send a messenger to

---

*Draper, p. 118.

Colonels Cleveland and Herndon of Wilkes County, and Major Joseph Winston of Surry County, North Carolina, urging them to raise a volunteer corps and share in this patriotic enterprise. McDowell was moreover requested to convey intelligence constantly to the "over-mountain." men of Ferguson's movements, and to preserve, as much as possible, the beeves of the Whigs in the upper Catawba, which would be needed by them.

Colonel Clarke took the mountain trails and returned to Georgia. Colonel Williams, who had a few years before resided in Orange County, North Carolina, conducted the Musgrove prisoners to Hillsboro, in that county.*

Ferguson continued his headquarters at Gilberttown. Major Dunlap, who was perhaps the most hardened of all the Tory leaders, and whom McDowell's men had severely crippled at Cane Creek, was on crutches at the house of William Gilbert, a loyalist. He had followed the fortunes of Ferguson in his northern campaigns, and Johnson, in his life of Greene, says, "Dunlap had rendered himself infamous by his barbarities." Numerous instances of his oppression and cruelty at Gilberttown are related by Draper, and he thus describes an attempt on Dunlap's life:

---

*Very many of the facts related by Draper are derived from a manuscript prepared by Captain David Vance, the grandfather of Senator Z. B. Vance, of North Carolina, which was preserved by Robert Henry, of Buncombe County. Both were American soldiers at King's Mountain.

"When Ferguson suddenly left Gilberttown on the approach of the over-mountain men, Dunlap was left behind. The avenger of blood was nigh. Two or three men from Spartanburg rode to the door of the Gilbert house, when the leader, Captain Gillespie, asked Mrs. Gilbert if Major Dunlap was not up stairs. She frankly replied that he was, supposing that the party were loyalists, and had some important communication for him. They soon disabused her of their character and mission, for they declared that he had been instrumental in putting some of their friends to death, and moreover had abducted the beautiful Mary McRea, the affianced of Captain Gillespie, as she would not encourage his amorous advances, and kept her in confinement, trusting that she would in time yield to his wishes; but death came to her relief; she died of a broken heart. They had now come for revenge, Gillespie particularly uttering his imprecations on the head of the cruel destroyer of all his earthly hopes. So saying they mounted the stairs, when Gillespie abruptly approached Dunlap as he lay in bed, with the inquiry: 'Where is Mary McRea?' 'In heaven!' was the reply. Whereupon the injured Captain shot Dunlap through the body, and quickly mounting their horses, Gillespie and his associates bounded away to their homes."

Gilberttown was to witness other tragedies in the near future, when the Whig leaders sat in judgment upon the murderers of McDowell's men. It was "a dark and bloody ground" where Whig and Tory alternately meted out vengeance to their captured foes.

Singular to relate, Dunlap did not die of this wound, but was concealed by his friends and turned up at Ninety-Six the ensuing March, where he went out with a foraging party of seventy-six dragoons. He was overtaken by Colonel Clarke and Major McCall at Beattie's Mill, in which he took refuge. He resisted until thirty-four of his men were killed and wounded, himself among the latter. The party then surrendered. "The British account of this affair stated that Dunlap was murdered by the guard having him in charge after the surrender; but such was not the fact," adds McCall, "for he died of his wounds the ensuing night." It is, however, justly surmised that he fell a victim to a just revenge and met a timely end.

We shall now endeavor to trace the events transpiring in the transmontane counties of Sullivan and Washington, North Carolina, and the regions of Rutherford, Burke, Wilkes, Surry and Tryon, from whence came the heroes and the men who were soon to make for themselves an immortal fame; also to look to Virginia, from which the "Campbells were coming" to the rescue of their neighbors and friends, and not forget the Spartan band from South Carolina, who joined the others to share in the glory of King's Mountain.

1780. The "over-mountain men" were so called from their location on the west of the Alleghany Mountains. North Carolina, at that time, extended from the Atlantic to the Pacific, and from the Virginia line on the north to a line south in latitude

35° 34″, extending from ocean to ocean, and took in all of that territory now embraced in the State of Tennessee.

Sullivan County was bounded by the Virginia line on the north, and just south of it was Washington County, both in North Carolina. North of the Virginia line and joining Sullivan County, North Carolina, was Washington County, Virginia. Sullivan and Washington counties, North Carolina, had been settled by Virginians who gradually made their way south along the slopes of the mountain, following the beautiful streams of the Holston, Watauga and Nollichucky and settling on their fertile valleys. Just south and southwest of these frontier settlements were the Cherokee Indians, extending in their domains to the Mississippi River. These Indians were at this time hostile to the whites, having been stirred up against them by British emissaries who had been sent among the tribe for that purpose. They had promised to invade the frontiers in the Fall, and to penetrate, if possible, as high up in southwest Virginia as the Chiswell Lead Mines, from which the Americans drew their supply of lead, and destroy the works and stores at that place.

Colonel John Sevier was the commander of the militia of Washington County, North Carolina, and resided on the Nollichucky River, from which circumstance he was familiarly known as "Nollichucky Jack."

Colonel Isaac Shelby was the commander of the

militia of Sullivan County, North Carolina, and Colonel William Campbell was in command of the militia of Washington County, Virginia, though his cousin and brother-in-law, Colonel Arthur Campbell, seems to have been his superior in rank in the county.

Colonel Benjamin Cleveland was the Colonel of the militia of Wilkes County, North Carolina, on the eastern slope of the Alleghanies, bordering on Washington County, Virginia, and Major Winston was from the adjoining county of Surry on the east.

Colonel Hambright and Major Chronicle were from Tryon County, North Carolina, and as we have seen before, Colonel Charles McDowell, and his brother, Major Joseph McDowell, were from Burke County, North Carolina, south of Wilkes, and Colonel Andrew Hampton was from Rutherford County. All these counties were contiguous.

1780. When Ferguson took post at Gilberttown in the early part of September, smarting under the remembrance of Musgrove's Mill, he paroled Samuel Phillips, who had been left at the mill wounded, and sent him with the verbal message to the "over-mountain men" that if they did not desist from their opposition to the British arms he would march his men over the mountains, hang their leaders and lay their country waste with fire and sword. It was a threat that Ferguson would have carried into effect if power and opportunity had been at his command. Phillips resided near Colonel Shelby's home in Sullivan County and soon communicated to him the message of Ferguson and the information he had in regard to Ferguson's command.

A few days after this message was received Colonel Shelby rode forty miles to a spot near the present site of Jonesboro, Tennessee, where he met Colonel Sevier and told him of the return of Phillips, and the information imparted to him.

These frontier men always acted upon the idea that it was much safer for their homes and their wives and children to meet a foe on his approach, and defeat him on his own territory, rather than allow him to make the seat of war in their own county; and these two men agreed at once that they would call together their own forces and endeavor, if possible, to procure assistance from Colonel William Campbell, to repel this threatened invasion. There was no time to lose; their safety was in the celerity of their movements and the boldness of their attack. It was agreed that the clans were to gather at the Sycamore Flats, on the Watauga River, below the present village of Elizabethtown, Tennessee, on the 25th day of September. Colonel Shelby immediately wrote to Colonel William Campbell, apprising him of the situation, and urged him to join the expedition with all the men he could raise. Captain Moses Shelby, a brother of the Colonel, was the messenger. Campbell did not at first approve the plan, and declined to go. Colonel Shelby then wrote a still more urgent letter, entreating him to come to the rescue of themselves and the Burke men, who were there as exiles among them and ready to join the expedition. Campbell was touched with this appeal to his generosity and gave his consent to the expedition. At a consultation of the field officers of his county it was arranged that half the militia should remain to repel the expected Indian invasion and the other half should join Shelby and Sevier.

At the same time Colonel Campbell sent an express to Colonel Cleveland, of Wilkes County, North Carolina, apprising him also of the situation and requesting him to meet them on the eastern side of the mountain with the militia of his county.

The time of assembling indicated was the 30th of September, the place was the "Quaker Meadows," in Burke County, North Carolina, the home of the McDowells, two miles north of Morganton.

Sevier found great difficulty in raising the necessary funds to properly equip his men, as his own means, which he freely offered, were small, and in this pressing emergency he applied to John Adair, the agent of North Carolina for the sale of lands in that county, for aid. Adair replied: "I have no authority to loan the money, but if the country is overrun by the British our liberty is gone. Let the money go too. Take it." Thus about twelve thousand dollars of a campaign fund was raised and ammunition and equipments were procured. Both Sevier and Shelby pledged themselves personally to return the loan or to have the act of the agent legalized by the Legislature of the State.

The appointment of the over-mountain men was kept. On the 25th day of September Colonel Campbell appeared at the Sycamore Flats with two hundred men and Colonels Sevier and Shelby with two hundred and forty men each. There Colonels McDowell and Hampton's party had been in camp for some time. The whole force at that place aggregated about eight hundred and fifty men. They were mostly mounted men and armed with the deadly Deckard rifle which I have described in previous pages.

They were expert in its use alike against the Indians and the wild beasts of the forest. Their muscles were strong and steady, their aim unerring. They feared no foe while the Deckard was in their grasp. It had been their defence against the savage foe; with it they had combatted the bear and the panther successfully; it had brought the deer and turkey for their subsistence; the loyalists had quailed before it at Musgrove's Mill and they felt confident that Britith valor and discipline would succumb before its deadly missile. Bayonets they had none, but the trees of the forest were a breastwork for refuge; they had no tents, but the deep blue sky of the mountains, bestudded with stars, was a canopy more splendid than oriental imagination could conceive. They had neither baggage wagons nor quartermaster's stores, nor commissary to provide them food. The noble horse which each man owned, and loved with an Arab's fondness, carried the wallet and the blanket: the one contained a supply of parched meal, and they trusted Providence to increase the store as necessity required; the other was the only covering from the winter's chill. Their dress was the hunting shirt made from woolen cloths manufactured by their wives and daughters, and the fur skin cap, taken from the animals of the forest, covered their heads. At their side in the belt was the tomahawk and the knife. With the little ax a brush arbor might be constructed and the knife was the camp tool for every purpose. A tin cup completed the outfit. The horses were to be subsisted on the grass which was at that time in luxuriant abundance all over the mountains and far off into the plains.

We can imagine these sturdy sons of the wilderness shouting welcome to every gathering band as it approached the camp and running to greet them hand in hand; how quickly and anxiously they inquired the news from Ferguson, and pressed around the camp-fires of McDowell to listen to the story of his exile and hear his plans for expelling the foe from their homes.

The exclamations of defiance and the voice of indignation were heard from every lip. The hand impulsively grasped the rifle, the eye flashed, restlessness and impatience characterized every action.

The glance of the men met the gaze of the leaders and unison was felt though only a smile or a nod was given. Their hearts were locked, as the shields of old, and nothing but death was to separate their strength.

When nearly ready to begin the march the sound of approaching voices was heard once more. The camp was astir; unexpected visitors were discovered in the distance; nearer they came and recognition was announced by a wild shout of joy, and Colonel Arthur Campbell led two hundred men more into the camp. One thousand and fifty voices now made the welkin ring with their glad acclaim. Colonel Campbell fearing that there might not be men enough to secure certain victory, determined, after Colonel William Campbell had left, to reinforce his strength. This being now done, he bade his men "Godspeed" and a hearty "good-bye" and returned to his home again.

As soon as Colonels McDowell and Shelby and Sevier had finally determined to attack Ferguson, Colonel McDowell hastened across the mountain to encourage the people, to obtain information and hasten the march of Cleveland and Winston to the place of rendezvous at the "Quaker Meadows."

Early on the 26th of September the little army was ready to begin its march and only one preparation for the journey was yet to be made. God's blessing must be invoked and His omnipotent protection supplicated. The Rev. Samuel Doak, the pioneer missionary of the Watauga settlements, was present. These stern, hardy, stalwart men, "true lightwood at heart," bowed their heads in reverence while the good man recounted to God the dangers with which they were threatened from the marauding hosts of the British in their front and the barbarous savage, little less wicked, in their rear, and repeating the promises of mercy with which the word of God abounded, he earnestly plead for protection and safety, in this time of need, and for guidance and victory to those who were marching to defend their homes and their families. As he proceeded his voice faltered but his faith grew stronger. He remembered the Midianites and the children of Israel hid in the holes of the mountains and the greatness of God's deliverance, and pausing for a moment, he exclaimed, "The sword of the Lord and of Gideon!" Tears stole down the furrows of the rough-skinned men of the forest but their faith was strengthened. The preparation was over, the march was begun.

The prayer was recorded in heaven. The answer came through the fire and smoke of battle on King's Mountain. Its voice was heard above the rattle of British muskets and the rifle's shrill crack on the ascending heights. The blasphemous boast of Ferguson, that he was on the "King's Mountain" and that God Almighty could not drive him from it, had been rebuked and his lifeless form lay prostrate on his chosen spot.

The march continued through the solitary wilderness along the mountain trails. That evening they reached the "resting-place,"* after a twenty miles march.

The next day they were delayed in slaughtering some beeves for the journey, and went only four

*In Cherokee, "Aquone."

miles, to the base of the Roan and Yellow Mountains.

The 28th September they ascended these mountains, following "Bright's trace." As they climbed higher the snow was shoe-mouth deep. On top they found a hundred acres of beautiful table-land; here was a bold spring and they struck camp.* When the troops paraded they fired off their rifles, and it is related that the air was so rarified there was little or no report.

While on this "bald" of the mountain the devil entered into James Crawford and Samuel Chambers and they deserted and made their way to Ferguson, hoping to save their lives by their treachery. It was therefore resolved to take a different trail from the one at first chosen, so as to baffle any spy Ferguson might send to intercept and watch their approach.

"Descending Roaring Creek eastwardly, they came to the North Toe River, running south, and a mile below passed Bright's place, now Avery's, thence down North Toe southwardly to a noted spring on the Davenport place (now the Childs' place), and rested at noonday." After a hard day's march they reached Cathey's, at the mouth of Grassy Creek,† and rested for the night. Here they ate their parched corn meal and the remnant of beef in their wallets.

On Friday, the 29th, the route lay up Grassy

---

*Most probably the Avery Spring at Cloudland Hotel, on the Roan.
†Near by what is now known as Spruce Pine P. O.

Creek to its head, and over Gillespie's Gap, on the Blue Ridge. Here they divided, Campbell following a trail six miles south to Wofford's Fort, the others to Hunnycut's Creek. At this latter place Colonel Charles McDowell rejoined the forces and imparted such information as he had acquired. He had sent James Blair to hasten Cleveland's march. Blair met Colonel Cleveland on the way, at Fort Defiance, but on his route Blair was waylaid by a stealthy Tory and wounded from an ambuscade.

On Saturday morning, the 30th September, the over-mountain men, passing over Silver and Linville Mountains, in an eastwardly course, and down Paddie's Creek, reached the "Quaker Meadows;" the hospitable home of Colonel Charles McDowell, and his brother, Major Joseph McDowell. Here the "fatted calf" was killed, the corn-cribs and smoke-houses thrown open, the camp-fires lighted and good cheer prevailed in that lovely valley. It was not long until another shout of welcome was heard echoing among the mountains and carrying glad tidings down the valley of the Catawba. Colonel Cleveland and Major Winston, with three hundred and fifty North Carolinians from the counties of Wilkes and Surry, were approaching the camp. They were kindred spirits from the mountains on the eastern slope, and were soon mingling joyfully with their comrades in arms.

Cleveland's regiment had marched up the Yadkin to the mouth of Warrior Creek, thence in a southwest course to old Fort Defiance, thence to Fort

Crider, where the village of Lenoir now stands, thence by way of Lovelady Ford on the Catawba, and passing the present site of Morganton to Quaker Meadows.* As they crossed Lovelady Ford, a stealthy Tory was lying in wait for Colonel Cleveland, and mistaking his brother Lieutenant Larkin Cleveland for him, shot Larkin through the leg, severely wounding him, so that he was left at McDowell's home. Another Tory had wounded Blair, the messenger that McDowell had sent to Cleveland. It was an internecine strife among these mountain men. This little army was now constituted as follows: North Carolinians under Shelby, Sevier, McDowell and Cleveland, nine hundred and eighty (980) men; Virginians under Campbell, four hundred (400) men, aggregating 1380 hardy and determined soldiers.

The weather had been fair, the air bracing and crisp. The men were cheerful and full of spirit; the horses fresh and active.

Sunday morning, October the 1st, 1780, dawned brightly upon the Whigs. The work of deliverance was a work of necessity. The horses were saddled and the march resumed.

Ferguson was almost in their grasp (as they supposed) at Gilberttown, and with eager footsteps they pressed forward for the prey. They passed Brindletown at noonday and camped in a gap of the South Mountain near where Colonel McDowell had pun-

---

*These routes can easily be traced on Kerr's large map of North Carolina.

ished Ferguson so severely when he went in quest of the Burke men. That evening it rained for the first time since they started.

Monday the rain descended all day and the army remained in camp. They were now in sixteen miles of Gilberttown and no commander had been chosen. A conference was held and Colonel Charles McDowell was selected to visit General Gates at Hillsboro and request him to send them a general officer.

Shelby proposed that during the absence of a general officer Colonel Campbell should command. He argued that all the field officers were from North Carolina, except Campbell, and it would be generous for them to elect him to that high position; that this would heal all jealousy and give them a trustworthy head, which was indispensable in the prompt execution of any plan they might adopt.

This counsel prevailed and Colonel Campbell accepted the honor conferred upon him. Colonel Shelby in 1823 explained his object in effecting this result by saying that he wished to displace Colonel McDowell, who by seniority of commission was entitled to the command; that "McDowell was brave and patriotic but too far advanced in life and too inactive for such an enterprise." This objection of age, however, was but a pretext, as Colonel McDowell was only thirty-seven years old. The truth was that Shelby considered him as lacking "in tact and efficiency." It was hoped too that McDowell would hasten back with General Morgan, whom the troops preferred above all others.

Colonel McDowell, than whom no braver man or purer patriot lived, looking steadily to the redemption of the land from the invaders, and sacrificing all personal considerations, submitted without murmuring to the counsel of his brother officers. He set off at once on his mission, leaving his men under the command of his brother, Major Joseph McDowell.

Colonel Campbell was now the commander-in-chief but subject to the council of the officers of this little army.

In order to trace the concentration of another clan, who were to become allies in this campaign, it is necessary to leave our friends, who were at Cane Creek, for a few days.

The digression is painful, because it necessitates the repetition of unpleasant incidents in the career of one who was soon to yield his life as a sacrifice on the altar of his country; one who was brave; one who, when his neighbors and friends were taking British protection around Ninety-Six, scorned to save his property by so base an act; one who left family, comforts and home to endure the hardships of the camp rather than be a slave of a tyrant at home. Whatever may have been his infirmities or his faults he was true to his principles and yielded up his life in the fight to maintain them. No nobler death could have befallen him, and we honor the man who fills a patriot's grave.

It will be remembered that Colonel James Williams, lately from South Carolina, though for some years previous a citizen of Granville County, North Carolina, where he was raised from boyhood, was sent with the Musgrove Mill prisoners to Hillsboro, North Carolina. While there he met Governor Rutlege, who was a refugee from his State, and on Colonel Williams' representations of his own conduct in the late engagement, the Governor, who had been invested with dictatorial powers, commissioned him as a brigadier general. It is alleged that these representations were not true; at any rate this appointment excited the jealousy of Colonels Lacey and Hill, who were then located with a detachment of troops in fork of the Catawba River and the "South Fork" of that stream. They were Sumter's command, Sumter being at that time wounded and not on duty. The piedmont section of South Carolina had been entirely overrun and the patriot band, under Lacey and Hill, had sought, with thousands of others, a refuge in North Carolina, where they found welcome and friends.

General Williams, before returning to duty, requested and obtained permission from Governor Nash to recruit one hundred men in North Carolina.*

---

*NOTE.—The following is the original order:

A. NASH TO COLONEL JAMES WILLIAMS.
(Original MS.)

HILLSBOROUGH, Sep. 8th, 1780.

SIR :—You are desired to go to Caswell County, and to such other counties as you think proper, and use your best endeavors to collect any number of volunteer horsemen, not exceeding one hundred, and proceed with them into such parts as you judge proper, to act against the enemy, and in this you are to use your own discretion. You may assure the men who turn out with you that they shall be entitled to all the advantages and privileges of militia in actual service, and that it shall be considered as a tour of duty under the militia law, they serving the time prescribed by law for other militia-men. All commissaries and other staff officers are required to grant you such supplies as may be necessary.

In getting your men you are to make no distinction between men already drafted and others; and in case of need, you are to impress horses for expresses and other cases of absolute necessity. A. NASH.

"Under this authority he enlisted these men, while encamped at Higgins' plantation, in Rowan County, North Carolina. Colonel Brandon and Major Hammond of his force were quite active in this service. His call for troops was dated the 23d of September, 1780. These new troops constituted the largest part of his force, and with this addition he marched to the camp of Lacey and Hill, and exhibiting his commission as brigadier general, demanded that they should put themselves under his command. This they refused, whether rightfully or wrongfully it is too late to determine now. Hot words ensued and Williams separated himself from them. It had been the design of Lacey and Hill to join General Davidson, who was posted at that time between Charlotte and Salisbury, North Carolina, and they had sent a messenger to him with this proposition. The messenger returned with the tidings which Davidson had received through Col. Charles McDowell, that a considerable body of men from the mountains were approaching Ferguson with a view of attacking him. That day Colonel William Graham and Lieutenant Colonel Frederick Hambright of Tryon County joined Lacey and Hill with sixty or more men. These with the one hundred men under Williams aggregated one hundred and sixty more North Carolinians who were soon to join the "over-mountain men."

Lacey and Hill now thought best to attempt a reconciliation with General Williams, which was finally accomplished by an agreement that they should elect a commanding officer. Information was now received through spies that Campbell's army was in the South Mountains of Burke County and advancing. The combined forces of Lacey, Hill, Williams and Graham immediately decamped, and crossing the upper forks of Dutchman's Creek proceeded to Ramsour's Mill, near where the town of Lincolnton, in Lincoln County, is now situated; from there they marched west, taking the Flint Hill road to "Flint Hill," in Rutherford County, now known as "Cherry Mountain," which is eight or ten miles east of what is now Rutherfordton in that county. Here on the 3d day of October they took up quarters and waited for information, and here it was that Colonel Charles McDowell called upon them on his way to see General Gates at Hillsboro.

The mountain men were then only sixteen miles distant, but as Colonel McDowell could not say whether Campbell had moved after his departure or not, they preferred to await developments.

At this time Campbell's men, as we shall briefly designate them for the present, were of opinion that the decisive struggle was to take place at Gilberttown and they began preparations for the battle. The troops were to be informed of the plans of their leaders and to be exhorted by them to be ready for duty. They were drawn up in a circle and Colonel Cleveland was the orator. Rude and uncultivated as he was, he had an earnestness and honesty in his language and manner that arrested the attention of his hearers, who were in the same sphere of intelligence as himself and as devoted to liberty as he.

His speech was short and pointed and plain. He said: "The enemy is at hand; we must be up and at them. I will be with you when the pinch comes. If any of you shrink from the battle and the glory you can now have the opportunity to back out and leave, and you may have a few minutes for consideration." "You who wish to back out will, when the word is given, march three steps to the rear and stand."

There was a pause for three minutes and the word was given, but not a man of that army moved— they "stood like a stone wall," with eyes that never quailed and nerves that never trembled.

The troops were then dismissed and in three hours the march down Cane Creek began. They came near to Gilberttown on the 4th day of October eager for the fray. They met Jonathan Hampton who first gave them the news that Ferguson had retreated in haste and intended to avoid an action.

On the 27th day of September Ferguson, in the hope of intercepting Colonel Clarke, who had been repulsed at Augusta, Georgia, and was retreating towards North Carolina, moved south from Gilberttown and halted on Green River, in what is now Polk County.

On the 30th day of September the two deserters, Crawford and Chambers, reached Ferguson's camp at James Steps' place, and apprised him that the over-mountain men were on his track.

Ferguson was alarmed. Many of his Tory allies were on furlough, and his ranks were thin. Messengers were sent in all directions to drum up the men on furlough, and a dispatch to Lord Cornwallis at Charlotte, acquainting him of the danger, was intrusted to Abram Collins* and Peter Quinn, Tories of that region, who promised to deliver it in person. Collins and Quinn took a direct course, crossing Second Broad at Webb's Ford, then by way of what is now Mooresboro to First Broad at Stices' Shoal, thence by Collins' Mill, on Buffalo. Coming to Alexander Henry's, a good Whig, they deceived him and were given refreshments, but some circumstance aroused Mr. Henry's suspicion after they left, and his sons followed to arrest them. Collins and Quinn got wind of the pursuit and were compelled to secrete themselves by day and travel with great caution at night, and by reason of these delays they did not reach Charlotte until the 7th day of October—the day of Ferguson's overthrow at King's Mountain.

Ferguson now gave out that he was in retreat for Ninety-Six, to delude the Whigs towards that route. On the 1st of October, the day the Whigs left "Quaker Meadows," Ferguson was at Baylis Earles', on Pacolet; thence he turned northwest to Denard's Ford, on the Broad River, where he issued the following proclamation to the country:

"GENTLEMEN:—Unless you wish to be eat up by an inundation of barbarians, who have begun by murder-

*Abram Collins was a noted counterfeiter after the revolution.

ing an unarmed son before the aged father, and afterwards lopped off his arms, and who, by their shocking cruelties and irregularities, give the best proof of their cowardice and want of discipline; I say, if you wish to be pinioned, robbed and murdered, and see your wives and daughters, in four days, abused by the dregs of mankind—in short, if you wish or deserve to live and bear the name of men, grasp your arms in a moment and run to camp. The 'Back-water men' have crossed the mountains; McDowell, Hampton, Shelby and Cleveland are at their head, so that you know what you have to depend upon. If you choose to be degraded forever and ever by a set of mongrels, say so at once, and let you women turn their backs upon you and look out for real men to protect them.

"PAT. FERGUSON,
"*Major 71st Regiment.*"

It was the appeal of a desperate man, who appreciated the danger that was rapidly approaching nearer to him. He uttered falsehood and exaggerated the situation that he might arouse a like feeling of desperation in the hearts of his Tory allies. But to an observant mind it was the cry of despair, the acknowledgment of ruin, the wail over his sinking fortunes.

From Denard's Ford* Ferguson moved, on Monday, the 2d October, only four miles and lay on his arms all night expecting an attack.† On the 3d October he marched east through Rutherford

---

*This was half mile below the present Twitty's Ford.
†Campbell's force was then at Cane Creek, one day's journey south from "Quaker Meadows."

County crossing Second Broad River, which runs north and south, at Camp's Ford, then six miles further crossing Sandy Run Creek, at Armstrong's, where they rested awhile; thence seven miles further to Buffalo Creek (according to Draper) and camped at Tate's place.*

At Tate's plantation Ferguson tarried the 4th and 5th of October waiting for intelligence from the Whigs. While there he sent the following dispatch to Cornwallis:

"My Lord:—I am on my march to you by a road leading from Cherokee Ford, north of King's Mountain. Three or four hundred good soldiers would finish this business. *Something must be done soon.* This is their last push in this quarter.

"Patrick Ferguson."

Up to this time Ferguson had escaped from his pursuers and evidently intended to reach Cornwallis if possible. He was then sixteen miles from "King's Mountain," which was to the southwest, while Charlotte, where Cornwallis lay, was directly east only thirty-five miles distant, and there were no forces, except a few militia, to intercept his march to that place. It may be, and it is probable, that Ferguson's pride outweighed his judgment and he determined to risk a battle rather than enter Charlotte a fugitive from the men he affected to

---

*This was in the southeastern portion of what is now Cleveland County, N. C.

despise ; or it may be that a destiny was shaping his ends which he felt but could not resist. The King's Mountain stood invitingly out to lure him to his fate, and in the vanity of his soul he believed himself invincible.

Whatever may have been the strange reason that impelled his conduct, Ferguson abandoned his intention to join Cornwallis. He passed to the southwest near where Whitaker's Station, on the Air-Line Railroad, is now, and on in the direction of Yorkville.

On this road, after crossing the creek, on the right hand, and two hundred and fifty yards from the pass, he came to "King's Mountain." This was on the evening of the 6th of October, 1780. Here he pitched his camp and uttered the impious boast that the "Almighty could not drive him from it."

The disappointment of Campbell's men was sore when they found the "game had fled," and their uncertainty and anxiety was increased when they learned that Ferguson had retreated towards Ninety-Six, giving out that he was on his way to that fort. The Whigs had nothing but rifles and could not subdue it. It seemed for a time that Ferguson had outwitted them and escaped.

The matter, however, was considered in the council of officers and it was determined to follow Ferguson even to Ninety-Six if necessary and strike him as best they could. Colonel Clarke had advanced further west, making his way to the

Watauga settlement, carrying his own and other Whig families with him. The news reached him of the expedition against Ferguson, and Major William Chandler and Captain Johnson of his party, filed off, with thirty Georgians, and joined Campbell at Gilberttown. A few days thereafter Major Chronicle, from the South Fork, in Tryon County, also joined him.

The Whigs did not tarry at Gilberttown. As soon as the resolution to follow was formed they set out on Ferguson's track following to Denard's Ford on the Broad River, where for a time they lost his trail.

I am informed that tradition accounts for this by the fact that Ferguson marched his men down in the stream to elude the pursuit of his foes and came out below the ford, then bore down the stream, instead of following the route southward towards Ninety-Six.*

Baffled by this ruse, many of the Whigs became discouraged and uneasy; many of the men were footsore from travel, and a portion of the horses gave signs of breaking down. They were now encamped at *Alexander's* Ford,† on Green River.

---

*I learned this from Colonel Frank Coxe, of Polk County, N. C.

†I find in the "North State" the following anecdote of Elias Alexander, which is worth preserving for its humor and to illustrate the feeling that continued after the war was over:

"Elias Alexander, of Rutherford County, was an old revolutionary Whig, who fought at King's Mountain, and died years afterward, with twenty-seven British and Tory buck-shot in his body. Old Major Green, of the same county, was a Tory, and was also in the battle of King's Mountain, on the Tory side. After the war Green was several times elected to the State Senate from Rutherford County,

A council was called and it was determined to select their best men, best rifles and best horses and expedite the pursuit, leaving those less strong to follow.

While Ferguson was encamped at Tate's place, on Buffalo, "an old gentleman called on him who disguised the object of his visit." On the next day, the 5th of October, after traveling twenty miles northeast, this old gentleman came to the camp of the South Carolina detachment at Flint Hill (or Cherry Mountain), and related how he had imposed on Ferguson under the disguise of being a Tory, and announced that Ferguson had sent to Cornwallis for aid, and that Ferguson had said he "had selected his ground, and that he defied God Almighty and all the rebels out of hell to overcome him."

That day, on the authority of Colonel Hill, it is stated, that Colonel Williams and Major Brandon of his company were missing and returned in the

---

and seemed invincible. In 1823, Alexander determined to have Green beaten and brought out his son as a candidate against him.

"Green became apprehensive of defeat and concluded that something must be done. He fell upon the idea of joining the Baptist Church, and in carrying out the project was immersed in the French Broad River. Alexander, somewhat discouraged at this turn, but nothing daunted, went to witness the ceremony. Leaning against an old tree on the bank of the river within speaking distance of the scene, he silently and doubtingly watched the process of regeneration.

"Everybody expected some kind of a declaration from him before the crowd dispersed. Just as Green was raised out of the water, wet as a rat, and gasping for breath, Alexander, who was very tall, and towered above the bystanders, slowly raised his hand and pointed at him, at the same time saying, in a loud and measured tone :

'There stands old Major Green, *now* neat and clean,
   Though formerly a Tory,
  The damndest rascal that ever was seen
    Now on his way to glory.'

"This furnished a campaign song and worked an overwhelming defeat of Green at the polls."

evening. Their actions aroused suspicion, and on being pressed by Hill and Lacey, they admitted that they had ridden across, southwest, to Campbell's camp, and that they were to join him next day at the old Iron Works on Lawson's Fork.

Hill discovering that Williams had misinformed Campbell as to the whereabouts of Ferguson, falsely stating that Ferguson had marched towards Ninety-Six, in order to induce Campbell to march to that point, where Williams' interest lay, instead of pursuing Ferguson, charged Williams with the fraud until he admitted it. That night Colonel Lacey, with a guide, made his way to Campbell's camp and acquainted him with the true location of the British army. For awhile Lacey was thought to be a spy, but finally he was enabled to impress Campbell with the truth of his statement, and in order to strike Ferguson, it was agreed between them to form a junction at Cowpens instead of the Iron Works, and to march on Ferguson at once.

Colonel Lacey returned next day to find the whole camp in a ferment of disorder. Williams was ordering the men to follow him to the Iron Works and on to Ninety-Six, while Hill was entreating them to join Campbell. At last the contending factions marched each to itself, when it was discovered that Williams had but few followers. Hill and Lacey calling on their followers, began the march for Cowpens. Colonel Williams was induced, by a sense of danger, to follow in the rear, but the men of the front derided his men during the march, and even threw stones at them. About sunset of the 6th of October, they all reached the Cowpens.

On the 5th of October, on Green River, and nearly all the night following, the Whig officers of Campbell's command were busy choosing the select men, rifles and horses for the fresh pursuit. Seven hundred were chosen, leaving six hundred and ninety (690) or more in the camp, others of the command having fallen by the way from weakness or sickness. These numbers are approximately correct.

Major Herndon, of Cleveland's regiment, was left in command of the footmen, with Captain Neal, of Campbell's regiment, in special charge of the Virginians, who were to follow. They were given orders to expedite their march as much as possible, and to follow the horse and support them if disaster should come. The seven hundred men, on the 6th of October, marched twenty miles by way of Sandy Plains to Cowpens, where they found Lacey, Hill, Williams and Graham. Here they slaughtered the fat beeves of Sanders, a wealthy Tory, who herded his cattle at the Cowpens, and pulled the fresh corn from his fields, and the men and horses ate and drank and were refreshed for the chase.

While here the crippled spy, Joseph Kerr, of Williams' command, who had been in Ferguson's camp at Peter Quinn's, six miles from King's Mountain, returned to communicate the news. It was deemed important, however, to obtain later tidings, and Major Chronicle suggested Enoch Gilmer, of the South Fork, as the man; for, said he, "Gilmer can assume any character that occasion may require; he could cry and laugh in the same breath, and all who saw it would believe he was in earnest; that he could act the part of a lunatic so well that no one could discover him; above all, he was a stranger to fear."

Gilmer left, and after traveling a few miles, entered the house of a Tory and assumed the disguise of a loyalist seeking Ferguson's headquarters, and soon won the Tory's confidence. From him he learned all about the movements of Ferguson in that region, and his communication with Cornwallis. Gilmer returned and reported. A council of war was held, all the officers being present except Colonel Williams. Campbell was retained as chief in command. The North and South Carolina men of Lacey's, Williams', Hill's and Graham's force numbered about four hundred, being about equally divided. The whole force amounted now to eleven hundred men.

As North Carolina had a little over two-thirds of the men in Campbell's command it is fair to presume that she had two-thirds of the seven hundred picked men who followed Ferguson, or four hundred and sixty-six men, to which add the two hundred men who joined at Cowpens and we have six hundred and sixty-six (666) men out of the eleven hundred at King's Mountain who were North Carolinians. As the proportion in Campbell's force was a little over two-thirds we may safely state that seven hundred were North Carolinians, and the others, except Clarke's thirty Georgians, were about equally divided between Virginia and South Carolina—two hundred each.

Here was the army that was to make the first turn in the tide of fortune which had been setting so steadily against the cause of liberty. North Carolina was furnishing nearly, if not entirely, two-thirds of that gallant band and she had contributed the money, $12000, by means of which the most of them were furnished with arms and ammunition. The expedition had been conceived by a North Carolinian. The maneuvering of the contending forces had all been in North Carolina, and that 6th day of October each army crossed the boundary line, after the fashion of honor, that the duel might be fought out of the State. How strange the circumstance! But at that date King's Mountain was assumed to be in North Carolina. It was, however, true to the laws of retribution that Ferguson and his marauders should perish in South Carolina, where they had forfeited their lives according to all law, human and divine, by the commission of every crime that depravity could suggest or ingenuity conceive.

The march from Cowpens to King's Mountain was by night; the rain began to fall and Campbell's men lost their way, so that when day dawned on the 7th of October, the rear of the Virginians was only five miles from Cowpens. Delay ensued until they were conducted by a guide to the main force. The column pushed forward again with spirit, going eastwardly. As they approached Cherokee Ford, on the main Broad River, Enoch Gilmer, the humorous spy, was sent forward to reconnoiter. He did not return, but as the vanguard came near they recognized the voice of Gilmer in the valley singing "*Barney Linn*," a jolly song of the day, and knew that the way was clear. Gilmer's heart was so glad that the chase was nearly over and the game almost in sight, that he had given vent to his soul in a mirthful song.*

The river was crossed and three miles further on they reached Ferguson's former camp. Here they halted and partook of a meal of Tory beef from the Cowpens and then dashed forward briskly through the rain that by this time was falling fast. The men sacrificed their own comfort by putting their blankets around their rifles to keep the powder dry. Gilmer had been sent in advance again. Halting at one Beason's, Campbell learned that Ferguson was only nine miles off and in camp. This freshened the zeal of pursuit and aroused the spirit of the Whigs. Revenge was almost in their grasp. As Campbell rode off a girl followed and calling to the Colonel she asked, "How many of you are there?" "Enough to whip Ferguson if we can find him," was the reply. A smile lighted her

---

*Draper relates many amusing anecdotes of this jolly and fearless Whig spy. He was from that portion of Tryon that is now Gaston County, North Carolina.

face (she was a Whig,) and pointing her finger in a direct line to King's Mountain, she said: "He is on that mountain." Swifter were the footsteps of the leaders, closer pressed the followers.

Three miles further Campbell rode up to the house of a Tory, and on entering found Gilmer partaking of the best in the house and hurrahing for King George, with two girls and the old woman waiting on him. Campbell couldn't resist the temptation to have some fun, and ordering a rope to be put around Gilmer's neck, had him marched up the road to be hung, the girls in the meanwhile weeping bitterly and begging for his life. Gilmer, after getting out of sight, began to laugh heartily and said: "Colonel, I found them such loyal friends I couldn't help, from pure sympathy, giving both the girls a smack."

Gilmer had derived all the information they needed as to Ferguson's exact location and the numbers with him, and that he was only a few miles ahead. The officers came together again for conference, and agreed upon the plan of attack, which was to surround the hill and press the enemy to the top and destroy him there. The men were informed of the plan and assured that there would be no danger of shooting each other, for they would all shoot upwards, as the hill ascends, and that the British shooting downwards would overshoot them.*

---

*Colonel Frank Coxe also informs me that an old soldier of the battle said the British shot from the hip, and that their aim was always too high.

Colonel William Graham was met here by a messenger to inform him that his wife was at the point of death, and with Campbell's advice and consent, he left to attend her bedside. The old hero, however, heard the guns before he was well away, and forgetting all else, returned to the battle and reached the mountain at its close. As Colonel Hambright was an elderly man, Campbell put Chronicle, the major, in command of the Lincoln County men. The whole-souled old Dutchman took no offence, and when Chronicle fell he led his men with spirit and courage, even refusing to leave the field after a musket-ball had penetrated his thigh.

In two miles of Ferguson's camp the Whigs captured a young man named John Ponder, and Hambright knew him as a Tory and had him searched. On his person was a dispatch from Ferguson to Cornwallis, telling him the situation and imploring help. Ponder, on being questioned in regard to Ferguson, said he was in full uniform, but wore a checked shirt over it. The jolly old colonel laughed, and in his broken English exclaimed: "Poys, hear dot! Shoot for the man mid the pig shirt."

In one mile of Ferguson's camp they met Henry Watkins, a Whig prisoner whom Ferguson had just released, and he was enabled to give them exact and accurate information. Hitherto the men had not been required to ride in order, but now they were drawn up in two lines, two men deep, Colonel Campbell leading the right and Colonel Cleveland the left. Then, as General Graham in his narrative says, "they moved up a branch and ravine, between two rocky knobs, beyond which the enemy's camp was in full view, one hundred poles (550 yards) in front of them." They had purposely approached the enemy by this route to cut off his retreat, if it should have been attempted.

"In the rear of the trees and bushes on the east side of King's Creek, a little above where the Quarry Road passes the stream, the Whigs arrived at 3 o'clock in the evening." The orders were given "to dismount and tie horses; tie up blankets and coats to the saddle," and a few men were detailed (who didn't stay detailed) to take care of the horses. Finally, "Fresh prime your guns; go in resolved to fight till you die or win."* The rain had ceased about noon that day, the sky was clear and a cool stiff breeze was blowing. The soldiers were comparatively dry and in readiness for the onset.

It seems, from the narrative of General Lenoir of North Carolina, that when in a mile of the camp of Ferguson, Major Winston, of Surry County, had been detached, with orders to make his way south of the Quarry Road and reach Ferguson's right, which movement, though very difficult, was accomplished successfully.

Ferguson was on King's Mountain in his lair like a wild beast that had been brought to bay.

---

*Draper, from whom this account is, in a great measure, condensed.

He showed no signs of fear. His little army was drawn up along the crest of the mountain from one end to the other. It was composed of one hundred Rangers, as they were called, who had been selected for their soldierly qualities from the King's American Rangers, the New Jersey volunteers and the Queen's Rangers. They were picked men who had undergone the severest discipline and were equal to any body of regulars in the English army. To these were added one thousand loyalists who had been recruited in South Carolina and North Carolina, principally from the region of Ninety-Six. These latter were called Provincials and had been well drilled. As far as their personal characters would permit they had been made efficient soldiers. This estimate of Ferguson's force is that given by Tarleton.*

The armies were therefore about equal in numbers, with the advantage to Ferguson of having chosen his ground for defence and having his troops well rested and fed. Neither had artillery or cavalry. It was a contest of the bayonet and musket on the one hand and the Deckard rifle on the other.

The men who fought were in contrast. The British force fought for the honor of their king or with the varied motives that actuated the American Tory—disappointed ambition, fear of punishment, or the opportunity for plunder. No noble sentiment was found in their hearts and they felt the disgrace of taking up arms in behalf of oppression and wrong.

*Tarleton's Campaigns, p. 156.

A very few may have been conscientious in their principles.

The Whigs fought for freedom; they fought to prevent the plundering horde from invading their peaceful and plentiful homes; they fought for religious liberty and for independence as a nation. They had no discipline nor drill, but every man knew that his duty was to stand by his comrade to the death; they had no bayonets, but they knew how to fight from tree to tree and to rally from every retreat. They knew that defeat meant ruin and capture meant torture.

With these sentiments and hopes to impel them and these discordant masses in front of them, we do not wonder that victory perched on the banner of the Whigs. No mercenary can stand before a man who is moved by the conviction of duty.

"Thrice armed is he who hath his quarrel just."

Ferguson viewed their approach with firmness and courage, but not with indifference or confidence. His last dispatch, by John Ponder to Cornwallis, indicated his apprehension of defeat. He was a Scotchman from the bonny hills and he knew that the gathering of the mountain clans foreboded evil to those who roused them to the battle. He knew that such men as had dogged him through the mountains and through the streams, through wet and cold, and were now deploying beneath his last bivouac, were men whom no danger could appall and no threat could intimidate.

What a sight to contemplate in this lonely mountain wilderness! No pyramids to look down upon them and challenge their claim to courage or incite them to glory; no forty centuries of battle scenes to provoke their emulation. It was untrained men, in the wilderness of a virgin region, who had come to contend for the land and the country on which they stood.

No maiden hand bore the wreath to crown the victor; no applauding thousands waited to honor the survivor of the carnage; no titles of nobility nor badges of knighthood were in the expectancy of the men who struggled for freedom. It was the conflict of men who came to contend for principle and who sought no reward but the "glorious privilege of being independent;" who courted no applause, and were content with the approval of a good conscience; who knew nothing of romance or fiction and lived only to love the women and the children they had left behind them.

It was fit that the God of battles should be the only spectator and that His omnipotent hand should crown whom He willed with the wreath of victory.

The spur of the mountain which Ferguson had chosen for the conflict runs from southwest ascending to the northeast. Its summit is about five hundred yards long and from seventy to eighty yards in width. A branch of Clarke's Fork sweeps around the northern declivity; at the northeastern extremity of the eminence the descent is precipitous; on either side were deep hollows parallel to the course of the mountain. The Whigs were drawn up near the southwestern extremity where the declivity is comparatively gentle. The army was divided into two corps. Campbell was to command the corps approaching from the south side of the mountain and Cleveland that from the north.

Winston had already made a detour in order to approach from near the northeastern extremity and Campbell now led his men in the following order: McDowell in advance, whose right joined Winston's left; Sevier, whose right joined McDowell's left; the right of the Virginians joined Sevier's left, so that the column from southwest to northeast stood Campbell first, then Sevier, then McDowell, then Winston.

On the north side of the mountain Colonel Hambright marched around the northeastern declivity, and his left joined Winston's right, Cleveland's left rested on Hambright's right, then Lacey on Cleveland's right, then Williams on Lacey's right, and lastly, Colonel Shelby at the southwestern extremity.

Campbell was to swing to the north with the left of his column and Shelby to the south with his right wing, so that their united columns should stretch across the mountain at its southwestern base. When all were in column at their respective positions, it formed a complete cordon around the mountain, and the coil was to be drawn closer and closer to the centre. If Ferguson pushed back one side, the other was to press his rear. The plan was admirable, and if executed was a sure success.

The diagram which we present illustrates the positions as above described.*

The Whigs marched in double column to their respective places, headed by the officers in command of each regiment.

Shelby and Campbell's men began the attack. As soon as the approach of the Americans was discovered, the drum beat to arms in the British camp, and the shrill whistle of Ferguson was distinctly heard,† notifying his men to take their respective places for the battle. "Orders had been given that when Shelby and Campbell were ready to begin the attack, they were to give the signal by raising a regular Indian war-whoop;" when this signal was given, the other columns were to press forward simultaneously. The enemy opened fire on Shelby first, and it was with difficulty that he restrained his men from returning it until the proper time. "Press on to your places," he cried, "and your fire will not be lost." Very soon Campbell's stentorian voice was heard, as they wheeled by the left into line, shouting, "Here they are, boys; shout like hell and fight like devils!" The Indian war-whoop reverberated through the valleys and hills and the battle was begun. DePeyster hearing the yell, recognized it as the same he had first heard on the 18th of August, and remarked to

---

*The map was made by General Joseph Graham from an actual survey made by him.

†Ferguson used a shrill whistle which he carried with him as cavalry use a bugle.

Ferguson, "These are those same yelling devils that were at Musgrove's Mill." Campbell pressing forward, was delayed in his march ten minutes by a swampy marsh in his front. Shelby going a short distance ahead received the first bayonet charge and was driven down the hill, but quickly reloading they gave the British a galling fire that drove them up the hill again. The trees, which retarded the charge of the Rangers, afforded a rampart for the riflemen, and from this cover they poured in the balls, each going with the marksman aim to its deathly work. The crest of the mountain was almost bare, and the British, unprotected when in column, were a splendid target for the mountaineers. Harry Lee said of King's Mountain that "it was more assailable by the rifle than defensible with the bayonet."

The battle now raged with fury from every side of the mountain as the coil drew nearer, and Ferguson, dashing from one side to another to rally his men or lead a charge, was typical of Satan when he cried, "Which way I fly is hell!"

The rattle of musketry, the keen crack of the rifle, the yells and whoops of the assailants, the commands of the officers, the groans of the dying, all mingled with one discordant noise around this little mountain, making a pandemonium in which devils might have disported themselves with joy. Many heroic deeds of daring were done, hand-to-hand conflicts were occurring on every side, splendid shots were being made, soldiers were leaping from rock to rock for shelter, the trees were being peeled by the bullets intended for the man behind them, the wounded were scrambling away for safety and the dead lay prostrate at every step; but amidst the infernal din the coil drew nearer still. As the British bayonets drove the men down one side, the Whigs from the other side shouted, "They retreat! they retreat!" and rushing to the British rear they poured in the bullets like hail on their backs.

At every repetition of this charge and counter-charge the ranks of the Rangers grew thinner and thinner. The Provincials, with butcher knives fitted to their guns as a substitute for bayonets, came to their assistance, but soon they too began to reel and stagger in the storm. The retirement before the bayonet created no panic, it was understood to be the order of the day, and then followed the fresh crack of the rifle and the advance again.

The Whigs kept out of the way of the bayonet and were comparatively unharmed, but there was no British foot swift enough to outstrip the bullets of the old Deckard, and every renewal of the charge came with weakened force.

Major Chronicle had led the South Fork boys up to the ascent on the northeast end, and turning to his men gave the command, "Face to the hill." It was his last speech. A ball struck him and he fell to rise no more.

The men, undaunted, pressed on under their brave old Colonel Hambright, with Joseph Dickson, Captains Mattocks, Johnson, White, Espey and

Martin at the head of their squads of men, each with a rifle in hand and doing the duty of a private in the fray. DePeyster was commanded to charge them, and firing a volley which killed Mattocks, the British pushed them back with the bayonet.

The old Colonel received a ball through his thigh which filled his boot leg with blood. His men begged him to retire. "No, poys, I vill stay as long as I can sit up," was the brave response of Hambright.

The coil was getting tight around the crest of the hill and at times Whig and Tory were going for the same tree or rock. The countersign of the Whigs was "Buford," a reminder of the massacre at the Waxhaws, and when this "shibboleth" was not given on demand, up went the rifle to the shoulder and the quickest was the survivor. The cloud of smoke was too thick to discern the white paper in the hat of the Whig or the bunch of pine in that of the Tory.

Relatives and acquaintances often recognized each other as the quarters grew closer. A Tory named Branson being severely wounded, seeing his Whig brother-in-law, Captain James Withrow, of Hampton's command, near by, solicited his help. "Look to your friends for help," was the reply.

Captain William Lenoir's company of Cleveland's command was left behind at Green River, but the Captain refused to remain and went forward as a private. He received two wounds, one in the side, another in the arm.

Colonel Sevier's North Carolinians were the first to reach the summit of the hill and hold their position; sheltered by the rocks around, they poured destruction into the British flank. Captain Robert Sevier, a brother of the Colonel, was mortally wounded as he was ascending the mountain.

Colonel Williams, who felt the mortification of neglect, fought with reckless desperation, pressing on into the thickest of the fight. He received a mortal wound and was borne unconscious to the rear. Water being sprinkled on his face he revived, and while gasping for breath he looked at the men around and said, "For God's sake, boys, don't give up the hill."

Shelby was now in conjunction with Campbell's column, getting nearer the summit. He constantly admonished his men "never to shoot till you see your enemy and never see him without bringing him down." Winston and McDowell were in close rifle shot and Cleveland had led his men up the steep acclivity in the rear of Ferguson's line. Colonel Lacey's horse had been shot but he was advancing on foot and driving the enemy before him.

The British were enveloped and the fire was so hot from every quarter and their ranks so thin, they were unable to compel the troops to renew the charge.

"The combat deepened."

The Provincials were now giving way on the southwestern side of the crest, pressed by Campbell, Sevier and Shelby, and taken in the flank by McDowell and Winston, and in the rear by Cleveland. Two white flags were raised in token of surrender, which Ferguson cut down with his sword. An officer remonstrated and begged that the carnage might cease, but Ferguson swore he "would never surrender to such banditti." Captain DePeyster, his second in command, seeing his men huddled on the crest and being shot down on every side, urged him to surrender. At length, being satisfied that all was lost, "Ferguson, with a few chosen friends, made a desperate attempt to break through the Whig lines on the southeastern side of the mountain and escape." As he went he cut and slashed with his sword, using his left hand, until the sword was broken.

To pass a file of mountain riflemen and live was more than man could do. Gillcland, one of Sevier's men, recognized Ferguson and "drew a bead" upon him, but his rifle missed fire. Calling to Robert Young, one of his comrades, "There goes Ferguson—shoot him," Young, drawing his rifle affectionately to his shoulder, replied, "I'll see what Sweet-lips can do." There was a flash, a sharp lingering crack, and Ferguson tumbled from his saddle. "Sweet-lips" had been true to her reputation. Others, too, had marked the "pig shirt" and revenged Hambright's wound by putting six or eight more bullets through that same "pig shirt." Ferguson fell near Sevier's column;

he was unconscious when he fell, and lived but a few minutes. The prayer of Parson Doak had been answered. Two Tory officers, Colonel Vezey Husbands and Major Daniel Plummer, who were with Ferguson, turned to flee, but both were shot dead.

Seeing their leader fall, the enemy began to break, and took refuge behind their wagons, where, for a short while, they renewed the combat, but being fired on from the rear by Cleveland, who had gotten close to them, they retreated into a sunken place or hollow. Few of the Rangers now survived and they were in terror. All order and organization was lost, and these wretched beings stood like a herd of deer in a corral, and were slaughtered in their tracks. "Buford!" "Buford!" "Tarleton's Quarters!" "Tarleton's Quarters!" rang with fearful tones in the ears of these perishing beings. The day of justice and judgment, awful in its reality, had come to them. Young Sevier, son of the Colonel, had heard of his uncle's death, and would not be restrained. "Standing erect, with deliberate aim he would bring down a Tory," to avenge the blood of the Seviers.

In vain were white handkerchiefs raised. Those who raised them became targets for the infuriated Whigs, and their holders fell beneath the signal. One man on horseback rode out with a white flag, but fell as he came in view; a second shared the same fate. The Wilkes men were lying in wait to shoot everything that made an attractive target. "Larkin Cleveland must be avenged before we cease firing!" "Chronicle and Hambright and Williams must have blood for blood!" Such was the maddened sense of these enraged men who had come for victory and vengeance. They determined that the work should be effectually done. The Rutherford men reminded each other of the cowardly assassination of their leader's son on Pacolet; they listened a moment and shot again. One more victim to the unbending law of retribution. Thus from lip to lip went tales of wrong, and from rifle to rifle came the voice of vengeance. The scene is too sad to contemplate—the curtain must fall. Major Evan Shelby shouted to the victims, "Throw down your arms!" It was instantly done, and rushing forward he implored his followers to shoot no more. The firing had almost ceased, but as stragglers, or those who were too weak to be in front, gained the crest, they emptied their rifles once more. Campbell, riding to the front, exclaimed: "For God's sake, quit! it is murder to shoot any more." DePeyster, a brave soldier, rode up to Campbell and said, "It is unfair." There was no time for argument. Campbell, addressing the enemy, ordered DePeyster to dismount, and called out: "Officers, go to yourselves; prisoners, take off your hats and sit down." The Whigs were then "drawn up and around them in a continuous circle, then double guards, and finally four deep." The game was bagged and the hunters stood around gazing at their victims. Now and then an old marauder or bushwhacker was recognized and his sin proclaimed. According to the enormity of their cruelties each wretch was endeavoring to hide behind his neighbor. A fearful reckoning was at hand. The arms were removed from the prisoners and strongly guarded that they might not be resumed in the confusion.

As Ferguson fell, his small silver whistle dropped from his pocket and was picked up by a Tory named Elias Powell, who lived in Caldwell County. It was preserved until Powell died in 1832, when his children took it west where it was lost.

Ferguson's sword was given either to Cleveland or Sevier, most probably the latter.

Such was the curiosity to see the dead body of Ferguson that many wounded soldiers had their friends to convey them to the spot that they might gaze upon it.

Ferguson was buried near where he fell. "No martial cloak" was around him; he was enclosed in a beef's hide and buried in a hole. It is discreditable, perhaps, to chronicle such a fact, but it seems to be well authenticated.

The envenomed hatred of Ferguson by the Whigs, whom he had so cruelly wronged, became a monomania and its cravings for revenge were insatiable.

Ferguson had two mistresses with him: the one, a red-haired woman, "Virginia Sal," was killed; the other, "Virginia Paul," survived and was indifferent to his fate. Tradition says that the former was buried in the same grave with Ferguson.

The engagement had lasted only fifty minutes when Ferguson fell, and that may be considered the end of the fight.

Not one of the enemy who were on the hill when the fight began escaped; there was a party of two hundred foragers out who left that morning and did not return.

From the many reports of the British loss I think that made by Colonel Shelby in a letter to his father, five days after the battle, is perhaps nearest to the actual facts. He says the loss of Ferguson's corps—the Rangers—was 30 killed, 28 wounded and 57 prisoners. That the loss of the Tories was 127 killed, 125 wounded and 649 prisoners; or both classed together, 157 killed, 153 wounded and 706 prisoners—total 1016. The official report of the Whig commanders, it was admitted, was exaggerated somewhat for effect. Of the Tories, three hundred were North Carolinians under Colonel Ambrose Mills.* The others were from South Carolina, mostly from the region of Ninety-Six, where Ferguson had his headquarters. The American loss was 28 killed and 62 wounded. The great disparity in the respective losses was attributable to the fine marksmanship of the mountain men, and that the British were huddled together when the close firing occurred.

The command of Chronicle, from Tryon County, suffered very much more than any of the others. Chronicle was killed, Colonel Hambright severely wounded, Captain Mattocks, William Rabb, John Boyd and Arthur Patterson killed, Moses Henry mortally wounded; Captain Espey, Robert Henry,

---

*He was hung at Biggerstaff's.

William Gilmer, John Chittim and William Bradley wounded. Four others of Captain Martin's company, names unknown, were wounded.*

Ferguson's personal effects were distributed as follows: Captain Joseph McDowell, of Pleasant Garden, first cousin of Major Joseph McDowell, who was in command of Colonel Charles McDowell's regiment, secured six pieces of his china dinner plates and a small coffee cup and saucer. These are still retained among his descendants. Colonel Shelby obtained the larger silver whistle; Colonel Sevier was allotted the silken sash and Ferguson's commission as lieutenant colonel, and DePeyster's sword; Colonel Campbell took his correspondence; the white charger, from which Ferguson was shot, was, by common consent, awarded to Colonel Cleveland, who had lost his horse in the battle and was too unwieldly to travel on foot.†

So much space has been devoted to this important battle that I cannot pursue the subject any more in detail. The heroes who fought it returned to their homes, feeling that they had been saved from calamities which only such a band of freebooters as the Tories could inflict. A few of these

---

*Major Chronicle was a young man of good family and more than ordinary intelligence. He was engaged to be married to a Miss Alexander of Mecklenburg County, and when killed was wearing a gold ring which she had presented to him. The ring is now in the family of her descendants of Charlotte, N. C., as I am informed. Miss Alexander subsequently married Judge Lowrie of North Carolina.

†Draper, pp. 307-'8.

Tories were hung for their crimes at Biggerstaff's, in Rutherford County, among them Colonel Mills. The other prisoners were sent to Virginia.*

"The victory at King's Mountain, which, in the spirit of the American soldiers, was like the rising at Concord, in its effect like the success at Bennington, changed the aspects of the war. The loyalists no longer dared to rise. It fired the patriots of the two Carolinas with fresh zeal. It encouraged the fragments of the defeated and scattered American army to seek each other and organize themselves anew. It quickened the Legislature of North Carolina to earnest efforts. It encouraged Virginia to devote her resources to the country south of her border. The appearance on the frontiers of a numerous enemy from settlements beyond the mountains, whose very names had been unknown to the British, took Cornwallis by surprise, and their success was fatal to his intended expedition. He had hoped to step with ease from one Carolina to the other, and from those to the conquest of Virginia, and he had now no other choice but to retreat.

"That memorable victory, Jefferson declared, was the joyful annunciation of that turn of the tide of success which terminated the revolutionary war with the seal of independence."†

North Carolina may glory in this decisive and splendid victory, which relieved her from further invasion of her western borders. Her sons had originated the campaign, her money equipped its

---

*Those who desire to continue the story can derive pleasure and profit perusing it in Mr. Draper's book.
†Bancroft, vol. 5, p. 400.

Hon. JOSEPH McDOWELL,
OF "QUAKER MEADOWS" BURKE COUNTY, N.C.
Hero of Ramsour's Mill, Kings Mountain and Cowpens
and Member of Congress.

soldiers, her sons constituted two-thirds of its army and most of its leaders were her citizens.

We yield to Virginia her full share of the glory, and accord to South Carolina praise for unexpected assistance which she so freely gave, but we must be pardoned for publishing the facts of history as they are, that North Carolina's name may not be obscured in the story of this great achievement.

NOTE.—A monument thirty feet high and constructed of granite blocks now stands upon the summit of King's Mountain to commemorate the deeds of the patriotic men who won this memorable victory. The Legislature of North Carolina appropriated $1500 to the work, and yet among the list of names chiseled on this monument the name of McDowell does not appear. The McDowells of Burke, in conjunction with Sevier, conceived the scheme and organized the American force which captured Ferguson and led the attack in the battle. Such are the egregious blunders and injustice which characterize history; such are the sins committed in its name.

CHAPTER IV.

Cornwallis Retreats from Charlotte to Winnsboro—General Morgan joins Gates at Hillsboro—Gates moves from Hillsboro to Charlotte—General Nathanael Greene supersedes Gates December 4th, 1780, at Charlotte—Personal Sketches of Greene and Cornwallis—Greene Moves to "Camp Repose" on the Pee Dee—Morgan sent to the Western Part of the State December 16th—Sketch of General Morgan—Lee's Legion joins Greene—Character of Lee—The North Carolina Riflemen join Morgan 310 Strong—The Fight at Hammonds' Store—Maneuvering of Tarleton and Morgan—Their respective Strength—Tarleton's Character—Battle of Cowpens January the 17th, 1781.

WHEN we took up the story of King's Mountain, Cornwallis was at Charlotte, North Carolina, where his army was every day subjected to insult and annoyance from the rancorous Whigs, who listened to no overtures of conciliation, and continued to shoot down his sentinels and foragers. General Davidson was, with his brigade of militia, between Charlotte and Salisbury, watching events. General Gates, with the scattered remnants of his army and some accessions of militia, was at Hillsboro. The Governor, Abner Nash, was exerting himself with patriotic energy to supply the wants of the army and place it again in the field. Public spirit was manifested by the people, and the officials seemed determined "to pluck safety from this nettle of danger."

The messengers whom Ferguson had sent to Cornwallis from Tate's plantation (in Cleveland

County now) narrowly escaped capture in the Whig settlement of Crowder's Creek, where the Scotch-Irish Presbyterians resided, and consequently they did not reach Cornwallis until the 7th day of October, while the conflict was raging on King's Mountain. Cornwallis appreciating Ferguson's danger, and suddenly aroused to the consciousness that an unexpected army had sprung up, from some unknown region, in front of him, immediately ordered Colonel Tarleton to hasten to his rescue. Tarleton left next morning.

The messengers, Collins and Quinn, returned with him as guides, and Tarleton intended to cross the Catawba at Armour's Ford, near the mouth of the South Fork. The ford was deep and the crossing proved dangerous, many of the advance guard being compelled to swim. It was resolved, therefore, to remain on the east side until morning; but the next day, before the water subsided, two men who had been near the battle, or perhaps some of the foragers who escaped, informed Tarleton of the disaster which had befallen Ferguson at King's Mountain, and he beat a hasty retreat to Charlotte,* arriving there the same evening.

Cornwallis was panic-stricken at the news of the destruction of his left wing, and his own exposure thereby to sudden attack. The Whigs purposely exaggerated the number of the army that had overwhelmed Ferguson, and conveyed to Cornwallis intimations that these men were marching westward

---

*General Graham in University Magazine, vol. 5, p. 101.

to join Davidson and attack the British at Charlotte. Ninety-Six was now at the mercy of these invincible mountain hordes and the British army could be cut off from its line of retreat. His lordship did not tarry to hear arguments on the other side; he thought "discretion was the better part of valor" in the emergency, and therefore ordered his whole army to be in readiness in one hour to begin the retreat to Winnsboro, in Fairfield district, South Carolina, about seventy miles south of Charlotte. The mud in the Black Jack (oak) country of the Waxhaws is proverbial for its sticky quality and the depth of its softness in rainy weather. It was then and is now a terror to all travelers, especially wagoners, who are compelled to pass through it in the winter. At this time, the 8th of October, the rainy season had begun, and the roads were almost impassable.

One McAfferty, a merchant of Charlotte, who was at heart a Whig, but who had remained in Charlotte to save his property, was selected as their guide. The retreat began at sunset on the evening of the 9th, taking the road leading to the old Nation Ford on the Catawba. "McAfferty led them the road to the right, about two miles below Charlotte, which went to Park's Mill. When they got near that place, he suggested that they were on the wrong road, and he must ride out to the left to find the right one, and in pretending to do this he escaped from them."*

*Joseph Graham's account.

The night was dark, and being near the hills of Cedar Creek, and floundering through the mud without guide or compass, the confusion was "worse confounded." In attempting to find roads leading to the left, so as to regain their proper route, they became separated and overcome by the fear that the Whigs had laid this snare to cover an attack. By midnight the two forces were three or four miles apart and did not succeed in reaching the Nation Ford road, and collecting their forces, until noon next day.

McAfferty had ridden all night to reach Colonel Davie's camp and inform him of the situation. Davie started in pursuit next morning, but found the cavalry so formidable in their rear that he was unable to make an attack. Davie returned to his camp, on Sugar Creek,* the same evening. The roads were so deep with mud that Cornwallis was ten or twelve days reaching Winnsboro.

This narrative of the British retreat is condensed from General Graham's article in the University Magazine. Tarleton denies that he returned to Charlotte. He says he received orders, at the Catawba, to cross the country and intercept the line of retreat of the main army, and he complains bitterly that not being present to get the Legion baggage off, he lost all his knapsacks, which were in the rear wagons that were left sticking in the mud. Graham says forty wagons. No doubt Colonel

---

*Tarleton places General Sumner at that time at Alexander's Mill, on a branch of Rocky River; p. 165.

Davie's cavalry enjoyed this "treasure-trove" and added it to his scanty supply.

Tarleton* says, "The royal forces remained two days in an anxious and miserable situation in the Catawba settlement, owing to a dangerous fever which suddenly attacked Lord Cornwallis, and to the want of forage and provisions." Tarleton himself had just passed through a spell of fever. "When the physicians declared his lordship could not endure the motion of a wagon, Colonel Lord Rawdon, the second in command, directed the troops to cross Sugar Creek."

Tarleton, in his usual vein of criticism, reflects on the judgment of Cornwallis for choosing Charlotte as the basis of operations against North Carolina, on account of the disloyalty of the people of that region, whose hostility to the British was so injurious and annoying to him, and for allowing Ferguson to march so far from the main army that he could not be supported when necessity required. Tarleton was of opinion that the invasion should have been attempted by Cross Creek (near Fayetteville), where the loyalists abounded, and would have assisted his march by communicating to him the movements of the American forces. At Charlotte the Whigs watched every suspicious person, and intercepted all communication with the country. To this cause is to be attributed the fact that Ferguson received no reinforcement.

It was the end of October before Cornwallis

---
*Page 167.

recovered entirely from his fever. His headquarters were now established at Winnsboro, which, as before stated, was seventy miles south of Charlotte. The region of South Carolina north of Ninety-Six, was abandoned. Camden on the right was in supporting distance, and the section around Winnsboro afforded provisions for the army during the winter. Cornwallis hoped to rest and recruit his army at this point, and be ready to renew his march into North Carolina in the spring. "The winter campaign was abandoned."*

His lordship, however, was not the sole arbiter of his own destiny. It was being "rough hewn" by the up-country men, who were gathering again to disturb his winter's repose, and force him a second time to navigate the miry roads that led him to the devoted province he fain would enter for conquest and glory. He had aroused the spirit of the hardy men of the mountains, who never waited for weather or the rules of warfare, as they are taught in books; men who had discovered their strength and were eager to encounter the British regulars, now they had "Burgoyned" Ferguson and his Provincials.

We shall leave his lordship to indulge in the dreams of a cozy fireside, while we visit the American lines and relate the preparations being made to disappoint these dreams and hopes of conquest.

General Gates was exerting himself with unusual energy, at Hillsboro, North Carolina, to reorganize

*Tarleton, p. 168.

his army and collect reinforcements. When he had begun his march to Camden, he had, fortunately, been compelled to leave two pieces of cannon behind for want of transportation. To these he added a few iron pieces, and thus was able to form a small park of artillery. On the 16th of September Colonel Buford, of Virginia, with the mangled remnant of his regiment and two hundred recruits, arrived in camp. Another small detachment from Virginia, without arms, came in a few days after. About fifty of Colonel Porterfield's regiment, that escaped from Camden, now joined this force and constituted the Virginia line.

About this time Colonel Daniel Morgan, a Virginian, who had acquired such harvests of laurels at Quebec and Saratoga, arrived in camp. His great reputation as a hard fighter and intrepid leader greatly encouraged the troops and revived the hopes of the people. He had only a few followers, young men who had come to share with him in service and honor. General Gates ordered four companies to be drafted from the regiments, to be equipped as light infantry and to form a partisan corps under command of Morgan. Colonel White and Colonel William Washington, who had been so roughly handled by Tarleton after the fall of Charleston, had seventy cavalry and these were added to this corps.* Colonel White, who was in disrepute, was granted leave of absence, and Colonel Washington was placed in command. To these were

*Johnson's Life of Greene, vol. 1, p. 313.

still added a small company of sixty riflemen under Major Rose.

North Carolina, whose military resources had been well-nigh exhausted by the capture of all her regulars at Charleston, and in supplying the militia who were under Caswell at Gates' defeat, was enabled, by extraordinary exertions, to collect a suit of comfortable clothing for each one of Morgan's command before they entered on the severe and active duties before them. She also supplied the other troops, but not so comfortably as Morgan's. Tents they had none, and blankets but a scant supply.

1780. Morgan's corps began its march for Salisbury from Hillsboro, North Carolina, on the 1st day of November, and the remainder of the army followed on the 2d day.

General Smallwood, who had been commissioned by the State, was in command of the militia and posted at Providence, six miles south of Charlotte. Morgan passed Charlotte and ventured to the neighborhood of Camden and occupied the ground which was the scene of the great misfortune in August.

Cornwallis heard with amazement that the invasion from the enemy to the south was substituted for his own invasion to the north, and began to realize that his conquest of South Carolina was far from completion, and that North Carolina defied his boasting threats.

The winter campaign of the Americans had begun when his lordship abandoned his own.

There was to be no repose for the distinguished convalescent.

Cornwallis had at this time about five thousand men at his various posts, and five hundred recruits had just reached him from the north.

On the 20th of November Colonel Sumter defeated Tarleton at Blackstocks, but himself received a ball through his right breast near the shoulder, which detained him for a length of time from service. Suspended between horses and guarded by one hundred faithful followers, he was conveyed to a place of safety in North Carolina.

The cavalry under Colonel Davie, and the militia under Davidson, whose term of service expired in November, returned home.* General Gates moved slowly westward, arriving at Charlotte the latter part of October. He recalled Morgan and Smallwood to that place and fixed his headquarters there.

This was the military situation when Major General Nathanael Greene, a native of Rhode Island and the trusted friend of General Washington, arrived at Charlotte on the 2d day of December, 1780, and assumed command on the 4th of the same month at that place.

Judge Johnson announces the appointment of General Greene and describes him personally as follows:

"The order of the commander-in-chief, which assigned General Nathanael Greene to the command of the South-

*General Joseph Graham.

ern Department, bears date the 14th day of October, 1780. Until that period his standing in the army was of the first order of respectability. He enjoyed the confidence of Washington and the country, and had ever discharged the duties of the man and the soldier with fidelity and ability. But no opportunities had yet been afforded him of displaying those eminent talents which then broke upon the American people and exhibited a splendor of military character excelled only by him whom none can equal.

"General Greene was at that time in the thirty-ninth year of his age; his stature about five feet ten or eleven inches; his frame vigorous and well proportioned; his port erect and commanding; nor was his martial appearance diminished by a slight obstruction in the motion of his right leg, contracted in early life. The general character of his face was that of manly beauty. His fair and florid complexion had not entirely yielded to the exposures of five campaigns; nor was a slight blemish in the right eye observed but to excite regret that it did not equal the benevolent expression and brilliancy of the left. Such is the portrait of the man. His manners were uniformly consonant to the gravity of his character and dignity of his station. Yet he could be cheerful, even to playfulness, and his intercourse with the world was marked with that unaffected urbanity of manners that flowed from the politeness of his heart. Whether grave or gay, he could accommodate himself to society with a grace and facility which may be acquired from long and general intercourse with polite circles, but which, in him, is to be attributed to rapid observation, a quick perception of propriety, and a mind well stored with sound and useful information.

"Advantages in early life he had none; born and raised in obscurity, without education and without society, he exhibited a striking instance of what good examples, sound principles, and native genius, and above all, industrious habits and a careful improvement of time can accomplish."*

Perhaps the best delineation of his military character was given by a British officer who opposed him in New Jersey. He writes:

"Greene is as dangerous as Washington; he is vigilant, enterprising and full of resources. With but little hope of gaining any advantage over him, I never feel secure when encamped in his neighborhood."*

General Washington thus bears testimony to his unselfish devotion to the cause of independence:

"There is no officer in the army more sincerely attached to the interests of his country than General Greene. Could he but promote those interests in the character of a corporal, he would exchange without a murmur his epaulette for the knob. For although he is not without ambition, yet ambition has not for its object the highest rank so much as the greatest good."

"Greene was born the 26th of May, 1742. His father was a miller, an anchor smith and a Quaker preacher. In early life he followed the plow and worked at the forge. His education was of an ordinary kind; but having an early thirst for knowledge, he applied himself sedulously to various studies whilst subsisting by the

---

*Life of Greene, vol. 1, pp. 1–2.
*Garden's Anecdotes, p. 76.

labor of his hands. Nature had endowed him with quick parts and a sound judgment, and his assiduity was crowned with success. He became fluent and instructive in conversation, and his letters, still extant, show that he held an able pen."*

With these precedents and such a character as we have seen portrayed by the leading historians of our country, he came to the South to contend with one of the best trained soldiers of England. He found the fragments of a defeated army, unclothed and without tents, in the midst of winter, with a scant supply of provisions in a country already exhausted by a hostile army; soldiers poorly equipped with arms, and dispirited by defeat and loss of confidence in their commander. He was to create an army out of this raw material and fight it against the veteran soldiers of England. This was all that stood between North Carolina and British conquest.

We have this sketch of the early life of Cornwallis, which will be interesting to a reader who follows his subsequent career:

"Earl Cornwallis, Viscount Brome, was born in Governor Square, London, December 31, 1738. He was educated at Eton. While at college, playing at hockey, he received a blow which produced a slight but permanent obliquity of vision. The boy who accidentally caused this was Shute Barrington, afterwards Bishop of Durham. After finishing his education he chose the army

*Irving's Washington, vol. 2, p. 8.

for his profession. His first commission, as ensign in the Foot Guards, is dated December 8th, 1756. His first lesson in war was as aid to the Marquis of Grandby in the contest between England and France in 1761. He had been elected a member of Parliament from Eye, and, upon the death of his father the following year, took his seat in the House of Lords. When in Parliament he was strongly opposed to the scheme of taxing America, but when the war came, as an officer of the army, he accepted active employment against the colonists. On February the 10th, 1776, he embarked for America in command of a division."*

Cornwallis was personally a very brave man and an accomplished soldier. While he did not individually commit acts of cruelty, he allowed his subordinates to do so without rebuke, and at times commended them for their conduct. He was a hard-hearted man, that never listened with pity to the supplications for mercy, and oppressed the people whom he conquered without compunction or compassion. He did not hesitate to violate his promises or break his engagements, if they stood in the way of his success. As a general he was vigilant and cautious, but slow. His judgment was not sound, and he was wanting in diplomacy or management. As a whole he was a military failure. He lost South Carolina and Georgia, and failed to overrun North Carolina. In Virginia he was captured and the cause he espoused went down beneath his banners. It may be that with an ordinary man like

*Wheeler's Reminiscences, p. 186.

General Lincoln for an opponent, he might have attained renown, but unfortunately for his fame he was opposed by a man who was by intuition a soldier, and by experience skilled in the art of war.

The first preparation made by General Greene for the campaign in North Carolina, which was soon to begin, manifested his foresight and military sagacity. The country through which the movements of his army, whether in advance or retreat, were to be made, was traversed by three large streams, the Dan, the Yadkin and the Catawba, and a knowledge of their crossings and the roads leading to their fords and ferries was indispensable to safety and success.

Colonel Edward Carrington of Virginia, Greene's Quartermaster General, an energetic, judicious and efficient soldier, was sent to make a thorough exploration and map of the Dan; General Stevens, at that time commanding a detachment of militia, undertook the same work on the Yadkin, and Kosciusko, the patriotic Pole, then chief engineer of the army, explored the Catawba. The historical retreat across these streams was made possible by the information which General Greene derived from these reports. The first duty of a good soldier is to make himself master of the geography of the country in which he is to maneuver. Looking to future necessities, General Greene also established magazines of stores and ammunition on the Roanoke and at Oliphant's Mill, on the upper waters of the Catawba River.

The first success of his little army was of a humorous character, and greatly enlivened the camp. Colonel Washington rode to Cleremount, in South Carolina, to attack a band of loyalists who held that fort. Not being able to storm it, Washington resorted to the stratagem of painting a pine log and mounting it on wheels, which he brought in sight of the besieged, threatening dire vengeance with his cannon if Rugely did not surrender immediately. The garrison was surrendered, and when disarmed was allowed to inspect the *cannon*.

'The whole number of regulars of all arms in Greene's camp did not exceed eleven hundred, and of these not eight hundred could be mustered with arms and clothing fit for duty. Some of Colonel Washington's cavalry were so naked that they were ordered back to Virginia to be clothed.

The provisions around Charlotte were nearly exhausted, and Colonel Thomas Polk, who was acting as Commissary General, reported that he could not gather more than a week's supply.

Colonel Polk resigned this place, and General Greene insisted on Colonel William R. Davie, who was just at this time without a command, taking the office of Commissary General. Colonel Davie reluctantly accepted, his nature being more adapted to field service and partisan warfare, but he yielded these objections and went to work with system and energy to find subsistence for the army; and to his timely efforts General Greene owed much of the success of his future operations. We have seen heretofore the adventurous skill and intrepidity of this distinguished North Carolinian, who was now to enter through his office into the most confidential relations with his commander, and who in after life was to have heaped upon him honors which seldom fall to the lot of man. Colonel Davie was, at this time, only twenty-four years old.

The selection of Carrington and Davie was the evidence of Greene's wonderful discrimination in the selection of men.

In order to subsist his army, General Greene selected the head of navigation on the Pee Dee River as a "camp of repose," where he could feed and rest and drill his little army. Kosciusko was sent to select and lay out the camp and explore the country.

The States had been called upon by Congress to provide subsistence directly to the army, and Colonel Davie was sent to the Legislature of North Carolina to urge compliance with this reasonable requirement. He met with a prompt and liberal support, and "arrangements were made to collect magazines at every court-house in the State, and officers appointed to register and report the produce on hand and the wagons and means of transportation in every county."

The next matter which strongly presented itself to General Greene was the re-establishment of the North Carolina Continental line. The whole of this class of the State's military force had been captured at Charleston, but it was estimated that two or three hundred had escaped or were left behind in North Carolina from sickness and other causes, and the supernumerary officers who had lost their commands at the reorganization were scattered through the country.

General Jethro Sumner, the senior officer on the Continental establishment in the State, was called upon to pay immediate attention to this matter, and strong appeals were made to the Governor to aid in this work.

There were various other matters requiring consideration, and it is said that Greene allowed himself not a moment's respite from the most intense application to business until everything necessary for the operations of an army, even down to an axe or a nail, had received his attention.

On the 20th of December the army, except Morgan's command, abandoned their huts at Charlotte and took up their line of march by Wadesboro to Haley's Ferry on the Pee Dee, where it was originally designed to be posted; but at the suggestion of Kosciusko they moved down the east side of the river to Hicks' Creek, nearly opposite the Cheraw Hill. General Isaac Huger, the only general officer, except Morgan, with Greene, was in command. Morgan had been appointed a Brigadier General by Congress, with a commission dating the 13th day of October, 1780. On the 16th day of December he was given a separate command by General Greene, and ordered to put himself on the left flank of Cornwallis.

The order itself is the best explanation of this movement, and it is given in full:

"CAMP CHARLOTTE, December 16th, 1780.

"You are appointed to the command of a corps of light infantry of 320 men detached from the Maryland line, a detachment of Virginia militia of 200 men, and Colonel Washington's regiment of light horse, amounting to from sixty to an hundred men. With these troops you will proceed to the west side of the Catawba River, where you will be joined by a body of volunteer militia under command of General Davidson of this State and by the militia lately under command of General Sumter.

"This force and such others as may join you from Georgia you will employ against the enemy on the west side of the Catawba, either offensively or defensively, as your own prudence and discretion may direct, acting with caution, and avoiding surprises by every possible precaution. For the present I give you entire command in that quarter, and do hereby require all officers and soldiers engaged in the American cause to be subject to your orders and command.

"The object of this detachment is to give protection to that part of the country and spirit up the people; to annoy the enemy in that quarter; to collect the provision and forage out of their way, which you will have formed into a number of small magazines in the rear of the position you may think proper to take.

"You will prevent plundering as much as possible, and be as careful of your provisions and forage as may be, giving receipts for whatever you take to all such as are friends to the independence of America.

"Should the enemy move in force towards the Pee Dee, where the army will take a position, you will move in such a direction as to enable you to join me if necessary, or fall upon the flank, or into the rear of the enemy, as occasion may require. You will spare no pains to get good intelligence of the enemy's situation, and keep me constantly advised of both your and their movements.

"You will appoint, for the time being, a commissary, quartermaster, and foragemaster, who will follow your instructions in their respective lines. Confiding in your abilities and activity, I intrust you with this command, persuaded," &c.

General Morgan was born of Welsh parents in Hunterdon County, New Jersey, in the winter of 1736, and was now forty-four years old, but his strength and his spirit was unimpaired, except from occasional attacks of rheumatism, which he had contracted at Valley Forge. His parents were poor and he had in early age wandered from them never to return. Fate brought him to Virginia, where he became a wagoner, and in that capacity was attached to Braddock's army. It was while here that he struck a British officer who insulted him, and for this manly act was condemned to receive five hundred lashes. He languished but recovered from this inhuman and barbarous punishment; his accuser afterwards admitting that he himself deserved the blow that he received.

Morgan was an Indian fighter of the frontiers, and when the revolution came it found him ready for war and enjoying the full confidence of his people. He entered the army and was captured in the assault on Quebec. After nearly a year's captivity he was exchanged, and feeling the love of his native earth, he fell upon the ground and cried, "Oh! my country." He did not kiss the earth as his mother, but embraced it as his home. In 1779 he retired from the army, but when Gates was defeated he offered his services and came to Hillsboro for duty. Gates had done him great injustice while serving under him in New York, but this he forgave. He is described as "tall, muscular, vigorous and active; trained from his childhood to an outdoor life of exertion which gave strength and elasticity to his limbs, with a clear and kindling eye, an open countenance full of character, but full too of good humor, with a keen rustic wit and a hardihood which secured him the first place in bold enterprises and athletic sports."*

General Greene reached his encampment the day after Christmas and immediately bent his whole energy and talent in improving his little army. He healed all jealousies, roused the spirit of the troops, sought for them food and clothing, nursed the sick, encouraged the feeble, and personally supervised every effort to bring them into soldierly training. Here these cold and hungry and naked troops found some repose in their huts, and had many of the social enjoyments of camp life. They soon became acquainted with their commander, and learned to love him and confide in him as their

*Greene's Life of Greene, vol. 3, p. 95.

leader. He had much magnetism about him, and all soldiers under his command drew closer to him and became devoted to his fortunes. Greene called this encampment the "Camp of Repose"; but while his soldiers were enjoying the repose, his fertile and active brain was conceiving stratagems and snares which were to perplex and worry his antagonist. From this camp Camden, Georgetown and Winnsboro were all in striking distance, and the lines of their communication exposed, while Morgan threatened the British left and cut off their foragers.

While at "Camp Repose" on the Pee Dee, Colonel Henry Lee, known as "Light-Horse Harry," and father of the late General Robert E. Lee, joined General Greene. Lee commanded a Legion composed of 300 men—150 infantry and 150 horse. Both men and officers were picked men; the officers were chosen in reference to their talents and experience; the men in proportion, from the regulars of the army. Virginia furnished twenty-five of these men. The Continental troops of the other Southern States had been sent south, and of course those States did not contribute.*

The uniform of Lee's Legion was exactly like that of Tarleton's, which made it difficult to distinguish them from each other.†

The horses for the three cavalry companies were procured in Maryland and were of the best the country afforded. It was all in all a magnificent

*Johnson's Life of Greene, vol. 1, p. 354.
†Johnson's Life of Greene, vol. 1, p. 453.

Legion, and we can well excuse the vanity of its colonel, whose tardiness of approach was attributed to his desire to be seen and admired of men on his march south. Lee had distinguished himself already as a dashing, intrepid soldier, and his advent was hailed with delight. He was young and handsome. Born the 29th January, 1756, he was just about to enter his twenty-fifth year. He was proud and brave but not generous; he was a genius, full of resources, and when acting independently, quick, restless and fierce. He was not just to his comrades when acting with others; self-willed and hard to be restrained. It is to be lamented that to so many virtues he added infirmities and faults which often exposed him to the severest criticism. He was, however, a sincere and ardent patriot and devoted to the cause he had espoused with so much fervor and zeal.

Lee reached the Pee Dee on the 12th of January, and with him came Colonel Green, of Virginia, with 400 men—a fine body of soldiers.

1781. General Greene immediately ordered Lee to join General Marion, which he did on the 23d January, and made with him a combined attack on Georgetown, South Carolina. The attempt was unsuccessful, after promising the greatest results; but it produced a panic among the British at that place which soon caused them to evacuate the town. Marion was thereby given greater latitude, and the troops were encouraged. Cornwallis discovered that Greene was never idle.

We shall now follow General Morgan to victory.

1781. Morgan's march led him across the Catawba River at Biggin's Ferry, just below where the South Fork River empties into that stream, and across the Broad River above the mouth of the Pacolet. He took post on the north bank of the Pacolet on the 25th day of December and began to gather forces and information. Many of the Whigs of upper South Carolina had been compelled, under duress, to take protection and give their paroles to be inactive, but seeing an opportunity now to recover independence, they began to embody for defence. Andrew Pickens was one of this class, and he determined to take all the risks and enter the field. After sending off their families to the mountains Colonel Pickens and Colonel McCall joined Morgan with 100 men. Colonel William Lee Davidson, of Mecklenburg County, North Carolina, also led to Morgan 120 men and returned to bring 500 more and thereby missed the battle of Cowpens.* He reached Morgan's camp on the 29th December. Major Joseph McDowell of "Quaker Meadows" also joined Morgan with 190 North Carolina riflemen from Burke County;† aggregating 310 men from North Carolina at that time with General Morgan, all of whom participated in the battle of "Cowpens."

Judge Johnson commits the unpardonable error of stating that Major McDowell was from South

---

*Johnson's Life of Greene, vol. 1, p. 362.
†Gordon's History, vol. 4, p. 31.

Carolina. It is passing strange that it could have been conscientiously committed, when we consider that Major McDowell had never quit the field after the battle of King's Mountain, in October, where he had so distinguished himself, and the further fact that after the war he had been a prominent member of the Congress of the United States from North Carolina, and, most probably, was personally known to Judge Johnson. It can only be excused on the ground of intemperate zeal on the part of that author to claim almost everything for South Carolina, regardless of the justice due his neighboring State. He shows but little appreciation, in his whole history, of the fact that North Carolina soldiers were foremost in every battle fought to redeem South Carolina from the conquest which followed the surrender of Charleston, and that her whole Continental line defended that ill-fated city to the last extremity when South Carolina troops refused to enter* that pitfall of Lincoln's folly.

Colonel Pickens' command proper was only 70 men.† He had recently escaped from captivity at Ninety-Six‡ and had no time to raise a force or to equip it when raised. Colonel McCall's Georgians were only 30 in number, but they were trained men, volunteers who had kept the field after the affair at Blackstocks. McDowell's 190 men were all mounted volunteers, hardy mountaineers who had fought at Musgrove's Mill and King's Mountain, riflemen,

*Johnson's Traditions, p. 308.
†Gordon, vol. 4, p. 31.
‡Gordon, vol. 4, p. 31.

with Deckards in their hands, and withal were as good troops as any that Morgan had in his command. The first dash that Morgan made at the British, McDowell's mounted men, under Colonel McCall, who ranked Major McDowell, constituted *two-thirds* of the force.

On the second day after Morgan's arrival at his camp, information was brought him that 250 Tories had advanced from the Savannah River to a point twenty miles south of him, and were committing outrages on the Whigs. Morgan detached Colonel Washington with 75 cavalry, McCall's small command, and McDowell's mounted men in quest of this party. The Tories, hearing of his approach, retreated to Hammond's Store, twenty miles further south, where Washington overtook them and immediately ordered a charge. It was a bloody retribution that so early overtook these marauders. The killed and wounded were 150, prisoners 40; the remainder escaped. These men, cowardly and vindictive, had come to plunder and oppress their neighbors, supposing that there was no resistance to encounter, and they fell victims of justice before an outraged foe. McCall's men remembered that Colonel Brown, the Tory who occupied Augusta, had, a few weeks before, brought twelve Whig prisoners into his house, where he lay wounded, and had them hung in his presence from the stairway, one by one, and other twelve he had delivered to his Indian allies, who tortured them to death at the stake. Such fiends deserved every vengeance that justice could inflict.

Morgan having some apprehension for the safety of Colonel Washington, who was near Tarleton's Legion of 250 cavalry, crossed the Pacolet and advanced to cover his retreat. This done he resumed his former post.

Lord Cornwallis was restless over these bold movements of his enemy, and concluded to open the campaign again which he had abandoned in the winter. General Leslie had been sent south with 2000 men as a reinforcement, and they were approaching Camden, as Cornwallis explained afterwards, to threaten Greene, and were to be moved rapidly across to Winnsboro, where the combined army was to be thrown forward between the Catawba and the Broad Rivers to separate Greene from Morgan, and Morgan was to be annihilated by a corps of the best troops, selected for that purpose, and under the command of Lieutenant Colonel Banistre Tarleton, a more vindictive and merciless marauder than Ferguson; but of a class usually chosen by Cornwallis to do the inhuman work which he was ashamed to do in person. His orders were to "push Morgan to the utmost." He did "push." Morgan in the race, but Tarleton was in *front* of it—just a little ahead of Washington's cavalry. He underrated Morgan, who, Bancroft says, "was at that time the ablest commander of light troops in the world; in no European army of that day were there troops like those he trained."*

*Bancroft's History, vol. 5, p. 480.

The vainglorious correspondence between Cornwallis and Tarleton reminds one of some of the ludicrous scenes in the comic opera of the "Grand Duchess":

1781. "Dear Tarleton," affectionately writes his lordship, on the 2d of January, "if Morgan is still anywhere within your reach I shall wish you to push him to the utmost. No time is to be lost!"

"My Lord," Tarleton responds, "I will either destroy Morgan's corps or push it to King's Mountain.

"I feel bold in offering my opinion, as it flows from well-grounded inquiry of the enemy's intentions."

"Dear Tarleton: You have understood my intentions perfectly."

Those "intentions" were understood to mean that if Morgan was overcome his corps was to be "destroyed" after the precedent set at the Waxhaws.

Cornwallis was to advance towards Charlotte a few days ahead of Tarleton, in order to capture the fugitives from Morgan's defeated army and prevent them from joining Greene; but without informing Tarleton of his change of mind, he concluded to await at Turkey Creek, forty miles north of Winnsboro, the result of Tarleton's expedition, having wisely considered that it was possible that as unexpected a reverse might attend Tarleton as that which overtook Ferguson.

On the 14th January, Tarleton crossed the Enoree and Tyger rivers above Cherokee Ford and northwest of it. These tributaries of the Broad flow east into that stream. On the 15th, Morgan was at Burr's Mill on Thicketty Creek. He there received information of Tarleton's approach with 1100 men and was anxious to avoid an action if possible. He sent a courier to Greene informing him of his desires and reminding him that he had previously urged that he be recalled to the main army, as the country was laid waste and no subsistence was to be found.

On the 15th, Morgan crossed Thicketty Creek and marched north toward the Broad, which here runs almost east, while in the evening Tarleton occupied the camp he left at Burr's Mill.

Tarleton's command consisted of 550 men which constituted his Legion, the 7th regiment of 200 men, the first battalion of the 71st regiment, the light infantry of the 71st, and some loyalists who were the "bummers" of that day. To this was added two field pieces served by a detachment of royal artillery; amounting in all to eleven hundred men, though Tarleton says he had only 1000 men.

Morgan's corps consisted of 320 men from the Maryland line, 200 Virginia militia, Colonel Washington's cavalry, 75 men—these making 575 men of all arms with which he started. To this were added McDowell's mounted North Carolina volunteers, 190 men, Davidson's Mecklenburg volunteers, a part of whom, however, were from Tryon—in all 310 North Carolinians, Pickens' South Carolinians, 70 men, and the Georgians under McCall, about 30. Sum total 985 men.

It is probable that a few Georgia militia were added to this command before the battle took place.

Banistre Tarleton was born in Liverpool, August 21st, 1754, and was not yet twenty-seven years old, but he was notorious even at that age—not famous but infamous. He had selected and trained his Legion and infused his own spirit and opinions into it. He set examples and they followed them. He declared "that severity alone could effect the establishment of regal authority in America," and exercised that severity without mercy or humanity whenever opportunity offered.

A writer who was cotemporary with him says: "It is difficult to speak with temper of a man whose invariable aim was to destroy, whose resentments were only to be appeased by an increasing flow of blood."*

The slaughter of Buford's men was so cruel and heartless that an American officer of undoubted integrity, who visited his wretched victims, declares that—

"Many of them were left in a perfect state of nakedness, having been stript of every article of clothing ; and that the wounds inflicted amounted on an average to sixteen to each individual."† Finally, "after partaking of the hospitality of the widow of General Richardson, he not only plundered the house and burned it, but spurned this venerable lady with his foot."‡

*Garden, p. 284.
†Garden, p. 284.
‡Garden, p. 284.

Such was the venomous character of the man who was nearing the Cowpens, and in sight of King's Mountain was burning with rage against Ferguson's conquerors. How many horrors were averted by his defeat no human wisdom can calculate.

Morgan's camp was at the Cowpens, "on a wide plain covered with primeval pines and chestnut and oak, about sixteen miles from Spartanburg, seven miles from Cherokee Ford on the Broad River, and a little less than five miles south from the North Carolina line."* It was also on the same ground where the "Backwater men" encamped the evening of the 6th of October and refreshed themselves for the night march in pursuit of Ferguson, and in Morgan's camp were a part of those same men who had brought him to bay and scattered his army to the four winds of heaven. Feeling the pride of conquest, they were ready to pluck fresh laurels for their brow by disposing of Tarleton as they did of Ferguson. McDowell's men were eager for the fray. Morgan's little army were in the best spirits over their recent adventure with the Tories, and the regulars were anxious to wipe out the recollection of Camden by a victory at Cowpens. Tarleton believed at that time that Cornwallis was in the rear of Morgan, instead of being a day's march southeast of him, waiting events at Turkey Creek; consequently Tarleton moved northwest towards the upper Pacolet to drive Morgan east into the

*Bancroft, vol. 5, p. 482.

snare they had set for him. Morgan had announced at Cowpens, to his army, his resolution to fight, and the cry to "lead them to victory" was the response from every lip. He therefore moved south on the 16th to intercept and fight Tarleton at the crossing of the Pacolet, but Tarleton, suddenly turning down from the upper Pacolet, crossed that stream above Morgan to its northern bank. This necessitated the falling back of Morgan to his former position at the Cowpens, where he determined to give Tarleton battle.

1781. Tarleton halted the evening of the 16th on the ground the Americans had left, and finding that Morgan had retreated, supposed that he intended to fly in order to avoid a battle. Early on the morning of the 17th day of January Tarleton resumed his march to overtake Morgan.

"It was 8 o'clock A. M. that the British army arrived in view of the Americans; and instead of overtaking his adversary in the hurry and confusion and fatigue of a flight, Tarleton found him rested, breakfasted, deliberately drawn up, every man at his post, and their commander in a popular and forcible style of elocution haranguing them."*

Tarleton had been five hours on the march through the darkness and his troops were much fatigued, but he determined to take advantage of the excitement and attack at once.

Morgan has been criticised severely by tacticians for his selection of ground, the Broad River being

*Johnson's Life of Greene, vol. 1, p. 372.

in his rear and his wings unprotected "in the air," but Morgan's genius rose above the rules of theorists and was successful. In defence of himself he wrote:

"I would not have a swamp in view of my militia for any consideration. They would have made for it and nothing could have detained them. As to covering my wings, I knew my adversary, and was perfectly sure I should have nothing but downright fighting. As to retreat, it was the very thing I wished to cut off all hope of. I would have thanked Tarleton if he had surrounded me with his cavalry. It would have been better than placing my own men in the rear to shoot down those who broke from the ranks. When men are forced to fight they will sell their lives dearly; and I knew that the dread of Tarleton's cavalry would give due weight to the protection of my bayonets and keep my troops from breaking as Buford's regiment did. Had I crossed the river one-half the militia would have immediately abandoned me."

The reasoning is sound and the result proved that it was correct.

There was a slope of three hundred and fifty yards gently ascending to an eminence on which Morgan had taken his ground. It was covered with an open wood. "On the crown of this eminence was posted 290 Maryland regulars, and in line on their right the two companies of the Virginia militia under Triplet and Tate and a company of Georgians under Captain Beattie, about 140 in the whole, making his rear line to consist of 430 men. This was commanded by Lieutenant Colonel Howard of Maryland."

In front of this line and about one hundred and fifty yards distant was the second line composed of 190 North Carolina militia,* all of whom had seen service and were good soldiers, and about 80 South Carolinians. Johnson puts this line as 270 men. I am persuaded, however, that it was stronger than this, because the Mecklenburg militia numbered 150 and perhaps only one-half, or 95, of McDowell's men were detailed as sharp-shooters in the front. This would leave 245 North Carolinians for the second line, and these added to the 70 South Carolinians would make the total 315 instead of 270 men, which is approximately correct. I judge this too from the gallant stand made by these troops, who were really veteran militia, except the new recruits recently organized by Pickens. It was these veterans who did the destructive work with their Deckard rifles that caused such slaughter among the British officers and threw them into confusion for want of orders and leaders. The militia, or second line, was put under the command of Colonel Andrew Pickens, of South Carolina, who was the ranking officer.

In front of the militia, and one hundred and fifty yards in advance, General Morgan posted 150 picked riflemen as sharp-shooters, whose orders were to shoot for the "men who wore the epaulettes"—kill the officers. It is probable, as we have seen, that

*Ramsay's South Carolina, p. 225.

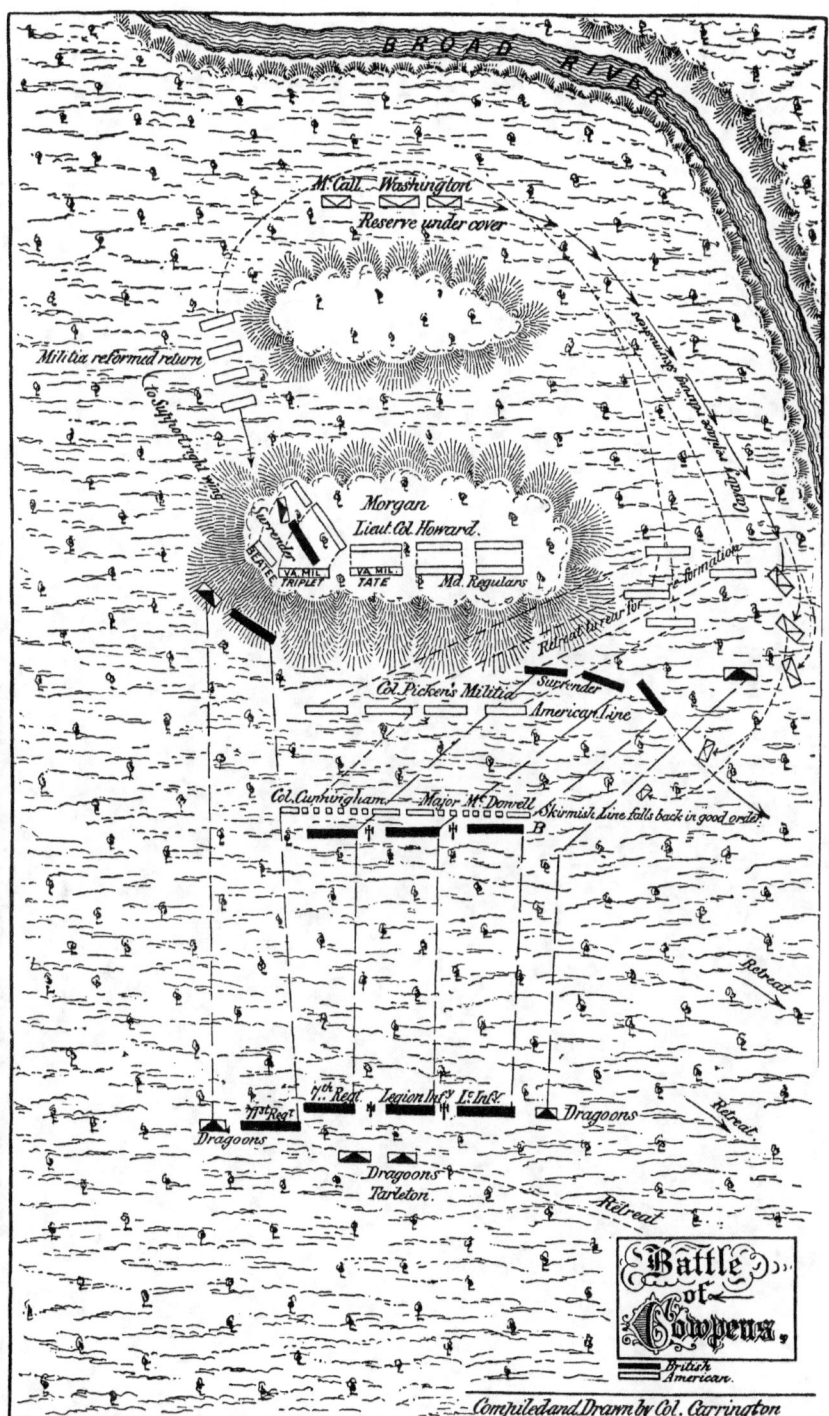

at least 95 of these men were North Carolinians; the other 55 were Georgians, remnants of Clark's command. The Georgians were on the right, commanded by Cunningham and Jackson, and the North Carolinians, under Major Joseph McDowell of Burke County, North Carolina, were on the left.

In the rear of the regulars, under Howard, the ground descended gently and then rose again to another eminence, and behind this eminence, and concealed from view and secure from the cannonade, was Washington's cavalry, numbering about 90, and McCall's mounted men, about 35, making only 125 cavalry, to oppose the Legion of 550 men.

The order to the sharp-shooters was to cover themselves by trees, if necessary, and not to fire until the enemy was in fifty yards; after the first fire they were to fall back, loading and firing until they came to the main line under Colonel Pickens, where they were to fall in with the militia. This would give the second line a force of 450 men at least.

The order to the militia or second line was to *deliver two deliberate charges at the distance of fifty yards and then retire* and take their post on the left of the regulars. If charged by cavalry every third man was to fire and two remain in reserve, lest the cavalry should continue to advance after the first fire, or these reserves were to fire if the cavalry wheeled to retire.

The orders to the regulars were to fire low and deliberately, not to break on any account, and if forced to retire to rally on the eminence in their rear.

The baggage and militia horses had been sent several miles to the rear under a small escort.

The order was then given to all the force to "ease their joints," that is, to assume comfortable attitudes until the enemy came in sight. All were in high spirits and full of confidence.

Morgan went along the lines encouraging the men and exhorting them to stand firm and assuring them that they were about to gain a great victory. No doubt too that all eyes had surveyed the King's Mountain, not far distant in their view, and gathered from that glorious field fresh inspiration to their courage. They were reminded that militia alone had defeated Ferguson and that Tarleton's troops were, many of them, only galvanized regulars recruited from the ranks of desperate Tories who cared to follow Tarleton more for plunder than for fight.

These noble men calmly surveyed the British as they deployed into line and waited their onset with the coolness of men determined to win.

Tarleton gives the formation of his troops as follows:

"The light infantry were ordered to file to the right till they became equal to the flank of the American front line; the Legion infantry were added to their left and, under the fire of a three-pounder, this part of the British troops was instructed to advance within three hundred yards of the enemy. This situation being acquired, the 7th regiment was commanded to form on the left of the Legion infantry, and the other three-pounder was given to the right division of the 7th; a captain with fifty dragoons was placed on each flank of the corps, who formed the British front line, to protect their own and threaten the flanks of the enemy; the first battalion of the 71st was desired to extend a little to the left of the second regiment and to remain 150 yards in the rear. This body of infantry, and near 200 cavalry, composed the reserve. During the execution of these arrangements the animation of the officers and the alacrity of the soldiers afforded the most promising assurances of success."

Tarleton now advanced to reconnoiter the American lines, but received a volley from the sharpshooters in ambush. The cavalry were ordered to dislodge them, but fifteen saddles were quickly emptied. The sharp-shooters then retired, slowly firing as opportunity offered, until they reached the main line of the militia.

The deadly aim of these riflemen, now for the first time encountered by Tarleton, so demoralized his cavalry that they could not be induced, after this, to charge upon them, and Tarleton complains severely against his troops for their consternation and want of daring. This rifle was an arm so destructive in the hands of men trained to its use in the hunting grounds of the mountains that it required the most desperate courage to advance within its range.

Tarleton's whole line now advanced steadily under the fire of their artillery until the "dead line" of fifty yards distance was reached, when the riflemen, obeying orders, took deliberate aim, "marking as much as possible the epaulette men," and fired upon their assailants.

As the shrill crack, sharp and thrilling, resounded through the forest, the officers of the British line reeled like drunken men, or threw up their hands in the agonies of death and fell to the ground, and the sting of the bullet caused many a brave soldier to recoil from the charge. Still these trained men pressed forward in the face of death and received a fire more galling than the first. With bayonets fixed they moved forward again, and the militia, obeying the instructions given them, retired behind the regulars and on to the eminence in the rear. But the work had been done by them; the mortal wound had been inflicted. The British were without officers and the line became a tumultuous mob, carried forward without method or order.

The regulars now received them, firing low and striking the moving targets as they ascended the slope. The line halted, but continued to fire for thirty minutes, but the fire grew less frequent and slower in repetition. Tarleton was soldier enough to know that this was the precursor of retreat, and quickly ordered up the 71st regiment into line and restored the attack; he also ordered the cavalry to sweep upon the American left and turn their right flank. A portion of Tarleton's dragoons had charged upon the militia in their retreat around the American left, and Colonel Washington, discovering the danger, made a furious charge from his covert under the eminence, and taking them by surprise, drove them in disorder to their lines. The militia were now enabled to make their way undisturbed, and in order, around the second eminence to the right flank of the American line.

Morgan, perceiving the threatened charge on his right flank, ordered the militia to form at right angles to the regulars and repel this assault of the cavalry. This movement of the militia was understood by the regulars as the signal for their retreat to the second eminence, and they fell back in order. Tarleton, supposing this meant flight from the field, was exultant with joy, and sounded the charge along his whole line. The Americans were now in line on the second eminence, with the militia in order, covering their right flank, and as the British rushed forward with a shout, to run over and trample down and bayonet the expected fugitives, they were shocked with a terrific fire from the whole American line.

Morgan, who kept close to his regulars, had marched slowly back with them and watched the place he had selected for a stand. As the line came to the spot he called out in a stentorian voice, "Face about, give them one fire and the victory is ours!" The British were coming on in great disorder, at only thirty paces distant, and many of the Americans fired with their guns in the position for the use of the bayonet. Colonel Washington had discovered the confusion of the enemy also, and cried out, "They are coming like a mob; give them one fire and I will charge them." As soon as the fire was delivered Morgan ordered a charge, and in a moment was upon the confused mass, striking them down on every hand. The British were so bewildered by this sudden onset, and thrown into such confusion by their loss of officers, that they fell on their faces in consternation and begged piteously for quarter. The cry was heard, "Give them Tarleton's quarters," but Colonel Howard, calling to his men, reminded them of their duty to a fallen foe. Hearing his voice his soldiers obeyed his order and spared the men, who, a few moments before, were impatient to repeat the carnage in which they had revelled at the Waxhaws.

The cavalry of the Legion seeing the riflemen in their front again, and witnessing the discomfiture of the infantry, could not be brought to the charge, but turning their heads they fled in confusion, trampling down their officers who vainly tried to rally them, and never stopped until they reached the camp of Cornwallis on Turkey Creek.

Washington had fallen upon the enemy's right and was making for the artillery. Morgan ordered one company to go to his support, and putting the prisoners under three other companies, he wheeled upon the 71st, which was still maintaining its ground. The British cavalry was gone, the militia disengaged bore down also on the 71st, and all hope of escape having vanished, Colonel McArthur surrendered, Colonel Pickens receiving his sword.

It was just at this time that Washington made so narrow an escape from death. The affair is thus related:

"Whilst Washington was engaged with the artillerists Colonel Tarleton, at the head of all the cavalry who would follow him, hastened to their relief. Washington perceiving his approach, ordered his men to advance, and dashed forward himself.

"Tarleton prudently ordered a retreat. Being of course in the rear of his men, and looking behind, he perceived that Washington was very near him and full thirty yards ahead of his troops. Attended by two officers he advanced to meet Washington.

" One of the officers led, and parrying a blow aimed at him by Washington, the sword of the latter proved of inferior temper and broke midway. The next effort must have brought Washington to the ground. But a little henchman, not fourteen years old, who was devoted to his master, and carried no other weapon but a pistol at his saddle bow, had pressed forward to share or avert the danger that threatened his beloved master, and arrived in time to discharge the contents of his pistol into the shoulder that brandished the sword over Washington's head. It fell powerless, but the other officer had his sword all ready to inflict the wound, when Sergeant Major Perry reached the side of his commander just in time to receive the sword-arm of the officer upon the edge of his extended weapon. The wound also broke this blow. But Colonel Tarleton in the meantime was securely aiming another from his pistol. The noble animal that bore Washington was destined to receive the ball that had, rather discourteously, been aimed at his rider. Poor Perry's destiny was bound up with that of his commander, for at the battle of Eutaw, when the latter was made prisoner, Perry, by the same discharge, fell under five wounds. We are uninformed, but believe that he never recovered from them."*

The victory was complete. Tarleton rallied, according to his account, fourteen officers and forty men and escaped from the field. Colonel Washington's cavalry were unable to catch him in the pursuit.

It was Miss Jones, of Halifax, North Carolina, who had the encounter of words with Tarleton about Washington. Tarleton, with a sneer of disdain, said he would like to see Colonel Washington of whom she spoke in such terms of praise. "You could easily have seen him by looking back at Cowpens," was the sarcastic reply.

The material results of this splendid victory were two field pieces, which had heretofore been captured at Saratoga, then retaken at Camden, and now by the fortunes of war were in the hands of Morgan again, eight hundred muskets, two stands of colors, thirty-five baggage wagons, one hundred dragoon horses and their equipments.

The battle lasted fifty minutes, about the same as the battle of King's Mountain. The American

---

*Johnson's Life of Greene, vol. 1, p. 382.

loss was comparatively small, the British, as usual, shooting too high. The whole loss of the Americans was only 11 killed and 61 wounded, no officer of rank being in the list.

The British loss was about 150 killed, 200 wounded and 400 prisoners. At least one-tenth of their killed and wounded were officers, picked off by the militia riflemen. Ten officers were found in front of the militia where they received the first fire, and to this was attributed the confusion that ensued as they advanced. The men receiving no orders, every man advanced at his will and the lines became confused.

Johnson, speaking of this fire, says: "At the assigned distance they delivered their fire with unerring aim and it was the magnanimous confession of a gallant officer of the Maryland line who fought on this day 'that here the battle was gained,' and the killed and wounded lying in their front fully justified the assertion."

The fatality among the British troops was wonderful, perhaps never equalled except at King's Mountain. There were about 650 infantry soldiers who bore the brunt of the battle and the killed and wounded were 350; assigning 50 to the cavalry, which is full enough, and we have 300 men, out of 650, killed or wounded. There was no slaughter here after the battle was over, either, as was alleged at King's Mountain. It was simply the "unerring aim" of the North Carolina and Georgia riflemen; for the Georgians were veterans and also armed with the rifle. Of the men who served under McDowell we have but little information, as no permanent records were ever kept of these numerous expeditions. We do know, however, that Captain Joseph McDowell, a first cousin of the Major, who was known as "Pleasant Garden Joe," was among the "bravest of the brave," and followed the fortunes of the Burke men into every conflict. He was so prominent as to have misled Wheeler into the error of assigning him to the command. I have, however, examined the evidence and it is conclusive that he did not command, but was only a captain, both at King's Mountain and Cowpens.

To this conclusion Mr. Draper has also arrived, after a most patient and exhaustive research. The evidence is chiefly the affidavits of men who applied for pensions and who speak of "Quaker Meadows Joe," or "General Joe," as their commander, for he was, after the revolution, made a general of militia. "Pleasant Garden Joe," Draper says, "was a physician and is regarded as having possessed the brightest intellect of any of the connection."

Thomas Kennedy was another captain. He was wounded at Ramsour's Mill, shared in the battles of Cane Creek and King's Mountain. He removed to Kentucky and served in the legislature and convention of that State, and was quite a prominent citizen.

David Vance, the grandfather of United States Senator Z. B. Vance and Congressman General Robert Vance, of North Carolina, was a conspicuous figure in all the campaigns, and to the Vance-Henry memoranda we are largely indebted for the information we have of these men. Vance was too modest to record his own exploits and they are lost. We also find mention made of Samuel Wood and Joseph White as captains in this command. Both followed the immigration west to the "dark and bloody ground" of Kentucky. Edmund Fear and John Ligman were also captains—the latter a prominent leader.

It is the fault of history to give too much prominence to commanders and ignore the men who died or fought to make them great, and in that way the truth is confounded. Colonel Andrew Pickens, by mere accident, outranked Major McDowell, and being in command, and from South Carolina, her historians are ever ready to ascribe all the glory of Cowpens to that State, when the fact is she had fewer troops present than either Georgia or North Carolina, and these were citizens who had, like Pickens, been forced to take British protection and had been quiet in the struggle. Finding an opportunity now to throw off the yoke, they enlisted under Pickens and figuratively fought "with halters around their necks," as Judge Johnson of that State relates.

I do not detract from the noble life and patriotic deeds of this gallant South Carolinian. No North Carolinian can afford to take one laurel from his crown of honor, for we shall see in the sequel that when he came to North Carolina, without troops, he was honored with position, and became so identified with North Carolina history that it is difficult to assign him, as a military chieftain, to our sister State. He won his spurs and his Brigadier General's commission at the head of North Carolina soldiers. North Carolina is entitled to share any honor that may be ascribed to him in this great struggle for independence.

In our zeal to give to North Carolina her proper credit for this victory, we must not forget to assign all the honor due the Maryland line and its distinguished commander, who afterwards became the Governor of his State. It was a Spartan band who had "pushed bayonets" (to use the phrase of that day) with the British at Camden and drove them from their front; they, with Dixon's North Carolinians, and the "blue hen's chickens" of Delaware, were the only mourners around the dying DeKalb; they alone had followed him to the death and avenged him with the blood of the men who murdered their fallen leader. Major Anderson of this line was the only officer who brought off an organized force from that ill-fated field, and all that remains of him is mingled with North Carolina soil at "Guilford Court-House," where he fell. No mark distinguishes his resting-place as yet, but it is a reproach which ought not longer to rest on his fellow-citizens, who followed after to enjoy the blessings purchased with his blood.

Another hero of this veteran band was Captain John Smith, who met the Honorable Lieutenant

Colonel Stewart, of the 71st, in personal combat at Cowpens, and when separated, was menaced with the promise, "we shall meet again." The promise was kept, and Colonel Stewart's sword is now in an American museum, instead of hanging in honor among the heir-looms of his family. North Carolina regulars came to Washington's rescue in the hour of his "extremest danger," and far from home, without a chronicler, these deeds of valor are only seen here and there through the crevices of histories which were opened to illuminate the conduct of others who stood by them. Let it not go unsaid that these brave Marylanders were the very heart of Greene's little army, that gave to it vitality and force, and that its blood moistened the soil of the Carolinas in every conflict from Camden to Eutaw. The names of Howard, and Anderson, and Ford, and Smith, all heroes indeed, should be emblazoned on imperishable granite, where they could be "seen and read of all men," as future generations may pass before it. Baltimore, "the Monumental City," has strangely forgotten the memory of those who gave this nation an existence and honored a few who repulsed simply an assault which was made upon it.

How bitter was the disappointment of the British commander at this defeat of his pet Lieutenant is reflected through the account of Stedman, who upbraids Tarleton with incompetency and rashness and depreciates him as a military leader.

"During the whole period of the war," he says, "no other action reflected so much dishonor upon the British arms. The British were superior in numbers. Morgan had only 540 Continentals, the rest militia. Tarleton's force composed the light troops of Lord Cornwallis' army. Every disaster that befell Lord Cornwallis after Tarleton's most shameful defeat at the Cowpens, may most justly be attributed to the imprudence and unsoldierly conduct of that officer in the action. It was asked why he did not consult Majors McArthur and Newmarsh, officers of experience and reputation who had been in service before Tarleton was born? * * * * * * Is it possible for the mind to form any other conclusion than that there was a radical defect, and a want of military knowledge on the part of Colonel Tarleton? That he possesses personal bravery, inferior to no man, is beyond a doubt; but his talents at the period we are speaking of never exceeded that of a partisan captain of light dragoons, daring in skirmishes."*

It is a singular coincidence in history that both the victor and the vanquished were severely criticised by their friends; but the strictures on Morgan were by scientific soldiers who never fought in a Parthian war or had the sons of the forest to compose their irregular lines. Irregular troops cannot be restrained or handled like the disciplined machinery of a continental line; they must have latitude for individual thought and be allowed some discretion themselves in the combat. Morgan, who had been one of these "irregulars" in early life,

---

*Stedman's History, vol. 2, p. 324.

was cognizant of these peculiarities and knew how to utilize them in times of danger.

This triumph of Morgan's was the most pronounced and brilliant of any achieved by the Southern army, prior to Yorktown. In fifty minutes a whole corps of the army of Cornwallis was destroyed, and this in the hearing of the British cannon. It was not Provincials or Tories who "fell on their faces and begged for quarters;" it was the flower of the British army; regulars, veterans,—men who had been soldiers "before Tarleton was born."

The humiliation of their prestige was the more keenly felt because they were routed by the "militia," whom they affected to contemn and despise.

Morgan had proved his skill and strategy in the field and in battle and demonstrated his wonderful influence over his troops; by the celerity of his movements, his unceasing vigilance and masterly tactics, he was now about to win for himself the honor of being the Xenophon of the Revolution.

We shall narrate the wonders of his retreat in the next chapter.

CHAPTER V.

Morgan's Retreat from Cowpens to the Catawba River—Sends his Prisoners by Island Ford to Virginia—He Crosses the Catawba with his Main Army at Sherrill's Ford January 23d, 1781—Cornwallis reaches Ramsour's Mill the 25th—Destroys all his Heavy Baggage—Greene meets Morgan the 30th at the Catawba: Orders the Army from "Camp Repose" to Join Morgan on the Yadkin—Battle at Cowan's Ford February 1st—Death of General William Lee Davidson—Frederick Hager, the Tory, Fires the Fatal Shot—Morgan Crosses the Yadkin at Trading Ford—The two Armies Unite Finally at Guilford Court-House February 10th—General Morgan Disabled by Rheumatism—Greene's Great Confidence in Him—Retreat of Greene into Virginia—Crosses the Dan, February 14th.

THE British army was resting quietly in camp on Turkey Creek, a tributary of the Broad River, in the northwestern corner of what is now York County, South Carolina, and only twenty-five miles from Cowpens, where the battle was fought, waiting, as his lordship says, for Leslie to reach him. The fright that followed King's Mountain had not entirely subsided, and he intended to secure his position and avoid another plunge through the blackjack mud before he advanced into North Carolina again.

He had confidence in "Dear Tarleton," too, and was, perhaps, sipping a glass of wine, of which he was very fond, to make his heart glad and put it in unison with the tidings which he was every moment expecting from that intrepid leader.

When the night gathered around his camp the sound of the cavalry approaching with rapid gait was heard, the wary sentinel challenged the advance, the countersign was exchanged, and then the news was broken: "Tarleton is defeated and his corps destroyed." No more revelry now; grief and dismay were written on every face; the guards were doubled and parties sent to gather more tidings from the battle. It came, but only sorrow was added to dismay. Cornwallis seems to have been dumbfounded by the appalling news, and not knowing what to do, he did nothing for a whole day, and that day Morgan made his escape and carried his prisoners out of the reach of British pursuit.

The battle began about half-past 8 o'clock in the morning—early for that season of the year—and was over by 10 o'clock. Morgan knew that Tarleton's cavalry had left without standing "on the order of their going," and that before the sun set Cornwallis would be apprised of the defeat of his troops; that if Cornwallis acted as his situation demanded he would at once advance northward to throw himself between Morgan and Greene and prevent a junction of their commands and, if fortune favored, overtake Morgan and rescue the prisoners and scatter his forces in the mountains. Morgan, therefore, immediately detailed Colonel Pickens to bury the dead and collect the wounded of both armies and provide them with what comforts he could from the captured stores and tents of the enemy, while he began the retreat. The day was spent in this work, and the unfortunate men were left in tents under a safeguard and a flag and Pickens, with his mounted command, made all haste to overtake his general.

Morgan had left before noon, taking the prisoners and cannon and captured muskets and ammunition along. The other wagons and all the heavy baggage that could not be removed were burned on the field. Morgan was still, however, encumbered with so many prisoners that his march was necessarily slow, but he persevered with all the energy possible, being aware that his safety depended on eluding the pursuit of the main army under Cornwallis. He intended, if Cornwallis got between him and Greene, to retreat into or across the mountains, if necessary, and either fight at some strong pass or make his way by a circuitous route into Virginia. But the fatal delay of one day by Cornwallis gave Morgan the requisite start, and he never lost the distance and advantage which was thus given him.

He left the battle-field shortly after noon of the same day it was fought and crossed Broad River, in Rutherford County, that evening. Early on the morning of the 18th Morgan resumed his march, going north towards Gilberttown; the same line of advance and retreat formerly travelled by the King's Mountain men, no doubt being guided by the McDowells who knew every path and strong position in the country. Patrols were sent out in the direction of approach of the army of Cornwallis and, on their return in the evening, Morgan was as much surprised as delighted to learn that not only had Cornwallis not moved yet, but that there were no signs of his moving. All was "supineness and indecision" around his camp.

At Gilberttown, three miles from where the town of Rutherfordton now is, Morgan "detached the greater part of his militia and a part of Colonel Washington's cavalry (as a guard) with the prisoners. The detachment took the Cane Creek road, through the ledge of mountains which divides the head-waters of the South Fork from the main Catawba, and then down the Catawba near where Morganton now stands, and on, until they crossed at the Island Ford. At this ford Washington's cavalry left the prisoners with the militia (under Pickens) and rejoined Morgan."* This reconciles the contention that Morgan crossed at Island Ford.

It was only this part of his force that crossed there, while he himself, with his main army, which he constantly kept between his militia and prisoners on the one hand and Cornwallis on the other, crossed at Sherrill's Ford, eight or nine miles further down the stream. He had approached Sherrill's Ford by taking the old Flint Hill road running east from Gilberttown and leading across the South Fork River, about one mile northwest of the present town of Lincolnton, at Gattis' Ford, to Ramsour's Mill, on Clark's Creek, which is about half mile

---

*General Joseph Graham in the University Magazine, vol. 5, p. 104.

from the junction of that creek with the South Fork. Morgan crossed at Sherrill's Ford on the evening of the 23d of January, 1781.

1781. At the Island Ford, on the east bank of the Catawba, "Major Hyrne, the Commissary of prisoners, received from Pickens the 600 prisoners," and they took the upper route, going northwest, into Virginia. Prisoners were generally kept in the neighborhood of Charlottesville, Virginia, at that date.

Returning now to the British camp we find that it was not until the 19th, the second day after the battle, that Cornwallis moved north, taking all his cumbrous baggage along, and with orders to the cavalry to return to his camp every night. He marched up the east bank of the Broad, crossing Buffalo and King's Creek, to the second, or little Broad River, where, hearing that Morgan had gone east, he turned to the northeast until he came to the old Flint Hill road, which Morgan had traveled, and thence down that road to Ramsour's Mill, on the 25th day of January, 1781. If he had made a forced march, even as late as the 19th, directly across from Turkey Creek, he could have easily reached Ramsour's Mill on the 20th, where he would have intercepted Morgan at this junction of their respective roads, and Tarleton censures Cornwallis for not moving in that direction. It is probable, however, that Morgan would have been early advised of this movement and escaped by the upper route. When Cornwallis reached Ramsour's Mill Morgan had crossed the Catawba River twenty-five miles beyond and was ready to turn the captured cannon on his British pursuers.

It is a common error, in the histories of this remarkable retreat, to attribute the escape of Morgan, from the pursuit of Cornwallis, to the sudden rise in the water of the Catawba. Providence may have confounded the judgment of Cornwallis and thus retarded his march, but up to this time, had not sent the floods to redeem the patriot host. Morgan outstripped the British army in the race and had a day of rest before resuming it again. The vigilance of Morgan was unceasing; he was soon informed that Cornwallis had stopped at Ramsour's Mill for reflection and he took advantage of it to rest his own troops on the eastern bank of the Catawba while the militia under Pickens were pushing the prisoners out of reach. Morgan was anxious to secure every one of them to exchange for the Continental line of North Carolina, captured at Charleston, who were then languishing and wasting away in the British prison ships. Greene had sorely lamented the paroling of the King's Mountain prisoners, by which he had lost the opportunity for exchange.

Cornwallis had lost the 17th and 18th of January in his camp waiting for Leslie, and when he did move he took six days of a circuitous route to reach Ramsour's Mill, which he ought to have reached in two. At Ramsour's Mill some fatuity overshadowed his reason and caused him to stop two days more.

On the 25th of January, the day that Cornwallis reached Ramsour's Mill, the news of Morgan's victory reached General Greene at his camp on the Pee Dee. His little army was immediately ordered to prepare to march to the assistance of Morgan. The troops were poorly clad and the winter was cold; but they received the orders of their commander with cheerfulness and confidence. The 25th, 26th and 27th of January were spent in energetic preparation for the march, and the most minute orders were given as to every detail before General Greene would consent to leave.

On the 28th, the day that Cornwallis left Ramsour's Mill, General Greene did what will be deemed by many the most imprudent act of his life. "With only a guide, an aid and a sergeant's guard of cavalry, he struck across the country to join Morgan and aid him in his arduous operations." The distance he had to traverse was one hundred miles; yet on the 30th we have his letters dated from Sherrill's Ford.* Erroneous traditions have crept into history that after Greene's arrival he and Morgan disagreed or quarreled, and that for this reason Morgan so soon retired from the campaign. Nothing is further from the truth. They were cordial, confidential and in entire accord. They both agreed that if Cornwallis resumed the pursuit, before the prisoners had been far enough away for security, that they would give him battle as he crossed the stream. They were in no hurry to leave.

*Johnson's Life of Greene, vol. 1, p. 403.
The proper name is Sherrill's, not Sherard's Ford.

The army of Greene had been ordered to march up the Yadkin (called lower down the Pee Dee) and to be in position near Salisbury to join Morgan, and were now on their way under General Huger.

Lord Cornwallis, having lost most of his light troops at Cowpens, determined to relieve himself of every possible encumbrance and enter with renewed ardor upon the pursuit of Morgan. Stedman says that—

"Previously to the arrival of the British troops on the banks of the Catawba, Lord Cornwallis, considering that the loss of his light troops could only be remedied by the activity of the whole army, resolved to destroy all the superfluous baggage. By first reducing the size and quantity of his own, he set an example which was cheerfully followed by all the officers in his command, although by so doing they sustained a considerable loss. No wagons were reserved except those loaded with hospital stores, salt and ammunition, and four empty ones for the accommodation of the sick or wounded. And such was the ardour, both of officers and soldiers, and their willingness to submit to any hardship for the promotion of the service, that this arrangement, which deprived them of all future prospect of *spirituous liquors*, and *even* hazarded a regular supply of *provisions*, was acquiesced in without a murmur."*

To this destruction of his whole material train and necessary outfit for a winter campaign is attributed the final discomfiture of Cornwallis at

---

*It is curious to read in this day of the great emphasis laid upon the loss of the liquors; Stedman gives it preference to "provisions."

Guilford Court House. The supplies he burned could not be replaced short of Wilmington, and thither he was compelled to go when a reverse met his arms.

While at Ramsour's Mill many of the Hessian mercenaries deserted, and some English soldiers; in all it is estimated that 250 deserted. This is accounted for first, on the ground that the Hessians found here a German-speaking population, and caring no more for British than American principles, they escaped and became laborers in the country. The English, it is said, rebelled at the loss of the porter* and rum—the "want of his gill of rum was more distinctly realized than the love of his King and country."

Finally the British army resumed its march on the 28th of January, taking the highway leading to Beattie's Ford, which is the direct route to Salisbury. This, however, was intended to deceive the Americans, as the real place selected for crossing was Cowan's Ford, a few miles lower down.

We do not know the exact numbers of the British army at this time. In a letter of Cornwallis, dated the 18th December at Winnsboro, he says: "I have a good account of our recruits in general, and hope to march from hence with 3500 fighting men." He lost, perhaps, 800 men at Cowpens, and received the 1500 men under General Leslie, and in round numbers must have had at least 4000 fighting men.

---

*NOTE.—The glass from the broken porter bottles were gathered for years by the potters to glaze their earthen-ware.

Sir Henry Clinton estimates it at "considerably above 3000, exclusive of cavalry and militia."

We must now look to the east and see what preparations were being made on that side of the Catawba to dispute the passage of the British army. General Rutherford was then a captive at St. Augustine and General William Lee Davidson, of Mecklenburg, had been appointed to the command of his militia district during his absence. This division, General Graham states, embraced the "old superior court districts of Salisbury and Morganton, now composing the fourth and fifth divisions of North Carolina militia, whose returns of effective men at this time (1821) exceed twenty thousand men."* As soon as General Davidson was informed of the advance of the British army he ordered out the next detachment, which was detailed for duty from the counties under his command, to rendezvous between Charlotte and the Catawba River. On the 19th he received information of Tarleton's defeat and hastened a letter, by special messenger, to General Greene on the Pee Dee. On the 21st a body of twenty Whigs brought in twenty-eight British stragglers whom they had picked up after the battle of Cowpens, and from them all the details were gathered.

I now incorporate the narrative of General Graham, which is so interesting that I need make no apology for doing so.

*University Magazine, p. 103.

"General Davidson was without cavalry and directed Adjutant Graham (afterwards General Joseph Graham), who had now recovered from his wounds received the 26th of September, to raise a company of cavalry, promising that those who furnished their own horses and equipments and served six weeks should be considered as having served a tour of three months, the term of duty required by the law. In a few days he succeeded in raising a company of 56, mostly enterprising young men, who had seen service, but found it difficult to procure arms. Only 45 swords could be produced, and one-half of them were made by the country blacksmiths. Only 15 had pistols, but they *all had rifles*. They carried the muzzle in a small boot, fastened beside the right stirrup leather, and the but ran through the shot-bag belt, so that the lock came directly under the right arm. Those who had a pistol carried it swung by a strap, about the size of a bridle-rein, on the left side over the sword, which was belted higher than the modern mode of wearing it, so as not to entangle the legs when acting on foot. They had at all times all their arms with them, whether on foot or on horseback, and could act as infantry or cavalry, and move individually or collectively as emergencies might require. With those arms, and mounted generally on strong and durable horses, with a pair of saddle-bags for the convenience of the rider and a wallet of provender for his horse, they were ready for service without commissary, quartermaster or other staff.

"General Davidson finding the enemy approaching so near, divided those under his command in order to guard the different fords on the Catawba. At Tuckaseege Ford, on the road leading from Ramsour's to Charlotte, he placed two hundred men under Colonel Joseph Williams, of Surry. At Tool's Ford seventy men under Captain Potts, of Mecklenburg,* at Cowan's Ford twenty-five men under Lieutenant Thomas Davidson, of Mecklenburg. With his greatest force and Graham's cavalry, he took post at Beattie's Ford on the road from Ramsour's Mill to Salisbury—being twenty miles above Colonel Williams. On the 31st of January the cavalry were dispatched over the river, and ascertained that the enemy were encamped within four miles. Within two miles they discovered one hundred of their cavalry, who followed them to the river, but kept at a respectful distance. The dispositions that were being made caused them to fear an ambuscade.

"The same evening General Morgan sent on the troops under his command with Colonel Howard, directly towards Salisbury. He himself and Colonel Washington came down to Beattie's Ford, about 2 o'clock, and in ten minutes General Greene and his aid, Major Pierce, arrived. He had been early informed of the movements of the British army and had first put his troops in motion, then leaving them under command of General Huger on their march towards Salisbury, he had come on to ascertain the situation of affairs, and give orders to the officers in this quarter; General Morgan and Colonel Washington met him at this place, by appointment. They and General Davidson retired with him out of the camp, and seating themselves on a log, had a conversation of about twenty minutes—they then mounted their horses, General Greene and aid took the road to Salisbury, Morgan and Washington took a way that led to the

---

*At Tuckaseege and Tool's fords, trees were felled in the road, and a ditch dug and parapet made. There was no such defences at the other fords.

troops marching under Howard. About the time General Greene had arrived the British vanguard of about four or five hundred men appeared on the opposite hill beyond the river. Shortly after their arrival, some principal officer with a numerous staff, thought to be Lord Cornwallis, passed in front of them at different stations, halting and apparently viewing us with spy-glasses. In about one hour after General Greene's departure General Davidson gave orders to the cavalry and about two hundred and fifty infantry to march down the river to Cowan's Ford, four miles below Beattie's, leaving nearly the same number at that place, under the command of Colonel Farmer, of Orange. On the march he stated to the commanding officer of the cavalry that, though General Greene had never seen the Catawba before, he appeared to know more about it than those who were raised on it, and it was the General's opinion that the enemy were determined to cross the river, and he thought it probable their cavalry would pass over some private ford in the night; and in the morning when the infantry attempted to force a passage would attack those who resisted it, in the rear; and as there was no other cavalry between Beattie's and Tuckaseege fords, he ordered that patrols who were best acquainted with the country should keep passing up and down all night, and on discovering any part of the enemy to have gotten over, to give immediate information to him. These orders were carried into effect. The party arrived at the ford about dusk in the evening, and after encamping it was too dark to examine our position.

"At Cowan's Ford the river is supposed to be about four hundred yards wide, of different depths and rocky bottom. That called the wagon ford goes directly across the river; on coming out on the eastern shore, the road turns down and winds up the point of a ridge, in order to graduate the ascent until it comes to its proper direction. Above the coming-out place a flat piece of ground, not much higher than the water, grown over with haw and persimmon bushes and bamboo briars, five or six yards wide, extends up the river to the mouth of a small branch and deep ravine.

"Outside of this the bank rises thirty or forty feet, at an angle of thirty degrees elevation; then the rise is more gradual. That called the horse ford, at the present time much the most used, comes in on the west at the same place with the wagon ford, goes obliquely down the river about two-thirds of the way across, to the point of a large island, thence through the island and across the other one-third to the point of a rocky hill. Though it is longer, this way is much shallower and smoother than the wagon ford, and comes out about a quarter of a mile below.

"From the information received General Davidson supposed that if the enemy attempted to cross here they would take the horse ford. Accordingly he encamped on the hill which overlooks it. Lieutenant Thomas Davidson's picket of twenty-five men remained at their station, about fifty steps above the wagon ford, on the flat piece of ground before described, near the water's edge.

"On the same day, as Cornwallis was marching to Beattie's Ford, about two miles from it at Colonel Black's farm, he left behind him, under the command of Brigadier General O'Hara, twelve hundred infantry and Tarleton's cavalry, which in the night moved secretly down to Cowan's Ford, only three miles below. The next morning at dawn of day, the 1st of February, 1781, he had his columns formed, the infantry in front with fixed bayonets, muskets empty, carried on the left shoulder at a slope, cartridge-box on the same shoulder, and each man had a stick about the size of a hoop-pole, eight feet long, which he kept setting on the bottom below him to support him against the rapidity of the current, which was generally waist deep, and in some places more. (It is stated by historians that the river was swollen so as to impede the passage of the British. The fact is, *it was fordable from the week before until two days after this time*, though a little deeper than usual. The cause of the enemy's delay must have been the disposition by General Davidson to guard the fords.)

"The command of the front was committed to Colonel Hall of the guards, who had for a guide Frederick Hager, a renegade Tory who lived within two miles of the place. They entered the river by sections of four, and took the wagon ford.

"The morning was cloudy, and a fog hung over the water, so that Lieutenant Davidson's sentinel could not see them until they were near one hundred yards in the river. He instantly fired on them, which roused the guard, who kept up the fire, but the enemy continued to advance. At the first alarm those under General Davidson paraded at the horse ford, and Graham's cavalry was ordered to move up briskly, to assist the picket; but by the time they got there, and tied their horses and came up in a line to a high bank above the ford, in front of the column, it was within fifty yards of the eastern shore. They took steady and deliberate aim and fired. The effect was visible. The three first ranks looked thinned, and they halted. Colonel Hall was the first man who appeared on horseback, behind, about one hundred yards. He came pressing up their flank on the lower side and was distinctly heard giving orders, but we could not hear what they were.

"The column again got in motion and kept on. One of the cavalry riflemen reloaded and aimed at Colonel Hall. At the flash of the gun both horse and rider went under the water, and rose down the stream. It appeared that the horse had gone over the man. Two or three of the soldiers caught him and raised him on the upper side.

"The enemy kept steadily on, notwithstanding our fire was well maintained. As each section reached the shore they dropped their setting poles, and brought their muskets and cartridge-boxes to their places, faced to the left, and moved up the narrow strip of low ground to make room for the succeeding section, which moved on in the same manner.

"By the time the front ranks got twenty or thirty steps up the river they had loaded their pieces and began to fire up the bank.

"The Americans receded a few steps when loading, and when ready to fire would advance to the summit of the hill, twenty-five or thirty steps from the enemy, as they deployed up the river bank. They had gained the ford and just commenced firing when General Davidson arrived from the horse ford with the infantry, and finding his cavalry on the ground he chose to occupy, and impressed with opinion given by General Greene, that the enemy's cavalry would attack them in the rear, he ordered Graham's men to mount and go up the ridge, and form two hundred yards behind. As they moved off, the infantry took their places, and the firing became brisk on both sides.

"The enemy moved steadily forward, their fire increasing, until their left reached the mouth of the branch upwards of thirty poles from the ford. The ravine was too deep to pass. The rear of their infantry and front of their cavalry was about the middle of the river, when the bugle sounded on the left, on which their fire slacked and nearly ceased. (They were loading their pieces.) In about a minute it sounded again, when their whole line from the ford to the branch advanced up the bank, with their arms at a trail. The hill was in many places so steep they had to pull up by the bushes.

"General Davidson, finding them advancing with loaded guns, ordered a retreat for one hundred yards. On gaining the point of the ridge their fire was so heavy that he had to recede fifty steps beyond the ground assigned for formation; he then ordered his men to take trees, and had them arranged to renew the battle.

"The enemy was advancing slowly in line, and only firing scatteringly, when General Davidson was pierced by a ball and fell dead from his horse.

("The General was shot with a small rifle-ball near the nipple of the left breast, and never moved after he fell. It was well known that their pilot, Frederick Hager, had a rifle of this description, and it was always believed that he shot him. Most of the other Tories returned at or before the close of the war, but Hager went to Tennessee and stayed there until some of the Davidson family moved to that country, when he moved, with eight or ten others, all fugitives from justice, and made the first American settlement on the Arkansas River near Six Post; married and raised a family there, and died in the year 1814. Major David Wilson and two others found the General's body in the evening, carried him off in the night and buried him at Hopewell Church, higher up on the Catawba River. The grave is yet known, and though Congress afterwards passed a resolution appropriating $500 for a monument, strange to tell, nothing is yet done to execute it.)

" His infantry retreated in disorder from the unequal contest. They dispersed in small squads, and took through the thickets in order to evade the enemy's cavalry. Graham's cavalry, which was formed about one hundred yards in the rear of where Davidson fell, moved off in order.

"At an early hour Cornwallis placed his remaining force in array on the face of the hill fronting Beattie's Ford, and as soon as the firing commenced at Cowan's Ford, made demonstrations of attacking the post at Beattie's. A company went into the water forty or fifty steps and fired. Four pieces of artillery fired smartly for thirty minutes, and his front lines kept firing by platoons, as in field exercises. It was only a feint, however. Few shots of the musketry reached the opposite shore, and the artillery did no injury but cut off the branches of some trees near our line, which was masked by the point of the hill from the enemy's fire. The ford was one hundred yards higher up then than now. When the British were deploying up the bank at Cowan's Ford, owing to the fog and density of the atmosphere, the report of the artillery and platoons at Beattie's Ford came down the river like repeated peals of thunder, as though it were within a mile, and was heard over the country, to the distance of twenty-five miles. Although it had no effect on our troops engaged at Cowan's (for they acted well under the circumstances), yet it had a wonderful effect on the people of the adjacent country. Hitching up their teams in great haste, and packing up their most valuable goods and some means of subsistence, the men who were not in service, and women and children, abandoned their homes, and drove off in different directions.

"In one hour after the firing the whole country appeared in motion, but unfortunately too many of them fled into the Salisbury road. The baggage and provision wagons had started from Cowan's as soon as the action began. Graham's cavalry maintained their order, and expected the enemy's cavalry would pursue the baggage.

"A disposition was therefore made by placing four men with good horses as a rear guard, and despatching two others to give directions to the wagon-master, if he heard firing in his rear, to cause the teamsters to cut the horses from their wagons and clear themselves. Moving on slowly, halting occasionally, and no enemy appearing, it occurred to the commanding officer that the enemy's design must be to take Colonel Farmer in the rear, at Beattie's Ford (if he had maintained his position against the tremendous cannonade). It was believed he had no intelligence of their being actually across below the ford. The cavalry filed off along a by-road to give him notice, intending to form a junction with the foot one and a half miles from the ford at a farm. An old lady (the only person at the place), informed them that shortly after the firing had ceased General Davidson's aid had given notice to the party at Beattie's and they had retired already some distance on the Salisbury road. Some rain had fallen, and the men were wet and cold, and both men and horses having had but a scanty supply of provisions at Cowan's the evening before, it was concluded to get some sustenance and take it off a mile or two in the woods and eat it. Videttes were ordered out, and, agreeably to rule in such cases, each right-hand file ordered to dismount and procure food for himself, comrade and their horses, while the left file held the horses. They had not gotten half their supply when one of the videttes gave notice that on the other side of the farm some men were in view, believed to be the enemy, but, having Hussar cloaks over their uniforms, could not be clearly ascertained, but by the tails of their horses being docked square off, which all knew was the mark of Tarleton's cavalry, they were instantly recognized, and orders given to mount, fronting the enemy. When all were in their places, they wheeled off, and up a lane, the whole British cavalry coming briskly round the farm on the other side. When Graham's party passed over a rise in the ground beyond the lane, they turned short to the right, and in twenty-five poles crossed a swampy branch. When the advance got over they wheeled to protect the rear, but the enemy were so eager in the pursuit that they did not discover them; but kept on, at a brisk gallop, along the Salisbury road. This was about two miles from Torrence's tavern, whither they were bound.

"The men who retreated from Beattie's Ford, and some of those who had been at Cowan's, and many others, some of them South Carolina refugees, as they arrived at Torrence's tavern, halted. Being wet, cold and hungry, they began to drink spirits, carrying it out in pailsful. The wagons of many of the movers with their property were in the lane, the armed men all out of order and mixed with the wagons and people, so that the lane could scarely be passed, when the sound of the alarm was given from the west end of the lane, '*Tarleton is coming!*' Though none had had time to become intoxicated, it was difficult to decide what course to pursue at such a crisis. Captain Nathaniel M. Martin, who had served under Colonel Davie, and six or eight others (armed as cavalry), rode up meeting the enemy, and called to the men to get over the fences and turn facing the enemy; that he could make them halt until they could be ready; some appeared disposed to do so; others, when they crossed the fence, kept on, some with their pails of whiskey. Martin moved forward until within fifty yards of the enemy. They halted near two minutes. Tarleton could readily discover the confusion and disorder that prevailed. One of his party fired a carbine and shot down Captain Martin's horse; he was entangled and taken prisoner, but escaped from the guard two days after. Tarleton and corps charged through the lane. The militia fled in every direction. Those who were on horse-back and kept the road were pursued about half a mile. Ten were killed, of whom several were old men, unarmed, who had come there in the general alarm, and a few were wounded, all with sabres. But few guns were fired. On the return of the dragoons from the pursuit they made great destruction of the property in the wagons of those who were moving; ripped up beds and strewed the feathers until the lane was covered with them. Everything else they could destroy was used in the same manner.

"At Cowan's Ford, besides General Davidson, there were killed James Scott of Lieutenant Davidson's picket, Robert Beaty of Graham's cavalry, and one private of General Davidson's infantry—in all, four. We had none wounded or taken. The enemy's loss, as stated in the official account, published in the Charleston Gazette two months after, was Colonell Hall of the guards, and another officer, and twenty-nine privates—thirty-one in all, killed, and thirty-five wounded. They left sixteen, who were so badly wounded they could not be taken along, at Mr. Lucas' (the nearest farm), and a surgeon, under protection of a flag, was left with them. Two wounded officers were carried on biers, and such of the other wounded as could not walk were hauled in wagons. Some of their dead were found down the river some distance, lodged in fish-traps and on brush about the banks, on rocks, etc. An elegant beaver hat, made agreeably to the fashion of those times, marked inside, "*The property of Josiah Martin, Governor,*" was found ten miles below. It never was explained by what means his excellency lost his hat. He was not hurt himself.

"When General O'Hara sent on Tarleton, his men kindled fires on the battle-ground to dry themselves, cook their breakfast, etc. They buried their dead, disposed of their wounded, and about midday he marched, and in the afternoon united with Lord Cornwallis at Givens' plantation, two miles from Beattie's Ford and one mile south of the Salisbury road. Tarleton joined them before night. It had rained at times all day, and in the evening and at night it fell in torrents.

"The men under Colonel Williams and Captain Potts, who were guarding at Tuckaseege and Tool's fords, had early notice of the enemy's crossing, and retired. The different parties met in the afternoon at Jno. McK. Alexander's, eight miles above Charlotte. By noon the next day all the men who were not dispersed were collected near Harriss' Mill, on Rocky River, ten or twelve miles from the enemy.

"On the 2d of February the morning was clear, though the roads very bad with the rain that had fallen the preceding night. The British army marched ten miles to Wilson's plantation and encamped. On their way they burnt Torrances' tavern (at that time kept by the widow Torrance; her husband had been killed at the battle of Ramsour's Mill), and the dwelling-house of John Brevard, Esq. (Mr. Brevard was the father-in-law of General Davidson, and at that time had several sons in the regular service. No other cause could be assigned for this barbarous mode of warfare.) Being now within twenty miles of Salisbury, the British General, not doubting that the rains and bad roads would obstruct the march of General Morgan as much as it did his own, on the 3d of February marched at an early hour. His pioneers opened a kind of track in the bushes on each side of the road for a single file. The wagons, artillery and horsemen only kept the road. By the time they got within eight miles of Salisbury, their line of march was extended four miles, but there were no troops near to intercept them. Their van arrived at Salisbury about three o'clock. Before the rear came in, Brigadier General O'Hara and the cavalry moved on. It was seven miles to the Trading Ford on the Yadkin, and it was getting dark when he came near. General Morgan had passed his regulars and baggage all over, and there remained on the south side only one hundred and fifty militia and the baggage-wagons of the troops which had escaped at Cowan's Ford, and some others. Finding the British approaching, the militia were drawn up near a half a mile from the ford, where a branch crosses, which was covered with small timber and bushes, and there was an old-field along the road in their front. When O'Hara came, twilight was nearly gone. The American position was low along the branch, under shade of the timber; that of the advancing foe was open and on higher ground, and between them, and the sky was quite visible. When they came within sixty steps the Americans commenced firing; the enemy returned it and began to form a line. As their rear came up they extended their line to the right, and were turning the left flank of the militia by crossing the branch above. This being discovered, a retreat was ordered, after having fired, some two, some three rounds. It was easily effected in the dark. They passed down the river two miles and crossed over, abandoning the baggage and other wagons which could not be gotten over, to the enemy, after taking out the horses. Two of the militia were killed. The loss of the enemy was not known, but from appearances of blood in different places, believed to be ten or twelve. They were by far the most numerous, yet from the positions of the contending parties, were most exposed. After the firing ceased the British marched on to the river, but found the water was too deep to ford, and still rising, and that General Morgan, encamped on the other side, had with him all the boats and canoes. General O'Hara returned to Salisbury the same night, notwithstanding the badness of the roads. Those under his command marched thirty-four miles in the course of this day and part of the night. On the 4th the army needed rest, and their commander being, it is supposed, undecided what course to pursue, they remained in Salisbury."

From Sherrill's Ford, on the 30th, General Greene writes General Huger explaining the military situation and ordering him to lead the army to the fords of the Yadkin and there await further orders.

In this letter General Greene expresses an apprehension that Arnold would make an incursion, by way of Wilmington and the Cape Fear River, and he directs that Colonel Lillington should call out the militia to oppose him. He closes by saying: "I am not without hopes of ruining Lord Cornwallis if he persists in his mad scheme of pushing through the country. Desire Colonel Lee to force a march to join us. Here is a fine field and great glory ahead." It is astonishing to discover how many varied circumstances are foreshadowed and orders given to meet them, and the many details and particulars discussed in this lengthy letter. Greene was not only comprehensive in intellect, but accurate and specific in his information, and sagacious beyond measure, ready for any emergency. In another letter of the 30th he mentions the fact that Cornwallis had arrived at Ramsour's Mill. This demonstrates that Cornwallis was not pressing the pursuit closely, and General Graham's narrative confirms this view. It is strange that Colonel Lee should have fallen into the common error of supposing that Morgan was saved from the grasp of Cornwallis by a flood of water. But it is appropriate to remark that Lee's "general inaccuracy," as Johnson calls it, is conspicuous through his whole Memoirs. He had the infirmity of Lord Erskine, of using the personal pronoun, first person, singular number, rather too often, and his memory was frequently treacherous in describing the acts of others. These defects are not perhaps inconsistent with patriotism or military skill, but are a little annoying to the patient investigator of truth. On the 31st of January, Morgan had gone to Beattie's Ford, six miles nearer Salisbury, and on that evening, perceiving that Cornwallis would force a passage at some of the numerous fords, all of which could not be defended, he moved silently away towards Salisbury, marching all night and a part of the next day, thus gaining a full day's march on the British army. When Cornwallis crossed at Cowan's Ford on the morning of the 1st of February, Morgan was well on his way to the Trading Ford, on the Yadkin, seven miles east of Salisbury, which he crossed on the evening of the 3rd.*

General Greene remained behind to bring off the militia, and directed them to rendezvous on the Salisbury road, sixteen miles from the river, and thither he repaired to await their coming. His danger was more imminent at this point than he apprehended. He was unattended, and only six miles in advance of Torrance's Tavern, where Tarleton, at noon, had scattered the carousing Whigs. He was unaware of Greene's proximity and of the fact that twenty of his troopers could easily have led Greene captive into the British camp. Here, perhaps, Divine Providence was more conspicuously displayed. At midnight of the 1st of February, Greene left the rendezvous, with his staff, for Salisbury. Johnson relates the story of

---

*NOTE.—Trading Ford is just below the railroad bridge on the North Carolina Railroad.

the General's reception at the Steele tavern so well that we give it in his words:

"On his arrival at Steele's tavern, in Salisbury, it was impossible not to perceive, in the deranged state of his dress and stiffness of his limbs, some symptoms of his late rapid movements and exposure to the weather; and to the inquiries of Dr. Read, who received him on his alighting, he could not refrain from answering, 'Yes, fatigued, hungry, alone and penniless.' This reply did not escape the quick ears of his benevolent landlady; and he was scarcely seated at a comfortable breakfast when she presented herself in the room, closed the door and exhibited a small bag of specie in each hand. 'Take these,' said she, 'for you will want them, and I can do without them.'"*

The meal being finished, he hastened away to overtake General Morgan.

Cornwallis made but little progress on the 1st, owing to the narrowness and badness of the private road he travelled from Cowan's Ford. He now added General O'Hara, with his mounted infantry, to his cavalry and ordered them to push forward rapidly to overtake the Americans, but this flying corps only came to Trading Ford in time to capture a few militia wagons that had been stuck in the mud, and for which the militia fired upon them from an ambuscade and killed about twenty, as related above.

Morgan had transferred his troops across the

---

*This lady was Mrs. Steele, the ancestor of Hon. John Steele Henderson, of this generation.

river on boats which Colonel Carrington had previously collected, and the cavalry forded the stream. So that if the Yadkin had been too high to ford the ferry-boats were, by General Greene's foresight, in readiness to put his army across. These boats, and all others for miles around, were secured on the eastern bank, and Morgan, complacently viewing the swelling tide between him and Cornwallis, halted for a much-needed rest. Frustrated in this attempt to overtake the Americans, O'Hara gave vent to his anger by opening upon them a furious cannonade. Morgan had none to reply, as he had sent the little three-pounders, called "grass-hoppers," which he captured at Cowpens, along with the prisoners to a secure retreat. Morgan would not be encumbered with artillery.

During the cannonade General Greene occupied a little cabin under a hill, only the roof being visible above it. Here, while issuing his orders, a cannon-ball struck the roof and scattered it in every direction, but Dr. Read, who relates the incident, says that the General "wrote on and seemed to notice nothing but his dispatches."

Cornwallis awaited O'Hara's return to Salisbury, where he came the same night. Having sent out reconnoitering parties higher up the Yadkin, and discovering that he could cross at Shallow Ford, Cornwallis put his army in motion on the 5th and crossed at that point on the evening of the 6th.*

---

*NOTE.—I follow General Graham in preference to Johnson as to the last two dates. Tarleton says it was on the 6th, but Graham, who was in their rear, says it was the 5th.

Greene had already sent forward Colonel Carrington and Captain John Smith, of the Maryland line, to secure the boats on the Dan and provide all possible facilities for crossing that stream, and had issued orders to Huger to press forward to Guilford Court-House, where a junction of the two armies was to take place. General Greene did not move from the Trading Ford until the evening of the 4th of February, 1781. The retirement was orderly and deliberate, and was not the "race" which some imaginative writers have colored with the figures of rhetoric. Greene was master of his own movements, and forced Cornwallis to change his.

After leaving Trading Ford, General Greene moved in a direction nearly north, as if he were making for the upper fords of the Dan, and Cornwallis pushed on with great spirit to intercept him on the way, but this was a part of the strategy of the American General, whose original purpose was to cross the Dan River lower down in ferry-boats.

At the forks of Abbott's Creek, a few miles from Salem (in Forsyth County now), he halted the army to obtain definite information as to the movements of the British, and then turning due east, he marched to Guilford Court-House, where he made the junction with his army, under General Huger, on the 10th of February.

On the 8th of February Greene had hoped to be able to fight Cornwallis at Guilford Court-House, where he formed a junction with his main army, and on that day addressed earnest proclamations to the militia to turn out and meet him there, and couriers were sent to Hillsboro to bring up a few troops who were left there, and further supplies of ammunition. As soon as Greene arrived at Guilford Court-House he began to reconnoitre the grounds and adjacent country.

"It was at this time that the celebrated position was selected, which directed the steps of Greene to this point a month after, when he found it advisable to give the enemy a challenge to battle; so truly did he exemplify the military maxim, that 'a good general will fight only when and where he pleases.'"*

But Greene was disappointed. The militia did not turn out with the alacrity that he expected, nor had the recruits and ammunition from Hillsboro arrived. About 200 of the Guilford militia, under Colonel James Martin, including the company under Captain Arthur Forbis, were, perhaps, the only reinforcements that responded to the call. As a reason for not having more men, Colonel Martin says "that guns were wanting by a number of the militia, and that he had to impress all he could to arm the few militia that did assemble." These men marched with Greene to the Dan and about half of them crossed the Dan into Virginia, as volunteers, and subsequently returned with him and participated in the battle at that place.

Greene called a council of war at Guilford Court-House and submitted to it the question of further

*Johnson, vol. 1, p. 425.

retreat or giving battle where they were. The council was unanimous that the army should retreat across the Dan. The returns of the army at that time showed that Greene had, of rank and file, of all arms, only 2036 men; of these 1426 were regulars. The Virginia militia, whose time had expired, were already discharged. The force of Cornwallis was ascertained to be 3000, all regulars, in the highest state of discipline and equipment. It is said that Greene would have risked a battle if he could have collected 1500 militia. He writes that retreat would depress the Whigs and encourage the Tories, and he believed, with his splendid cavalry, in which arm of the service he had great confidence, that he could prevent a route of his army in any event; he also expressed great sympathy for Mecklenburg and Rowan counties, which he desired to protect from the ravages of the enemy.

The resolution to retreat was, however, adopted, and General Greene made his dispositions accordingly. The Dan was to be crossed at Irwin's Ferry, seventy (70) miles from Guilford Court-House, and Colonel Carrington was sent to secure all the boats and make every preparation necessary for the army to cross.

"'The route of retreat being determined, the place of crossing designated and measures taken for the collection of boats, General Greene formed a light corps, consisting of some of his best infantry, under Lieutenant Colonel Howard, of Washington's cavalry, the Legion of Lee, and a few militia riflemen " (most probably the Guilford men who joined Greene at the court-house), "making in all seven hundred. The troops were to take post between the retreating and advancing army, to hover around the skirts of the latter, to seize every opportunity of striking in detail, and to retard the enemy by vigilance and judicious positions; while Greene, with the main body, hastened towards the Dan, the boundary of his present toils and dangers."*

General Morgan, who was at that time prostrated with a severe attack of rheumatism, contracted in his late retreat by exposure to wet and cold, was offered the command of these light troops, but was reluctantly compelled to decline the honor. His sufferings at the Catawba River were intense, often compelling him to abandon duty and seek comfort in a bed or an ambulance. He had in former years suffered greatly from this painful malady, and it had now returned upon him with more distressing symptoms. He had not only to refuse this command, but to retire, by slow and easy marches, taking rests by the way at the hospitable homes of his friends, to his own home in the western part of Virginia.

There was no man in Greene's army, or perhaps in the whole service, so fitted to command such a force, in the execution of the duty assigned them, as Morgan, and there was no associate of General Greene's who so entirely possessed his confidence and enjoyed his friendship.

*Lee's Memoirs, p. 236.

Greene, not being well acquainted with the mode of warfare on the frontiers and in the South, was greatly dependent on Morgan for advice and counsel in this respect, and the splendid achievement at Cowpens and the masterly retreat to the Catawba, had so impressed General Greene with the pre-eminent abilities of Morgan that he leaned upon him, in this hour of need and this crisis in the affairs of the country, as a brother and a friend. His distress and disappointment was strongly manifested when General Morgan communicated to him the condition of his health and his determination to retire temporarily from service. In the sequel it will be seen that Morgan's heart was still with his friend, and that he wrote him letters containing valuable suggestions, upon which General Greene did him the honor to act.

Upon Morgan's declining this important command, it was tendered to and accepted by Colonel Otho Williams, of the Maryland line.

In order to deceive Cornwallis, who was then at Salem, about twenty-five miles west of Guilford Court-House, Williams made a sudden movement north as if to secure the upper fords of the Dan and cross them in front of the British army. The British commander, mistaking this detachment for the main body of the American army, hastened forward to cut it off from escape by these fords into the mountains of Virginia, which he supposed they were endeavoring to reach for safety. In the meantime, Greene, with the remainder of the army, marched rapidly to Irwin's Ferry, according to his original design, and crossed the Dan in safety.

The strategy was completely successful, and Williams now changed his course, and annoying the advance of the enemy, which camped in sight of him every night, he finally reached the vicinity of the Dan on the 14th day of February, and having received the joyful news that Greene had crossed that day, Williams, leaving his camp-fires burning, stole away from Cornwallis, who reached the bank of the river on the next day, the 15th, only to see the last of Williams' command ascending the hill on the opposite side.

The 15th February, 1781, found Greene and his united army at the end of their long and toilsome retreat, and with an impassable barrier between him and his adversary. Cornwallis, crest-fallen, outwitted and desperate, knew not what to do. His subsequent movements manifest indecision, want of purpose and a knowledge of the great danger in which he was placed by the Fabian tactics of his wily antagonist. He was in an enemy's country, his winter supplies all burned, the militia were "swarming in his rear," recruits were increasing Greene's army, his base of supply was far away and his foe refused to fight until he selected his own time and place. A beleaguered situation indeed!

CHAPTER VI.

Greene on the Dan—Cornwallis at Hillsboro—General Andrew Pickens, of South Carolina, selected by a Brigade of North Carolina Militia at Shallow Ford, to lead Them—Movements of General Richard Caswell with the Militia in the East—"Council Extraordinary," its Acts—General John Butler's Movements—Major Craig, of the British Army, enters Wilmington January the 29th, 1781—Letter of Governor Abner Nash—Greene Recrosses the Dan February 23d, 1781—Graham's Dash at Hart's Mill—Pyle's Defeat, 25th February, 1781—Affair at Whitsill's Mill, March 6th—Lieutenant Colonel Webster's Marvelous Escape from Death— Reinforcements Reach General Greene at High Rock Ford, on Haw River, Sunday, March the 11th, 1781.

THE final conclusion of Cornwallis was to march to Hillsboro, then the capital of the State, and the recent headquarters of the American army, at that time quite an important place. It was also in easy distance of the Scotch settlements, whose inhabitants were generally loyalists or neutrals in the fight.

His lordship, after taking one day of repose, began his march on the 18th to Hillsboro, where he "raised the royal standard," and invited, by his proclamation, "all liege subjects to prove their fidelity by contributing their aid in restoring the blessings of peace and order in their convulsed country."*

"In the camp of Greene," says Lee, "joy beamed on every face, as if every man was conscious of

*Lee's Memoirs, p. 251.

having done his duty; the subsequent days to the reunion of the army on the north of the Dan were spent in mutual gratulations; with the rehearsal of the hopes and fears which agitated every breast during the retreat, interspersed with the many simple but interesting anecdotes with which every tongue was strung."

But Greene relaxed no vigilance nor neglected any precaution against surprise. The waving of a handkerchief by a patriotic lady on the North Carolina bank of the river announced the retrograde movement of Cornwallis. Major Pierce, of General Greene's staff, with a select party, were sent to reconnoiter and give intelligence, while Colonel Williams and Colonel Campbell, two eminent North Carolina militia officers, with their faithful adherents on horseback, patroled and guarded the passes, and Otho Williams, with his light troops, were thrown across the stream to harass his lordship's retreat.*

Leaving the two contending armies watching each other, and preparing for the conflict, which must sooner or later occur, it is necessary to narrate events transpiring elsewhere in North Carolina which influenced, to a great degree, the subsequent results of the unfinished campaign.

The militia, who had defended the fords of the Catawba, had made good their retreat to the Rocky River, a western tributary of the Yadkin, which traverses from west to east the present county of

*Johnson's Life of Greene, vol. 1, p. 448.

Cabarrus, North Carolina, but which at that time was a part of Mecklenburg County. They were advised as to the location of the British army, and Captain Joseph Graham, who had been sent to reconnoiter, followed in its rear; but beyond the capture of half a dozen stragglers, and killing a Tory or two in arms, was not able to do more than gather information.

About the 10th of February the militia were in camp near Shallow Ford, on the Yadkin. General Davidson had been killed, and "no small contention" had arisen between the different colonels of the regiments as to the seniority of their commissions and their right to command. But this contention, hot as it was, did not lead to a separation. The fervent patriotism of these brave men rose above self and State, and the difficulty was happily and generously settled by electing Andrew Pickens, of South Carolina, who had recently been appointed Brigadier General, to the command. Pickens was at that time a refugee in North Carolina, accompanied by not exceeding forty (40) South Carolinians and Georgians; among the latter was Lieutenant Jackson, afterwards Governor of that State.

Lieutenant Jackson was appointed Brigade Major. Rev. James Hall, then of Rowan, was selected as chaplain. "The only infantry in the brigade was placed under the command of Colonel Locke of Rowan County, and Major John Caruth of Lincoln County." This statement is taken from General

Graham's narrative, written in 1821, and he adds a note in which he says:

"This circumstance (the election of Pickens to the command) has occasioned every professed writer of history to represent these troops as South Carolina militia, whereas they were simply the brigade of Davidson, from Mecklenburg and Rowan, the field officers of which conferred the command on General Pickens, who was with them as a refugee, to avoid conflicting claims of rank among themselves, *there not being forty South Carolinians* in the body of 700 men."

The Tory bullet that killed General Davidson, the absence of General Rutherford, who was a prisoner, and the magnanimity of the North Carolina soldiers—coincided to place General Pickens in command of a full regiment of splendid troops, who followed him with unswerving devotion in the short but brilliant campaign which followed.

This organization being completed, the brigade marched, via Salem, to Guilford Court-House, where, "learning that Greene had passed the Dan and Cornwallis had retired to Hillsboro, they moved slowly towards the enemy."

General Caswell was now engaged in calling out the militia in the middle and eastern part of the State and had succeeded in collecting a considerable force with which he was threatening the left flank of Cornwallis. General Greene was, at this period, apprehensive that Cornwallis would march into Virginia by way of Halifax, North Carolina, crossing the Roanoke at that place. Kosciusko had been sent to that point to throw up breastworks and General Greene was resolved to prevent the enemy getting possession of that town if possible. "Being accessible from the ocean, having a very fertile country around it, convenient to Chesapeake and possessing the only manufactories in the State, it was too strong a military point to surrender without a struggle."* As we have but little information in regard to the whereabouts of General Caswell when the battle of Guilford Court-House was fought, a month later, I am of opinion that he was at Halifax for the defence of that place, to which General Greene was so anxiously looking. I find the following order from Governor Abner Nash to General Caswell, in the 4th volume of the University Magazine, which throws considerable light on the movements of troops in North Carolina during February and March, 1781:

"NEWBERN, February 23d, 1781.

"Major General Caswell will march the detachment of militia now assembled and assembling to Halifax, or to such other parts as the motions of the enemy or the exigency of the public affairs may require. He will also take such measures for posting these, as well as the militia of Halifax district, in such a manner and fortify in such places as he shall deem best for the public security. He will take such order respecting the militia, in Hillsboro and the other western districts, as shall seem expedient. The General will also, on his arrival at

*Johnson's Life of Greene, vol, 1. p. 434.

Halifax, call on the other members of the "Council Extraordinary" to meet, and he will pursue such further steps as may be concluded on by the said council, for the further operations of the militia against the enemy. General Lillington having the command of the militia in the district of Wilmington, and there being no occasion for the presence of any other general officer there, Brigadier General Caswell* will serve in the army to the westward and take his orders from the Major General, who will also commission the officers for the Light Horse corps in such way (agreeable to the resolve of the General Assembly) as he shall deem best for the public service.

"The General will endeavor to have General Butler supplied with ammunition as speedily as possible, and he is earnestly requested to send forward, with dispatch, any important intelligence he may receive respecting the motions of the enemy.

"A. NASH."

It is more than probable that Caswell, as Major General, detached General Butler and General Eaton, with their brigades, to the assistance of General Greene (as they were at Guilford Court-House) and remained himself in the command of the eastern part of the State, with Halifax as headquarters. This is in accord with the general scope of Greene's plan for preventing the invasion of Virginia by that route.

It is much to be lamented that General Caswell did not have sufficient sagacity to place these brigades under the command of some one of the

---

*He was the son of Governor Caswell.

numerous Continental soldiers, from Washington's army, who were then in the State. It was the appointment of General Stevens, of Virginia, to command her militia, that caused that particular brigade in her service to do such noble work at Guilford Court-House. But Governor Caswell had more genius for the forum than for the field; in the former he was foremost in zeal and devotion to American liberty, but as a soldier he obtained but few honors on the field of battle. There was a jealousy in the minds of the militia against the veterans, and Caswell seems to have shared in it to a great degree.

General Greene was anxious that Brigadier General Jethro Sumner, of Warren, who had greatly distinguished himself in the New Jersey campaign under Washington, should command the North Carolina troops who were to join him, and wrote to General Sumner suggesting that he should make this known to General Caswell.

In a letter from General Sumner to General Greene, dated February 24th, 1781, he says:

"I received yours of the 10th inst. on the 21st, and immediately, through Major Hawkins, aid to Major General Caswell, I proffered my assistance and sent expresses to Lieutenant Colonel Ashe and Major Murfree, who, by the temporary arrangement of the officers of the North Carolina line, present in the State, were to take charge of two of the regiments, to acquaint them without delay that it was your wish that they join the militia camp to render such assistance as may be in their power. * * * I await General Caswell's sentiments respecting myself. However, since I wrote him, I am informed by Major Eaton* that General Jones† is desirous that I take charge of the brigade of Halifax, which I believe will amount to 1500 or 1800 men. I shall make it my business to see General Jones to-morrow and shall, if I have the offer of that brigade, inform you. I am satisfied it will meet the approbation of the great majority of the officers and soldiers of that brigade—I mean as a Continental officer, who, two years ago, the militia were very averse to."

The information alluded to was that "General Jones was sick and compelled to return home, and that he would have been exceedingly happy to have given the command of his brigade to you (Sumner) provided he had continued with it, but as he is obliged to return, the command devolves on General Eaton,‡ who insists on taking it."

The services of General Sumner were not accepted, and there is some ground for believing that they were repelled with circumstances calculated to offend that gallant and distinguished officer.

On the 11th March, General Sumner writes Governor Abner Nash:

"Second thoughts are often best; therefore, I now write under apprehension that my attending you, where General Caswell may be, will be injurious to my character, and perhaps hurtful to his. For my part, I declare

*Pinkethan Eaton.
†Willie Jones.
‡Thomas Eaton.

that I wish to render service to my country at this alarming crisis. Believe me, I only wish to have no enemy."

Neither the expressed wishes of General Greene nor the desires of the Governor prevailed. Caswell seems to have been inexorable. Neither Sumner, Ashe nor Murfree were given commands, but the militia were left under inexperienced officers in this great crisis of the State, when discipline and military skill were so essentially necessary to success. It is useless to conjecture what might have been the result at Guilford Court-House if the North Carolina militia had been commanded by Sumner and Ashe, as the Virginians were by General Stevens. We can only regret that such a patriot as Governor Caswell should have been so narrow and contracted in his views and so obstinate in maintaining them.

The Legislature of North Carolina met at Halifax the 18th day of January, 1781, and directed their attention at once to the defence of the State. "Bills were passed for giving greater efficiency to the militia and for the reorganization of the Continental battalions; the latter, nominally six, were reduced to four and provision made for speedily filling up the ranks to the proper complement." "The Board of War" was discontinued. By an extraordinary stretch of authority, whose only palliations were the crisis and the purity of their motives, they established a "Council Extraordinary," to consist of three persons of integrity and abilities such as the General Assembly can have the greatest confidence in, and invested the actual Governor, Nash, and this council, with the powers of government, "after the expiration of his, Nash's, official term," *provided* the invasion of the enemy should prevent the holding of elections and the meeting of the Assembly at the usual time. After thus guarding against the chances of war, the Assembly closed the session February 14th, 1781.

The "Council Extraordinary," newly created, consisted of General Richard Caswell of Lenoir County, Colonel Alexander Martin of Guilford County, and Mr. Bignal of Newbern. This "Council Extraordinary" succeeded to all the powers of the recent "Board of War" and "Council of State," and was required to keep a journal.

This renewed expression of confidence in Colonel Martin is evidence of his constancy and fidelity to the cause of independence. He may not have been adapted by nature to the duties of a soldier, but his fidelity as a citizen and civilian were never questioned.

I have not been able to trace the history of Mr. Bignal.

The formation of this "Council Extraordinary" was analogous to the action of South Carolina, which had clothed Governor Rutlege with dictatorial powers: "*inter arma leges silent.*" Happily for the State these powers were not abused. It was to this "Council Extraordinary" that Governor Nash alludes in his order to General Caswell, and which, it seems, was about to assemble at Halifax.

In the meantime, on the 29th day of January, 1781, Major James H. Craig, with an English force, took possession of Wilmington. Greene no doubt had some intimation of this movement before it was made, but supposed it was to be under the command of Arnold, and attended with the atrocities which characterized his expedition into Virginia. Cornwallis, of course, was cognizant of this part of the plan of invasion into North Carolina, and expected to open a communication with Major Craig, through the loyalists of the Cape Fear, who abounded in that region, though they had not embodied to any considerable extent since the battle of Moore's Creek. They were waiting the advent of the British army, and, for the present, contenting themselves with predatory excursions here and there in that region.

The American troops had suffered painfully in their long marches through the mud and ice of a dreary winter, more severe than usual at this period. The Maryland line, which had been exposed without tents ever since Morgan left Charlotte in December, and which had now been in retreat from the 17th day of January to the 15th of February, were the greatest sufferers. After Greene crossed the Dan an inspection of the line showed 861 men fit for duty, and 274 in the hospitals.

General Greene writes Washington a doleful account of the condition of the army. We copy it:

"IRWIN'S FERRY, Feb. 15th, 1781.

"The miserable situation of the troops, for want of clothing, has rendered the march the most painful imaginable, many hundreds of the soldiers tracking the ground with their bloody feet. Your feelings for the sufferings of the soldier, had you been with us, would have been severely tried."

How little does the average reader appreciate the privations and exposures of the soldier! They turn from it with impatience to listen to the tale of combat and the shout of victory, and, too often, amid the comforts of home, are disposed to criticise the errors of the field. The endurance and fortitude of these soldiers are as noble evidences of their true manhood as their most splendid exploits on the field of battle. Under excitement one may be nerved to deeds of daring, but to submit to privation and nakedness and hunger, in the cheerless inactivity of a bivouac, requires the sternest stuff that men are ever made of.

On the 17th the report exhibited, of men fit for duty: infantry, 1078, artillery 64, cavalry 176, Legionary infantry 112—1430 in all.

It would be a story too tedious and vexatious to recount all the perplexities of General Greene at this time. Arnold had invaded Virginia and plundered Richmond; the whole State was in terror at his approach, and the reinforcements intended for Greene's army were diverted to the James River. The militia of eastern North Carolina were marching to the assistance of their neighboring State. Finally, when the Baron Steuben had organized 400 regulars, under Colonel Richard Campbell, and 2600 militia, and had them on their way to camp, the whole militia turned back on a false rumor that Cornwallis had retreated to Wilmington, and only Campbell persevered in the march and reached Greene.*

Maryland had early adopted the policy of enlisting for the war, and to that fact may be assigned the splendid heroism of her troops in the South. Virginia and North Carolina only partially adopted this policy, and the Continental line of the latter was now in prison, and the militia of both States being generally called out for six weeks, spent one-third of this time in getting to camp and the other two-thirds in calculating the day of their return. They came without drilling or discipline, with only ordinary guns, without bayonets or equipments, and were a poor match for veteran soldiers, armed and equipped for battle. It was this short-sighted policy that prolonged the struggle for independence, and for a long time held the event of it in doubt. Colonel Lee very truthfully remarks that the exposure of such undisciplined troops to the attack of trained soldiers was murder. The riflemen of the mountains, the volunteers of King's Mountain and Cowpens, were not of this class, and

---

*Richard Campbell was afterwards killed at Eutaw, and must not be confounded with Colonel William Campbell, who commanded at King's Mountain.

we will discover Greene's mistake in supposing that the ordinary militia could be depended on like these highland hunters.

As soon as General Stevens had conveyed the Cowpens prisoners to a place of safety he joined Greene's army, and being authorized to raise troops for six weeks' service, soon raised 1000 men from the counties in Virginia around Greene's camp. With the reinforcement of Colonel Richard Campbell's regulars and Stevens' militia, and the brigade of North Carolinians under Pickens, Greene determined to recross the Dan, and on the 23d day of February he entered North Carolina again. This was three days after Cornwallis entered Hillsboro. His lordship was greatly encouraged by the numbers of men who flocked to Hillsboro from curiosity or for gain, and he offered "guineas and lands to those who would enlist under his banner;" but it was only a day or two subsequent that he sorrowfully wrote to the British ministry that he was "surrounded by timid friends and inveterate enemies." His lordship also did the region of Orange and Guilford counties the distinguished honor of declaring, "I could not get one hundred men in all the Regulators' country to stay with us even as militia."* It was another "Hornet's Nest" his lordship had gotten into. There was one regiment of the British army under Colonel Hamilton, formerly of Halifax, North Carolina, *called* the North Carolina regiment, but it was like the street in

*Cornwallis to Clinton, April 10th, 1781.

Damascus, only *called* straight. This regiment was formed at St. Augustine, Florida, from renegades who came in from every quarter, and with but a small proportion from North Carolina. Colonel Hamilton, however, was an English gentleman of culture and refinement, and was honorable and brave as a soldier, never allowing his troops to plunder or murder. He was for years English Consul at Norfolk, after the revolution.

Before Greene recrossed the Dan, Colonel Otho Williams, with the same detachment which was placed under him to cover the retreat, was pushed forward with orders to hang on the enemy's flanks and watch his movements, and if the British army started for Wilmington, to harass and retard its march. Lee and Washington, with their cavalry, were also directed to watch every opportunity to strike the enemy and overawe any rising of Tories in the lower settlements. General Butler was, at this time, marching up the Cape Fear with his brigade of militia, and at one time Lee thought of joining him and making a sudden attack on the British.

General Pickens did not remain idle, and, as we stated, had marched with his North Carolina brigade of infantry, under Colonel Locke of Rowan, and cavalry under Graham, towards Hillsboro in search of adventure, and with him was McCall of South Carolina, with about thirty cavalry and a few Georgians. Cornwallis was scarcely encamped at Hillsboro before Pickens' command was hovering around him in sight of the town. On reaching Stony Creek, ten miles from Hillsboro, General Pickens sent Captain Graham forward with twenty cavalry and twenty infantry, under Captain Richard Simmons, to examine the position of the enemy and to strike a blow if practicable. Captain Graham discovered a detachment of British soldiers, numbering twenty-five men, at Hart's Mill, on the Eno, one mile and a half from Hillsboro. He concealed himself for the night, and as soon as it was light enough for the riflemen to see the sights on their guns, he made a sudden onset upon them, taking them entirely by surprise, and captured their captain, sixteen privates of the regulars and two Tories. One sergeant and eight privates were left on the ground killed or wounded. This was a brilliant opening for the Whigs, and threw the British camp into consternation for awhile. The whole of Tarleton's cavalry were paraded and sent in pursuit, but in vain. Captain Graham baffled his pursuers and reached the camp in safety. Judge Johnson falls again into an egregious error in ascribing this *coup de main* to Captain McCall of his own State, when in fact he was ten miles from the scene. This is a second glaring injustice done to North Carolina; for this success, though comparatively small, was greatly commended by General Greene and caused rejoicing all around the camp. It was a gem of a skirmish, and shone brightly, if not with extended effulgence. In reflecting on these injustices done one State by another, we cannot refrain from quoting from Judge Johnson himself the tacit acknowledgment of his fault. He says:

"There is and perhaps ought to be a clannish spirit in the States of the Union which will ever dispose the writers they produce to blazon, with peculiar zeal, the virtues and talents of the eminent men of their respective States. It is a tendency so natural to man that religion, the retirement of the cloister and the barefooted friar, who has renounced the world, acknowledge its influence in exaggerated eulogies on a patron saint or beatified brother. And it will probably happen that, in future times, *the States that have produced the ablest writers will enjoy the reputation of having produced the ablest statesmen, generals and orators.*"

South Carolina did not lack for an "able writer" or a "clannish spirit" in the distinguished biographer of General Greene.

Graham and his men had just tumbled down for a little rest after this arduous duty, when they were startled by the cry, "Tarleton's coming!" The whole camp was astir in a moment and put in readiness to receive the charge; when, to their great joy, it was discovered to be Colonel Harry Lee and his cavalry, who had started to surprise this same detachment at Hart's Mill.*

On the night of the 21st of February, General Greene, attended by a small escort of dragoons, crossed the Dan and visited Pickens and Lee to confer with them as to the future movements of the army and the proper measures to annoy the enemy. Having spent the greatest part of the night in anxious consultation, Pickens and Greene

*Graham, in University Magazine.

"wrapped up in their cloaks and shared the same blanket in a refreshing nap."

Pickens being the superior officer, was given the command of Lee's Legion as well as his own brigade, as one corps, and both officers were exhorted to harmony and good will. This visit was another of Greene's bold enterprises, which to us, at this day, appears almost reckless, yet, as he returned safely next morning, we must admit he did not err in his calculations.

About the 21st or 22d February, General Pickens was apprised of the advance of Colonel John Preston and Colonel William Campbell (he of King's Mountain fame) with a reinforcement to join his command, and on the next day perhaps, for we cannot fix the exact days, the General also was informed that Tarleton, with his cavalry, four hundred infantry and two pieces of artillery, had left Hillsboro in the direction of Haw River to the west.

Being apprehensive that Tarleton would fall in with these approaching reinforcements, and feeling strong enough now to cope with him, Pickens called in his forces and set out in pursuit of Tarleton.

They found he had crossed the Haw River, and at noon of the 25th of February, they were so near to him as to capture two of his officers who had lingered behind, and while eager in the pursuit, and with even the order of attack arranged, a most singular occurrence happened, which defeated all their ardent hopes of destroying this "scourge" of the British army. As Johnson says that Lee's account of "Pyle's Defeat," sometimes termed "Pyle's Massacre," is inaccurate and fanciful, I will do as I have done before—give the unvarnished story as it is related by Joseph Graham, who prepared it for Judge Murphy, to be incorporated into a history of North Carolina. Resuming the narrative at the junction of Lee's force with Pickens, he writes:

"The whole army moved a few miles and encamped at an adjacent farm for the night. The next day it was in motion, in different directions, nearly the whole day; but did not go far, beating down nearer Hillsboro. The two corps kept near each other, though they moved and camped separately, as they had done the previous evening. Reconnoitering parties, which were sent out in the evening and had returned in the night, gave notice of a detachment passing from Hillsboro towards the ford on Haw River.

"Pickens and Lee put their forces in motion at an early hour, and came into the great road eight miles west of Hillsboro, near Mebane's farm.

"The whole of the militia cavalry, seventy in number, that had swords, were placed under Captain Graham, and in the rear of Lee's horse. Such of Graham's men as had not swords were ordered to join another company. They followed the enemy's trail on the road to Haw River, with the cavalry in front.

"During the whole day's march every man expected a battle and hard fighting. Men's countenances on such occasions indicate something which can be understood better than described in words. The countenances of the whole militia, throughout the day, never showed better.

"Lee states (page 311) that Pyle's men, on seeing the militia in the rear of his cavalry, recognized and fired on them.

"The true statement of this is, that Major Dickson, of Lincoln, who commanded the column on our right (when the disposition for attack had been made at the last farm), had been thrown out of his proper order of march by the fences and a branch, and when Pyle's men were first seen by the militia they were thought to be the party under Dickson, which had come round the plantation and gotten in the road before them. On coming within twenty steps of them, Captain Graham discovered the mistake; seeing them with cleaner clothes than Dickson's party, and each man having a strip of red cloth on his hat. Graham, riding alongside of Captain Eggleston, who commanded the rear of Lee's horse, remarked to him: "That company are Tories. What is the reason they have their arms?" Captain Eggleston, addressing a good-looking man at the end of the line, supposed to be an officer, inquired, "To whom do you belong?" The man promptly answered, "A friend to his majesty." Whereupon Captain Eggleston struck him over the head. The militia looking on and waiting for orders, on this example being set, rushed on them like lightning and cut away. The noise in the rear attracted the notice of Lee's men, and they turned their horses short to the right about five steps, and in less than a minute the attack was made along the whole line. The same page* states that ninety loyalists were killed. The next day our militia counted ninety-three dead, and there was the appearance of many more being carried off by their friends. There were certainly many more

*Referring to Lee's Memoirs.

wounded. When Lee and Pickens retired, it appeared as if three hundred might be lying dead. Many, perhaps, were only slightly wounded and lay quietly for security.

"At the time the action commenced, Lee's dragoons, in the open order of march, extended about the same distance with Pyle's men, who were in close order, and on horseback; and most of them having come from home on that day, were clean, like men who now turn out to a review. Lee's movement was as if he were going to pass them five or six steps on the left of their line. When the alarm was given in the rear, as quickly as his men could turn their horses, they were engaged; and as the Tories were over two to one of our actual cavalry, by pressing forward they went through their line, leaving a number behind them. The continual cry by the Tories was, 'You are killing your own men! I am a friend to his majesty. Hurrah for King George!' Finding their professions of loyalty, and all they could say were of no avail, and only the signal for their destruction, twelve or fifteen of those whom Lee's men had gone through, and who had thrown down their guns, now determining to sell their lives as dearly as possible, jumped to their arms and began to fire in every direction, making the cavalry give back a little. But as soon as their guns were empty, they were charged upon on every side by more than could get at them, and cut down in a group together. All the harm done by their fire was that a dragoon's horse was shot down. Falling very suddenly, and not moving afterwards, the rider's leg was caught under him, and by all his efforts he could not extricate himself, until the action began to slacken, when two of his comrades dismounted and rolled the horse off him. Lee's men had so recently come to the South that they did not understand the usual marks of distinction between Whig and Tory, and after the first onset, when all became mixed, they inquired of each man, before they attacked him, to whom he belonged. The enemy readily answered, 'To King George.' To many of their own militia they put the same question. Fortunately no mistakes occurred, though in some instances there was great danger of it.

"At the close of the action the troops were scattered and mixed through each other—completely disorganized. General Pickens and Colonel Lee gave repeated orders to form, but the confusion was such that their orders were without effect. These officers appeared sensible of the delicate situation we were in. If Tarleton, who was only two or three miles off, with nearly an equal force, had come upon us at this juncture, the result must have been against us.

"Lee's men, though under excellent discipline, could with difficulty be gotten in order. The commandants exhibited great perturbation, until at length Lee ordered Major Rudolph to lead off and his dragoons to fall in behind them; Captain Graham received the same order as to the militia dragoons, and by the time the line had moved a quarter of a mile there was the same order as when we met Pyle. Lee himself, while they were forming, staid in the rear of his own corps and in front of Graham's, and ordered one of the sergeants to go directly back and get a pilot from among the Tories, and bring him forward without delay. The sergeant in a short time returned with a middle-aged man (his name _____ and he lived near that place), who had received a slight wound on the head, and was bleeding freely. The sergeant apologized to his Colonel because he could find none who were not wounded. Lee asked him several questions relative to the roads, farms, water-courses, etc.; how O'Neal's plantation (where Tarleton then was) was situated: whether open, woods, hilly or level, etc. After answering the several questions, and after an interval of about a minute, while Lee appeared to be meditating, the man addressed him: 'Well, God bless your soul, Mr. Tarleton, you have this day killed a parcel of as good subjects as ever his Majesty had.' Lee, who at this time was not in the humor for quizzing, interrupted him, saying: 'You d——d rascal, if you call me Tarleton I will take off your head. I will undeceive you: we are the Americans and not the British. I am Lee of the American Legion, and not Tarleton.' The poor fellow appeared chop-fallen.''*

Colonel Pyle and his men were misled by the uniforms of Lee's Legion, both his cavalry and infantry being dressed in short green coats, with other distinctions resembling the uniform of Tarleton's Legion.

Pyle, though wounded with many cuts of the sabre, crawled into a pond of water, where he concealed himself and was afterwards rescued by his Tory friends and survived.

In Governor Swain's lecture on the War of the Regulation, I find this allusion to Colonel Pyle:

"The forced requisition of a wagon and team from

---

*NOTE.—The scene of Pyle's defeat is very near the present town of Burlington (formerly "Company Shops"), on the North Carolina Railroad, in Alamance County.

John Pyle, exhibited in our last number, shows the severe process which secured his allegiance. His followers, who, with him, rendered such fearful retribution in the sanguinary conflict with Pickens and Lee, on the 25th February, 1781, were fellow-sufferers in the ravages of Tryon in 1772. Colonel Pyle was a physician and an amiable man, and for faithful and skillful services, rendered to wounded Whigs at the battle of Cane Creek, a few months after his discomfiture on Haw River, was pardoned by the executive authority."

Colonel Pyle had been a Regulator, and, after the battle of Alamance, Governor Tryon had impressed his wagons and other property. He subsequently took the oath of allegiance, and feeling conscientiously bound by it, became a Tory in the revolution. Perhaps many of his followers owed their apostacy to the same causes.

Tarleton was only a mile or two in advance. Pickens ordered his column to move forward, and about sunset his scouts came in view of the enemy's camp, who seemed to be resting in a state of security. After a conference it was decided to postpone the attack until morning, as the troops were weary with marching and hungry for food. Patrols and sentinels were placed in every direction to prevent intelligence reaching Tarleton's camp; but during the night a messenger reached him from Cornwallis, who had been informed of the movement of Pickens. Tarleton was ordered to return to Hillsboro in haste. So urgent was the command that several couriers had been dispatched with the same message. Tarleton obeyed the order by decamping at 2 o'clock in the morning and riding with all speed towards Hillsboro. Pickens followed, but only to get in sight of Tarleton as he entered the town.

The sanguinary destruction of Pyle's command had the effect of striking terror into the hearts of the Tories of Randolph and Chatham, and so completely subdued their spirit that they never embodied again during the war. There were marauding parties of banditti who stole and plundered, but their forces were never again brought together as a military organization. The good name of the American troops suffered, even in the estimation of their friends, for this bloody slaughter of the Tories; but in extenuation of the fierce passions of that hour, it must be remembered that Tarleton had been the first to inaugurate this unsparing and merciless warfare, the summer before, at the Waxhaws, and many of the North Carolinians who faced Pyle's command had friends and relatives among the slain who were hacked to pieces on that unfortunate day. "Tarleton's Quarters" had become a proverb in the American army; it was the watchword of revenge—the spirit of memory that never slept in the hearts of our people; by it "they nursed their wrath to keep it warm," and, in muttering tones around the camp-fires of the bivouac, they vowed that vengeance should be meted out, "an eye for an eye," when the auspicious day should come to put their enemies in their grasp. Neither discipline, nor authority, nor humanity could stand before the dreadful wrath which the blood of Buford's men had stirred within their hearts. "Blood for blood," was the cry of the men who that day hacked the Tories, and now and then "Tarleton's Quarters" put fresh strength into the sabre arm which seemed to grow weary of slaughter and death. Buford, too, was a Virginian, and Eggleston and Armstrong did not keep their swords at rest while the memory of the slaughter was fresh in their minds. It was a dreadful day, sickening to the heart; but how many other tales of butchery it prevented can only be known by the Omniscient One. If Pyle had succeeded in joining Tarleton, and Preston, Armstrong and Winston had fallen into his hands next day, as he expected, the tears would only have been transposed from Tory to Whig homes, and the weeeping and lamentations would have made patriots, instead of traitors, shudder at the result. Whatever may be said of the deed itself, the results were most salutary to the American cause, and it may, in this instance, perhaps, be claimed that

"All's well that ends well."

Tarleton had marched to intercept the detachments of militia under Preston, Armstrong and Winston who were on their way to reinforce Pickens; and the massacre of Pyle's was the fortunate circumstance, from the British standpoint, that prevented the extermination of Tarleton's command. Some destiny shaped the ends of this bad man so strangely that he seems to have been excepted from the just and certain laws of righteous retribution. He survived the war, lived to an old age, and requited the affection of Cornwallis by exposing his errors and magnifying his faults.

General Greene was again in North Carolina, and evidently was making preparation to attack Cornwallis or repel his lordship if attacked by him. He was expecting reinforcements every day and was strong enough already to choose his battle-field and the day of battle. In the meantime, he was goading and harassing and irritating the British commander until his enemy was growing obstinate and desperate—the frame of mind that precedes mistakes and destruction. His foraging parties were cut off, his camp insulted, his reinforcements hacked to pieces, and even Tarleton and his famous Legion were not strong enough to stand before the detachments sent to annoy him. He was compelled to leave his camp at Hillsboro and seek a more friendly region. On the 26th of February, Cornwallis left Hillsboro and marched to Alamance Creek, in what is now Alamance County, but was then the southeastern portion of Guilford County. This was a little south of west from Hillsboro, a good day's journey, and on the direct road to Salisbury. It was designed, too, to put Greene in doubt, whether the British commander would retrace his steps to Salisbury or move suddenly to the Cape Fear and fall back on Wilmington. Greene was anxiously watching the movement and awaiting impatiently the arrival of the North Carolina and Virginia brigades of militia, then well on their way to his camp, in order that he might resume the offensive and defeat either of the movements of the enemy. But he was also, as ever, alert to prevent surprise, knowing that Cornwallis was in a mad state of mind and ready to do even a rash act. His orders to Otho Williams and Pickens, who commanded the two detachments in the front of the British camp, the one being on one side of the Alamance Creek, the other on the other side, was to be wary and watchful and let not the slightest motion of the enemy be unobserved.

Greene was now at his camp at Speedwell Iron Works, on the upper waters of Troublesome Creek, thirty miles distant. The two brigades of Virginia militia under Stevens and Lawson, and the two brigades of North Carolina militia, were marching on a highway, running west, from a point below Hillsboro, to join Greene at his camp. The nearest point that this road came to the camp of Cornwallis was twenty-five or thirty miles, and in a northwardly direction. The command of Williams lay between that point and Cornwallis. The roads from the camp of Williams and from the camp of Cornwallis to that point intersected each other at Whitsill's Mill, which was on the direct route that Cornwallis would travel to strike the approaching militia. It was soon developed that he was at last aroused to energetic action, and that he came to Alamance as a crouching spot, from which he might pounce upon the prey as it passed, all unconscious of danger, as he thought, within the length of his spring. If the militia were scattered and the 3000 arms which they were bringing to camp destroyed, Greene would be forced to cross the Dan again and North Carolina would be at the mercy of the British crown. These were the anxious hopes that agitated the bosom of the British commander and brought victory to his imagination once more.

The line of march of the militia was a hazardous one, but General Greene was so much impressed with the idea and apprehension that Cornwallis would escape, that he resolved that they should approach by the nearest route. In order to guard against the possibility of their falling a prey to a sudden dash from the enemy, General Greene moved his camp down and across Troublesome Creek, fifteen miles, and put himself about the same distance from Cornwallis. Colonels Williams and Pickens were between them on the flank of the enemy. The American commander was confident that Cornwallis could not move without the knowledge of Williams and Pickens, and that they could impede his march until the militia could escape; or if Cornwallis forced Williams and Pickens into a sudden or precipitate retreat they could fall back and join him, and their combined forces could so retard the enemy that he could not reach the reinforcements. Greene now waited anxiously at his camp, at Boyd's Mill, on Reedy Fork, seven miles above Whitsill's Mill, for the event of these several dispositions of his troops.

Cornwallis, in the meantime, maneuvered constantly, so as to impress Williams with the idea that he was about to begin a retreat to Cross Creek (now Fayetteville), on the Cape Fear River; but on the 6th day of March, when least expected, the British commander made a sudden dash north, hoping to outstrip Williams to Whitsill's Mill, on Reedy Fork, and passing on ten miles further, and directly north, to intercept the train of the American reinforcements at High Rock Ford, on the Haw River, which ford they would necessarily pass on their route to the permanent camp of Greene at the Speedwell Iron Works, further up that river. Cornwallis had scarcely moved out of his camp before the intelligence of it reached Williams, who was then on his left flank, and the race for Whitsill's Mill was immediately begun. It was "neck and neck," on parallel roads—Williams flying, with his light troops, to the rescue of his friends; Cornwallis dashing through every obstruction, with reckless speed, to reach the prize his heart had so anxiously coveted. Williams was unincumbered and full of vigor; Cornwallis, though obliged to move his trains with his army, was desperate and determined. As the patrols and scouts passed from the one column to the other, apprising each of the advance of his competitor, the race grew more animated, the competitors more earnest and resolute; the goal was now getting nearer and the excitement greater, when Williams, putting forth his whole energy, urged his men to a triumphant speed and dashed down the hill and across the Reedy Fork as the enemy appeared upon the crest in their rear, entering from the other road.

Williams drew up his forces on the north bank of the stream and gave the British a warm reception. The enemy was checked; he had failed in his purpose to separate Williams from Greene.

Williams was now in seven miles of Greene, at Boyd's Mill, and soon informed him of the occurrences of the day. Sending orders to Williams to fall back north, towards the High Rock Ford, on Haw River, where he proposed to meet him, General Greene at once moved in that direction for the protection of the advancing reinforcements. The British commander finding that his stratagem had not succeeded, fell back to his old encampment.

The fight at Whitsill's Mill was sharp and severe—bloody while it lasted.

Lee, in his Memoirs, relates the thrilling story of Colonel Webster's almost miraculous escape in the skirmish:*

"The British van appeared, and after a halt for a few minutes on the opposite bank, descended the hill, approaching the water, when, receiving a heavy fire of musketry and rifles, it fell back, and quickly reascending, was rallied on the margin of the bank. Here a field officer rode up, and in a loud voice addressed his soldiers, then rushed down the hill at their head and plunged into the water, our fire pouring upon him. In the woods occupied by the riflemen stood an old log school-

---

*Lee's Memoirs, p. 266.

house, a little to the right of the ford. The mud stuffed between the logs had mostly fallen out and the apertures admitted the use of the rifle with ease. In this house twenty-five (25) select marksmen, of King's Mountain militia, were posted by Lee, with orders to forego taking any part in the general resistance, but to hold themselves in reserve for any particular objects. The leading officer, plunging into the water, attracted general notice, and the school-house party, recollecting its order, singled him out as their mark. The stream being deep and the bottom rugged, he advanced slowly, his soldiers on each side of him, and apparently some of them holding his stirrup leathers. This select party discharged their rifles at him, one by one, each man sure of knocking him over; and having reloaded, eight or nine of them emptied their guns a second time at the same object. Strange to tell, though in a condition so perilous, himself and horse were untouched; and having crossed the creek, he soon formed his troops and advanced upon us."

In a note Colonel Lee says:

"The twenty-five riflemen were selected for their superior excellence as marksmen. It was no uncommon amusement among them to put an apple on the point of a ramrod, and holding it in the hand, with the arm extended, to permit their comrades, known to be expert, to fire at it, when many balls would pass through the apple; and yet Lieutenant Colonel Webster, mounted on a stout horse, in point-blank shot, slowly moving through a deep water-course, was singled out by this party, who fired *seriatim* thirty-two or thirty-three times at him and neither struck him nor his horse."

This wonderful escape is only equaled by that of Washington at Braddock's defeat. It seems marvellous, yet we cannot doubt its truth.

Cornwallis now "withdrew from his camp on the Alamance to Bells' Mill, on Deep River," not far from where Jamestown now is, "with the resolution of restoring by rest the strength of his troops, and of holding it up for that decisive day which, from his knowledge of the character of his adversary, he was assured would arrive as soon as he had acquired his expected reinforcements."*

The reinforcements, approaching, now continued on their way unmolested and reached Greene's camp at High Rock Ford, on the Haw River, on Sunday, March the 11th, 1781.† This was only four days before the great battle at Guilford Court-House, which I will attempt to describe truthfully and impartially in the succeeding chapter.

*Lee's Memoirs.
†Johnson's Life of Greene, vol. 1, p. 472.

CHAPTER VII.

North Carolinians with Greene at the Battle of "Guilford Court-House"—Virginians with Him—The Troops constituting His Regular Army—The Number and Character of the Troops under Cornwallis—Description of the Battle-Ground—Description of the Battle—Defence of the North Carolina Militia—Incidents and Anecdotes of the Battle—Results of the Battle in its Effect on the Military History of the Country—Mr. Benton's Review of the Importance of this Battle—The Precursor of Yorktown—The Lesser the Father of the Greater Event.

The battle of Guilford Court-House, fought on Thursday, March the 15th, 1781, between the American forces under Major General Nathanael Greene, and the English forces under Lord Cornwallis, was, in my opinion, second in its results to no battle of the revolutionary war. It was the only pitched battle fought on the soil of North Carolina, between the two regular contending armies, of any magnitude, and for that reason is more conspicuous in North Carolina history than any other event of that period.

It has been described by Lee and Campbell, Virginians, who participated in it, on the American side, and in their respective narratives they have severely reflected on the conduct of the North Carolina militia, who formed the first, or front line of Greene's army, and received the cannonade and first fire of the enemy. General Greene, though abstaining from the use of harsh language, has adopted that account and reported the militia as delinquent in duty in the fight; and for these reasons North Carolinians, without investigating the correctness of these statements, or considering the sources where they originated, or reflecting upon the extenuating, if not the justifying, circumstances which surrounded these troops, have suffered mortification at this supposed dereliction of duty on the part of their fellow-citizens.

These statements of Lee and Campbell have been repeated so often, and have been so greatly exaggerated by subsequent historians, especially by Johnson in his "Life of General Greene," that it seems almost presumptuous to question their correctness. It is the more embarrassing because our own writers have carelessly fallen into this beaten track of error and repeated this story literally from others, until we are condemned "out of our own mouths." I shall not, however, shrink from the task of endeavoring to unfold the whole truth of history, and to publish important facts and circumstances which have either been intentionally or criminally suppressed by these historians, who have gone before, and also to show that much of the glory of this battle belongs to other classes of troops, from North Carolina, who participated in it and whose identity, as North Carolinians, has been overlooked by historians because their names were not on the muster-rolls of the regular army, and who, though embodied as North Carolina soldiers, were fighting under commanders from other States.

There were three English historians, all soldiers, participating in this battle on the side of the crown, to-wit, Colonel Tarleton, Colonel Stedman and Sergeant Lamb, who have given their account of the struggle. Their testimony is entitled to respect, especially that of Stedman, whose fairness and honesty is admitted by American historians.

There is another source of information open to us in the cotemporaneous literature of that day, written by the soldiers engaged in the battle, many of them afterwards distinguished in church and state, and, last of all, is tradition, coming down to us from trustworthy sources. We may add to this positive testimony, the natural evidence which is always truthful and cannot be neglected by any reasonable tribunal investigating truth.

To all these sources of information I shall appeal for truth, and for justice to North Carolina, with the confidence that very much, if not all, the odium attached to her militia will vanish away, and that the honorable part borne by her other volunteer troops, in this battle, shall be established beyond cavil or doubt.

On the 10th day of March, 1781, on Saturday before the battle, General Greene wrote to Governor Jefferson, of Virginia, as follows:

"Every day has filled me with hopes of an augmentation of my force; the militia have flocked in from various quarters, but they come and go in such irregular bodies that I can make no calculation on the strength of my army, or direct any future operations that can insure me success. At this time I have not above 800 or 900 of them in the field. Yet there have been upwards of

5000 in motion in the course of four weeks. A force, fluctuating in this manner, can promise but slender hopes of success against an enemy in high discipline, and made formidable by the superiority of their numbers. Hitherto I have been obliged to effect that by *finesse* which I dare not attempt by force. I know the people have been in anxious suspense, waiting the event of a general action. But let the consequence be what it may, nothing shall hurry me into a measure that is not suggested by prudence, or dictated by the interests of the Southern department.

"General Caswell is on his way with a considerable force of the Carolina militia; and Colonel Campbell,* with the Virginia regulars, I expect, will be up in a few days. When this force arrives, I trust I shall be able to prescribe the limits of the enemy's depredations, and *at least dispose of the army in such a manner as to incumber him with a number of wounded men.*"†

From this we learn that the militia with Greene had recently been as many as 5000 at one time, of which number there were less than 1000 Virginians.

The "*finesse*" to which Greene alludes was getting rid of mounted militia, who, Greene alleged, consumed the forage of the country and made it difficult to support his cavalry. For dispensing with this class of troops, who, from long custom in that kind of warfare, were active, rapid and vigilant, besides being hardy and courageous, General Greene has been severely censured. His whole

---

*Richard Campbell.
†Johnson's Life of Greene, vol. 1, p. 473.

correspondence shows in what low esteem he held the citizen soldiery, and with what distrust he looked upon them. He seems to have made one exception, if Johnson is correct. This was General Pickens' command of North Carolinians, "on whose services he could depend from day to day."

But it seems, that on that 10th day of March, there were still 800 or 900 militia with General Greene, and as the Virginia reinforcements had not reached his camp, and those who were with him at Halifax had remained behind,* it is to be presumed that nearly if not quite all of these militia were North Carolinians. These were the men left after General Greene had gotten rid of the "mounted militia" by *finesse*, and were no doubt hardy infantry and followed the fortunes of the American commander to Guilford Court-House, though he gives no names of these officers, and no muster-rolls show who they were. They were an unknown factor in that important conflict of arms.

Occasionally we can get glimpses of facts in the voluminous pages of Johnson, who had access to all the papers of General Greene, which throw much light on the number and character and individuality of the troops engaged, though his conclusions are so paradoxical that we cannot trust to their correctness. We can only gather together isolated facts, from here and there, and draw from them our own inferences. From Johnson's account of the battle one would infer that there were no

*Johnson, vol. 1, p. 471.

North Carolina troops present except the two brigades of militia under Butler and Eaton, which reached Greene on the 11th of March, and that these ran without firing a shot. This is the absurd and arbitrary assertion which he makes.

I shall now extract the real truth, or very much of it, in regard to the North Carolina troops in this battle, from Johnson's own statements, made elsewhere, and disconnected with the battle.

In his account of the battle of Hobkirk's Hill, fought the 25th day of April, 1781, he uses this language:

"The only militia force then with the army consisted of 254 North Carolinians; 150 of these, under Colonel Read, had joined Greene *soon after he crossed the Dan, and had faithfully adhered to him from that time.* They were *volunteers*, men of the *first respectability*, and much might have been expected of them in action."*

Honorable George Davis, of Wilmington, kindly furnishes me the following sketch of Colonel James Read:

"WILMINGTON, N. C., February 9th, 1888.
"HON. D. SCHENCK, *Greensboro, N. C.:*

"MY DEAR SIR :—It affords me pleasure to give you what meagre information I possess about Colonel James Read, of the Continental army, who was my great-uncle, the brother of my maternal grandmother. He was born in the town of Armagh, Ireland, but at what time, and

*Vol. 2, p. 77.

when he emigrated to North Carolina, I do not know. From the fact that he threw himself early and heartily into the patriot cause, I infer that he must have been here some years before the revolution—long enough to have identified himself thoroughly with our country and people. On the 7th of July, 1776, he was commissioned a Lieutenant; and on the 8th day of July, 1777, a Captain in the 1st Regiment of North Carolina troops, commanded by Colonel, afterwards General, James Moore. I have no account of his military services, beyond what is related in McRee's Life of Iredell, vol. 1, pages 494, 499, 504, 545, 546. He was with Greene at Guilford Court-House and Hobkirk's Hill, and was reputed to have behaved well on both occasions. After the war he stoutly opposed the adoption of the Federal Constitution by North Carolina, and so drew upon himself the animadversion of Archibald Maclaine. (Life of Iredell, vol. 2, p. 219.)

"In 1785, under an act of the General Assembly passed in 1784, Colonel Read was appointed, under the authority of the State, Collector of the Port of Brunswick, which position he held until the adoption by this State of the Federal Constitution, when that office was superseded by the authority of the United States. In 1790, Wilmington was made the port of entry for the Cape Fear, and he was appointed Collector of that port by President Washington. This office he held until his death in 1802 or 1803. He lived and died in Wilmington. He was never married. Colonel Read had no relatives in this country, except his young sister Sarah, whom he brought over from Ireland, and who married my grandfather, Joseph Eagles. He had a brother, Andrew Read, who was a Colonel in the British army, but he never served in America, but was stationed in India, where he died without issue."

Greene recrossed the Dan the 23d of February, and these men joined him "soon after." They were "volunteers," not militia, and men of the "first respectability" and had "faithfully adhered to Greene," and beyond question were in the battle at Guilford Court-House; but the account of that battle, by either Johnson or Lee, may be searched in vain for any mention of these "faithful volunteers."

Here, then, we have 150, as a remnant of Read's volunteers; in all probability they numbered 200 at the battle of Guilford Court-House.

At another place* we are informed that on the 25th day of February, the day of "Pyle's defeat," Pickens' command was reinforced by "two detachments of 100 each under Majors Winston and Armstrong," both of North Carolina. Here then, were 200 more North Carolina "volunteers" who joined the American forces and "adhered faithfully to Greene." Draper, in his biography of Major Winston, says positively that he "shared in the battle of Guilford."†

Major Winston was conspicuous for his bravery at King's Mountain, and led the van of the attack on the rear of the hill. He was a member of Congress from North Carolina in 1793, and again in

*Volume 1, p. 455.
†King's Mountain and Its Heroes, p. 455.

1803. He lived near Germantown, in Stokes County, and died in 1814, leaving a large family.*

It is not only true that these riflemen of Surry were present, but they were the very last to leave the field, after Tarleton's final charge which dispersed the American forces on the left; for in that charge Talliaferro, of Surry, was killed, and Jesse Franklin, afterwards Governor of North Carolina and United States Senator from this State, made a very narrow escape. The narrative of these occurrences is given by Caruthers, in his Sketches of North Carolina, second series, upon the authority of the present Judge Jesse Franklin Graves, a grandson of Governor Franklin, than whom no better man or purer Judge now adorns the bench of the "Old North State."

In "Tarleton's Campaigns," page 320, we find the official report of the killed and wounded in the battle of Guilford, by Otho Williams, Deputy Adjutant General. It contains this statement:

"The North Carolina cavalry, commanded by the Marquis Bretigny, lost one man killed and one man wounded." We learn elsewhere† that this company consisted of 40 men.

From Colonel James Martin's application for a pension under the act of 1832, we learn that his force, about 200 strong, joined Greene at Guilford Court-House on the 10th February, and that about 100 of them were still with Greene at the battle.

*Wheeler's History, vol. 2, p. 149.
†Gordon's History, vol. 4, p. 54.

Ramsay, in his Annals of Tennessee, page 251, also says that "in response to Greene's earnest entreaties, a few of the pioneers of Tennessee were under Greene's command at the hotly-contested battle of Guilford Court-House."

"These men were under Charles Robertson," and were all North Carolinians. They numbered perhaps 100 men.

To sum up the organized "volunteer" force of North Carolinians, in the Battle of Guilford Court-House, of whom no official report gives any account, we have the following:

Colonel Read's men,	200
Major Joseph Winston's men,	100
Major Armstrong,	100
Forbis' men from Guilford,	100
Sevier's men under Robertson,	100
Total,	600 men.
Add to these the North Carolina cavalry,	40 men,
And we have a total of	640

North Carolina volunteers who were in this battle, besides the 1000 militia who joined Greene on the 11th day of March. The failure of Lee, in his Memoirs, or Campbell in his letter,* to mention these troops or their organizations, or the absence of their names from the official report, are scarcely to be considered as evidence against my position,

*Gibbs' Doc. His. (1857) p. 139.

as but few persons are mentioned in the official report, except those on the muster-rolls of the army. It is as well established that Thomas Watkins, with a militia company of dragoons, from Prince Edward, Virginia, was present at this battle, as it is that Lee's Legion was there,* and yet this troop of Watkins is nowhere mentioned by Lee or Campbell, or in Greene's official report. It is also well established that Watkins' dragoons did gallant service in the charge on the Guards, and remained to cover Greene's retreat after Lee had, without orders, left the field.†

I think it but fair to infer from Greene's letter of the 10th of February, when all his forces had rejoined the main army, that the "800 or 900" militia, as he termed them, included the 600 whom we have been able to trace directly to him, and that, in fact, instead of 600, there were "800 or 900" North Carolina volunteers, select, good infantry, who remained with Greene after the "mounted infantry" had left.‡

The brigade of North Carolinians under Pickens were not in the battle of Guilford. Their term of service ended on the 3d of March, but they remained a few days hoping to join in a general battle, and at last, by General Greene's order, they marched, in companies, for Rowan, Mecklenburg and Lincoln, where they were directed, should occasion require,

*Foote's Sketches of Virginia, 1st series, p. 403.
†Johnson, vol. 2, p. 20.
‡Johnson, vol. 1, p. 470.

to embody again, and hang on the flanks of the enemy if he retreated in that direction. There were, however, a number of individuals of this North Carolina brigade, who remained for the battle; among them Abram Forney, of Lincoln County, ancestor of the present Judge Shipp, and of General Robert D. Johnson and Captain J. F. Johnson, of Birmingham, Alabama, late of Charlotte, N. C. Abram Forney was an old Indian and frontier fighter and could not endure the idea of missing his favorite pastime. He was on the front line and fired until the point of the British bayonet was too close for further amusement. There were others, of that Mecklenburg and Lincoln Legion, who were with Forney, but I cannot gather their names. There were also many individual riflemen of the surrounding country who, as soon as Greene advanced to Guilford Court House, repaired to the "shooting-match," as they designated it; some of these we may mention by name in subsequent pages.

It has been previously stated that the North Carolina militia who joined General Greene at High Rock Ford (or Troublesome Creek, according to General Graham), consisted of two brigades of 500 men each. The aggregate, however, was 1060. The one was under Brigadier General John Butler, of Orange County, one of the old Regulators, who had adhered to his ideas of resistance to tyranny, from Alamance, in May 1771, to that time. He had been in arms from the beginning of the war and had recently been at Gates' defeat and escaped capture. He is represented as a man of great courage and much force of character. He was very popular with his neighbors and retained their respect by his honest and straightforward dealings with them. There was no time during the revolutionary war when the name of General Butler was not conspicuous in North Carolina, as a patriot and soldier. He never laid down his arms until independence was declared and won. The militia who served under him at Guilford Court-House were from Orange, Granville and Guilford counties.

General Thomas Eaton, who commanded the other brigade, had been prominent in the civil and political service of the State. In 1775 he was one of the councillors of the Provisional Government in North Carolina, of which Cornelius Harnett was the "head."*

In 1776 he was Colonel of a battalion of militia and was ordered out to repel a threatened invasion by Sir Henry Clinton, on the Cape Fear.† He was at the battle of Briar Creek, under General Ashe, March the 3d, 1779, and narrowly escaped capture.

In the "Life and Times of Iredell,"‡ we find this anecdote about him:

"Eaton (afterwards General) was at Briar Creek. He had a very small foot and wore a boot of unusual finish

---

*Moore's History, vol. 1, p. 197.
†Moore's History, vol. 1, p. 215.
‡Vol. 1, p. 408, note.

and neatness. In the haste of his flight he left his boots behind; they were recognized and purchased of a soldier by Colonel John Hamilton, who afterwards commanded a regiment of loyalists in the British service. After the war, at a dinner party at Willie Jones', Colonel Hamilton, with some good-humored raillery, produced the boots and passed them to their former owner, who, greatly incensed, threw them across the table at Hamilton's head."

General Eaton was the ancestor of the late Honorable William Eaton, of Warren County, Attorney General of the State.

The aggregate of the North Carolina troops who were in the battle of Guilford Court-House was, approximately, 1700 of all arms.

We shall now endeavor to ascertain the troops from Virginia, outside of the regulars, who composed the army of General Greene.

On the 25th day of February, after the "Hacking Match," as Pyle's defeat was called, Johnson says:*

"But notwithstanding the approach of darkness, the American commander resolved not to rest until he had thrown himself between Tarleton and the approaching reinforcements. For this purpose the detachment was ordered to proceed, and a place of encampment being selected, three miles in advance of the British party, Pickens halted for the night and made every arrangement for attacking the enemy by the break of day.

*Vol. 1, p. 455.

Never was there a more fortunate step taken than this; for one mile beyond the American encampment, Colonel Preston" (of Virginia), "with 300 respectable followers, had halted for the night, and at small intervals beyond him were two other small detachments of about 100 each, under Majors Winston and Armstrong."

Colonel William Campbell, of Washington County, Virginia, did not arrive at the camp of Pickens, in Guilford County, near Alamance, until about the 3d of March. He was on his way the 25th of February, as we learn by the following letter from Martin Armstrong to him:

"FEBRUARY 25TH, 1781.

"DEAR COLONEL:—Yesterday I had an express from Colonel Locke's camp; he is at the High Rock Ford on Haw River; General Pickens is near Hillsboro, and by this time considerable strong; General Greene on his march towards the enemy, with a number of the Virginia militia and regulars; General Butler, with the Orange district militia, lies below Hillsborough, and by every intelligence, the enemy are penned up in that town. It is generally supposed that a reinforcement is on its march to the assistance of the British; *our people are gathering from all quarters*, and the enemy's pickets are constantly harassed by our reconnoitering parties. The arrival of your troops would add vigor to us and discourage the enemy, who, no doubt, have heard of your being on your march towards them. Pray send back this express as quick as possible. I shall endeavor to have some meat for you at Bethabara; meal and corn you can have a plenty, but meat is scarce. However, I shall try my best. This day Colonel Preston, I think, will join General Pickens; if any extraordinary news comes to hand before you arrive at Bethabara, I shall let you know by another express.

"I am, in haste, sir, your humble servant,
"MARTIN ARMSTRONG."

Lee, in relating the dash of Cornwallis on the 6th of March, says:

"The left of our light troops was composed of militia who had lately joined under Colonel Campbell, one of the heroes of King's Mountain, relieving Brigadier Pickens and the corps who had so faithfully adhered to General Greene during the trying scenes just passed. Campbell's men were part of the conquerors of Ferguson; better suited, as has been before observed, for the field of battle than for the security of camp. In this quarter, through some remissness in the guards, and concealed by the fog, Lieutenant Colonel Webster, commanding the British van, approached close before he was discovered."*

Johnson, relating the junction of Colonel William Campbell with Greene's army, states:†

"The gallant Colonel Campbell, who had promised a reinforcement of one thousand hardy mountaineers, flushed with the capture of an entire army on King's Mountain, had, *almost desperate with mortification*, presented himself *with only sixty followers.*"

*Lee's Memoirs, p. 265.   †Johnson, vol. I, p. 469.

The reason for this disappointment was, that the Cherokee Indians, instigated by British emissaries, had suddenly appeared on the western frontiers, and almost every available man of that portion of the State was called out to repel the invasion.

This fact, too, accounts for the absence of Sevier's and Shelby's men, who were engaged in the same service. These latter spared a company, under Robertson, for General Greene, as we have seen.

It is worthy of observation that, though Campbell brought fewer men to the field than any other leader, he is made one of the most conspicuous figures in the battle. His reputation was made by commanding leaders subordinate to him in rank, and all his command was, for convenience of narrative, called "Campbell's Corps."

The next volunteer corps of Virginia was a battalion of riflemen under Colonel Charles Lynch.

I have not been able to find in Johnson or Lee, who give particulars, or in any general history, an estimate of their number.

In a note, p. 269, Lee says: "Colonel Lynch had lately joined, commanding one of the battalions of Virginia militia which arrived" (on the 11th March) "under Brigadier Lawson," and Johnson says they were all volunteers and riflemen. It may be safe to estimate them between one and two hundred men, say 150.

This was the Colonel Charles Lynch who gave the name of "Lynch law" to the summary punishment of violent and desperate criminals.

He was of Quaker descent and an ardent Whig; he folded up his non-combatant principles when they were in the way of his patriotic impulses. He inflicted these punishments generally on the worst class of Tories; but to his character for mercy, be it said, he did not take human life. In Judge Lynch's court there generally sat as associates Robert Adams and Thomas Calloway, and an old song commemorating their judgments ran thus:

> "Hurrah for Colonel Lynch, Captain Bob and Calloway,
> They never turned a Tory loose
> Until he shouted liberty."

Colonel Lynch died October 29th, 1796, aged 60 years.*

There was a company of militia dragoons from Prince Edward County, Virginia, commanded by Thomas Watkins, with Lieutenants Philemon Holcomb, Charles Scott, and Samuel Venable, and among the privates was the giant Peter Francisco, long the sergeant-at-arms of the House of Burgesses in Virginia. They did gallant service, as we shall see. They perhaps numbered 50 men.†

The militia of Virginia which joined Greene on the 11th March, and constituted the brigades of Stevens and Lawson, has been variously estimated. Gordon fixes the number at 1693,‡ Johnson, who underrates the number of Greene's forces of every

---
*Robert Carroll in Chicago *Inter-Ocean.*
†Foote's Sketches of Virginia, first series, p. 403.
‡Gordon, vol. 4, p. 54.

corps, puts the number "as two brigades of 600 each."*

The aggregation of Virginia forces under Greene, outside of the regular army, is—

Colonel William Preston's command,	300
Colonel William Campbell's command,	60
Colonel Charles Lynch's command,	150
Watkins' dragoons,	50
Virginia militia,	1693
Total,	2253

Greene's regular troops were as follows:

Virginia brigade, two regiments, under Colonel Green and Lieutenant Colonel Hawes, commanded by Gen. Huger of South Carolina.	778
Two Maryland regiments of regulars, under Lieutenant Colonel Howard and Colonel Ford, forming a brigade under Otho Williams, to which were attached Kirkwood's Delawares, the remnant brought off from Gates' defeat, in all	630
The artillery consisted of four (4) six-pounders under Captain Anthony Singleton and Lieutenant Finley, with sixty matrosses† from Virginia and Maryland.	60
Lee's cavalry,	75
Washington's cavalry,	90
Lee's infantry,	82
Total,	1715

*Vol. 2, p. 3.   †Artillerymen.

These are the figures of Johnson as to the regulars, which, I suspect, are too small.

To make a summary of Greene's forces, we have

North Carolinians,	1700
Virginians,	2253
Regular army,	1715
Total,	5668

In my opinion, this is more probably under the true figures than over it, as there were so many irregular troops, going and coming, that it is impossible to locate them at any one place.

Turning to the camp of Cornwallis at Bell's Mill, on Deep River, I will endeavor to ascertain the number and character of the troops composing the British army, though I find it a most difficult and complex problem to solve. I do not know that I can do better than condense the argument in the words of Johnson :*

"It is no easy undertaking to determine the number of men brought by the enemy into the battle of Guilford. The assertion of Lord Cornwallis that they amounted to only 1360 is sneered at by Sir Henry Clinton, and not even contended for by the British historians. It is an unfortunate fact, for the support of this assertion, that he admits a loss of more than 500 killed and wounded, and yet admits a total on the 1st of April of 1723. Deduct from this number Hamilton's loyal regiment, which does not appear to have been in the action, and there will still remain more than 2000 exclusive of the artillery.

*Vol. 2, pp. 3-4.

It is also observable that Colonel Tarleton admits his cavalry to have amounted to 200, and yet the whole Legionary corps is set down in Cornwallis' account at 174. By the army returns of the 1st March, it appears that his total was 2213, which will leave 2000 after deducting Hamilton's regiment. Sir Henry Clinton supposes that Lord Cornwallis ought to have had with him, after the affair of the Cowpens, 3000 men, exclusive of cavalry and militia, and General Greene constantly insists that his force, when at Hillsboro, as ascertained from his daily rations and other means resorted to by military men, exceeded 2500 and approached 3000. No author, that we recollect, ventures to state it at less than 2000."

It is probable that Cornwallis had at least 2000 men engaged in the fight, with Hamilton's loyalists in charge of his baggage in the rear.

These were all veteran soldiers, inured to war by long experience and inspired to deeds of glory by the history and traditions of these regiments.

The brigade commanded by Lieutenant Colonel James Webster was composed of the 23d and 33d regiments of infantry.

The 23d was the regiment of the Prince of Wales and was known as the "Welsh Fuzileers." They bore the motto of the Prince—*Ich dien* (I serve)—on the buttons of their uniform.*

Sir William Howe was its Colonel in 1775, with Nesbett Balfour Lieutenant Colonel, and William Blakeny, Major.

*I have one of these buttons in my possession.

The 33d regiment was one of the most honorable in the English service. It was the old regiment of Cornwallis and was his pet and pride. In the British Army Records we find that on the 21st March, 1766, Charles E. Cornwallis was appointed its Colonel, and that he was made Lieutenant General, August 29th, 1777. Its other officers were Lieutenant Colonel James Webster and Major William Dansey. Captain Frederick Cornwallis commanded one of the companies in the regiment.

The 71st was a Scotch regiment. It seems from the "Historical Records of the British Army" that it was newly reorganized in October, 1775, specially for service in America. They wore "green plaid pants, close fitting red vests and high fur caps." They were Highlanders. Their officers in 1779 were Colonel Simon Fraser, afterwards Major General, Lieutenant Colonel Archibald Campbell and Major Alexander McDonald.

This regiment was composed of two battalions, one of which, under McArthur, was captured at Cowpens.

Next to the 71st was the Hessian regiment—a brutal and ignorant mass of Dutchmen, who had been hired as slaves, and, as Lee expresses it, "mechanized" into soldiers.

The contract of the English Government with the Prince of Hesse was, that the Prince

"Should receive as Levy money for every foot soldier 30 Crowns Bunco, at 53 Holland Stivers the Crown."

Three men wounded were to be reckoned, as usual, for one man killed. "Those that are killed shall be paid at the rate of the Levy money."*

The Prince was an avaricious man, loving money more than subjects or human life, and complained that these "mercenaries were not killed in sufficient numbers to replenish his empty treasury." The English always reported the missing as wounded, and saved two-thirds of the "Crown's Bunco."

The 71st regiment and Bose's regiment of Hessians were under Major General Leslie.

Brigadier General O'Hara supported Webster with the 2d battalion of Guards and the Grenadiers. After O'Hara was wounded, this battalion was under the immediate command of Lieutenant Colonel Robert Stuart. "He was fifth son of Robert Stuart, seventh Baron Blantyre, in the Peerage of Scotland. The present Baron Blantyre is his grand nephew."†

The 2d battalion of the Guards was in command of Lieutenant Colonel Norton. Both battalions were of the best material and under the most accomplished officers.

Tarleton's Legion was not equal in material to the other regiments. He had seriously injured its *esprit de corps* by recruiting its ranks with Tories.

The artillery was commanded by Lieutenant

---

*New York His. Soc. Collection, 1879, vol. 11, p. 348.
†I am indebted for this information to David Hutcheson, Esq., Assistant Librarian of the Congressional Library.

McLeod, with Lieutenant O'Hara, a spirited young officer, as second in rank. Lieutenant O'Hara was unfortunately killed in the opening cannonade.

The field of battle is undulating ground, mostly covered with forest. If we approach it, as Cornwallis did, from the westward, until we come in sight of the first American line of battle, we come first to a small creek, a tributary of Horsepen Creek, and generally known as Little Horsepen. It runs a little west of north, and is about five or six hundred yards in front of the American line. After crossing the creek we climb a long, gently-ascending hill, with fields on either side, making an open country of from four to five hundred yards wide, and skirted by primitive forest. Half way up this hill, on the southern side, is the Hoskin's farm house, which is still standing, and occupied by the grandchildren of the proprietor who owned it in 1781, and, to whose credit be it said, he never allowed the face of the battle-field to be changed any more than was absolutely necessary.

At the end of the field on the east, the road—which in 1781 was known as the old Salisbury or New Garden Road—enters a dense forest of sturdy oaks, where the ground is nearly level, and this forest extended on both sides to the Bruce Road, which is, by measurement, 750 yards distant. There is a slight ascent from the mouth of the forest for 295 yards, and from there to the "Bruce Road" the road is nearly level. Near the Bruce Road begins the descent of a steep hill about 125 yards long, then across a valley 100 yards wide. On either side of this part of the road were old fields; that on the northern side is intersected by a deep ravine, in which, in wet weather, is a running rivulet. Along the road on the north side, and enclosing one of these fields, was a fence grown up with a thick hedge row. Pursuing the road further, we cross a small branch, coming from the south and forming a second valley at an acute angle to the road; then ascending a short, steep, rocky ridge about fifty yards, we come to the intersection of the "New Salisbury Road." This is a high point overlooking the whole field of battle. From this eminence, which is at the end of a ridge, the descent is steep to the valley of Hunting Creek, one hundred yards distant; then crossing a little fertile valley, the ascent is at first steep, then gradual to Guilford Court-House, four hundred (400) yards off.

From the front line to the court-house is very little less than a mile. A log house, tradition says, stood on the south side of the old Salisbury road just opposite the fork made by the Bruce road, and a spring was used at the foot of the hill, which is now called the "Clyde Spring,"* so well known for the purity and refreshing coolness of its water.

Guilford Court-House was the capital of Guilford County, which then embraced Davidson and Alamance. It had perhaps two or three hundred inhabitants, the court-house, jail and a large coppersmith shop being its principal buildings; the

---

*This spring is now beautifully adorned, by a generous donation from Mr. William P. Clyde to the Guilford-Battle Ground Company.

Lindsays, Whittingdons, Bevills, and Colonel Hamilton, a rich man of his day, being among its citizens. Its name, after the revolution, was changed to Martinsville, in honor of Governor Alexander Martin. In May, 1809, the court-house was moved to Greensboro, five miles southwest, and the old town soon went to decay. It is now a wheat field, there being no vestige of it remaining except an ancient well of pure water, still used, and the scattered rocks and debris of the court-house and jail, and pieces of copper which never corrode.

Tradition has much to say of "Uncle Mose," an old slave, who was chief artificer in this curious old shop, and who was allowed one quart of whiskey per day to counteract the fumes of heated copper.

There was an old grist-mill that stood on the west side of Hunting Creek, north of the old Salisbury road, which belonged to Colonel Hamilton. This was a great convenience to the town and a place of note in 1781. The race that conveyed the water along the hillside is still visible. It lay in the line of Greene's retreat from the old field where the last stand was made, and some graves, near by, are marked with rude headstones of common rock. Who rest there only eternity's roll-call will divulge.

In approaching the description of the battle of Guilford Court-House, I am forcibly impressed with the confession made by Judge Johnson as to the confusion of history in regard to that event, and I may, therefore, be pardoned for attempting to draw my own conclusions instead of "taking up" and repeating what has been said by "other writers." That author says:

"Like most other interesting battles, the descriptions handed down to us are very confused, and although all the incidents may be gathered from a careful examination of the several accounts, the connection and dependence of the several incidents are involved in much obscurity. This is the necessary result of the manner in which such narratives are collected and transmitted. *Each party publishes an account most favorable to himself;* these are taken up by writers under the influence of opposite partialities and *seldom collated by those who follow* with the patience necessary to the attainment of truth. Nor is it always practicable for the most laborious investigation to detect the errors or impositions practiced upon the public, since it is in the power of parties interested to conceal material facts, at least from the existing generation, and as to motives, by a comparison with which alone can a fair estimate of the merits, talents and success of the parties be formed, *they* may forever lie in the bosom that conceived them."

The Memoirs of Lee are roughly handled by Johnson, and Johnson in turn has been roughly handled by the critics, who accuse him of magnifying his hero and disparaging all others who are rivals for the honors of history gathered around him. The truth is not yet established by the verdict of history and the matter is open for further testimony and additional argument. No one need be deterred from entering this field of discussion and contributing what facts he may have collected or presenting such conclusions as have been formed in his mind.

We have seen that General Greene had examined this battle-field carefully, on the 10th of February, and pronounced it one of the most desirable for the character of his troops and the number of his army. It afforded a forest where the militia could fight from tree to tree for shelter and be protected from the charge of cavalry; and for the same reason a solid column of bayonets could not be kept together among the undergrowth and trees. The roads that concentrated from the north, northeast and east, all afforded safe lines of retreat, for his army, to his supplies and reinforcements.

It was in a country loyal to the American cause, where, as Tarleton says, the British "had no friends or partisans, at this period, except those included within the extent of the royal camp."

The British commander had burned all his heavy baggage and stores at Ramsour's Mill, and had consumed nearly all his medicines and much of his scant supply of ammunition.

If he were now crippled in battle and incumbered by his wounded, he must fall a prey to the gathering hosts of militia who were preparing to fall upon him on every side, or he must make a precipitate and inglorious flight to the sea, where he could find protection from his ships.

The only escape left for his lordship was by winning a decisive victory like that at Camden,

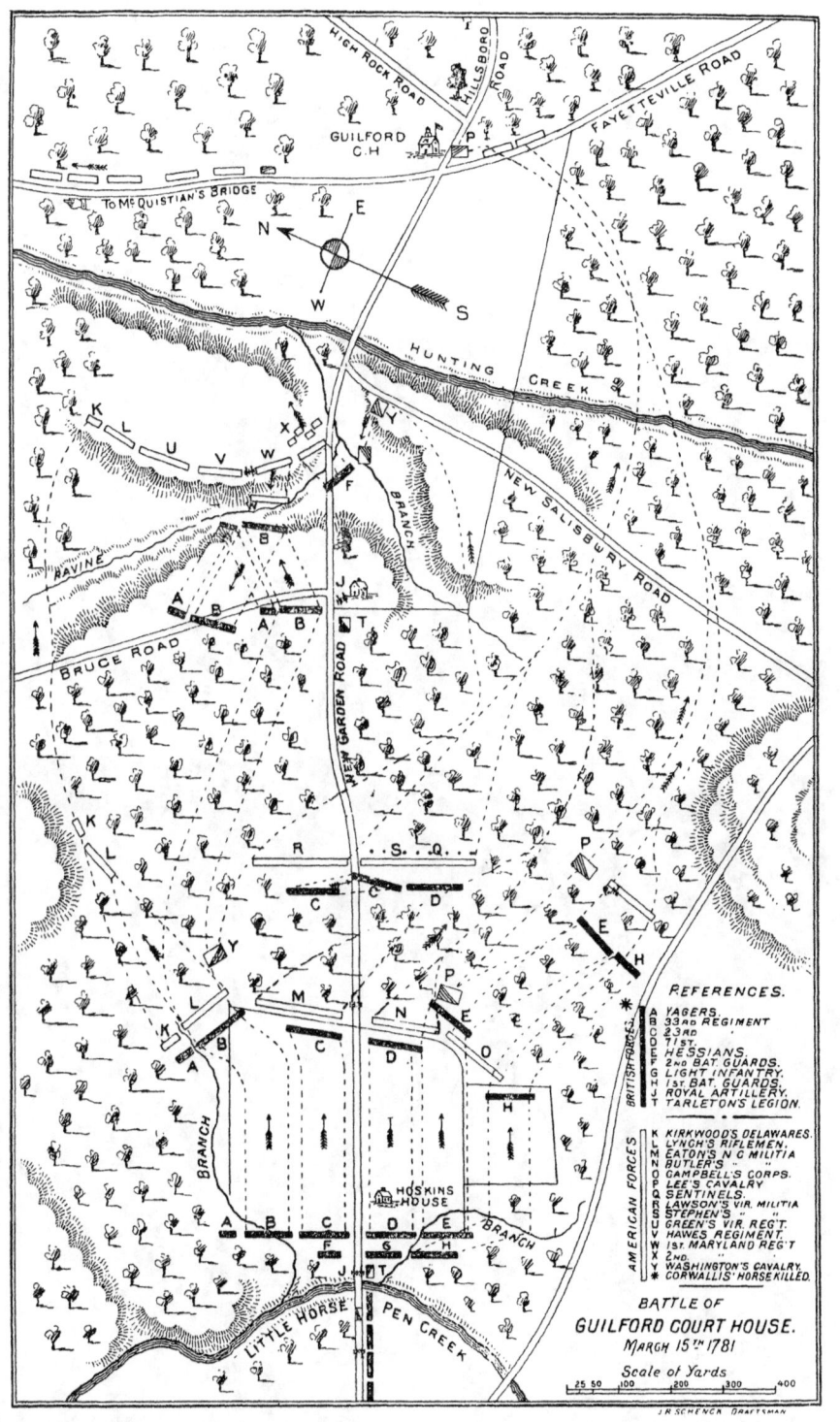

and against this General Greene had made most certain provisions. He would risk his militia, but he knew that his Continentals, who could not be broken, and his superior cavalry, were able to secure him a safe retreat and constitute a nucleus around which a fresh army could soon be collected and organized.

The order of battle chosen by the American commander was the same which General Morgan adopted at Cowpens, and the progress and result were expected to be the same. With Morgan in command, who had dash and confidence, almost to recklessness, or with Tarleton for an opponent, who had more spirit than endurance, no doubt that the British would have been driven from the field; but it does not follow, therefore, that Greene committed a mistake.

On the 20th of February, General Morgan writes to General Greene:

"I have been doctoring these several days, thinking to be able to take the field, but I find I get worse. My pains are now accompanied with a fever every day. I expect Lord Cornwallis will push you until you are obliged to fight him, on which much will depend. You have, from what I see, a great number of militia. *If they fight, you beat* Cornwallis, *if not, he will beat you*, and perhaps cut your regulars to pieces; which will be losing all your hopes. I am informed, among the militia, will be a number of old soldiers. I think it would be advisable to select them from the militia and put them in the ranks with the regulars. *Select the riflemen also and fight them on the flanks* under enterprising officers, who are acquainted with that kind of fighting, and put the *remainder of the militia in the centre, with some picked troops in their rear with orders to shoot down the first man that runs.''*

Greene was most confidential with Morgan, and Morgan's experience in fighting Southern militia, in his earlier days, gave much weight to his advice.

Greene formed his first line in exact accordance with the advice of Morgan. The North Carolina militia were placed in the centre, General Thomas Eaton's brigade, from Halifax and Warren counties, was placed at a right angle to the old Salisbury or New Garden road, behind a rail fence which separated the woods from the fields. Eaton's left rested on the road. General John Butler's brigade, from Orange, Guilford and Granville, continued the line on the south side of the road, Butler's right resting on the road, and his whole line being behind a zig-zag rail fence, the fashion of that day. On the left of Butler's line was the separate command of Colonel Arthur Forbis, of Alamance, in Guilford County, which consisted of about 100 men, Scotch-Irish Presbyterians; Forbis himself being an elder in the pastorate of Doctor David Caldwell.

Between the left of Eaton's brigade and the right of Butler's brigade, in the old Salisbury road, and a little in advance of the militia line, were placed two six-pounder cannons, under the command of Captain Anthony Singleton, a Virginia officer.*

---

*Lee's Memoirs, p. 275. Johnson's Life of Greene, vol. 2, p. 6.

The artillery was thus supported by the North Carolina militia, and, in fact, formed a part of that line. It was compelled to act in concert with the militia, and to be observant of and governed by its movements—to stand when it stood, and retire when it retired. Singleton would necessarily be cognizant of the orders given this line, and be acquainted with their conduct in the battle.

On the right flank of Eaton's brigade a " covering party," as it was called in that day, was placed. It was under the command of Colonel William Washington, of the cavalry, and consisted of Kirkwood's Delawares,* "The Blue Hen's Chickens," about eighty (80) in number, and a battalion of riflemen under Lynch, about 200. They were

---

*The State of Delaware furnished one regiment only, and certainly no regiment of the army surpassed it in soldiership. The remnant of that corps, less than two companies, from the battle of Camden, was commanded by Captain Kirkwood, who passed through the war with high reputation : and yet, as the line of Delaware consisted of but one regiment, and that regiment reduced to a captain's command, Kirkwood never could be promoted in regular routine—a very glaring defect in the organization of the army, as it gave advantages to parts of the same army denied to other portions of it. The sequel is singularly hard. Kirkwood retired, upon peace, a captain; and when the army, under St. Clair, was raised to defend the west from the Indian enemy, this veteran resumed his sword as the eldest captain of the oldest regiment. In the decisive defeat on the 4th of November, the gallant Kirkwood fell, bravely sustaining his point of the action. It was the *thirty-third* time he had risked his life for his country ; and he died as he had lived—brave, meritorious, unrewarded Kirkwood. *Lee's Memoirs, p. 185, note.*

Captain Kirkwood was a relative of Colonel Julius A. Gray, of Greensboro, whose grandfather visited Captain Kirkwood at Hillsboro, North Carolina, in 1780.

extended in the woods obliquely to the main line, and its right rested near a swamp in a little valley. In the rear of the angle formed by the militia and the "covering party," and in the woods, was the cavalry command of Colonel Washington.

On the left of Butler's line, and obliquely to it, in the woods, was another "covering party," under the command of Colonel William Campbell, of Virginia—he of King's Mountain fame—and in the rear of the angle formed by these two lines was Lee's Legion cavalry, his infantry being in the line of the "covering party."

The strength of this covering party is estimated by Johnson as only two hundred and fifty, all told, which a moment's reflection will show to be incorrect; but he has been followed by most subsequent historians, who have not been interested in correcting the error, supposing it to be immaterial. It is, however, very material to North Carolina, because her troops formed a large part of that corps, and have been ignored in the reports of the battle.

We have seen in a former page that Colonel Preston joined Pickens on the 25th of February with *three* hundred (300) "respectable followers,"* and they adhered to Greene's army until after the battle, and were under Campbell. I am of opinion, however, that Preston's battalion did not exceed two hundred, which was the strength of Lynch's other Virginia battalion.

Campbell had sixty men, and Lee's Legion

*Johnson, vol. 1, p. 455.

infantry numbered eighty men. These low estimates would aggregate three hundred and forty men, and to these must undoubtedly be added the riflemen of Surry, under Major Armstrong,* 100 men, and Major Joseph Winston 100 men,† making a total aggregate of five hundred and forty (540) men.

In the rear of this line, in the forest, under the gentle slope of the hill, and about three hundred yards distant to the east, was posted the Virginia militia. On the south side of the road, with its right resting at a right angle on the old Salisbury road, was Stevens' brigade. In the rear of this brigade was "a line of sentinels extending from right to left at about twenty yards distance from the line. These were chosen, confidential men, selected by General Stevens on personal knowledge, and posted there with orders to shoot down any individual who broke from the ranks. This may appear to have been a strong measure, but it is one which, with irregular troops, or troops composed of diversified materials, ought never to be omitted. The good effects of it will be presently seen."‡

Stevens, "who had been stung by the recollection of the inglorious flight" of his militia brigade at Gates' defeat, had frequently expressed his determination to have them shot down if they

---

*I am convinced that this was Martin Armstrong.
†Johnson, vol. 1, p. 455.
‡Johnson, vol. 2, p. 6.

repeated the disgraceful conduct; but the gallant stand of his brigade at Guilford Court-House is not wholly due to this line of executioners, in the rear, as Johnson supposes. Among the troops of Stevens were many veterans of the army of Washington whose terms of service had expired, and on their return they had been hired as substitutes, or called in occasionally by the draft or by volunteering. It was to these that Morgan alluded in his letter to Greene. Stevens was an accomplished officer and had the entire confidence of General Greene, and his heroic conduct on this field is deserving of honor and praise.

On the north side of the "old Salisbury road," in the forest, with its left resting at a right angle to the road, was Lawson's Virginia brigade of militia. Lynch's battalion had been detached from it, and to this is probably due the weakness of its resistance, as it lost only one man killed in the battle.

The third and last line was drawn up in an old field, around the brow of a hill, in semi-circular form, on the north side of the old Salisbury road.

I have located the second and third lines at the places indicated by Johnson and Lee, and they are at least five hundred and fifty (550) yards apart by actual measurement. I am quite familiar with every foot of the battle-ground and visit it very often. I have measured all the distances on it.*

---

*Johnson puts this distance at 300 yards, which is just about half of the real distance.

This was the line of Continental troops, or regulars, and included two brigades. The first brigade, on the right of the line, was composed of two Virginia regiments, the one under Colonel Green, the other under Lieutenant Colonel Hawes, the whole commanded by Brigadier General Huger of South Carolina. These troops, as an organization, had not yet been in battle. The second brigade was composed of the first and second Maryland regiments, the first was under Colonel Gunby, at the opening of the battle, the second under Colonel Ford; the whole commanded by Colonel Otho Williams, a veteran soldier of the Maryland line.

The First Maryland was the finest regiment in Greene's army, and had seen service under Washington in all his New Jersey campaigns. It came South, under DeKalb, after the fall of Charleston, in May, 1780. It bore the onset of the whole British army, with the aid of Dixon's North Carolina battalion, at Gates' defeat, and Major Anderson, of this regiment, was the only officer who retreated with an organized force to Charlotte. Under Lieutenant Colonel Howard it charged and routed the British regulars at Cowpens and finished the defeat of Tarleton on that auspicious day. It was about to add another laurel to its wreath of glory.

The Second Maryland was a new levy and had never been in battle before, and did not remain very long in this one.

Greene placed two pieces of artillery between the

flanks of these two brigades, at the sharp curve, of the semi-circle, around the hill.

General Greene, during the battle, was with the Continental line, eight hundred and fifty yards from the front, with the forest intervening, and did not have personal observation of the battle until its tide flowed to his position.

Leaving General Greene's army in position, with the exception of Colonel Lee, who, as an advanced guard, brought on the battle, before falling back into the line, I will take the reader to the camp of Cornwallis on Deep River, which was twelve miles nearly west from Guilford Court-House. The British commander correctly interpreted the advance of Greene, to a point so near his camp, as a challenge to battle and immediately prepared to accept it.

Early on the morning of the 15th March, 1781, which was Thursday, he sent back his baggage to Bell's Mill, under the escort of Colonel Hamilton's regiment of loyalists and a few infantry and cavalry, and advanced with his main army directly towards Guilford Court-House by the route which intersects the old Salisbury road at New Garden Quaker Meeting-House.

Lee, with his dragoons and infantry, and a detachment from the riflemen under Campbell, were sent out by Greene to reconnoiter and report the position and movements of the enemy. They met Tarleton in the advance, at the point where the present New Garden Meeting-House stands, between four and five miles from Greene's camp, and where the Deep River road intersects the old Salisbury road. Here a very sharp skirmish took place. Lee at first made a brilliant charge, driving Tarleton before him, but, venturing too far, he received a galling fire from the advanced infantry, and was compelled to retreat precipitately. Colonel Lee relates that it was in the early morning, and his horse became so badly frightened at the sheen of the British muskets that he was compelled to dismount and change to another in the thickest of the encounter. Lee retreated, reaching the American line sometime before the battle, and took the position assigned him on the left.

Captain Tate of Virginia, so distinguished at Cowpens, received a ball which broke his thigh; Lieutenant Snowden, of the Legion infantry, was severely wounded also and left behind. The British suffered more severely. Captain Goodricks of the Guards was badly wounded and quite a number killed.

At the cross-roads, near the Quaker Meeting-House, off from the side of the Salisbury road, in a little cove at the head of the hollow or valley, are the graves of about twenty soldiers who were buried there after the skirmish; friend and foe alike awaiting the final trumpet sound which shall summon them to the common array before the Judge of all the earth.

The British now pursued their march unmolested until they wound around a valley which leads to Little Horsepen Creek; descending this in a gentle slope, between the hills, they soon came to the creek and in sight of the American line. Singleton opened on them with his six-pounders, and the British responded with their three-pounders, and a lively cannonade ensued. The British, in the meantime, marched rapidly into the valley of the creek, and, under cover of the hill, "displayed" their line.

"The 71st regiment, Scotch Highlanders, known as the 'King's Own Borderers,' and the Hessians, known as the Regiment of Bose, but commanded now by Major DuBuy, formed on the right, or south of the old Salisbury road, and at a right angle to it. These were under the command of Major General Leslie, and constituted the force that was to assail the American left. They had in reserve, as a support, the first battalion of Guards, under Lieutenant Colonel Norton.

"Colonel Webster was directed to form the 23d and 33d regiments on the left of General Leslie's division,[*] and on the left or north side of the old Salisbury road, and at a right angle to it. Brigadier General O'Hara was directed to support Colonel Webster with the second battalion of Guards and the Grenadier company of the Guards. Whilst these troops were forming, the Yagers and the light infantry of the Guards remained near the guns in the road, but when the line moved on they attached themselves to the left of Webster's brigade. The artillery, under Lieutenant McLeod, proceeded

[*]Tarleton, p. 272.

along the high-road; the dragoons likewise could only move in column in the same direction, and Lieutenant Colonel Tarleton was ordered to keep his regiment in reserve till the infantry should penetrate through the woods to the open ground near the Court-House, where the country was represented to be more favorable for the operations of cavalry."*

Colonel Carrington gives the following official figures as containing the number of these respective organizations on the first day of March, 1781, to-wit:

23d Regiment,	258
33d Regiment,	322
71st Regiment and 2d Battalion,	212
Regiment of Bose,	313
The Yagers,	97
British Legion,	174
Total,	1376

This does not include the First Battalion of Guards, the artillery or the Grenadiers, whose numbers are not given.

Thus was the front of battle formed, by the British commander, in the valley of Horsepen, a bright and sparkling rivulet, which went on its racy way all unmindful of the bloody carnage which was soon to crimson and pollute its crystal fountains. It was at noon when the scarlet uniforms and burnished arms of the British soldiery

*Tarleton, pp. 272-3.

were glistening in the sunlight of that beautiful day. Not a furrow had been turned in the fields; not a bud was yet seen upon the trees, nor a flower in the valleys; but the first warm sunshine of spring was beginning to cast its rays upon the earth and enliven nature into activity again after a dreary winter of repose. It was not a day that suggested the conflict of arms or the shedding of blood, but rather the lassitude of peace and the dreaminess of rest; but war, like death, "has all seasons for its own," and places its iron hand on every scene of beauty and loveliness without consideration or remorse.

The last remnant of the Continental army in the South was now arrayed in front of the British commander, and he fondly hoped that its rout or captivity would be succeeded by the fall of Virginia and the subjection of the States.

It was a supreme moment in the life of Cornwallis and the crisis in the revolution. This victory won, there was no foe to obstruct his passage into the defenceless province of Virginia; North Carolina would be at the mercy of the Crown, and Georgia and South Carolina, already prostrate and subdued, could never rally for defence again.

Should Greene be beaten, Cornwallis could take up his triumphal march to the sea to be welcomed by the English fleets which rode unchallenged in the harbors of Norfolk and New York.

The prisoners of war at Charlottesville, Virginia, would be set free to plunder and pillage their captors. France, capricious and fickle, would forsake the waning fortune of the colonies, and, making peace for herself, leave her allies to their fate. Washington would be crushed by the army of Clinton in his front and that of Cornwallis in his rear, or be driven into the frozen regions of the North for refuge. Congress would be scattered from its halls and carry dismay wherever they fled for safety.

These were the precious hopes and dazzling visions that stimulated the ambition and nerved the hand of Cornwallis for the battle now before him. The greater the odds against him, the greater would be the glory of his triumph and the more important its results.

Not only hope and glory allured him to battle, but retaliation and revenge rankled in his heart and drove him to desperate deeds. His lieutenants, Ferguson and Tarleton, had been defeated and humbled by the militia of North Carolina whom they despised, and British pride demanded that the insult be avenged.

Every officer and soldier remembered King's Mountain and Cowpens, and were eager to wipe out the disgrace of those disastrous fields.

Nothing but news of misfortune had gone to Clinton from the army of invasion since the frosts of October, 1780, had chilled their zeal, and the great rival of Cornwallis was secretly gloating over the misfortunes of his personal and political enemy.

The recovery of prestige and the restoration of

royal confidence added a powerful incentive to the achievement of victory.

Cornwallis resolved, therefore, that "he would conquer or die" on this field, and the reckless exposure of his person during the battle indicated the determination with which he entered the conflict.

None the less was the appreciation of the American army and its officers of the decisive crisis which was now upon them.

General Greene, the confidential friend and trusted counsellor of Washington, had been selected by him as the commander-in-chief of the Southern Department of the American army. Their friendship had begun at Boston with the first enthusiastic outburst of the revolution, and had steadfastly matured in the camp and the council.

He had been intrusted with almost dictatorial powers, and he knew that the eyes of the confederation were upon him. He was fully aware of the discipline and strength of the magnificent soldiery in his front; that they were led by men whose honor was dearer, by far, to them than life, to whom disgrace and defeat meant ruin and shame. Greene knew the desperate straits to which he had driven his adversary, and the obstinacy that characterized his nature. He sadly knew the want of discipline in his own hastily-gathered forces, and how inferior were their arms; that the larger part of them had never faced a British column with their dreadful "push of the bayonet"; that few of his militia had ever endured the suspense and terror of a cannonade, while compelled to inaction themselves. He hardly hoped for victory; but he was confident that he could wound and cripple his adversary and prevent that adversary from destroying his army.

He trusted that the militia would so stagger and demoralize the British columns that when they encountered his regular troops they would fall a prey to the Continental line as they did at Cowpens. Desiring that in all things this battle should be a repetition of that, he seems to have endeavored to imitate Morgan in the details and particulars of that splendid achievement.

"When his arrangements were completed, Greene passed along the first line. The day was hot, and, holding his hat in one hand, he was wiping the perspiration from his ample forehead with the other. His voice was clear and firm as he called his men's attention to the strength of their position, and, *like Morgan at the Cowpens*, asked only THREE ROUNDS. 'THREE ROUNDS, MY BOYS, AND THEN YOU MAY FALL BACK!' Then taking his position with the Continentals, he held himself in readiness to go wherever his duty might call him."

The only error in this statement is that it was TWO, not *three*, rounds which Greene required. The quotation above is taken from "The Life of Major General Nathanael Greene," by his grandson George Washington Greene, vol. 3, page 196.

The error was from inadvertence, not intentional; for on pages 143–4 of the same volume, the author gives this account of Morgan's speech and requirement of his troops at Cowpens. Addressing the militia, Morgan

"Bade them call to mind his own long experience and unvarying fortune, and exhorted them to take confidence from his example, be firm and steady and above all aim true. 'Give me TWO FIRES, *at killing distance,' he exclaimed, 'and I will make the victory sure!'"*

The author says he received the knowledge of this incident from "tradition"—no doubt a direct tradition from his grandfather, and handed down from sire to son as one of the circumstances of this battle often repeated around the fireside.

It is a fact so significant as to become a pivotal one in the further narrative of this battle. I verily believe that "upon this rock" the North Carolina militia may rest their vindication against the aspersions cast upon them in history, and that neither the excuses and pretexts of defeated soldiers, nor the jealousies of States, nor the slander of enemies, nor the oft-repeated misrepresentations of careless and superficial writers, can drive them from this solid foundation of eternal truth and justice. When this incident and order, now established in history, shall be accepted as truth, it is easy to demonstrate, from the testimony of eye-witnesses and participants in this battle, that the requirement of General Greene was fulfilled; that the order given to the North

Carolina militia by him in person was obeyed, and that their

> "Twice-lit tongue of bolted flame
> Blazed full upon their foemen."*

I propose to fortify my position, that General Greene gave this order, or made the requirement of only "*Two Fires*" from the North Carolina militia, by the testimony of other authors and writers.

Johnson, in his Life of Greene, vol. 1, p. 378, says, that the

"Orders to the first line (at Cowpens) were to deliver *two* deliberate discharges at the distance of fifty yards and then to retire."

Lee, in his Memoirs, page 227, repeats this speech in these words:

"If you will pour in but *two* volleys, at killing distance, I will take upon myself to secure victory."

All historians agree that "two rounds" were required by Morgan, and then the militia were to fall back.

In further confirmation of George Washington Greene, that this same order was given the North Carolina militia at Guilford Court-House, I add other testimony. Garden, who was one of Lee's Legion, and heard the speech, says:

*J. W. Rumple, poem on this battle.

"The North Carolina militia were assured by General Greene that if they would only preserve their station long enough to give their enemy *two fires* they should obtain his free permission to *retire from the field.*" *Garden's Anecdotes, p. 40.*

Gordon's History, vol. 4, page 55, has also this language:

"General Stevens had the address to prevent his brigade from receiving any bad impression from the retreating North Carolinians by giving out *that they had orders to retire* after discharging their pieces. To cherish this idea he ordered his men to open their files to favor their passage."

It is evident that General Stevens and his whole command were apprised of the order to the North Carolina militia (as they should have been) to prevent surprise and panic in their ranks by the retreat of the North Carolinians in their front. Gordon affects to believe this was a ruse of General Stevens, but in this he is manifestly in error. The order was given just as General Stevens communicated it to his command.

Rev. E. W. Caruthers, D. D., who wrote the Life of Rev. Dr. David Caldwell in 1842, had been over the battle-field of Guilford Court-House very often in company with the soldiers who participated in the battle and had conversed with many old people of the neighborhood who knew its history from their cotemporaries, and was therefore familiar with the incidents and traditions of the battle. Robert Rankin, a member of the Buffalo Church, often pointed out the different localities of the field, especially on the left, where Rankin fought under Colonel Campbell among the North Carolina riflemen. With this familiar knowledge of events, Dr. Caruthers assumes, in his Life of Caldwell, as an established fact, known by everybody, that the militia were ordered to fire twice and then retreat. Speaking of Captain Forbis' command, page 236, he says:

"They stood firm until they had fired *twice*, according to orders."

Again, he says:

"They were placed in the front rank, stood firm and fired the number of times prescribed in the general order. Forbis himself fired the first gun in that division, and killed his man."

There are several incidental allusions to this "order" to fire twice, and always as one of the unquestionable facts connected with the battle.

It is not, however, emphasized because the Doctor was writing the biography of a minister of the Gospel, and not a defence of the North Carolina militia, and the order was only a collateral fact in the narrative.

Subsequently, in 1856, Dr. Caruthers, in his Sketches—Second Series—vindicated the North

Carolina militia from the charge of inefficiency in the battle.

It was indeed a fact well known, and often spoken of by old persons to succeeding generations; and it is incomprehensible that a circumstance so well known and understood should have been omitted in his Memoirs, by Colonel Lee, who must have been cognizant of it, for he was on the front line when the order was given. It is inexplicable that Johnson, too, who had access to General Greene's correspondence and papers, should have suppressed it, while he gives great prominence to the like order of General Morgan at Cowpens.

I have in my possession also an interesting letter from Captain James F. Johnson, of Charlotte, North Carolina, giving me the statement of Abram Forney, of Lincoln County, who remained from Pickens' brigade to participate in the impending battle. Forney states distinctly that it was "two rounds," and adds that his portion of the line obeyed the order.

There can be nothing settled, by testimony, more certainly than the fact that the North Carolina militia were, by the *personal order* of General Greene, directly instructed *to fire twice*, and assured that he required no more of them. And it is the failure to observe and state this all-important fact that has placed these troops in a false light before their posterity. When we reflect for a moment, this order is so reasonable and natural that we cannot doubt the truth of the assertion that it was given.

The North Carolinians were armed with their hunting rifles. They carried their powder in a powder-horn with a charger attached. Their bullets and patching were in a pouch to their left side, and the tallow to grease the patching under a spring in the stock of the rifle. To load a rifle required that the powder be measured in the charger and poured carefully into the small muzzle bore of the rifle. The patching was to be greased and placed over the muzzle and the ball placed upon it and pressed into the gun. A knife was then used to cut off the surplus patching. The ball was to be rammed down the gun with a ramrod, which was then to be replaced in the thimbles along the barrel. The last operation was to prime the pan in the flint and steel lock before the rifleman was ready to fire upon his enemy. The operation required at least three minutes to perform it.

If the British line were fired upon at fifty yards, they could be over the intervening ground in less than fifty seconds, or if at one hundred yards, in one and a half minutes. So that, unless the British line was repulsed in its advance by the deadliness of the fire, they would be upon the militia before it was possible to load three times, or, if the operation of loading were delayed, by trepidation or accident, before they could fire twice.

It is evident that General Greene, as well as every reasonable person, expected that the militia would give way whenever the bayonet did reach them; for against it they had no arm of defence nor discipline to beat it back. Johnson well remarks, in speaking of the terror of the bayonet, that "nothing but the absolute subjection of every human feeling to the restraints of discipline can dissipate the real or imagined terrors of such a conflict;" and Lee has said that "to expose militia to such a charge, without discipline or arms to repel it, is murder." Therefore, General Greene instructed them, so they could understand it, to fire until the bayonet did reach them, which he calculated would be two rounds, and then to retire. Otherwise it would have been to expect more of them than of the conquerors of Ferguson at King's Mountain.

The sequel will show that the North Carolinians disobeyed no order in retreating before the bayonet, and that they performed the whole duty required of them, and if the day had gone as did Cowpens, the order of Greene to the militia would, most probably, not have been suppressed.

General Greene having now retired to the Continental line, exhorted the second Maryland, which was a fresh regiment, though regulars, to firmness and courage. He was no more on the front line, and as to its conduct he could only afterwards speak from hearsay.

The British army having completed its array, advanced with that steadiness and coolness characteristic of veteran and disciplined soldiers. The ground, on the north side of the road, is comparatively level for several hundred yards in front of the position occupied by Brigadier General Eaton's brigade, and being an open field, the line of the enemy, with their bright uniforms, presented a tempting mark to the riflemen. Impatient to fire and have time to reload for a second discharge, they threw in their first fire at one hundred and fifty yards—a distance at which an ordinary rifleman could bring down a turkey or a deer at almost every shot, and it is not surprising that they felt sure of hitting the scarlet body of a British soldier.

Lieutenant Colonel Webster, seeing the effect of this first fire, and desiring to reach the militia before it could be repeated, rode to the front and gave the order to charge and he himself headed the advance.

Colonel Tarleton, who was in the road, in the rear of Webster's brigade, and in full view of its advance against Eaton's brigade, thus describes the scene transpiring before his eyes:

"The *order and coolness* of that part of Webster's brigade which advanced across the open ground *exposed to the enemy's fire cannot be sufficiently extolled.* The extremities were not less gallant, but were more protected by the woods in which they moved. The militia allowed the front line to approach within 150 yards before they gave their fire."

Stedman, the English historian, who was the

Commissary General of Cornwallis, and was also a spectator of the scene, repeats this account of Webster's advance and vouches for Tarleton's general description of the battle. Colonel Lee, who knew Stedman's character well, and the incidents of the whole campaign, in correcting an unintentional error into which Stedman had fallen about the defeat of Pyle, says: "I have acknowledged my conviction of Stedman's impartiality and respect for truth." Therefore, this account of Tarleton's comes endorsed by Stedman, and Stedman's character is endorsed by Lee.

Tarleton's statement is a prominent and important fact, because, if "the order and coolness of" Webster's brigade under the fire of the North Carolina militia cannot be "sufficiently extolled," the fire must have been very deadly and continuous.

Tarleton and Stedman would not acknowledge the insufficiency of the English language to describe this charge unless it was made in the face of a galling and destructive fire. The tribute to the "coolness and courage" of Webster's brigade involves the highest tribute to the firmness of the North Carolina brigade.

Another English historian, Lamb, who was at that time an officer of the Thirty-third regiment and participated in this charge, has also quoted Tarleton's language with approbation, and in order to give further and greater emphasis to the coolness and courage of Webster's brigade, he says:

"As the author belonged to Colonel Webster's brigade, he is enabled (and the reader will naturally expect it of him) to state some circumstances, unnoticed by any historian, from his own personal observation. After the brigade formed across the open ground, Colonel Webster rode on to the front and gave the word, 'Charge!' Instantly the movement was made in excellent order at a sharp run, with arms charged; when arrived *within forty yards* of the enemy's line it was perceived that their whole force had their arms presented and resting on a rail fence, the common partition in America. *They were taking aim with the nicest precision.*

" ' 'Twixt host and host but narrow space was left—
A dreadful interval, and front to front,
Presented, stood in terrible array.'

"At this awful period a *general pause* took place; both parties surveyed each other a moment with most anxious suspense. Colonel Webster then rode forward in front of the Twenty-third regiment and said, with more than his usual commanding voice, which was well known to his brigade, 'Come on, my brave Fusileers!' This operated like an inspiring voice. They rushed forward amidst *the enemy's fire. Dreadful was the havoc* on both sides.

" 'Amazing scene!
What showers of mortal hail, what flaky fires!'

"At last the Americans gave way and the brigade advanced to the attack of the second line."*

Lamb wrote his work in 1809, after seeing other

*Lamb's History of the American Revolution, p. 361.

accounts of this battle, and felt constrained to give his personal recollections of this particular part of the engagement, because he was an active participant in it and no other historian had described the action in detail in that part of the field. This author is one of the highest respectability and is frequently quoted by American historians. In Carrington's "Battles of the American Revolution," a standard work of recent date, copious quotations are made from Lamb. He is also quoted by George Washington Greene in his biography of the General. Lamb's work was published by subscription, and among the list of subscribers are most of the noblemen and *literati* of his day. Lamb was a teacher in a high school in Scotland and a man of letters as well as a soldier.

Can any one doubt the truth of such a statement, coming from a participant in the scene, who gives such emphasis and particularity to details, and who is of unimpeachable character for truth and intelligence?

I can safely rest the reputation of that part of the North Carolina militia under General Eaton, on these splendid tributes to their courage and firmness.

It establishes the fact that they had fired once and reloaded, and when the enemy were in forty paces were resting their rifles on the rails and aiming with the "nicest precision" at their foe. So appalling was their martial array that even the

British veterans, who had faced so many dangers from Quebec to Camden, paused and stood aghast at the spectacle, and that only the magic voice of their commander, accompanied with his reckless exposure in their front, could prevail upon them to advance.

The "havoc" was great, says Lamb, and we may well believe it. Riflemen who could take a squirrel's head from the highest tree would not be likely to miss a scarlet uniform at forty paces.

In Foote's Sketches of Virginia, Second Series, p. 149, is a biography of the Rev. Samuel Houston, a Presbyterian minister, whose simple epitaph tells the story of his useful and honorable and pious life:

SACRED

TO THE MEMORY

OF THE

REV. SAMUEL HOUSTON,

WHO IN EARLY LIFE WAS A SOLDIER OF THE REVOLUTION,

AND FOR 55 YEARS A FAITHFUL MINISTER OF THE

LORD JESUS CHRIST.

HE DIED ON THE 20TH DAY OF JANUARY, 1839,

AGED 81 YEARS.

Mr. Houston was a student at Lexington Academy, but responded to a call for volunteers, and was one of General Stevens' command at this battle, and kept a diary of his movements from February 26th to March 23d, in which are related many interesting incidents. He was fond of telling the story of this battle, and thus describes its opening:

"The Virginia line was in the forest, the Carolina militia partly in the forest and partly in the skirt of the forest and partly behind the fence inclosing the open space, across which the British force was advancing with extended front.

"*According to orders*, the Carolina line, when the enemy were *very near*, gave their fire, which on the *left of the British line was deadly, and having repeated it, retreated.* Some remained to give a *third fire* and some made such haste in retreat as to bring reproach upon themselves as deficient in bravery, while their neighbors behaved like heroes."

Here is a direct confirmation of Lamb's account of the "deadly fire" on Webster's brigade, and a positive assertion that the fire was "repeated," and that some remained to fire the third time, and that they acted "according to orders."

That there was "haste in the retreat" when it began, is conceded; but no military man or intelligent reader of the history of militia contests would have expected it to be otherwise. The Virginians and North Carolinians, being undisciplined troops, were alike disorderly when retreating from the field. The North Carolinians had done all they were commanded or instructed to do, and hastened to the rear, where they were ordered to rally again. Mr. Houston was frank and just as well as truthful, for in describing the advance of the British on Stevens' brigade, after the North Carolinians retreated, he relates as the first fact occurring that "our brigade Major, Mr. Williams, fled."

The Rev. J. Henry Smith, D. D., one of the most distinguished ministers of the Presbyterian Church in the South, and for twenty-five years pastor at Greensboro, North Carolina, has seen Mr. Houston in his old age and knew his character well, and testifies to the great esteem and reverence in which he was held by all who knew him. He was one of the leading spirits of the Presbyterian Church in Virginia in his day.

These men of North Carolina did their duty, and after firing every shot possible, before the bayonet was upon them, *obeyed orders*, and retreated behind the second line, who were in readiness to give the enemy a similar reception.

On Butler's side of the road the North Carolina militia and Forbis' volunteers gave the British a bloody repulse. The Scotch Highlanders, a regiment of Leslie's brigade, rested its left on the New Garden or old Salisbury road, and therefore was immediately in front of Butler's militia, chiefly from Orange, Granville and Guilford.

Captain Dugald Stuart, who commanded a company in the 71st regiment (called "Scotch Highlanders") on that day, when writing to a relative in Guilford County under date of October 25th, 1825, uses the following language:

"In the advance we received a very *deadly fire* from

the Irish line of the American army, composed of their marksmen, lying on the ground *behind a rail fence.*

"*One-half the Highlanders dropped on that spot.* There ought to be a very large *tumulus* on that spot where our men were buried."*

This letter was written by Captain Stuart to a relative in Guilford County, who had suggested that most of the Highlanders had been killed in the charge on the Continental line, and these particulars were given to correct that error.

The centre of the State had among its population, at that period, many Irish and Scotch-Irish, and for that reason the militia line was called the Irish line.

The *tumulus* to which Captain Stuart refers is, no doubt, the two large graves, sixteen feet square and six feet deep, near the Hoskins residence, which were filled with the dead bodies of the English army, thus confirming Captain Stuart's memory in regard to it.

A further confirmation of this positive statement of Captain Stuart is an extract from " Brown's History of the Highland Clans," as quoted by Caruthers, vol. 2, p. 134:

"The Americans, covered by a fence in their front, reserved their fire till the British were in thirty or forty paces, at which distance they opened a destructive fire, which annihilated nearly one-third of Webster's brigade."

The Highlanders, however, were under Leslie,

*Caruther's Sketches, Second Series, p. 134.

instead of Webster, that day, but joined Webster's right.

The Hessians were opposed by the left of Butler's brigade and the volunteers under Forbis. These latter, Lee confesses, were firm and never gave way except to sullenly and slowly retreat before the English bayonet, and adhered to Campbell's command to the very last.

It was a North Carolina rifle that brought down the first English officer in this battle.

Colonel James Martin, in his petition for a pension, thus describes the scene:

"I was posted on the front line with a company commanded by Captain Forbis, a brave, undaunted fellow. We were posted behind a fence, and I told the men to sit down until the British, who were advancing, came near enough to shoot. When they came within about 100 yards, a British officer with a drawn sword was driving up his men. I asked Captain Forbis if he could take him down. He said he could, for he had a good rifle. I told him to let him come in fifty yards and then take him down, which he did. It was a Captain of the British army, and at that instant General Greene sent his aid-de-camp to me to go to him, and I went and asked him his command. He told me as he had begun battle, and I had not a complete regiment, he wished me to go with Major Hunter to the court-house, and in case of defeat to rally the men, which we did and collected about 500 and were marching them to the battle-ground when I met General Stevens, of the Virginia corps, retreating. I asked him if the retreat was by General

Greene's orders. He said it was. I then retreated with him and ordered the men to repair to the Troublesome Iron Works to outfit, as he had ordered me, which we obeyed."*

It was stated by Peter Rife, of Virginia, one of Lee's Legion, to Caruthers, that he witnessed the fact with his own eyes, that the men of Guilford fired till the Hessians mounted the fence, and then clubbed their rifles and fought them back, hand to hand. When asked if this was not done by Campbell's men, he replied indignantly, "No, it was the North Carolinians. I sat on my horse and saw them with my own eyes."

Caruthers then remarked to him, " According to history, the North Carolina militia did nothing on that occasion," and he replied with some sternness: "Whoever says the North Carolina militia did nothing on that day, says *what is false, for I know better.*"†

I quote further from Caruthers :‡

"William Montgomery, of Guilford County, who was one of Captain Forbis' company and one of the four who stood by him to the last, when describing the scene in after life, usually illustrated it by saying that, after they delivered their first fire, which was a deliberate one, with their rifles, the part of the British line at which they aimed looked like the scattering stalks in a wheat field, when the harvest man has passed over it with his cradle."

*Wheeler's Reminiscences, p. 414.
†Caruthers, Second Series, p. 132.
‡Caruthers, Second Series, p. 134.

As evidence of the coolness and pluck of the men of Alamance, Caruthers relates the following anecdote:

"William Paisley, father of the Rev. Samuel Paisley, who is yet living, was one of Captain Forbis' neighbors and one of his firmest men. He was one of the last to leave the ground, and when about to retreat, on looking under the smoke, the British were so near that there seemed to be no chance of escape; and dropping on the ground, he lay with his face in the leaves as if he were dead. Supposing that he was dead, they rushed by without noticing him and engaged with the Virginians. As soon as they had done so, he got up, and on looking around he saw a British soldier who was a very large man, and so much afraid of the rifles that he was keeping a tree between him and danger, peeping first from one side and then the other. He said he thought he would give the cowardly dog one 'pop' at all events, and leveling his rifle he laid him on the ground at the foot of the tree."

Caruthers adds the personal testimony of numerous others, either soldiers who participated in the battle or visitors to it next day, and with whom he had conversed, confirmatory of the deadly effect of the fire from Butler's brigade and Forbis' men. Many of these soldiers survived and were cotemporaries of Doctor Caruthers, who was for many years the distinguished pastor of Alamance Presbyterian Church and successor to Doctor David Caldwell.

I copy from "Jefferson's Correspondence," vol. 1, p. 213, the following letter:

"Richmond, March 21st, 1781.
"*To His Excellency the President of Congress:*

"Sir:—The enclosed letter will inform you of the arrival of a British fleet in Chesapeake Bay.

"'The extreme negligence of our stationed expresses is no doubt the cause, as yet, why no authentic account has reached us of a general action, which happened on the 15th inst., about a mile and a half from Guilford Court-House, between General Greene and Lord Cornwallis. Captain Singleton, an intelligent officer of Harrison's artillery, who was in the action, has this moment arrived here, and gives the general information that both parties were prepared and desirous for action; the enemy were supposed about twenty-five hundred strong, our army about four thousand; that after a very warm and general engagement of about an hour and a half, we retreated about a mile and a half from the field, in good order, having, as he supposed, between two and three hundred killed and wounded—the enemy between five and seven hundred killed and wounded; that we lost four pieces of artillery; *that the militia, as well as regulars, behaved exceedingly well;* that General Greene, he believes, would have renewed the action the next day, had it not proved rainy, and would renew it as soon as possible, as he supposes; that the whole of his troops, both regulars and militia, were in high spirits and wishing a second engagement; that the loss has fallen pretty equally on the militia and regulars; that General Stevens received a ball through the thigh; Major Anderson, of Maryland, was killed, and Captain Barrett, of Washington's cavalry; Captain Fauntleroy, of the same cavalry, was shot through the thigh and left on the field.

"Captain Singleton, having left the camp the *day after*

the battle, does not speak from particular returns, none such having been then made. * * *

"I have the honor to be, with very high respect and esteem, your Excellency's most obedient and most humble servant, "TH. JEFFERSON."

The statement of Captain Singleton, who commanded the artillery, which was stationed immediately between the two North Carolina brigades on the front line, and had the best opportunity to observe their conduct, and who was a Virginian, in no way partial to North Carolina, "*that the militia, as well as the regulars, behaved exceedingly well*," is certainly entitled to very great weight on this disputed point. He was not only an eye-witness and participant in the battle, but his movements depended on the action of the North Carolina militia and his own safety was involved in their conduct. I cannot imagine a witness whose testimony could be more pertinent and reliable than that of Captain Singleton.

We may further consider that he did not leave Greene's camp until the day after the battle, and had therefore an opportunity to converse with his fellow soldiers about its incidents and occurrences and to get a correct impression of the conduct of the troops. He was no doubt a messenger to convey tidings of this battle to Governor Jefferson, and had no motive to conceal the truth and every inducement of honor to tell it. His other statements in regard to the battle are correct, and why should we suspect that he prevaricated in this one? Where is the motive or the reason for any such suspicion? There was no man in Greene's whole command who bore a higher character than Singleton or who more heartily despised a falsehood.

Jefferson could not have misunderstood him, eager, as he evinces himself to be, for news from the battle. We may imagine that the two talked long about it, and if Singleton had said that the North Carolina militia shamefully fled and lost the battle, Jefferson would not have been slow to hear it and denounce it. The conclusion is, that Singleton spoke the truth.

I have thus endeavored to sustain, by the testimony of credible witnesses, the affirmation that the North Carolina militia performed the duty assigned them, in this battle, by the order of General Greene, delivered to them in person, on the field, and that this duty was well performed by giving the enemy two well-directed and "deadly" fires.

To summarize the argument on the first point, that the order, to fire twice and then retire, was given to the militia, we have the uncontradicted testimony of Garden, who heard it, of George Washington Greene, who received it as a family tradition, and of Caruthers, who heard it from numerous soldiers who were in the battle. No author nor writer has ever contradicted or doubted the testimony, and the characters of the witnesses are above reproach. The fact is, therefore, established, as far as human testimony can establish any fact.

On the other point, that the order was obeyed in letter and spirit, we have the testimony of the English authors Tarleton, Stedman and Lamb, who were present and either participating or observing the facts about which they wrote, and of Captain Dugald Stuart, whose men fell under this "deadly" fire.

On the American side we have the testimony of the Rev. Samuel Houston, a man of exalted character and an eye-witness of what he relates; of Captain Anthony Singleton, of the artillery, who was in line with the North Carolina militia; and Peter Rife, a soldier, who denounces as false the assertion "that the North Carolina militia did nothing." All these are Virginians—fellow-citizens of Lee and Campbell; Rife, a soldier in Lee's command.

To these we may add the evidence of William Montgomery, of Guilford County, who was well known to persons yet living, and whose character as christian, patriot and soldier no man would dare assail where Montgomery was known.

With such a "cloud of witnesses," may we not be pardoned for disbelieving the account written by Lee in 1809, twenty-eight years after the battle, from memory alone? That memory, too, was so treacherous and inaccurate, in regard to this very battle, that, in describing the positions of the American troops, he placed Lawson's brigade of Virginia militia on the front line, and speaks of it as receiving the charge of Webster's brigade; and placed all the North Carolina militia on the south side of the New Garden road—errors so palpable that no subsequent author has ever repeated them If Lee could not even remember where the North Carolina militia were, how could he recall the picture of their flight, as he rhetorically describes it? The errors of Lee, in his Memoirs, are so numerous that Johnson, after exposing many of them, speaks of the "general inaccuracy" of the whole narrative. But Lee has written so charmingly that his book has become a popular favorite, and, indeed, when he is accurate, no one describes the incidents of that period with more force and beauty than he.

Campbell's statement is contained in a letter written to the Rev. Mr. Cumming, in September, 1781, and says "a whole brigade of North Carolina militia abandoned their party from the first onset."* Lee does not confine the abandonment to one brigade, but includes both in his exuberant fancy. Of such like inconsistent accusations it was said, in Holy Writ, "but neither so did their witness agree together." Both Lee and Campbell profess to describe what they saw, but they did not see it alike, or did not see it at all.

We will resume the narrative.

The British not only received a galling fire from the front, but Washington's corps on the right and Campbell's on the left poured in a heavy fire on their flanks.

*Gibbs' Doc. History.

It was so heavy on the left flank that Colonel Webster wheeled the 23d and 33d regiments to the left, so as to face Lynch and Kirkwood, while the Light infantry of the Guards and the Yagers, under General O'Hara, turned obliquely across the field and formed to their extreme left, and the front of the battle, at that point, was nearly at a right angle to the former line. This movement left a vacancy in the British line next to the old Salisbury road, formerly Webster's right flank, and into this the Second battalion of Guards was marched and continued to move eastwardly, resting their right on the road.

Lynch and Kirkwood being hard pressed, retreated under cover of Washington's cavalry and formed on the extreme right of Lawson's brigade of Virginians.

Colonel Webster was now free to readjust his old line and make it co-extensive with the Virginians in his front, the only change being that the Second battalion of Guards now formed his right.

The North Carolina militia had left the field and retreated towards the Court-House. Their retreat was disorderly and resulted in a flight. They were without discipline, and the flight became a rout, and in this consisted their misfortune that day; one common to militia everywhere.

On the left of the American line the militia had generally been driven from their position, but the fire from Campbell's corps became so deadly that Colonel Norton, with the First battalion of Guards, was ordered to join the British line on the right and oppose themselves to Campbell.

As the Hessian regiment passed the line of the militia, it wheeled to the right, and, in line with Norton, faced Campbell. Campbell was reinforced by many of Butler's brigade, who retreated in that direction, and by all of Forbis' men, who formed on Campbell's right. Lee's Legion was on that flank. The 71st Regiment, of Highlanders, continued on its course up the road and soon engaged Stevens' brigade of Virginians.

It had been the intention of Campbell to fall back and put his corps in line on the left of Stevens, but the Hessians passed so rapidly in his front as to cut him off. He was also delayed by his conflict with Norton on the left. The riflemen, retiring deeper into the forest, took to the trees and made it so hot for the Guards that they were compelled to retreat in great disorder. Cornwallis came in person to their rescue, and by riding in their front and exposing himself to imminent danger, succeeded in rallying them. The Hessians being now joined again by the Guards, made a combined charge and drove Campbell to the south, and entirely separated his command from the American army, so that in fact two distinct battles were raging at the same time.

About one-quarter of a mile on the southeast of

Campbell's first position, Cornwallis, who was following up Norton and the Hessians, had a large iron-gray horse shot from under him. The spot is now marked by a persimmon tree, a century old, whose identity is well authenticated by tradition.

Campbell would retreat and fire, then the British would fall back, and using the bayonet, push the riflemen back again; so it raged and alternated between them until Campbell was driven to a high range of hills, or a little mountain range, as it is sometimes called, about one mile from Campbell's first position. Here the riflemen began to gain a decided advantage and to drive the Hessians before them, when Lee, unexpectedly, left Campbell's flank and Tarleton appeared on the scene.

We must now return to the front of the Virginia line.

The British artillery had advanced, supported by Tarleton's Legion. Lieutenant O'Hara of the artillery had been killed early in the action. Cornwallis had abandoned the right and come to the left of his line, riding a dragoon's horse.

Singleton had retired with his guns and taken his position on a high ridge to the left of the Maryland brigade, where the new Salisbury road intersects the old Salisbury road, west of Hunting Creek, and quite a commanding eminence.

The right of the British line being weakened by the engagement of the Hessians and First battalion of Guards with Campbell's corps, the 23d joined the 71st in its assault upon Stevens, while Webster assailed Lawson with the 33d, in conjunction with the Light infantry and Yagers on his left, and the Second battalion of Guards on his right.

Lawson's brigade soon gave way, and in its retreat wheeled upon its left flank as a pivot, so as to bring the brigade to the south side of the road, in the rear of Stevens, and thence moved along that side of the road, avoiding the field at the Bruce road, and clinging to the forest to escape from Tarleton's dragoons. Washington conducted them to the new Salisbury road, and Kirkwood and Lynch marched to a position on the right of the Continental line; Washington remaining on the ridge in the new Salisbury road, where he could overlook the field and protect the left flank of the Continental line.

The contest between Stevens' brigade and the 71st and 23d was protracted and stubborn.

Mr. Houston, who was in this brigade, says that they drove the British back three times and were as often compelled to retreat before the bayonet. Lee having gone south with Campbell, and the left of Stevens' brigade being thus without any protection, Tarleton was ordered to charge them on that flank, and they were compelled to give way. General Stevens had, in the meantime, been shot through the thigh and was unable to remain on the field.

Colonel Webster having driven Lawson from his

front, moved rapidly through the forest in a direct line with the 33d and the Light infantry and Yagers. The Second battalion of Guards were dropped, perhaps, to assist in the assault on Stevens.

Webster soon reached the Bruce road, on the western edge of the old field, in which the Continental line was drawn up.

They were about 200 yards apart at this point of the American line. The hill from either position descends rapidly, and in the valley was a ravine where the water runs in wet weather. The old field had not been in cultivation for some years, and was grown up with weeds, and here and there were small scrubby pines and bushes, but not so as to obstruct the view across it.

Colonel Webster did not stop to count the odds against him, or to wait for the Second battalion of Guards, but immediately sounded the charge in front of the 1st Maryland regiment and Hawes' Virginians. The Americans waited for the charge until the British line was within forty (40) paces of their front, when they poured in upon them a most destructive fire, and followed it up with the "push of the bayonet," as they did at Cowpens. Webster's line at first recoiled, then broke and fled in disorder to the forest, out of which they had emerged.

The Marylanders followed up this brilliant charge until the British troops under Webster were routed and scattered in the forest. Colonel Webster himself received a musket-ball in his knee, from which he died a few weeks thereafter.*

The battle on the American side had so far been a counterpart of Cowpens, and it only remained for Greene to push his victory to completion as Morgan did. To do this, however, would have required a general advance of the whole Continental line. If the movement succeeded, the victory would be complete and glorious, but if his left were to give way, or it should be true, as he then feared, that Campbell had been driven from the field and the Hessians were coming on his flank and rear, then the advance would have been a disaster.

Prudent and cautious, as well as brave and stubborn in fight, Greene determined not to risk his army for glory—not to sacrifice the only remaining army in the South to personal ambition. The conduct of the 2d Maryland soon demonstrated the wisdom of his decision. The 1st Maryland was ordered to fall back to its original strong position on the brow of the hill across the ravine. It had hardly begun this retrograde movement before the Second battalion of Guards, now under Lieutenant Colonel Stuart, O'Hara being wounded, swept around the hill, at the fork of the Bruce road, and moving along the valley, to the right and south of the old Salisbury road, struck the 2d Maryland regiment, under Colonel Ford. Scarcely any resist-

---

*I have in my possession a silver knee buckle, with the initial W on it, found near this spot.

ance was made by this regiment; it is not even said in history that they fired a gun.

Colonel Washington, who was on the ridge above this little valley with his cavalry, witnessed this inglorious flight of the Marylanders. He had with him one company of North Carolina cavalry, forty men, under the Marquis of Bretigny, and a fine company of Virginia volunteer cavalry from Prince Edward, under Captain Thomas Watkins, and in this company was Peter Francisco the giant.*

Washington sounded the bugle for a charge, and pushing down the slope of the ridge, leaped across the branch in his front and rushed in a full gallop upon the rear of the Guards, and passing through, slew them right and left. Lieutenant Holcomb, of Captain Watkins' company, relates "that the strong arm of Francisco leveled three of the enemy during one charge and eleven before the fight was over."

In Foote's Sketches of North Carolina† it is said:

"The carnage was dreadful. At this time it was that Lieutenant Holcomb related to Dr. Jones, of Nottoway, that the noted Francisco performed a deed of blood without a parallel. In that short rencountre he cut down eleven men with his brawny arm and terrible broadsword. One of the Guards thrust his bayonet, and, in spite of the parrying of Francisco's sword, pinned his leg to the horse. Francisco forebore to strike, but assisted him to extricate his bayonet. As the soldier turned and

---

*Foote's Sketches of Virginia, First Series, p. 403.
†Foote's Sketches of North Carolina, p. 278.

fled, he made a furious blow with his sword and cleft the poor fellow's head down to his shoulders."

Washington had hardly passed, like a destroying angel, through this devoted regiment of gallant Englishmen, in this valley of death, before the 1st Maryland arrived on the scene. It wheeled to the south and rushed like a whirlwind on Stuart's left flank, bearing down all before it, slaughtering its victims and piling up its sacrifices as it rolled on. But still Stuart refused to fly. He stood like a lion at bay and repelled the fury of his adversaries. Cornwallis arrived at the fork of the road and looked down upon the struggle with dismay. Then galloping down the hill to the old white oak at its base, (now decaying under the weight of a century of years), looked into the face of the unequal combat. Reascending the hill, he ordered Lieutenant McLeod, who had come up with the artillery, to open with grape-shot upon the mass of struggling soldiers beneath him. O'Hara, who lay bleeding in the road, remonstrated and begged that his men be spared, but Cornwallis was determined and desperate and repeated the order. O'Hara hid his face in his hands and refused to witness the slaughter. The remedy was dreadful and sanguinary, but it was effectual. The combatants separated and the few brave men that escaped the awful carnage came, limping up the hill, for protection behind the guns which had so recently been trained upon them.

Colonel Gunby had been unhorsed early in the charge, and Lieutenant Colonel John Eager Howard,* the same who had handled the regiment so skillfully at Cowpens, took the command. Major Anderson, of this regiment, was killed. Lieutenant Colonel Stuart, of the Guards, was also among the slain. Johnson gives this thrilling account of his death:

"Two combatants particularly attracted the attention of those around them. These were Colonel Stuart of the Guards and Captain John Smith† of the Marylanders, both men conspicuous for nerve and sinew. They had also met before on some occasion, and had vowed that their next meeting should end in blood. Regardless of the bayonets that were clashing around them, they rushed at each other with a fury that admitted of but one result. The quick pass of Stuart's small sword was skillfully put by with the left hand, whilst the heavy sabre of his antagonist cleft the Briton to the spine. In one moment the American was prostrate on the lifeless body of his enemy; and in the next was pressed beneath the weight of the soldier who had brought him to the ground. These are not imaginary incidents—they are related on the best authority."

---

*NOTE.—On the 14th of November, 1781, Greene, writing to a friend about Colonel Howard, said: "He deserves a statue of gold no less than the Roman and Grecian heroes." Colonel Howard was, after the revolution, Governor of Maryland and served in Congress.

†Captain Smith survived the struggle for liberty. I have in my possession a sword exhumed near the scene of this conflict, in 1866, which is undoubtedly the one Colonel Stuart wore. It is beautifully chased with a coat of arms and is of the finest steel. Its scabbard is German silver.

The separation of the combatants enabled General Greene to restore order to his line. The two pieces of artillery, lost at the new Salisbury road, were regained and placed on the left flank in the old Salisbury road. The 1st Maryland was substituted on the left of the line for the 2d Maryland, which had fled. Lynch and Kirkwood formed the centre, with the other two pieces of artillery under Lieutenant Finley. Hawes' and Green's regiments were on the right; Colonel Washington with his cavalry was in the concavity of the semi-circle in the rear.

Webster had rallied on the British left, and had made an unsuccessful charge, on Hawes and Kirkwood, and been repulsed. The remnant of the Second battalion of Guards, though few, had come into line. The 71st and 23d, now disengaged, were coming up on the right. A cannonade and occasional musketry fire were going on across the ravine between the contending forces.

Lee had suddenly left Campbell, without warning, and was now an idle spectator of this scene from the Court-House hill, across Hunting Creek, without notifying Greene of his presence, or offering to cover the flanks.* Tarleton had been sent hurriedly to bring Norton, with the First battalion of Guards, to the field for a final onslaught on the American line, and finding that Campbell was unprotected, had ordered the Hessians to fire, and then rushed on the riflemen under cover of the

*Johnson, vol. 2, p. 14.

smoke and cut them to pieces. Colonel Campbell never forgave Lee this desertion. He retired from Greene's army shortly after in disgust.*

Colonel Campbell, with his Virginia and North Carolina riflemen, were the last to fire a gun on this bloody field, and were still firing when Greene sounded the retreat. They became scattered after the charge of Tarleton upon them, and made their way, as best they could, to the camp of Greene next day.

The American commander, having now lost his militia from the field, and the 2d Maryland also, and Campbell's fate being unknown, and Lee inactive in the fight, perceived that the enemy were about to outnumber him in the charge, which they were preparing, and concluded to save his army by a timely retreat.

Green's regiment of Virginians were thrown in front to hold the line, while Washington covered the retreat through the rear of the old field and across the valley of Hunting Creek, until they came to the high-road leading north to McQuistian's Bridge, on Reedy Fork Creek, three miles distant.

Green checked the feeble pursuit of the enemy, and Washington easily drove Tarleton back to his lines, while General Greene leisurely pursued his retreat to Reedy Fork, where he waited to collect his stragglers and rest his men. He himself was so prostrated by the long and arduous labors

*Draper, p. 394.

24

through which he had been passing for weeks, that, in this hour of relaxation, he fainted from sheer exhaustion, and for awhile was unconscious. He wrote his wife after the battle that he had not taken off his clothes for six weeks.

Lee, though in half a mile of the rear of Greene's retreating army, did not join it, but pursued his own line of retreat by the High Rock Ford road, and came into camp twenty-four hours after Greene.

Cornwallis, who had but little means of transportation, and a very scant supply of provisions and medicines, found his ammunition nearly exhausted, more than one-third of his force (over 600) killed or wounded. Stuart was cold in death; O'Hara and Howard wounded and sick; Webster, the pride of the army, valiant in battle and wise in council, had received a mortal wound; and the mournful spectacle of the dead and dying, on every hand, was enough to dishearten the British commander. He gathered his wounded, as best he could, and buried his dead, and realizing that his only safety was now in flight, he left the field on the 17th, and placing those of his wounded, whom he could not transport, in care of the humane Quakers at New Garden Meeting-House, he hastened to put the Deep River between him and his adversary, and gave no rest to his feet until he reached the fork of that river, with the Haw, at Ramsey's Mill. Here he could burn a bridge behind him on either stream, as necessity required. From thence he fled to Wilmington, leaving the corpse of Webster in North Carolina, near Elizabethtown. He had died near town while swung in a litter between two horses. He literally died in the flight.*

In the evening of the battle the weather turned suddenly cold and a heavy rain began to fall, lasting through the whole night. Many wounded died from the dreadful exposure.

The next morning after the battle, as was the English custom, Cornwallis sent his officers to the few prisoners he had captured with offers of liberty and money, if they would join his service. They

---

*I am indebted to Colonel T. D. McDowell, of Bladen County, for the following account of Colonel Webster's death:

"ELIZABETHTOWN, March 20th, 1888.
"*Hon. D. Schenck:*
"DEAR SIR :—The postmaster has handed me your letter dated in February. I have just received it, and give you what information I can in regard to Colonel Webster.

"It seems in those days the army had no ambulances, as at the present day, and the wounded men were carried on a litter swung between two horses. It was in this manner that Colonel Webster was carried on the retreat from the battle of Guilford Court-House. On ascending the hill at Baker's Creek, five miles above Elizabethtown, it was first discovered that he was dead. The army marched on through the village and camped two miles below on Brown's Creek, on the plantation belonging to the Waddell family. Lord Cornwallis stopped in the village and got his supper.

"Captain James Childs, who was well known to the old citizens of Hillsboro, told me that he was a small boy, and going to the Waddell mill, with a bag of corn on a horse, had to pass along by where the army was camped, and he saw the corpse of Colonel Webster lying on a litter between two pine trees. (I have frequently seen the stumps of the trees.) When the late Judge Toomer was comparatively a young man, he, in company with several other gentlemen, spent a night with Mr. Waddell during our court week, and allusion being made to Colonel Webster, it was proposed that they should dig open the grave (as the spot was well known to an old negro man belonging to the Waddell family). They found the body with the sword lying beside it. It looked quite natural, until a puff of wind scattered it like dust. The exact spot is now known to no one—though it is certain he is buried near the stumps referred to.

"If this information is of any service to you, you are welcome to it.
"Very respectfully,
"THO. D. MCDOWELL."

had been confined all that dreary, rainy, cold night in a rail pen, herded like cattle, and listened to these appeals with silence and sullenness. They were then told that the American army had been routed and Greene had fled from the State, but still these staunch old Whigs, drenched with rain and shivering with cold, maintained their stolid indifference.

Just then the sound of the morning guns from Greene's camp came reverberating from the hills. An old Tar Heel, who had squatted in a corner of the rail pen, heard the familiar signal, and, rising with a smile, he cried out: "LISTEN, BOYS! THE OLD COCK IS CROWING AGAIN," and a shout of defiance went up from the rail pen that convinced the English officer that patriotism, in the old North State, was above the temptation of bribery or the intimidation of British power.

That "old cock" Nathanael Greene, and the "blue hen's chickens" around him, continued to crow until Cornwallis was admonished of his sins and his danger, and prepared for flight.

Eager to meet the American army, which he had been pursuing for two months through mud and rain, thirsting for the glory of annihilating his foe, Cornwallis had marched out from his camp with fluttering banners and martial music to accept the challenge of the American General; he looked with pride on the veteran soldiers of his line and the splendid officers who led them; the half-clad soldiers of the American army and the untutored militia of the State were contemptible in his eyes. The scene at Camden was to be repeated—the militia would flee at his approach, the Continentals would be outnumbered and crushed, and Tarleton would revenge the defeat of Cowpens by putting the retreating masses to the sword; Greene would forsake the field and find a refuge in the mountains of Virginia, and the Royal government would be restored in North Carolina.

These were the exultant visions that floated before his lordship's eyes as he gave the command, "Forward for Guilford Court-House!"

He sought the American army and advanced upon the militia, but he found them in "forty paces, with their rifles resting on the rails," and aiming with the "nicest precision" at his line, and the next moment there was "havoc" in Webster's brigade. He looked to the right and witnessed one-third of the Highlanders drop; he galloped his charger into the midst of the fight, but in a moment was unhorsed by the riflemen on the flank; in fury he rode to the valley where his Guards were weltering in blood, and returned to shoot them down in promiscuous carnage with his own guns; he called for Webster to lead the last charge for victory, but found him in the hands of the surgeon; he looked for O'Hara and saw him bleeding at his side; to the inquiry for General Howard came the response, "wounded and carried to the rear;" gazing anxiously at the Guards, who were emerging from the smoke and carnage under the hill, he missed the stalwart figure of Stuart, now stiff and cold in death. Still he hoped for the realization of his dreams when he saw the Americans turn from the field of blood, and calling for Tarleton, he ordered him to charge the retreating foe. Tarleton came with a rifle-ball through his hand, but was met by Green and Washington and hurled back to his commander with disordered ranks.

The visions of glory had vanished; the truth came rushing over his mind that the victor of this battle was not the man who held the field, and that the ground on which he stood would soon become the scene of his captivity if he tarried to rest his bleeding cohorts.

Greene had lost but three hundred and twenty (320) men, and by the evening of the 17th, he found still around him 1350 Continental soldiers, more than 1500 militia, and the 600 riflemen.

An American officer relates that his compassion was so excited by the pitiable condition of the English army, in their retreat, that he had no heart to strike them a blow. The roadside was strewn with the dead who had vainly tried to drag their wounded bodies along with the retreating army.

The march was tracked by the blood that flowed from the wounds of those who were borne in litters, and here and there a soldier, wounded and forsaken, begged for mercy and protection. When pressed in their camp at Ramsey's Mill, they made a hurried flight across the bridge and burned it behind them. Reaching Cross Creek (now Fayetteville), his lordship expected to glide safely down the Cape Fear in boats; but found Lillington's militia lining the river and ready to pick off his men from every covering on the banks. Sadly he resumed his mournful march and only found safety under his guns at Wilmington.

Cornwallis had boasted, in the spring of 1780, that he was only waiting for the harvest to ripen in North Carolina, to subsist his troops, and he would then hasten to effect its subjection. The harvest had ripened, but his lordship had not garnered the sheaves; he came to the fields of Mecklenburg, but a voice from King's Mountain sent dismay and terror to the hearts of his reapers and they forsook the State.

Another spring had come with its sunshine and warmth, and the earth was waiting for the seed. The furrows were drawn but the sowers were freemen still; the summer came and patriots rested undismayed under the shade of their own vines and fig trees; no royal standard floated over their heads and North Carolina, yet, was free. Georgia and South Carolina were trodden under foot, but the proud hearts of the "Old North State" were never humbled before the British throne. They declared for liberty and maintained it, unsubdued, to the end. The Battle of Guilford Court-House made it impossible that another British soldier should invade her soil, and thenceforth she had peace and rest and a free government for her people.

No longer able to maintain the conflict in the Carolinas, his lordship continued his flight to Yorktown, and before the frosts of October had tinged the leaves of the forest, he marched out of his breastworks an humbled and heart-broken captive, and with the surrender of his army came independence to the colonies.

The fatal wound to royal authority, from which it lingered, and lingering died, on the 19th day of October, 1781, was given at Guilford Court-House on this 15th day of March, 1781.

There are many interesting anecdotes and incidents of this bloody battle preserved by the various writers who have attempted to describe it, each illustrating some characteristics of the struggle or the men who were engaged in it.

Cornwallis had two horses shot under him and made two narrow escapes from death or capture.

Lamb, who was in Webster's brigade on the left, relates the following incident as occurring after Eaton's brigade had retreated and the British were about to assail the front of the Virginians under Lawson:

"On the instant, however, I saw Lord Cornwallis riding across the clear ground. His lordship was mounted on a dragoon's horse, his own having been shot; the saddle-bags were under the creature's belly, which much retarded his progress, owing to the vast quantity of underwood that was spread over the ground; his lordship was evidently unconscious of his danger. I immediately laid hold of the bridle of his horse and turned his head. I then mentioned to him that if his lordship had pursued the same direction he would, in a few moments, have been surrounded by the enemy, and perhaps cut to pieces or captured. I continued to run along the side of the horse, keeping the bridle in my hand, until his lordship gained the 23d regiment, which was at that time drawn up in the skirt of the woods."—*P. 362.*

Tradition fixes the point where the second horse of his lordship was shot as on the right of Lawson's brigade, probably a shot from Lynch's or Kirkwood's men.

"The next escape from danger by Lord Cornwallis, took place at the foot of the steep hill just beyond the fork of the Bruce road, near the ancient white oak which still marks the spot.
"Cornwallis came down from his post at the fork of the Bruce road, to the ravine below, to see the condition of the battle, and under the cover of the smoke, rode up to that old white oak, just in the skirts of the fiery contest. Washington, who had drawn off his troops, was hovering round to watch his opportunity for another onset, and approached that same oak unperceived by his lordship; stopping to beckon on his men to move and intercept the officer, then unknown to him, he happened to strike his unlaced helmet from his head. While he dismounted to recover it, a round of grape from the British artillery so greviously wounded the officer next in command to Washington, that, incapacitating him to manage his horse, the animal wheeled around and carried him off the field, followed by the rest of the cavalry, who,

unhappily, supposed that the movement had been directed. Thus Cornwallis escaped."

General Greene was not exempt from peril during this sanguinary battle. Johnson relates his escape during the conflict with the Continental line, as follows:

"Such also had been the apprehensions for the consequences of the defeat of the second battalion of the Guards, that the first battalion had been ordered up from the left and had reached the New Garden road, on which Greene was anxiously observing the progress of events. The bush on the roadside had so effectually concealed the advance of this corps from view that General Greene had approached within a few paces of them, when they were discovered by his aid, Major Morris, and pointed out to him. He had the presence of mind to retire in a walk; a precipitate movement would, probably, have drawn upon him a volley of musketry."

The death of Colonel Arthur Forbis was tragical and cruel. After he had fallen with two bullets, one in the neck, the other in his leg, and after he had endured all the horrors of that dreadful night of cold and rain, a Tory by the name of Shoemaker, a weaver from the neighborhood of Alamance, who was plundering, came near to Forbis, who begged him for water. Shoemaker, recognizing him, cursed him and thrust at him with a bayonet, which passed entirely through his leg. Another Tory, more humane, brought water in his hat and administered to the famishing soldier.

On the same day, Miss Montgomery, who was searching for her brother, discovered Colonel Forbis, and helping him on her horse, she held the bridle, and led the horse towards home. At a point near where Holt's Chapel now is, two miles east of Greensboro, they were met by the wife of Colonel Forbis, who was starting to look for him. She did not recognize the pallid face and sunken eyes of him who was so dear to her, when in a feeble voice he said, "Bettie, don't you know me?"

Colonel Forbis was carried to his home, and Doctor Caldwell, both a Doctor of medicine and of divinity, with his son, attended him. They insisted on amputating the leg, but the Colonel replied: "I want all my body to be buried together," and refused. He lived three weeks. His remains are buried in the cemetery at Alamance Church, five miles south of Greensboro. The citizens of Guilford County erected a handsome marble monument over his grave, and a granite monument has been erected by the "Guilford Battle-Ground Company," who own the battle-ground, on the battle-field, to his memory. He was not more than thirty-five years old when killed. "Shoemaker" was soon found at his home, one night, by the Whigs and hanged to a tree near an old church. The door of the old church was used as a litter to convey his body to his family.

Cornwallis makes the following official report of his losses in this battle:

"Return of the Killed, Wounded and Missing of the Troops under the Command of Lieutenant General Earl Cornwallis, in the Action at Guilford, March 15th, 1781.

"*Royal Artillery*—One Lieutenant, one rank and file, killed; four rank and file wounded.

"*Brigade of Guards*—One Lieutenant Colonel, eight Sergeants, twenty-eight rank and file, killed; two Brigadier Generals, six Captains, one Ensign, one staff officer, two Sergeants, two drummers, one hundred and forty-three rank and file, wounded; twenty-two rank and file missing.

"*23d Foot*—One Lieutenant, twelve rank and file, killed; one Captain, one Sergeant, fifty-three rank and file, wounded.

"*33d Foot*—One Ensign, one Sergeant, nine rank and file, killed; one Lieutenant Colonel, two Lieutenants, three Ensigns, one staff officer, one Sergeant, fifty-five rank and file, wounded.

"*71st Foot*—One Ensign, one Sergeant, eleven rank and file, killed; four Sergeants, forty-six rank and file, wounded.

"*Regiment of Bose*—Three Sergeants, seven rank and file, killed; two Captains, two Lieutenants, one Ensign, six Sergeants, three drummers, fifty-three rank and file, wounded; one Sergeant, two rank and file, missing.

"*Yagers*—Four rank and file, killed; three rank and file, wounded; one rank and file, missing.

"*British Legion*—Three rank and file, killed; one Lieutenant Colonel, one Sergeant, twelve rank and file, wounded.

"*Total*—One Lieutenant Colonel, two Lieutenants,

two Ensigns, thirteen Sergeants, seventy-five rank and file, killed; two Brigadier Generals, two Lieutenant Colonels, nine Captains, four Lieutenants, five Ensigns, two staff officers, fifteen Sergeants, five drummers, three hundred and sixty-nine rank and file, wounded; one Sergeant, twenty-five rank and file, missing.

"OFFICERS: NAMES KILLED AND WOUNDED.

"*1st Royal Artillery*—Lieutenant O'Hara, killed.

"*Brigade of Guards*—Honorable Lieutenant Colonel Stuart, killed; Brigadier Generals O'Hara and Howard and Captain Swanton, wounded; Captains Schultz, Maynard and Goodricke, wounded, and since dead; Captains Lord Douglass and Maitland, Ensign Stewart and Adjutant Colquhoun, wounded.

"*23d Foot*—Second Lieutenant Robinson, killed; Captain Peter, wounded.

"*33d Foot*—Ensign Talbot, killed; Lieutenant Colonel Webster (since dead), Lieutenants Salvin, Wynyard, Ensigns Kelly, Gore and Hughes, and Adjutant Fox, wounded.

"*71st Foot*—Ensign Grant, killed.

"*Regiment Bose*—Captains Wilmousky (since dead), Eichendrobt, Lieutenants Schwener and Graife, Ensign de Trott (since dead), wounded.

"*British Legion*—Lieutenant Col. Tarleton, wounded.

"J. DESPARD,
"*Deputy Adjutant General.*"

Cornwallis also reports that he captured four brass cannons, six-pounders, mounted on traveling carriages, with limbers and boxes complete.

Of the British officers wounded, the following died: Colonel Webster, Captains Schultz, Maynard and Goodricke. General O'Hara was so badly wounded that his recovery was long in doubt. General Leslie's health gave way under the exposure and fatigue, and he was obliged to retire a long time from service. General Howard, who was without a regular command, it seems, was only slightly wounded. Colonel Tarleton received a rifle-ball through his right hand (his unlucky member) in the morning encounter.

Johnson says that "the American killed and wounded could never be ascertained with precision. That the returns of the day could furnish no correct idea on the subject, for one-half the North Carolina militia, and a large number of the Virginians, never halted after separating from their officers, but pushed on to their homes."

This proportion of the North Carolina and Virginia militia is too large. It is based on the reports made on the 17th, and many of these men came in afterwards. The North Carolina militia, being nearer home, could the more easily return. The Virginians left by whole companies, in the face of raging officers, and, Mr. Houston says, they hid in the mountains, so that for years they feared the approach of officers.

The North Carolinians, whose term of service was only six weeks, and four of which had expired, supposed they would escape censure and punishment; but they were mistaken in this. The law followed them and brought them back to service, where, as we will see in the sequel, they became brave and disciplined soldiers, who wiped out their disgrace in blood, and returned, after twelve months (such of them as did not sleep under the sod of South Carolina and Georgia), crowned with honors and welcomed with the plaudits of their fellow-citizens. They added training to courage and made the best of soldiers.

It is probable that Greene's loss was about three hundred besides the militia.

The American commander having collected his stragglers and rested his soldiers an hour or two, continued his march to the Iron Works, on Troublesome Creek, where he was soon after joined by Lee.

The next day the soldiers were all in the best of spirits and anxious to be led again against the enemy, some to acquire more glory, others to retrieve the reputation that they had lost. Greene, however, knew that his enemy was fatally wounded, and that his losses would compel a retreat instead of a pursuit, and spent his time in reorganizing his little army, preparing ammunition and getting ready to follow the British forces.

While he is resting we may contemplate the splendid results of this fatal blow to British prestige and power in North Carolina, and its bearing on the subsequent military events which followed.

Stedman wrote "that a victory achieved under such disadvantages of numbers and ground was of the most honorable kind, and placed the bravery and discipline of the troops beyond all praise; *but* the expense at which it was obtained rendered it of no utility."

Tarleton says: "The position and strength of General Greene at the Iron Works, on Troublesome Creek, did not invite the approach of the British army; Earl Cornwallis, therefore, commenced his march on the 18th* for Deep River, on his way to Cross Creek."

Fox, in the British Parliament, contended that the victory was Greene's. He argued that "if the British army had been vanquished, they could only have left the field and fled to the coast, precisely the measure Cornwallis was compelled to adopt," and exclaimed, "Another such victory would destroy the British army!"

Senator Benton, in his eulogy on Nathaniel Macon, the great Commoner, who was a soldier under Greene up to February, 1781, takes occasion to discuss the historical results of this battle. It is so lucidly and eloquently told that I offer no apology for incorporating it in my narrative:

"In the year 1778 the Southern States had become a battle-field, big with their own fate, and possibly involving the issue of the war. British fleets and armies appeared there, strongly supported by the British cause; and the conquest of the South was fully counted upon. Help was needed in these States; and Mr. Macon, quitting college, returned to his native county in North Carolina, joined a militia company as a private, and marched to South Carolina, then the theatre of the enemy's

*He sent off his wounded on the 17th.

operations. He had his share in all the hardships and disasters of that trying time; was at the fall of Fort Moultrie, surrender of Charleston, defeat at Camden, and in the rapid winter retreat across the upper part of North Carolina. He was in the camp on the left bank of the Yadkin when the sudden flooding of that river, in the brief interval between the crossing of the Americans and the coming up of the British, arrested the pursuit of Cornwallis, and enabled Greene to allow some rest to his wearied and exhausted men. In this camp, destitute of everything and with gloomy prospects ahead, a summons came to Mr. Macon from the Governor of North Carolina, requiring him to attend a meeting of the General Assembly, of which he had been elected a member, without his knowledge, by the people of his county. He refused to go, and the incident being talked of through the camp, came to the knowledge of the General. Greene was a *man* himself, and able to know a *man*. He felt at once that if this report was true, this young soldier was no common character, and determined to verify the fact. He sent for the young man, inquired of him, heard the truth, and then asked for the reason of this unexpected conduct—this preference for a suffering camp over a comfortable seat in the General Assembly. Mr. Macon answered him, in his quaint and sententious way, that he had seen the faces of the British many times, but had never seen their backs, and meant to stay in the army till he did.

"Greene instantly saw the material the young man was made of, and the handle by which he was to be worked. That material was patriotism; that handle a sense of duty; and laying hold of this handle, he quickly worked the young soldier into a different conclusion from the one that he had arrived at. He told him he could do more good as a member of the General Assembly than as a soldier; that in the army he was but one man, and in the General Assembly he might obtain many, with the supplies they needed, by showing the destitution and suffering which he had seen in the camp; and that it was his duty to go. This view of duty and usefulness was decisive. Mr. Macon obeyed the Governor's summons; and by his representations contributed to obtain the supplies which enabled Greene to turn back and face Cornwallis, fight him, cripple him, drive him further back than he had advanced (for Wilmington is south of Camden), disable him from remaining in the South (of which, up to the battle of Guilford, he believed himself to be master), and sending him to Yorktown, where he was captured, and the war ended.

"The philosophy of history has not yet laid hold of the battle of Guilford, its consequences and effects. *That battle made the capture at Yorktown.* The events are told in every history; their connection and dependence in none. It broke up the plan of Cornwallis in the South and changed the plan of Washington in the North. Cornwallis was to subdue the Southern States, and was doing it, until Greene turned upon him at Guilford. Washington was occupied with Sir Henry Clinton, then in New York, with 12,000 British troops. He had formed the heroic design to capture Clinton and his army (the French fleet co-operating) in that city, and thereby putting an end to the war. All his preparations were going on for that grand consummation when he got the news of the battle of Guilford, the retreat of Cornwallis to Wilmington, his inability to keep the field in the South, and his return northward through the lower part

BATTLE MONUMENT 1888. FLAG POLE. KEEPER'S LODGE. CANNON MADE IN 1774.
BATTLE-FIELD OF GUILFORD COURT HOUSE SEPTEMBER 9-1889.

of Virginia. He saw his advantage—an easier prey, and the same result if successful. Cornwallis or Clinton, either of them, captured, would put an end to the war. Washington changed his plan, deceived Clinton, moved rapidly upon the weaker general, captured him and his 7,000 men, and ended the Revolutionary War. *The battle of Guilford put that capture into Washington's hands;* and thus Guilford and Yorktown became connected; and the philosophy of history shows their dependence, and that the lesser event was father to the greater.

"The State of North Carolina gave General Greene 25,000 acres of western land for that day's work, now worth a million of dollars; but the day itself has not yet obtained its proper place in American history."—*Benton's Thirty Years in the U. S. Senate, p. 115.*

I shall reserve for the next chapter the further movements of General Greene and the vigorous measures adopted by North Carolina to prosecute the war.

It is gratifying to close this chapter with the freedom of North Carolina from British invasion, which never again desecrated her soil.

CHAPTER VIII.

The Retreat of Cornwallis from Guilford Court-House—Pursued by General Greene—Disbandment of the Militia—Colonel James Read's Command from North Carolina Remains with Greene—The Militia who Fled from Guilford Court-House Reorganized as Part of the Continental Line under Major Pinketham Eaton—Battle of Hobkirk's Hill—Fall of the British Outposts—Splendid Courage and Dash of the North Carolinians at Augusta, June 5th, 1781—Death of Major Eaton—Greene Retires to the High Hills of Santee, 16th July, 1781.

THE "Speedwell Iron Works," on Troublesome Creek, was the camp of General Greene, to which he retired, reaching there on the morning of Friday, the 16th of March, 1781. He remained here until the morning of Tuesday, the 20th of March.

The disorder and derangement incident to such a fierce and sanguinary battle had to be repaired. The Americans carried their powder and lead and bullet moulds along with the army and manufactured their cartridges in the camp. Greene had lost his two ammunition wagons and the remnant of cartridges contained in them, and one of the first duties of his soldiers was to mould musket and rifle balls for the next battle.

The second duty was to reorganize his Virginia and North Carolina militia, who had only been called out for a six weeks' "tour." Much of this short time had already expired, and he could not hope to retain them long. The North Carolina militia who had fled from the field after the battle and went to their homes, which lay in a day or two of march from the battle-field, were about four hundred and fifty or five hundred. Some few had reported after the main army reached the camp. About five hundred and fifty Virginians fled from the field who never returned, and after they reached the camp they left by regiments, while their commanders were "raging" at their perfidy. Every one of Colonel McDowell's[*] regiment of Virginians left in this way, but the gallant Colonel adhered to Greene after his men were gone.

Mr. Houston, in his Diary, gives a most amusing account of this stampede, or, to use the ingenious circumlocution of Colonel Lee, this "voluntary and customary return of the Virginians to their homes."

Generals Butler and Eaton were immediately sent after the recreant North Carolinians, and the remainder were, it seems, attached to Colonel Read's volunteer corps and marched with General Greene in pursuit of Cornwallis. March the 21st, Greene writes to Colonel Lee, whom he had thrown forward to gain intelligence:

"Your letter, dated at New Garden yesterday, has this moment been received. Our army marched yesterday in the direct route for Magee's Ordinary, near the headwaters of Rocky River, which will be twelve miles from Bell's Mill. We expect to get two or three miles beyond

[*] Close kinsman of the North Carolina McDowells.

Passley to-night. We have got provisions to draw, cartridges to make, and several other matters to attend to, which will oblige us to halt a little earlier than common. I beg you will try to forward me the best intelligence you can get of the enemy's situation this morning and whether they move or not. *I mean to fight the enemy again*, and wish you to have your Legion and riflemen ready for action on the shortest notice. Lord Cornwallis must be soundly beaten before he will release his hold."

This was the spirit of the American commander, and demonstrated that he was the real victor at Guilford and was ready to renew the combat, while his antagonist was using every artifice to avoid the contest and, redeeming the time in rapid retreat, always keeping a stream between him and his pursuer.

Cornwallis at first crossed to the southwestern bank of the Deep River, as if he intended to march for Salisbury, but suddenly recrossing that stream, he moved down its eastern bank, having the Haw River to his left and the Deep River to his right, and nearing their junction at Ramsey's Mill. Arriving here, he threw a temporary bridge across the Deep River, there being one already across the Haw, so that if the American army pressed him he could retreat by either outlet and burn the bridge behind him. Here at Ramsey's Mill he paused to reorganize his forces and repair his damage as much as possible and to gather what provisions he could for his further retreat. He had left the wounded American prisoners at Guilford Court-House, and those of his own wounded who could not be transported, about eighty, at New Garden Meeting-House. The British army had neither courage nor spirit left. Their condition was mournful indeed, and all their energies were directed to the one idea of reaching a port of safety.

On the 30th day of March the terms of service of the Virginia and North Carolina militia expired and they insisted on their discharge. General Greene was much distressed over this loss, but seeing it inevitable, under the call of enlistment, submitted as gracefully as possible, and returning his thanks to those who had adhered to him, they were allowed to return to their homes. Colonel Read, of North Carolina, who commanded a volunteer force of two hundred men, spoken of in a former page, was the only North Carolina organization which voluntarily remained with the American commander and continued to share with him in the subsequent successful campaign in South Carolina.

It seems very difficult to trace the history of this command. I find the following letter from Colonel James Read to General Sumner, dated February 27th, 1781, from "Miller's tavern":

"Since I had the pleasure of seeing you at Halifax, the Assembly honored me with the command of a regiment of horse. As I had your approbation to accept a command in the militia, I did not think it necessary to trouble you about this command particularly."

This is the only communication I can find in regard to it, either by Colonel Read or any one else.

On the 29th March, General Greene writes General Washington:

"In this critical and distressing situation I am determined to carry the war directly into South Carolina. The enemy will be obliged to follow us or give up his posts in that State. If the former takes place, it will draw the war out of this State and give it an opportunity to raise its proportion of men. If they leave their posts to fall, they must lose more than they can gain here. If we continue in this State the enemy will hold their possessions in both."

Colonel Hampton, of South Carolina, had visited Greene at the Iron Works, and made him acquainted with the condition of affairs in South Carolina, and urged him to return to that State.

Before entering upon another campaign, however, General Greene deemed it proper to give a short repose to his wearied troops and to gather supplies for that part of his journey which lay through a comparatively barren country between the Yadkin and Camden, and consequently the American commander did not renew his march until the 6th of April,* the day before Cornwallis reached Wilmington.

Neither was General Greene unmindful of the vicissitudes of war and the necessity of providing a line of retreat and stores for his army, should he be forced to seek shelter again in North Carolina. It was this provident characteristic that enabled

*Lee's Memoirs, p. 325.

him to make his former wonderful retreat before the British army. To Colonel Wm. R. Davie, his Commissary General, was intrusted the important service of collecting magazines on the banks of the Catawba, and measures were adopted for establishing a considerable depot at Oliphant's Mill.*

As all the artillery was lost, Captain Singleton was dispatched to Prince Edward Court-House, Virginia, to obtain whatever pieces could be procured from that quarter.

Perhaps it will be appropriate here, before tracing the progress of Greene, to record something of the North Carolina militia who "deserted their colors" and "returned" to their homes; for these same men will make a conspicuous figure in the history which is to follow.

During the administration of Governor Nash, the Legislature of North Carolina passed an act to punish those of her citizens who refused to perform the military duty required of them. It provided that—

---

*On Tarleton's Military Map, Oliphant's Mill is located in Iredell County, North Carolina, where Buffalo Creek runs into the Catawba River, on the present Western North Carolina Railroad; but the Hon. Wm. M. Robbins, who has made some research, for the author, as to its location, can hear of no tradition of a mill of any kind at this point. But on the opposite side of the Catawba River, in Catawba County, on Ball's Creek, there was, many years ago, Iron Works, which continued to a recent period of time, and I am much inclined to the opinion that Oliphant's Mill was located at this Iron Works, which would be an appropriate place for the repair of arms and the storage of provisions.

"Those persons who have been lawfully drafted and have neglected or refused to march and go into actual service on due notice, or find a substitute, as is therein directed, shall be held and deemed *a Continental soldier for twelve months;* and that those persons who have deserted their colors, when in actual service, shall be held and deemed a Continental soldier during the war."*

William Hooper writes Mr. Iredell on the 29th day of March, 1781, from Halifax, North Carolina, that—

"'The Council Extraordinary' have passed an order to take from every inhabitant a fifth part of his provision for the use of the army; *and that every man who abandoned his post in the last action, should be enrolled in the Continental army for twelve months.*"

On the 6th day of April, 1781, Thomas Gilchrist writes to Mr. Iredell from Halifax, North Carolina, that—

"Part of the scattered militia from Guilford Court-House were rendezvousing here at the time your letter came to hand by one of them (a captain). These militia are now marched under the command of Colonel Linton and are sentenced to twelve months' duty, as Continentals, for their desertion."

On the 13th of April, Major Pinketham Eaton writes General Sumner from Chatham Court-House:

*Johnson, vol. 2, p. 181.

"I this day received of Lieutenant Colonel William Linton, one hundred and seventy (170) men turned over into the Continental service, but am without a single officer to assist me. I shall, by General Greene's orders, march them immediately to headquarters."

On the 11th of April, General Butler writes General Sumner from Ramsey's Mill:

"We have now in the field 240 men of those who fled from the field on the 15th ulto. They are for one year, and will in a few days join headquarters. My orders were to inform you from time to time of their numbers, in order that you might send on as many officers as are necessary to command them. Major P. Eaton, Captain James Read, Captain Yarborough and Lieutenant John Campbell, are in service and mean to continue, with your leave."*

In less than one month after the battle these men had been collected for duty. They were neither cowards, as we shall see, nor did they avoid arrest or flee from the State; they were undisciplined men, who returned to their homes instead of their camp. They were ashamed of their conduct and willing to redeem their reputations. We shall soon find them organized as Continental soldiers under the gallant and ill-fated Eaton.

The Continental Congress had passed an act, after the compression of the regiments, in May, 1778, requiring North Carolina to raise four (4)

*These are the titles and rank held in the Continental line.

more regiments or battalions for the Continental service, for twelve months. Brigadier General Sumner, of Warren County, was given the command of this new brigade, and the Continental officers who had lost their positions by the "compression," and those who might be exchanged from prison, were to be assigned to duty in these regiments. General Sumner entered upon this important duty with systematic energy and patriotic spirit. These regiments were to be raised by volunteering, or, if this failed, by draft.

A rendezvous, for these levies, was appointed in the several districts of Wilmington, Newbern, Halifax, Hillsboro and Salisbury, and the militia officers were ordered to assemble their commands and return their respective quotas and have them in readiness by the 25th April, 1781.

The voluminous correspondence of General Sumner with Colonel Nicholas Long, the Commissary General of the State, Major Eaton, Colonel Hal. Dixon, General Butler and numerous subordinate officers, discloses the insuperable difficulties which prevented the consummation of this plan at that time; want of arms and clothing being the greatest, while other parts of the State were disloyal and refused to respond. In the meantime, General Sumner, anxious to render service to his country, had offered to command a brigade of militia under Greene, but for some unfortunate and inexplicable reason the offer was declined.

One of the four regiments was to have been

cavalry, but no effort, it seems, was made to raise it. The total inability of the State to equip cavalry was probably the reason for abandoning it.

In a letter of General Sumner's, without date, he alludes to the fact that General Greene had instructed him to make "an arrangement for the Continental line," and "that he had met the officers of the State, who could convene at Halifax the 23d January, 1781, but the difficulty of making the formation, at this time, was that the dates of the officers' commissions who were in captivity could not be procured. However, they had formed a *temporary* arrangement of the officers present to receive the four regiments ordered to be raised by the State. Since the arrival* of the officers who were in captivity we have been as expeditious as desirous in making a re-arrangement of the line of officers. Colonel James Armstrong, Colonel Gideon Lamb, Lieutenant Colonel James Thackston, Lieutenant Colonel William Lee Davidson, Captain Micajah Lewis and Captain Francis Childs resigned, to be recommended by the board of officers, at Halifax, to Congress, to permit them to retire on half pay. Lieutenant Colonel Wm. Lee Davidson, Colonel Gideon Lamb and Captain Micajah Lewis are since dead."

February 24th, 1781, General Sumner writes General Greene that he

*In June, 1781.

"Had sent expresses to Colonel Ashe* and Major Murfree†, who were, by the *temporary* arrangement of the officers of the North Carolina line, present in the State, to take charge of two of the regiments, to acquaint them without delay that it was your wish that they join the militia camp to render such assistance as may be in their power. Major Dixon‡ and Major Armstrong‖ are to take charge of the other two regiments. Major Dixon is in your camp, who is Inspector General of militia, and promised me to join that camp upon a general rendezvous. Major Armstrong is with the forces from the district of Salisbury. A large number of the officers of the State are, to my knowledge, already in the militia camp."

I quote this letter entire, so far as it refers to the organization of the regular troops, to show the changes that afterwards occurred; for when the three regiments moved, in July, they were commanded respectively by Colonel John B. Ashe and Majors John Armstrong and Reading Blount, as General Sumner's correspondence shows. How it was that Murfree did not reach the rendezvous from Newbern, or did not take the command assigned him, I am not able to solve.

While General Sumner was still exerting all his power to collect the new levies and provide them with arms, Major Pinketham Eaton, who was at or near the camp of General Butler, on Deep River, was ordered to march and join the army under General Greene, with the, now, re-assembled militia

*John B. Ashe. †Hardy Murfree.
‡"Hal" Dixon. ‖John Armstrong.

from Guilford Court-House, and we will have to trace their history as a part of that magnificent little army which was, so soon, to redeem South Carolina and Georgia from the British power.

1781. On the 17th day of April, Major Dixon, as Inspector General, was ordered to forward two subaltern officers to Major Eaton, "who was informed that more of the militia were on their way to his command."

Eaton was detained until about the 23d of April before he began his march to South Carolina, and did not reach General Greene until about the 16th of May, when his command was attached to Lee's Legion as one of the corps which was to act against Augusta.*

On the 6th day of April, General Greene detached Colonel Lee, with orders to seek General Marion and make a junction with his forces. He was directed, however, to follow in the track of Cornwallis as far as Cross Creek, in order to produce the impression that the American army would follow in that direction to Wilmington.

From Cross Creek, Lee moved east rapidly, then south, crossing Drowning Creek, then by Marion Court-House to Pope's Ferry, on the Great Pee Dee, where, on the 14th day of April, he formed a junction with General Marion. Marion furnished the boats, which he had concealed, to cross the stream, and with their joint force they made a hurried march almost west to Fort Watson, on the

*Johnson's Life of Greene, vol. 2, p. 126.

Santee, below Camden and below the confluence of the Wateree and Santee.

On the 7th day of April, General Greene crossed the Deep River with his army and moved west in a direct line to Mark's Ferry on the Yadkin; then south, crossing Rocky River and Lynch's Creek, to Camden, which vicinity he reached on the 19th day of April.

Lord Rawdon, who was in command of that post with 900 men, had been informed by the numerous Tories in that State of General Greene's approach, and, much to Greene's surprise, had six days' notice of his coming and had called in detachments from the Saluda and Broad until his force was fully equal to Greene's army. In addition, he had strengthened his fortifications so that it was impossible to take them by storm. Nothing was left but to set down and endeavor to entice the British commander into battle. With this view, on the 20th, Greene advanced to a hill on the Waxhaw road, in half mile of Rawdon's breastworks, but the challenge was not accepted. He then moved his army one and a quarter miles and took post on a rising ground of moderate elevation, known by the name of "Hobkirk's Hill," with his left covered by an impassable branch and his right approaching a thicket almost impenetrable.

General Greene had lost his four six-pounder cannons at Guilford Court-House, all he had, but "order had been taken for procuring from Oliphant's Mill, at the head-waters of the Catawba, two pieces that had been forwarded to that place for repair." One of these he sent to Marion, who had advanced towards Camden, on the fall of Fort Watson (which was the 23d), in order to intercept the approach of Colonel Watson's force, which was marching to reinforce Rawdon. Greene, unfortunately, was too confident of the power of General Marion and Colonel Lee to prevent that officer from getting into Camden, if Marion could have a piece of artillery to counteract the artillery of Watson. I state this with some precision, because Greene has been much criticised for parting with this artillery, which he needed so badly at Hobkirk's Hill. General Greene also knew that Colonel Harrison was on his way from Prince Edward Court-House with two other pieces of artillery; these reached him on the 23d. The piece of artillery intended for Marion was sent to Rugeley's Mill, under escort of the North Carolina militia of Read's command. These troops General Greene designed to send as a reinforcement to General Marion, and Colonel Carrington, in order to get them together at a safe spot, retired eight miles further off than Rugeley's Mill, at a place called Upton's Mill, and this made it difficult for Greene to communicate with him. The consequences of this mistake, on the part of Carrington, who was in command of this detached corps, exhibited themselves in the hurry in camp, on the morning of the battle, which occurred on the 25th.

I take from Johnson, page 77, the following estimate and classification of Greene's force. He says:

"The whole regular infantry of the American army, at the battle of Hobkirk's Hill, was 843 present and fit for duty. The cavalry consisted of two regiments, White's and Washington's, but actually it numbered only 87, and 56 only of these were mounted. The artillery also nominally constituted a regiment, and was commanded by Colonel Harrison in person; but actually there were not men enough to fight three pieces; after detaching Finley, not above 40. *The only militia force then with the army consisted of* 254 *North Carolinians.* One hundred and fifty of these, under Colonel Read, had joined Greene soon after he recrossed the Dan, and *had faithfully adhered to him from that time.* They were volunteers, men of the first respectability, and much might have been expected of them in action. The rest had escorted the supplies sent to the army by Colonel Davie."

Perhaps the most intelligible account of this battle is given by Colonel Lee. He was not a participant, and could, therefore, be impartial to all. I give his account in the following words:

"The position of Greene was upon a ridge covered with uninterrupted wood, the Waxhaws road running directly through it; his army resting with its left upon the swamp of Pine Tree Creek, where the ridge or eminence was easiest of ascent, and extending to the right to woods uncovered by water-courses or any other obstructions. In this quarter the American position was easiest assailed, but the probability of an undiscovered approach was not so encouraging. Therefore, Lord Rawdon preferred the route to our left, inasmuch as an

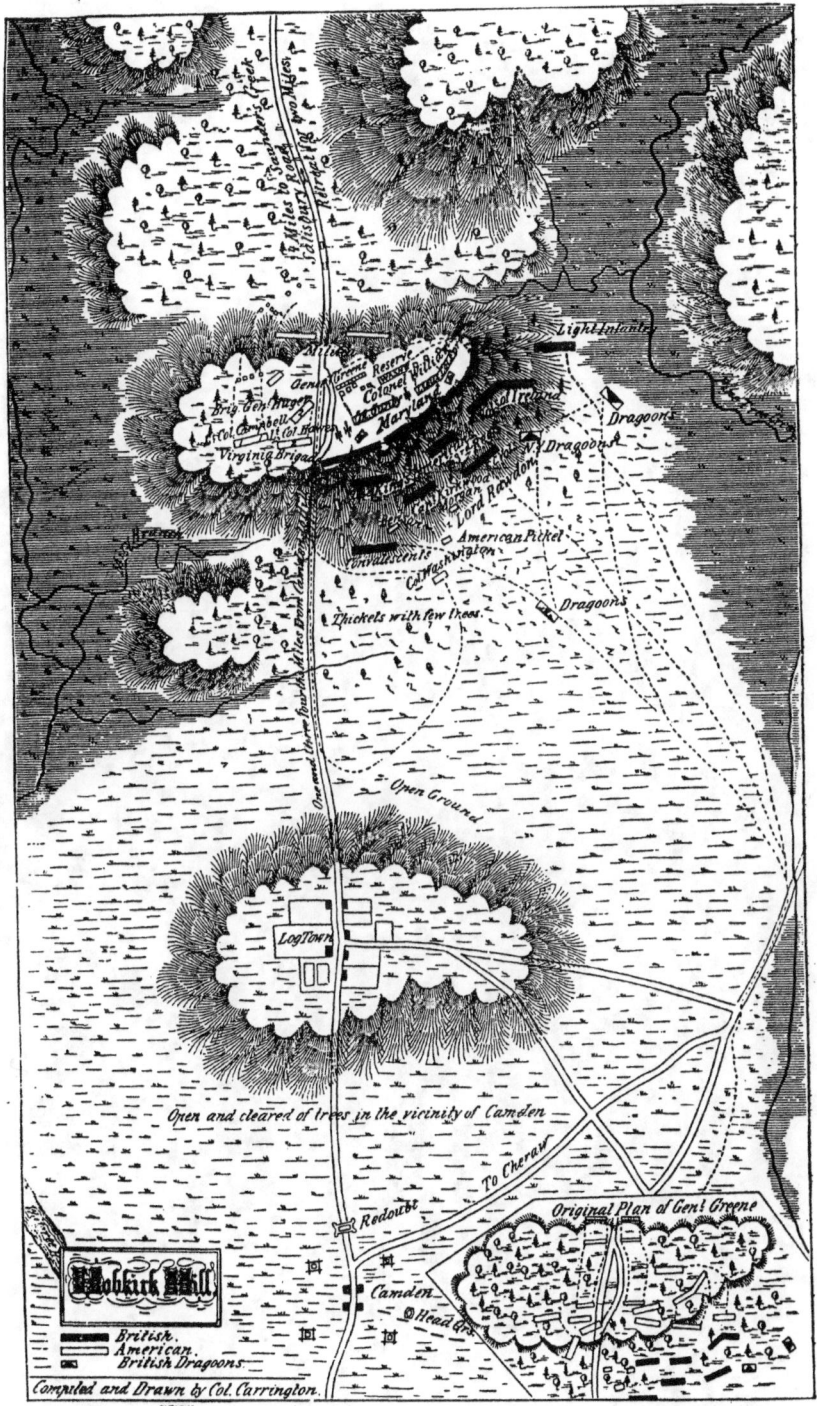

unexpected assault upon our camp was a leading feature in his plan.

"In the morning Carrington joined, with a comfortable supply of provisions, which had been rather scarce during the late hurried changes of position. These were issued, and, of course, engaged a portion of the troops, while the residue were employed along the rivulets in washing their clothes, an occupation which had been for some days past impracticable.

"Absorbed in these employments, the period was very propitious to the enemy's object. His advance was never discovered until his van fell upon our pickets. The two in front commanded by Captain Benson, of Maryland, and Captain Morgan, of Virginia, received him handsomely; and, retiring in order, disputed bravely every inch of ground, supported by Kirkwood with the remains of the Delaware regiment. This rencounter gave the first announcement of the contest at hand. Disposed for battle by the order of encampment, the American army, notwithstanding its short notice, was quickly ranged for action—an event, although unexpected, of all others the most desirable; because, in all probability, the readiest for the production of that issue so anxiously coveted by the American General.

"During the contest with the pickets, Greene formed his army. The Virginia brigade, with General Huger at its head, having under him the Lieutenant Colonels Campbell and Hawes, took the right; the Maryland brigade, led by Colonel Williams, seconded by Colonel Gunby, and the Lieutenant Colonels Ford and Howard, occupied the left. Thus all the Continentals, consisting of four regiments, much reduced in strength, were disposed in one line, with the artillery, conducted by Colonel

Harrison, in the centre. The reserve consisted of the cavalry, under Lieutenant Colonel Washington, with a corps of North Carolina militia, about two hundred and fifty, commanded by Colonel Read.

"The British General, pushing before him the pickets and Kirkwood, pressed forward to battle. The king's American regiment on the right, the New York volunteers in the centre, and the sixty-third on the left, formed the line of battle. His right wing was supported by Robertson's corps, and his left by the volunteers of Ireland. The reserve consisted of the South Carolina regiment, with a few dragoons, all the cavalry then at Camden. Greene, examining attentively the British disposition, discovered the very narrow front which it presented, and gratified as he was with the opportunity, so unexpectedly offered, of completing, by one blow, his first object, he determined to avail himself of the advantage given by the mode of attack.

"He directed Lieutenant Colonels Campbell and Ford to turn the enemy's flank; he ordered the centre regiments to advance with fixed bayonets upon him ascending the height; and detached Lieutenant Colonel Washington with his cavalry to gain his rear. Rawdon no sooner cast his eyes on our disposition than he perceived the danger to which his unequal front exposed him, and bringing up the volunteers of Ireland into line, he remedied the defect, seized by Greene, in time to avert the expected consequence.

"The battle opened from right to left with a vigor which promised a keen and sanguinary contest; but the superiority of our fire, augmented by that from our well-served artillery, must have borne down all opposition, had the American line maintained itself with becoming firmness. On the right Huger evidently gained ground; Washington was carrying everything before him in the rear, and Lieutenant Colonel Hawes, with fixed bayonets, conformable to order, was descending the hill ready to fall upon the New York volunteers.

"In this flattering movement, the veteran regiment of Gunby, having first joined in the fire, in violation of orders, paused; its right falling back. Gunby unfortunately directed the disordered battalion to rally by retiring to its right company. Retrograde being the consequence of this order, the British line, giving a shout, pressed forward with redoubled ardor; and the regiment of Gunby, considered as the bulwark of the army, never recovered from the panic with which it was at this moment unaccountably seized. The Virginia brigade, and the second regiment of Maryland, with the artillery, notwithstanding the shameful abandonment by the first Maryland, maintained the contest bravely. Williams and Gunby, assisted by Lieutenant Colonel Howard, who had so often and so gloriously borne down with this very regiment all opposition, vainly exerted themselves to bring it to order. Not the menaces of the one, nor the expostulations of the other, and the exhortations of the third, not the recollection of its pristine fame, could arouse its cowering spirit. The second Maryland, which had from the commencement of the action acted with gallantry, feeling severely the effect produced by the recession of the first, became somewhat deranged; and Lieutenant Colonel Ford being unluckily wounded while endeavoring to repress the beginning disorder, this corps also fell back.

"Rawdon's right now gained the summit of the eminence, flanking Hawes' regiment, which had undeviatingly held its prescribed course, although early in the action abandoned on its left by the first Maryland, and now but feebly sustained on the right by the first Virginia—for this corps had now begun to recede, notwithstanding its preceding success. Greene recalled Hawes, our only unbroken regiment, and finding every effort to reinstate the battle illusory, wisely determined to diminish the ills of the sad and unaccountable reverse by retiring from the field. Orders were given to this effect, and Lieutenant Colonel Hawes was commanded to cover the broken line.

"The retreat was performed without loss, although the enemy continued to pursue for a few miles. Washington, with his cavalry, retiring from the rear the moment he discovered that our infantry had been forced, came in time to contribute greatly to the safety of the army, having necessarily relinquished most of the fruits of his success. Checking the enemy's efforts to disturb our rear, he at length, by a rapid charge, effectually discomfited the British van and put a stop to further pursuit.

"General Greene, having passed Saunder's Creek, about four miles from the field of battle, encamped for the night, and on the next day proceeded to Rugeley's Mill. The loss sustained by the respective armies was nearly equal. On the side of America, two hundred and sixty-eight were killed, wounded and missing; on the side of the enemy, two hundred and fifty-eight, including the prisoners brought off by Lieutenant Colonel Washington and those paroled by him on the ground. The British lost no officer of distinction, which was not the case with us. The wound of Lieutenant Colonel Ford proved mortal; and Captain Beatty, of the first Maryland, was killed, than whom the army did not possess an officer of more promise."

Gordon says "the militia was coming into action, when suddenly a number of the Americans began to retire, though the danger was not apparently great, and everybody seemed ignorant of the cause."*

In the Life and Times of Iredell† it is said: "North Carolina soldiers followed Greene's flag to the close of the contest; and I believe that a careful examination will disclose the fact that their number has been carelessly stated and greatly underrated by our historians. Colonel Read's regiment of North Carolinians, under the command of Colonel Washington, greatly distinguished themselves at the battle of Hobkirk's Hill."

The most brilliant conduct in this unfortunate battle was that of Captain John Smith and his light infantry company. This was a company of 45 select Irishmen, detailed from the Maryland line, not one of whom was over thirty years old. They were intended for critical service in the absence of the Legion of Lee.

When Greene had withdrawn his line and formed it again in rear of his first position, it left the artillery, three pieces, exposed to imminent danger. Captain Smith, with his company of Irishmen, was ordered to defend and secure it at all hazards. The British were ascending the hill with loud shouts, and Coffin, in command of their cavalry, was charging up the road to join in the pursuit. "The matrosses were now quitting the drag-ropes, when General Greene galloped up alone, his aids being

*Gordon, vol. 4, p. 83.   †Vol. 1, p. 504.

in other portions of the field, and dismounting and seizing the drag-ropes with one hand, whilst he held his horse with the other, exhibited an example which the most timid could not resist. Smith's men arrived, and gathering the drag-ropes in one hand and holding their muskets in the other, they were dragging off the cannons when Coffin rushed up with his cavalry. Smith immediately forming his company in rear of the artillery, poured such a deadly fire into Coffin's face that he retired in confusion. Again Coffin rallied his men and with determined courage rushed upon the devoted band, but only to be sent back with shame and defeat. Three times it was renewed with the same result, but in the intervals they continued to remove the guns farther from danger. At length the British infantry advanced and their marksmen in the wood soon began to sacrifice this heroic company; Smith himself was wounded and his 45 men had been reduced to 14. At this instant Coffin charged upon them again and *all* were either killed or captured. Captain Smith fell into the hands of the enemy. The artillery was for a moment lost, but at this crisis Colonel Washington returned from his circuit in the rear, and in a moment was upon the enemy with his cavalry. They fled before his impetuous onset, and the artillery was redeemed."

Greene had led a Virginia regiment to the charge, twice that day, in person, and exposed himself with reckless courage to the fire of the enemy. He seems to have become desperate over the failure of his favorite regiment, the 1st Maryland, which had become panic-stricken in the very moment of victory. Even these men, victors of Cowpens and saviors of Guilford Court-House, fled before the charge of the British regulars; a most amazing fact, but one that teaches us the duty of charity to the conduct of others, who, under more trying circumstances, might imitate the example.

A court-martial was convened for the investigation of Gunby's conduct, and its finding was that "Gunby's spirit and activity were unexceptionable; but his order for the regiment to retire was improper and unmilitary, and in all probability the only cause why we did not obtain a complete victory."

In August, Greene wrote "that he found him more blamable than he had represented him in his public letters." Poor fellow! brave, but imprudent and unwise, he lingered awhile with the army, and being mortified by assignment to duty in the rear, he retired from the service, leaving the regiment under Howard, who was the favorite son of fortune.

It is due to Colonel Gunby to say, that Colonel Lee, an accomplished and scientific soldier, defends him and says that "Howard performed the same movement at Cowpens that Gunby attempted to repeat at Hobkirk's Hill"—which is true.

Bancroft censures Greene for "weakening himself irretrievably" by sending Washington to the enemy's rear and having no protection from the dangers of disaster, and characterizes this maneuver as "inconsiderate confidence;" but Bancroft is not an admirer of General Greene.

Stedman's comment on the result was, that "the victory at Hobkirk's Hill, like that at Guilford Court-House, although most honorable and glorious to the officers who commanded, and the troops that were engaged, produced no consequences beneficial to the British interest."

My admiration for the enthusiastic courage and distinguished patriotism of Captain John Smith, "the hero of Hobkirk," constrains me to incorporate the following account of him, which I find in Johnson's Traditions of the Revolution, by Joseph Johnson, M. D., of Charleston, South Carolina:

"CAPTAIN JOHN SMITH.

"The first Maryland regiment, commanded by Colonel Gunby, was very highly considered by General Greene; ever ready to encounter danger at the word of command, and ever ready to lead in battle, under the most discouraging circumstances.

"It had conquered at the battle of Cowpens, and acquired the highest distinction at the battle of Guilford; yet, at the battle of Hobkirk, near Camden, they had been thrown into confusion and retreated disgracefully. Captain John Smith, commanding a light infantry company in that regiment, was not with them at that time. He was particularly distinguished at the battle of Guilford, as well as that of Hobkirk.

"At the head of his company he charged the enemy's line at Guilford, encountered Colonel Stuart, of the Guards, in the open field, and slew him. He also slew, as the British asserted, on that occasion, two or three of Stuart's men. He had been detached from the Maryland line by General Greene, at Hobkirk, for the protection of the artillery, and not only avoided their disgrace on that occasion, but acquired additional honors.

"His company then consisted of forty-five men, they were all Irishmen, and all under thirty years of age. They continued to defend the retreating artillery, and finally preserved it till Washington came up with his cavalry at the critical moment when Smith's men, having been reduced to fifteen, the enemy overpowered them, and all were either killed or taken prisoners. Smith was wounded and captured among the survivors. On being carried into Camden, Lord Rawdon ordered him into close confinement, under a misrepresentation of his conduct at Guilford, where he was said to have killed two or three men after they had surrendered. The charge having been disproved by the united testimony of Greene, Washington and Howard, he was sent down to Charleston on parole and on foot.

"Some persons connected with the British army, in disguise, calling themselves Whigs, seized him a few miles below Camden, stripped him, tied him up and whipped him with switches on his bare back.

"On his arrival in Charleston, his character for bravery being known, he became intimate with a number of British officers of kindred spirits, equally honorable and equally brave.

"Dining one day with some of them, an officer was introduced, whom he immediately recognized as one of those who had treated him so ignominiously. Smith took occasion to say that their whole deportment to him had been so honorable, that it was a pity that any dishonorable fellow should intrude among them. The officers called upon him to explain, as they suffered no such intrusion into their society.

"He accordingly pointed out the man, and declared the treatment received from him and his associates, while a prisoner on parole.

"'Then kick him, Smith,' was the general reply; and Smith had the gratification of kicking the rascal out of the company.

"Many years after these events I knew Captain Smith well; he was styled 'the hero of Hobkirk,' and commissioned by President John Adams in the armament against France."

But great as the mortification and disappointment of General Greene was, at his defeat, it did not alter his plan to drive the enemy from Camden. On the day after the battle he wrote General Marion, "We are now within five miles of Camden, and shall closely invest it in a day or two again." To the French minister he wrote, "We fight, get beat, rise and fight again."

There is one feature of Greene's usual consolatory letters that is "conspicuously absent" from his correspondence in regard to Hobkirk Hill. He had no militia to scold; no scape-goat of citizen soldiery.

He tried the militia in front at Guilford Court-House and on them he put the blame. He thought to reverse it at Hobkirk Hill, but the result was worse, and subsequently at Eutaw he returned to the plan of Cowpens and Guilford. There was a

Higher Power whose wisdom and providence was ordaining all these things for good, and though mysterious in His ways, the liberty of a mighty christian people was "worked out" through all these tribulations and delays.

It is not my purpose to record all the subordinate military movements and actions of General Greene's army in South Carolina, but only such as will disclose the part taken by North Carolina in this eventful campaign. I shall, therefore, only give a rapid review of those minor affairs, that the reader may not lose the thread of the history.

On the 26th the news of the fall of Fort Watson reached the army of Greene at Gum Swamp. "It was joyfully announced in orders next day and the names of Marion and Lee were given out as the countersigns in honor of the captors of that fortification."

Greene, with all his greatness, was capricious and irritable. His ill humor led him into inconsistencies, which it had been well that his biographers had not made public. In five days after this brilliant achievement of the modest and devoted Marion, General Greene writes to President Reed:

"Generals Sumter and Marion have a few people who adhere to them, perhaps more from a desire and opportunity of plundering than from any inclination to support the independence of the United States."

If there was one trait in Marion's character conspicuous above all others, it was his pure and simple devotion to principle and his abhorrence of the "plunderer" in warfare. No opportunity for plunder was ever afforded by him. A more unfounded and grosser wrong was never done to an unselfish patriot and his followers than this. It was, I regret to observe, a custom of General Greene, to reflect on Southern soldiers, when writing private letters to his Northern friends. Pity it is that the unguarded expressions of his great mind, when irritated by disappointment, should have been paraded as history. No doubt that General Greene himself regretted these expressions in after life. I allude to them "more in sorrow than in anger," but this peculiar characteristic is necessary to be understood in order to weigh correctly similar expressions of his in regard to North Carolina troops.

Colonel Watson, whose junction with Rawdon General Marion and Colonel Lee had in vain endeavored to prevent, entered Camden on the 7th of May. With this substantial reinforcement, which gave him a superiority over Greene, he marched out to give him battle, but the American commander skillfully avoided action.

The British commander, having lost Fort Watson on the Santee, and finding his communication with Charleston entirely cut off, determined to abandon Camden.

"On the 10th May, after destroying all public buildings and stores, and many private houses, the British abandoned Camden never to hold it again."

On the 11th the post at Orangeburg, held by

sixty British militia and twelve regulars, surrendered to Sumter. Rawdon marched down the Santee on the north side, anxious to save the garrison at Fort Motte, to which Marion had laid siege. To hasten its surrender, Rebecca Motte, the owner of the house in which they were quartered, on the 12th, brought into camp a bow and a bundle of Indian arrows, and when the arrows had carried fire to her own abode, the garrison of 165 men surrendered. Two days later the British evacuated their post at Nelson's Ferry. On the 15th, Fort Granby, with 352 men, capitulated. General Marion turned his army against Georgetown, and on the first night after the Americans had broken ground, the British retreated to Charleston. The troops under Rawdon did not halt until they reached Monk's Corner."*

Thus, in less than one month after General Greene appeared before Camden, he had compelled the British General to evacuate that important post, forced the submission of all the intermediate posts, and was now upon the banks of the Congaree, in the heart of South Carolina, ready to advance upon Ninety-Six (the only remaining fortress in that State, except Charleston, in the enemy's possession), and to detach a force against Augusta, in Georgia; comprehending in this decisive effort the completion of the deliverance of the two lost States, except the two fortified towns of Charleston and Savannah—safe because the enemy ruled at sea.†

*Bancroft, vol. 5, p. 500.   †Lee's Memoirs, p. 352.

General Pickens, with such force as he had collected in the upper districts, had been ordered to concentrate his force before Augusta, then defended by Colonel Brown, an American loyalist.

General Greene now attached Major Pinketham Eaton, of North Carolina, with his 200 men, militia from Guilford Court-House, to Lee's Legion, and commanded Lee to join Pickens at Augusta.

On the 21st Lee captured Fort Galphin, below Augusta, by a stratagem. Appearing before it with a very small force, the garrison sallied out in pursuit, when Captain Rudolph, who was concealed, rushed into the fort. Those outside surrendered. This gave the Americans "powder, ball, small arms, liquor, salt, blankets," and other valuable and much needed articles.

The defences at Augusta were Fort Cornwallis, in the centre of the town, and Fort Grierson, a half mile up the Savannah River. The regulars were with Brown in Fort Cornwallis, and the loyalist militia in Fort Grierson.

It was determined by General Pickens to attack Fort Grierson first, and carry it by storm. Colonel Lee gives the following graphic account of the affair, which took place June the 5th, 1781:

"Brigadier General Pickens, with the militia, was to attack the fort on the north and west; Major Eaton, with his battalion of North Carolinians, by passing down the north side of the lagoon, was to approach it on the south, co-operating with the militia; while Liutenant

Colonel Lee, with his infantry and artillery, was to move down the lagoon on its southern margin, parallel with Eaton, ready to support his attack if required, or to attend to the movements of Brown, should he venture to leave his defences and interpose with a view to save Grierson. The cavalry, under Eggleston, were ordered to draw near to Fort Cornwallis, keeping in the wood and ready to fall upon the rear of Brown, should he advance upon Lee. These arrangements being finished, the several commandants proceeded to their respective points. Lee's movement, open to view, was soon discerned by Brown, who was drawing his garrison out of his lines, accompanied by two field pieces, and advancing with the appearance of risking battle to save Grierson, now assailed by Pickens and Eaton. This forward movement soon ceased. Brown, not deeming it prudent, under existing circumstances, to persevere in its attempt, confined his interposition to a cannonade, which was returned by Lee, with very little effect on either side. Grierson's resistance was quickly overpowered; the fort was evacuated; himself, with a Major and many of his garrison, killed; the Lieutenant Colonel, with others, taken; and the few remaining, by reaching the river, escaped under cover and concealment of its banks to Fort Cornwallis. Lieutenant Colonel Brown, perceiving the fall of this post, withdrew into his fort, and apprehending, from what he had seen, that he had to deal with *troops fitted for war*, applied himself to strengthening his situations.

"Whatever was attainable in the town, and necessary to his defence, was now procured, and every part of the works requiring amendment was repaired with industry. These exertions on the part of the enemy could not be counteracted ; all now to be done was to assume proper stations for close investure, and by regular approaches, to compel his surrender.

"In the late contest our loss was trivial—a few wounded, and fewer killed. But, unhappily, among the latter was Major Eaton, of North Carolina, who had served only a few weeks with the light corps, and in that short period had endeared himself to his commandant and fellow-soldiers by the amiability of his manners. *He fell gallantly, at the head of his battalion, in the moment of victory.*"

Major Pinketham Eaton was the intimate friend of General Sumner, and in one of his late letters had said, "I shall not be happy until I am in your command again."

He began his military career as a Captain in General Sumner's regiment, the third; his commission as Captain was dated the 16th of April, 1776, and on the 22d November, 1777, he was promoted to be Major. He had been General Sumner's most active assistant in raising the new levies, and was the first officer of the Continental line assigned to active service in the campaign of 1781. His early promotion and the admiration which General Sumner had for him, is sufficient evidence of his skill and courage as a soldier, and Lee testifies to his great amiability of temper, which had endeared him to his late comrades.

Colonel John Armstrong, in a letter to General Sumner, dated June 13th, 1781, says:

"I have the disagreeable news to inform you of the death of Major Eaton. He was wounded at Augusta, taken prisoner and surrendered up his sword, and was afterwards put to death with his own sword. This I have by a letter from Captain Yarborough."

Captain Yarborough, as we have seen, was one of the Continental officers of Eaton's command, while at Deep River, and continued with him to Augusta.

Colonel Grierson, for whom the fort was named, was captured in the further progress of the assault, and a similar death was awarded to him by his captors, no doubt, in retaliation for the abominable murder of Eaton; though Grierson's cup of iniquity had long been full.

The splendid courage and dash of the command of Eaton, composed, as it was, *entirely of the militia* who had fled to their homes from Guilford Court-House, cannot be too lavishly extolled. Native courage was common to them all, but they needed discipline, drill and experience to make them soldiers.

It gives me the greatest pleasure to trace the history and march of these patriotic men direct from Guilford Court-House to this bloody baptism of fire at Augusta, and this pleasure will be heightened by the continued observance of their subsequent and glorious achievement at Eutaw Springs.

Pickens now pressed the siege against Fort Cornwallis with all diligence and activity. It was approached by earth-works on the south side until the parallels drew near to the fort. Colonel Brown, who defended the fort, was fertile in resources, brave to a fault, and an obstinate and determined foe. Nothing that genius, labor and desperation could accomplish, was left undone to strengthen his position, and for two nights in succession he made reckless sallies on the besiegers, but was driven back by the discipline and valor of the Legion infantry.

General Pickens, gathering from Lee the idea of erecting what was known as the Maham Tower, at once put a force to collecting logs, which were notched firmly together as a pen, and the enclosure was filled with rock and earth. To conceal this work it was located behind a house, and was not discovered, even by the vigilance of Colonel Brown, until late in the second day, when the tower had nearly reached its desired height. Brown, judging that this queer military *tumulus*, which overlooked and commanded the inside of his fort, must be destroyed or his fate would be sealed, mounted two of his best pieces of artillery on platforms, at the angle of the fort, nearest the town, and opened upon it a furious and incessant cannonade; but the American six-pounder, from its lofty height, soon silenced the artillery of the fort and made sad havoc with the works, for protection, inside the fort, and uncovered its magazine.

The situation was almost hopeless for the Tory commander, but his undaunted courage still prompted him to resistance. Another desperate assault was made on the night of the 29th of May. It met a bloody repulse by the militia and Rudolph's company of the Legion. Pickens now pressed forward his approaches with renewed zeal and resolution. On the 4th of June Pickens and Lee were ready to make the final assault, and the troops were in the highest spirits. The Georgia militia anticipated a bloody revenge on the commander, who had hanged thirteen of their number with remorseless cruelty. The regular troops, who had been laboring all day and fighting all night, were impatient for the final struggle, and all seemed to be concentrating on a day of carnage and retaliation; for no authority nor officer would be respected when the men were once in the heat of blood and the presence of death. All human pity would be smothered in the struggle for the mastery, and men, losing their superiority over the inferior animals, would, like them, only remember their wrongs and the opportunity to revenge them with blood.

The American commander having witnessed the fury of the assailants of Fort Grierson, and being willing to avoid such another scene of slaughter at Fort Cornwallis, sent a final demand to Colonel Brown for surrender. Negotiations followed, which resulted in a capitulation of the fort and garrison on the 5th June, 1781.

The officers and soldiers who surrendered were to be conducted to such places as the commander-in-chief of the American army should direct, and the officers to be indulged in their paroles.

At the appointed time the garrison marched out. Colonel Brown was placed in the care of Captain Armstrong, of the Legion, with a safe-guard to protect him from the violence of the enraged Georgians, whose disappointment only whetted their appetite for his blood.

Colonel Lee kept Brown at his headquarters until next day, when he was sent down the river to Savannah as a paroled prisoner, under care of Captain Armstrong.

Georgia was now redeemed, and the unrestrained rejoicing of the Whigs evinced the spirit with which they received the gladsome news. The English power was confined to Savannah, and the Indian allies of the British fled to their wigwams in the pathless forests of the frontier. The loyalists sought refuge within the British lines, or hid themselves in the swamps from the avengers of blood. The names of Pickens and Lee and Clarke were idolized, and pæns of praise, to them, were sung at every fireside.

On the 6th June, Lee recrossed the Savannah River and hastened to join Greene, on the 8th, who was then laying siege to Ninety-Six. General Pickens, after securing the baggage and stores, followed on the same day, the 8th.

Lord Rawdon, who was at Charleston, heard with consternation of the fall of Augusta, and was impatiently awaiting reinforcements to enable him to march to the rescue of Ninety-Six. These reinforcements landed on the 3d of June, and on the

7th his lordship set out for the relief of Ninety-Six with three Irish regiments, just arrived, and was joined by some other troops from Monk's Corner, giving him a total of 2000 men.

General Sumter advised General Greene, on the 11th, of Rawdon's approach. Sumter, Pickens and Marion were sent immediately to Rawdon's front to impede his progress and give all the time possible to Greene to press the siege. Colonel Cruger, who was a faithful and skillful officer, declined with contempt all conditions of surrender and exerted every nerve to defend his fort to the last extremity.

About the 15th, one attired as a farmer rode into the American camp, representing himself as a friend, and, as was usual, moved among the troops, when, at last coming near the front line, he spurred his horse to a fearful speed and dashed through the fire of sentinels and pickets, until, unharmed, he entered the open space between the contending lines, where he took from its concealment a letter, and holding it aloft to the view of the besieged, he rushed for the gate of the fort, where he was given a vociferous welcome. But a few minutes more elapsed until the ground almost trembled under the shouts of triumph inside the fort. Rawdon had communicated to them the joyful news that he was at Orangeburg, on his way for their rescue, and would soon relieve them from danger.

On the 18th General Greene made an assault upon the fort, but it was repulsed with great loss to the American troops. He has been severely censured by historians for this useless sacrifice of human life. The American loss was 185 killed and wounded, the enemy's loss only 85 men.

On the 19th of June, General Greene, being advised of the rapid advance of Rawdon with an army superior to his own in numbers, withdrew from Ninety-Six and retreated in the direction of Charlotte, North Carolina, crossing the Enoree, Tiger and Broad rivers.

On the morning of the 21st the British army reached Ninety-Six. A few hours were spent in rejoicing, but in the evening of the same day, notwithstanding the fatigue of his soldiers, the intrepid Englishman sounded the signal for an advance, hoping to overtake the American army and destroy it. On the Enoree he encountered Colonels Washington and Lee, who were covering the retreat. He soon learned that General Greene was beyond his reach, and finding that the American cavalry were superior to his own and likely to greatly harass his weary army, he beat a hasty retreat to Ninety-Six. Here, after reflecting on the situation and seeing the unsupported condition of this outpost, so long held by his troops, but now in imminent danger, he determined to evacuate the place and fall back to his line on the coast.

The light troops of Lee harassed his retreat, to some extent, but he soon reached Orangeburg, where, on the 8th of July, he made a junction with Lieutenant Colonel Stewart. No further attempt upon him was made by the American Generals.

The heated season was now oppressive, and sickness began to show itself alarmingly among the American troops. General Greene, therefore, determined to withdraw his troops from the field and rest his little army on the high hills of the Santee, south of Camden, which was a healthful region and a strategic position from which he could command the State.

We shall leave him here, the 16th of July, and return to North Carolina to trace the history of the three new battalions of the Continental line, commanded respectively by Colonels John B. Ashe, John Armstrong and Reading Blount, which formed the splendid brigade of General Jethro Sumner.

CHAPTER IX.

General Jethro Sumner Raises a Brigade of Continental Troops in 1781—His Correspondence in Regard Thereto—Marches, in July, 1781, to Join General Greene—Colonel John B. Ashe, Major John Armstrong and Major Reading Blount, his Lieutenants—Brigade Numbers 800 Men—North Carolina Militia Join Greene—General Sumter, of South Carolina, Recruits his Brigade in Rowan and Mecklenburg Counties.

IT is somewhat discouraging to discover the many errors that have crept into history in regard to the general events in North Carolina during these stirring times; and it is surprising to find how little of history has been recorded in regard to General Sumner and his Continental brigade.

Governor Graham, though generally accurate, in his lecture on General Greene, fixes General Sumner as one of the captives at Charleston in May, 1780; and Moore, the historian, says he was at Gates' defeat at Camden, in August, 1780. Both these statements are incorrect. General Sumner was at that period in North Carolina endeavoring to recruit the levies for the new Continental regiments. Various letters to and from him in his voluminous correspondence show this.

General Sumner was called to command the North Carolina militia, at Charlotte, in August, 1780, when they were left without a leader, after Gates and Caswell had fled to Hillsboro; but he left that camp when, through somebody's influence, the Legislature had him superseded by General Smallwood, of Maryland, an officer much inferior in talent and military genius to Sumner, and withal not a citizen of the State. After retiring from this militia command, General Sumner renewed his exertions, against all obstacles, to hasten the drafts and collect volunteers for his brigade. He was constantly in correspondence with General Greene, LaFayette, Steuben, and Washington himself, in 1780 and 1781, showing the esteem these great men had for his worth as a soldier. He also constantly wrote letters to the commanders of the military districts, urging them to complete the drafts, and visited various sections of the State in prosecution of his noble work. He was applying in all directions for arms, and even as late as July the 1st, after his battalions were ready to move, they were delayed for want of muskets. At one time, so hopeless was the prospect for arms in North Carolina, that General Sumner was ordered to join the Baron Steuben in Virginia, as the only hope of arming his men. The history of these events are obscurely traceable through this voluminous correspondence, and as far as the limits of this book will allow, I will endeavor to note the progress and trials which marked the completion of the three North Carolina Continental regiments.

The first order was, that the drafts should be at the places of rendezvous by the 25th of April, 1781, and General Greene was urging the fulfillment of this order with constant importunity, but at that date nothing scarcely had been accomplished. The militia officers were "lazy," some disloyal, others feared unpopularity, those drafted deserted, some had no clothing, all were without arms, and a thousand excuses and misfortunes brought disappointment and failure to the hopes of General Sumner. To Colonel John Armstrong, who was at Salisbury April 30th, General Sumner writes:

"I wrote you a few days ago respecting the drafts of the district of Salisbury remaining in Salisbury until further orders. Since then I have received several expresses from General Greene. You are to march the drafts of Salisbury to Harrisburg, in Granville County, by companies and officered."

On May 1st, he writes General Greene that the "small-pox was raging at Hillsboro, and that there could be no collection of stores there; that General Jones, who had gone to Virginia to procure arms, had returned without success."

May 6th he writes General Greene:

"I have not been able, sir, to arm, of the drafts, more than sixty."

On the 22d May, Major Dixon writes General Sumner from Hillsboro:

"We are scarce of arms, and what we have are bad. I expect the troops from Caswell County Thursday. They are pretty well clothed."

On the 22d of May, Colonel John Armstrong writes Sumner from Salisbury:

"Since my last, I have received about 30 men of the drafts of this district. I expect 50 more, and by the last of this month I think I will have 200 in all, if they come according to promise. I have received 50,000 cartridges for the use of your brigade, which I intended to bring with me to your headquarters, but I understand by Captain James Read (recently sent to Salisbury on special mission by General Greene) 'that it is General Greene's express orders for the Salisbury drafts to join him soon.' If I march southward I will leave 20,000 cartridges with Captain Gamble, Quartermaster, in Salisbury, to be delivered to your order."

May 26th, Armstrong writes again:

"Our army to the southward is in great spirits and increasing very fast. General Greene's heavy baggage and artillery that lay high upon the Catawba is ordered to camp. *I shall start for camp to-day*, and will take every opportunity to write you. I am so unhappy not to be under your immediate command."

But Colonel Armstrong did not start on the 26th of May.

June the 13th, he was still at Salisbury, and writes General Sumner:

"I am almost ready to march, with 200 good men of this district. *I sent on 180 before.*"

Who went on with these 180 men is not recorded. I presume they left on the 26th May.

In examining the applications for pensions under the act of 1832, I find that of John Wilfong, of Lincoln, now Catawba County, who was the great-grandfather of the late Major General Stephen D. Ramseur, of the Confederate army. Wilfong was one of the volunteers at King's Mountain, and was wounded in the arm. He states that—

"In July, 1781, I volunteered for ten (10) months with Captain Cowan and Lieutenant George Hammond, who marched from Lincoln County, to near Augusta, then joining the army of General Greene, thence to Eutaw Springs, and was in that battle."

I think it probable that most of the levies in the Salisbury district were volunteers; the Whigs abounded in that portion of the State more than any other.

June 19th, General Sumner seems to have written an appeal to the people to raise the new levies. A copy, in his handwriting, is among his papers. It is evident that the General fought better than he wrote. His orthography is hardly tolerable, and the chirography is worse—a heavy, large handwriting, irregular and not well constructed; but the matter is vigorous and strong. He recounts the "savage waste and destruction of the enemy in making their way, the indefensible father, the aged mother, the loving sister appealing with groans and wringing hands to their friends to preserve their innocence and virtue from pollution."

On the 20th of June, General Sumner writes to General Greene:

"CAMP HARRISBURG,* June 20th, 1781.

"DEAR SIR:—I enclose a return of the drafts collected at this place. Colonel Armstrong I expect in two or three days with the troops of the district of Newbern. On his arrival I shall immediately form the *second* regiment. I have, sometime since, wrote Major Eaton† for a return of those men under his command with you, and to have *them* arranged as the *first* regiment, *together* with those of the district of Salisbury; and I have directed him to report to me the number and companies, and the part wanting to complete the regiment, to be made here. Captain Doherty, who attends at Wilmington district rendezvous, has orders to repair to general rendezvous with what drafts have been received from that district, and a general order has been issued to the several districts that a diligent officer remain at each district rendezvous to receive drafts from such counties as have not yet delivered its drafts to the Continental officer.

"I shall, as soon as possible, march to join the Baron Steuben in Virginia, having no prospect of being supplied with arms, &c., in this State.

"I received yours of the 20th instant, and shall pay our respects to the contents.

"The Marquis, by last accounts, was in twenty miles of Lord Cornwallis, who was in the vicinity of Petersburg; that a very respectable force of riflemen had

---

*Harrisburg was in Granville County. It was a camp and depot of provisions.

†He had not, it seems, yet heard of Eaton's death.

joined the Marquis last Wednesday. I shall, in a few days, be able to give you a more particular account of their maneuvers. Major Craig, at Wilmington, continues his ravages for thirty or forty miles up Cape Fear, with little or no opposition. His Excellency, the Governor, a few days since, sent me orders to march all the drafts collected to Duplin; but, sir, it was so incompatible with my orders that I did not do so, and, at that time, I was not joined by Major Dixon with the Hillsboro drafts, neither were those of Edenton come up. I have heard nothing of this matter since.

"Permit me to congratulate you on the very consequential success the army immediately under your command have had in South Carolina and Georgia.

"I am, sir, with regard and esteem,
"Your very obedient servant,
"JETHRO SUMNER."

Fortunately Virginia was able to furnish the muskets so essentially necessary, and by this generosity Sumner's brigade was enabled to join Greene instead of Steuben. Some of the trials incident to raising recruits is graphically set out in the following letter:

"DUPLIN, June 22, 1781.

"SIR:—I embrace the opportunity of Colonel Kenan's going to the Assembly to inform you that the tumults in this part of the country have been the cause of the drafts, and everything in relation thereto, being delayed and more out of order here than in any other part of the State.

"We have at present some little respite from the cursed Tories, but cannot say they are entirely subdued.

The draft was made in Duplin, but more than half of them have been among the Tories, or so disaffected they will not appear. The number that we ought to have here is about seventy men, and there has not above twenty-four yet appeared, and about twenty from Onslow. The men have been so harassed by being kept in arms, that hitherto they could not attend to providing the clothing required by law, and without clothing the men cannot march, as not one among them have a second change, and some have hardly duds to cover them. The Colonel has used all possible means to urge the people to clothe their soldiers, and when this is done I will march with the few we have.

"If an opportunity offers from your camp towards Wake, I should be glad to hear from you. If it is directed to the care of Colonel Kenan, he will forward it to

"Your humble servant,
"GEORGE DOHERTY."

Captain Doherty was one of the officers of the Continental line and had been in General Sumner's old regiment.

June 29th General Sumner informs Baron Steuben that General Greene had just ordered the North Carolina brigade to join him in South Carolina, as the enemy had been largely reinforced. He urges the Baron, notwithstanding this, to forward arms to him.

Major Reading Blount was in Salisbury on the 29th of June, attending to the organization of the *third* battalion, and writes to General Sumner:

"I am sorry to inform you that there is no account of those parties yet that were expected when you left here. In case any should come in a short time, it would be out of my power to have them equipped, unless you send me an order from General Greene for that purpose, as he has given Gamble orders not to issue cartridges or stores of any kind to any order but his own. But should troops come on before I get such an order, I shall run all risks of taking them, if not to be had other ways."

Colonel John Armstrong had, at last, gone forward, with orders to incorporate Major Eaton's command with those men who accompanied him from Salisbury, and on the 1st day of July had reached "Camp Big Springs, 20 miles from Broad River," "half way between Nation Ford on the Catawba, and Fish Dam Ford on Broad," and gives General Sumner the following information:

"We are now in camp half way between the Nation Ford on the Catawba, and Fish Dam Ford on Broad River, in a fine situation; plenty of good water. It hath one failing—it will not make grogg. The General seems very uneasy about the delay of the drafts of Salisbury district and the desertions that frequently happen by reason of the forced number of Tories into the service, and as soon as they receive the bounty they desert. I have received nigh 300 men and will not have above two hundred in the field. I did everything in my power to bring out the drafts of this district, but all to no purpose; there is one-half at home yet, and remain without molestation; as for clothing, there was little or none sent, fit for a negro to wear, except from Rowan. I am sorry that I ever had anything to do with such slothful officers and neglected soldiers; there is a number of them now almost naked, and when cold weather sets in they must be discharged, for no officer would pretend to put them on duty. The neglects that we have labored under heretofore, together with the present, makes the service very disagreeable to every officer in camp; we are without money, clothing, or any kind of nourishment for our sick, not one gill of rum, sugar or coffee, no tents or camp kettles or canteens, no doctor, no medicine. Under these circumstances we must become very indurable.

"I wish it had been my lot to have gone with you to Virginia, where we would have been under your immediate care, and shared the fate of the other drafts and other officers of the State. I am fully satisfied that you were not acquainted with our circumstances here, or otherwise it would have been removed. I have received yours of the 12th inst., directing me to order the Lewis' to the field again; one is dead, the other is a member of the Assembly, and Joel resigned and denies serving any longer; I am afraid that in a short time you will have but few officers in the field, by reason of the shameful neglect of the State. We seem rather a burden than a benefit to them; we are tossed to and fro like a ship in a storm. We cannot learn what has become of Major Eaton's men; Saunders has a few to the southward of this.

"McCree, Lytle and Brevard were sent back with the prisoners, to Salisbury; I have about ninety (of Eaton's men) in camp. I will do my best to gather them all to camp, if possible, and make you a full return."

Since the gallant Major's death, on the 5th of June, at Augusta, his command seems to have been broken into several detachments, and Colonel Armstrong had not been able to gather up more than "ninety" of them. The others were to the "southward."

Colonel Armstrong disappears now from our correspondence until after the battle of Eutaw Springs. In July, 1782, he apologizes for delay and excuses himself on the ground that he "had the misfortune to be wounded in a duel with Major Lewis, and that his wounds were not yet well." It may be it grew out of the order alluded to in the above letter.

General Sumner was at Frohawk's Mill, in Mecklenburg County, on the 16th July, lamenting the delay of Major Murfree and Captain Doherty; but his heart, no doubt, leaped for joy when he received the gladsome intelligence, contained in a letter from "J. Pryor, Charlottesville, Virginia," dated July 19th, saying:

"Some days since I was ordered by the Honorable Major General Marquis de Lafayette to send on 300 stands of arms to you by the most safe and convenient route. The movements of a detachment of the enemy on the south side of James River proved a great obstacle, but since hearing they had passed toward the southward, I have ventured them on under the care of Mr. Edward Moore, whose precaution and diligence, I am in hopes, will convey them safe, and in time, to your camp.

"*Two hundred and fifty-three* of the arms *are very fine and complete*, sent from Philadelphia, intended for Virginia new levies, of which I must beg the greatest care be taken. Forty-seven are not so complete."

It was these fine muskets that did the fine work at Eutaw Springs.

Colonel John B. Ashe was ready, on the 14th day of July, to march for Greene's camp, and received from General Sumner the following order, to be executed on his arrival:

"You are to take charge of all the Continental troops from this State in camp now, under the command of Major John Armstrong, and incorporate them as of the *first regiment* of the four Continental regiments of Continental troops of this State."

On the same day, 14th of July, Sumner writes Governor Burke a letter, dated from Salisbury:

"My expectation of being supplied with arms is now otherwise, 300 wanting repairs. We shall, however, be able to march, three hundred (300) rank and file, equipped, except bayonets, this evening (14th July) or very early to-morrow morning. I shall leave Major Hogg and Major Blount at this place, who are to follow as soon as a number of these muskets can be put in repair. I have left Captain Chapman at Harrisburg Station, who is also to act as a detail officer there until further orders. Major Murfree, of Edenton district, and

Captain Doherty, have not yet joined me, but might be far advanced on their march."

General Sumner had reached Hanging Rock, South Carolina, by July 30th, as he informs Governor Burke.

I copy the following from Major Blount:

"SALISBURY, August 1st, 1781.

"SIR :—I have the pleasure to inform you that Captain Goodman arrived at this post on the 28th (July) with about 120 men, on the same day the *arms arrived* from Virginia, which I shall take on to you unless ordered to the contrary. I shall be able to leave this place in about five days, and not sooner. Many of the soldiers are barefooted and can't march without shoes. I have procured an order from the clothes General for as many shoes as will do them by sending to Davidson's for them.

"You should have been furnished with a general return of what men there are at this post, but Captain Goodman has not time to make one since he arrived. If you have any order relative to the arms or the troops, I should be happy to receive them as soon as possible.

"I am sir, yours,

"READING BLOUNT.

"To General Sumner."

General Sumner had now taken the field in person, his Lieutenants, Ashe and Armstrong, were with him, and Blount was ready to follow from Salisbury in five days.

From the foregoing correspondence we learn that, June 13th, 1781, Colonel John Armstrong had
   sent forward to Greene's camp, - - 180
He followed very soon with - - - 200
General Sumner left Salisbury, July 14th, with 300
August the 1st, 1781, Major Blount had ready
   to march, - - - - - - - 120

   Total, - - - - - - 800
The Guilford Court-House militia, with Greene
   were - - - - - - - - 90
"To the southward" there was another detachment of this milititia, about - - - 110

   Aggregate, - - - - - - 1000
men, whom North Carolina sent forward from the 6th of April to the 1st of August, 1781, as regulars. Perhaps 200 deserted or were unfit for active service, leaving at least 800 effective men with Greene, in August, 1781, under the command of General Sumner.

We have no further correspondence showing the route taken by these troops. Fighting and marching were resumed, and the pen, never fertile in Sumner's hand, seems to have been put away. They no doubt reached General Greene's camp at the High Hills of the Santee in a fortnight, and while in this salubrious location and enjoying immunity from battle, they received training, drilling, and exercise necessary to "mechanize" the soldier. Then they met with the men of Eaton's battalion and heard them recount their exploits at Augusta, and repeat the sad tale of their leader's death, and how his comrades of all arms grieved over his untimely fate. These new levies learned from the old veterans, who had followed Greene so long, that the British were not invincible, even with the bayonet in their hands, and were encouraged to imitate the day of Cowpens. They saw what splendid soldiers experience and discipline had made out of the militia of Guilford Court-House, and how nobly those men had wiped out their reproach in the charge on Fort Grierson, and they were eager to share in that glory on the next field of battle. Sumner, thoughtful of all their necessities and comforts, rigid in discipline, sharing in their toil and privations and giving them an example of endurance and courage, infused into them his own heroic spirit. Ashe, Armstrong and Blount, all veteran soldiers, who had passed through the dangers of many battles, with reputations for exalted courage, were models for their imitation, and that *esprit de corps*, so necessary to confidence, and combined attack or defence, was generated among officers and men around the camp-fires of the "Hills," and on the parade grounds of the regiments. Mutual acquaintance, friendship and State pride grew up among them and united them as one man, in one cause, with one glorious end in view—the independence of the American colonies.

In addition to this brigade of North Carolina regulars, there were five hundred North Carolina militia who joined General Greene* at this camp, but it was not possible to arm but two hundred of them. North Carolina had sent more troops to the field than the General Government and the States combined could arm.

These, however, were not all the North Carolinians in this camp. General Sumter had been authorized by Governor Rutlege to raise a brigade of regulars and most of these men had been recruited in North Carolina. I state this upon the authority of Joseph Graham, and it is fully sustained by cotemporary evidence. In the University Magazine, June, 1856, the narrative of General Graham is published as follows:

"Shortly after the battle of Guilford (March 15th, 1781), Governor Rutlege, of South Carolina, who had been invested with full power by the Legislature of that State, authorized General Sumter to raise a brigade of State troops for the term of ten months, each man to find his own clothing, horse, arms and equipments, but to be found in forage and rations by the public, and receive a grown negro for his pay. Colonel William Polk, Wade Hampton, William Hill and Middleton, commanded. The greater part of the regiments of Polk, Hampton and Hill *were raised in the, then, counties of Mecklenburg and Rowan*, between the Yadkin and Catawba. The act of Assembly of North Carolina, 1781, exempted those counties from levies, for the Continental line, which had furnished men for General Sumter. Many of them might be considered

*Johnson, vol. 2, p. 208.

as seasoned to a camp life, and from the services they had seen, accustomed to endure hardships and privations and encounter dangers. How well they acted their part in the summer of 1781, until after the battle of Eutaw, is recorded in the history of the war within the State of South Carolina. They sustained considerable loss of both officers and men in that action, in the autumn; but suffered much more from the climate in that low country. Many of them never returned."

In another communication from General Graham, published in the University Magazine of October, 1855, he says:

"It may further be remembered that the brigade of State troops raised by the State of South Carolina, in the spring of 1781, where each man furnished his own horse and military equipments, the regiments commanded by Colonels Polk, Hampton and Middleton, were mostly raised in the counties aforesaid.

"It is admitted that some, of both officers and soldiers, of the militia of South Carolina, were as brave and enterprising as ever went to a field of battle, but those well affected to the cause of independence *were but few in number.*

"The most of the lower districts (except Marion's brigade) were endeavoring to save their property, either by moving to North Carolina or Virginia, or the greater number by taking protection from the enemy.

"From the conduct of the few, before alluded to (who were not disaffected), Ramsay's History gives character to the whole militia of the State, when it is well known a great majority of them saw little military service. The counties of Mecklenburg and Rowan not only furnished the greater part of the troops commanded by General Sumter, but it was in all cases his place of retirement when menaced by a superior force of the enemy, and from whence he mostly organized and set out on his several expeditions.

"The writer, finding those things unfairly represented, has undertaken in his plain way to present a more correct account of several transactions than has heretofore been given, and to take notice of some which have been entirely omitted, which, in his opinion, are worthy of being preserved.

"For the truth of the facts he states, he appeals to those who were present on the several occasions related, of whom, it is believed, more than a hundred are living.

"Some of the details may appear minute and trivial, but not so to those who were present, and it is expected the present generation will read with some interest the part their fathers and relatives acted in those times, more especially when they have a personal knowledge of the very spot where each transaction took place."

CHAPTER X.

Battle of Eutaw Springs, Fought the 8th day of September, 1781—
The Noble Part borne by North Carolinians in this Battle—
Greene Retires to the High Hills of the Santee—Hears of the
Fall of Yorktown—The War Virtually Ends.

WE now return to the movements of General Greene. On the 22d of August he issued an order to his troops in these words:

"The army will march to-morrow morning by the right, in the following order: The North Carolina brigade, two pieces of artillery; Virginia brigade, two pieces of artillery; Maryland brigade; the baggage in the usual order according to the line of march. The General will beat at 4 o'clock, when all the small guards will join their corps; the assembly in forty minutes after, and the march at 5 o'clock."

The two armies were only sixteen miles apart, but the Santee intervened, and it was not safe to attempt its passage in the face of the enemy. The route, therefore, lay up the Santee and above the junction of the Congaree and Wateree; then crossing the Wateree first and descending its southern side, then crossing the Congaree—in all a circuit of seventy miles. The weather was so sultry that the army only moved in the cooler hours of the day, in the morning and evening.

As soon as Stewart was informed of Greene's movement, he fell back down the Santee, to Eutaw

Springs, forty miles distant, in the direction of Charleston.

Lord Rawdon had, previously to this, sailed from Charleston for England, but was captured by a French vessel on his way and was now a prisoner. He was an unwilling witness to the surrender of Yorktown, and returned, a captive, with Lord Cornwallis.

He was a fit subject of retaliation for the execution of Colonel Isaac Hayne, but Colonel Fanning, the Tory leader, about this time, made his celebrated incursion to Hillsboro and carried off Governor Burke. This gave the British a hostage for the life of Rawdon, and, perhaps, saved his lordship from the gibbet.

General Greene's march was necessarily slow. On the 28th of August he reached Howell's Ferry, where he received intelligence that the enemy had been reinforced and were making preparations for a permanent post at Eutaw. It did not seem to occur to the British commander that Greene would have the temerity to attack him in his camp, but that was exactly what Greene was preparing to do.

The American commander sent back all his heavy baggage, on the line of retreat, under a suitable guard, mostly militia, and took with him only two wagons, ladened with hospital stores and *rum* (the latter, in that day, considered the most indispensable article for an army, next to medicines).

On the 5th of September General Greene, in his order of the day, informed the army of a brilliant victory of General Francis Marion, over a British convoy of three hundred men, in which twenty of the enemy were killed and eighty wounded, with inconsiderable loss to the American force.

The victory was announced in glowing words and aroused the greatest enthusiasm and confidence in the hearts of the army, and they were eager for an opportunity to add more victories to the campaign.

On the 7th day of September, General Marion joined General Greene at Burdell's plantation.

Colonel Stewart lay in fancied security at Eutaw, wholly unapprised of the approach of his adversary. Every messenger or scout from his army had been captured or killed by the vigilance of the Americans, and no tidings had reached him.

On the morning of the 8th, Colonel Stewart had sent out his "rooting party," as they were called, to gather sweet potatoes for his army, and these the advance of Greene's army discovered, and, after a feeble resistance, captured.

The same morning, however, two deserters from Greene's forces made their way to the British camp and communicated the news of the proximity of the American army. Colonel Coffin, commanding the British cavalry, was sent immediately to reconnoiter the situation, and coming in contact with the American vanguard, soon gave information of the fact.

Colonel Stewart began at once to dispose his

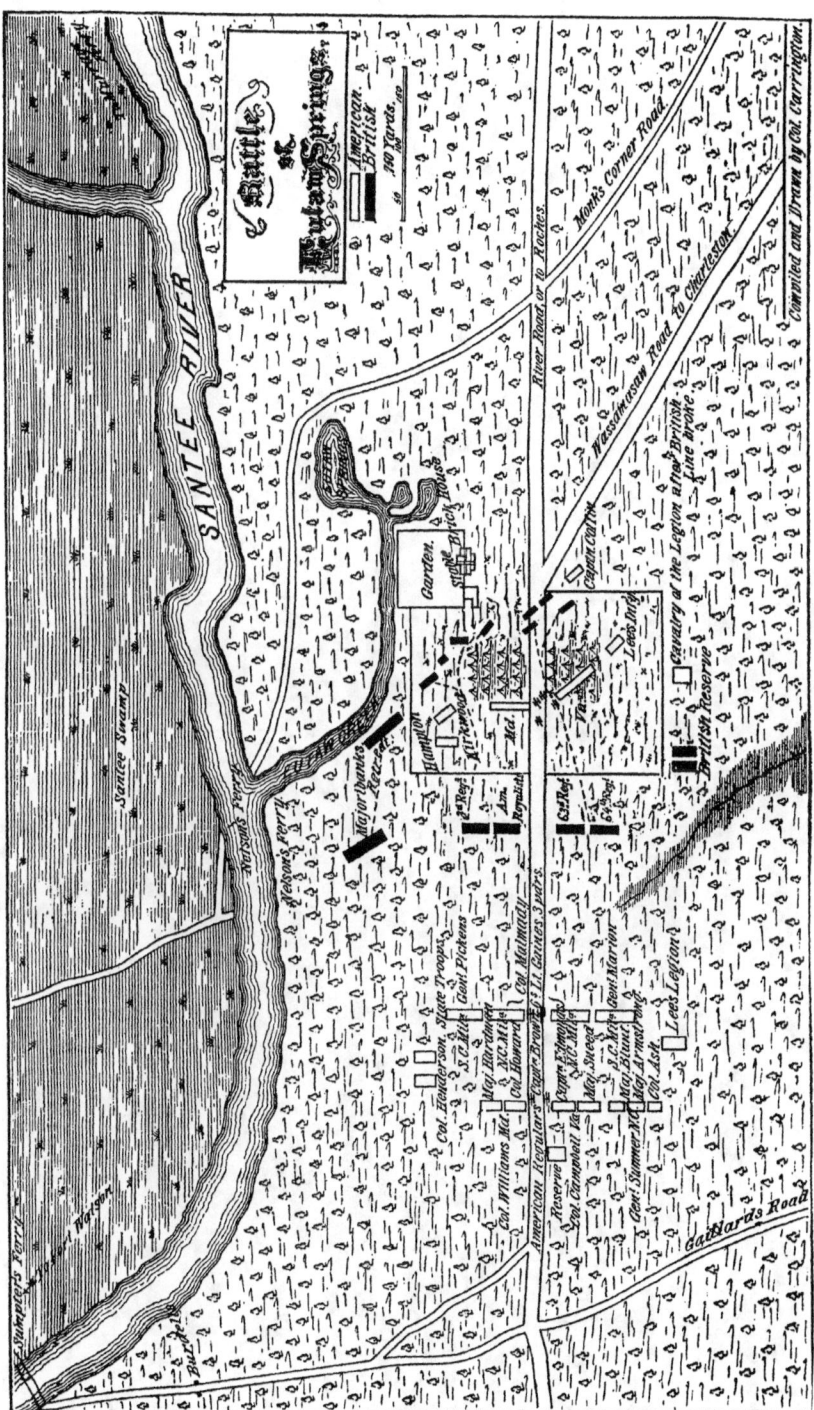

troops for battle. Few situations were more favorable for defence.

"On the right was the Eutaw Creek, which, issuing from a deep ravine, ran under high banks, thick bordered with brush and underwood. The only open ground was a large field which had been cleared of its timber on both sides of the road, and this was commanded by a brick house two stories high, with garret windows, which answered the purpose of a third story, and with walls thick and strong enough to withstand the light artillery of the Americans. In the rear of the house there was a garden surrounded by a strong palisade, and covering the space between it and Eutaw Creek. A barn and some smaller buildings near it afforded good rallying points in case of disaster. The approach to the rear was embarrassed by springs and deep hollow ways, and on the right by the ravine from which the creek flowed, and a thicket, rendered almost impenetrable by a low shrub, called, in the language of the country, 'black-jack.' On every side the woods came down in dark masses to the border of the clearing. Midway through the clearing, and dividing it into almost equal parts, a road had been recently opened, which, forking directly in front of the house and garden, and about fifty yards from them, formed two branches, one of which led to Charleston, and the other to a plantation on the Santee. The British camp lay in the field under cover of the house and on both sides of the road, and when the troops marched out to form for battle their tents were left standing."*

Colonel Stewart, as was the usual custom of British officers, drew up his army in only one line of battle, with a strong reserve in the rear to act as emergencies might require. This line was in the woods, a few hundred yards west of the open field, where they had their camp, and extended on both sides of the Congaree road, with the artillery in the centre, and moving along this highway. Eutaw Creek covered the right wing effectually, the left was in the woods to the south of the road and covered by the cavalry under Major Coffin, a dashing and skillful officer. Major Majoribanks, the hero of the battle, was in command of the right wing, with his troops protected by the thick growth along the bank of Eutaw Creek, and the scrubby black-jack oaks which extended out a short distance from the creek bank. It was impenetrable by cavalry, and almost unassailable by infantry. To the south and left of the light infantry battalion, under Majoribanks, came, in their order, Cruger's command, which was composed of several broken corps, then the "Buffs," with their left resting on the Congaree road. To the south of the road were the 63d and 64th, two veteran regiments. Two separate bodies of infantry in the rear formed the reserve. A small detachment of infantry was thrown in front of the line of battle as skirmishers, with orders to fall back into the main line.

*Greene's Life of General Greene, vol. 3, p. 388.

The British officer, fully realizing the strategic importance of the brick mansion-house in his rear, as a rallying point in which a small garrison might, in case of disaster, be thrown, ordered it to be occupied, together with the barn, outhouses and palisaded garden, and this judicious foresight saved his army from utter destruction.

The British troops were well armed, and equipped with every necessary military outfit, and were inured to service and under the best discipline. It was, indeed, what, in this day, is called a "crack corps" of soldiers. Many of them were American loyalists and deserters, good marksmen, whose deadly aim was severely felt in the action. They were aware, to use a common figure of speech, that they fought with "halters around their necks," and that the penalty of desertion would be promptly meted out to them if captured. They, therefore, went into the fight to win or die.

The approach of the American army was from the west along the Congaree road. General Greene had placed his militia in front at Guilford Court-House, and he was discomfited; at Hobkirk's Hill, he reversed this order, and his front line was composed of his veteran troops; but still fortune forsook him and the disaster was worse than at Guilford; now, at Eutaw, the American commander determined to re-assume the arrangement made at Guilford Court-House, by again placing his militia in the front line. The militia, at this time, under Greene, had the advantage over those at Guilford, in that they had seen service and been trained in his camp, on the Santee, for the duties of the field. They were, in fact, well-drilled troops, and as the tide of victory had steadily set with the American army, they were inspired with the spirit of triumph and were impatient to end the long struggle by one determined effort to destroy the British army.

They were fresh from the rest, and strong from the plenty they had enjoyed in camp. Physically, they were in the best trim for the fight and eager for it to begin.

"Greene, wishing his troops to form with coolness and recollection, halted his columns, and after distributing the contents of his rum casks, ordered his men to form in order of battle."

"The column of militia, when displayed, formed the first line; the South Carolinians, in equal divisions, on the right and left, and the North Carolinians in the centre. General Marion commanded the right, General Pickens the left, and Colonel Malmedy, a French nobleman, who held a commission from North Carolina, commanded the centre. Colonel William Henderson, with the South Carolina State troops, including Sumter's brigade, 'covered' the left of this line, and Lieutenant Colonel Lee, with his Legion, 'covered' the right."

"The column of regulars, also displayed into one line (the second); the North Carolinians, under Brigadier General Jethro Sumner, occupied the right, divided into three battalions, commanded respectively by Colonel J. B. Ashe and Majors John Armstrong and Reading Blount; the Marylanders, under Colonel Williams on the left, divided into two battalions, commanded by Colonel Howard and Major Hardman; the Virginians in the centre, under command of Colonel (Richard) Campbell, were also divided into two battalions, led by Major Sneed and Captain Edmonds. The two three-pounders, under Captain Gaines, moved in the road with the first line, which was equally distributed to the right and left of it; and the two six-pounders, under Captain Brown, attended the second line in the same order. Colonel William Washington still moved in the rear in columns, with orders to keep under cover of the woods, and hold himself in reserve."*

The American army had begun its march at 4 o'clock in the morning, but it was 8 o'clock before the advanced parties of the British army were driven in and the battle begun in earnest. "The day was clear and calm and the sun was rising in a cloudless sky."

The advanced guard of the British was encountered by Lee's Legion and Colonel William Henderson of the South Carolina State troops (mostly North Carolinians, as we have seen).† Coffin was soon thrown into confusion and fled pell-mell, leaving forty prisoners behind him.

---

*Johnson, vol. 2, p. 223.
†Colonel Henderson was in command of Sumter's brigade. Sumter had not recovered from his wound.

The regular lines, as before indicated, were formed, and "a steady and desperate conflict ensued" between the militia in the front line, North and South Carolinians, and the veteran regulars of the British service. The duel between the artillery was "bloody and obstinate in the extreme; nor did the American artillery relax for a moment from firing until both pieces were dismounted and disabled. One piece of the enemy shared the same fate."

The gallant and glorious record of the citizen soldiery of the Carolinas is thus described by Johnson: "Nor had the militia been wanting in gallantry and perseverance. It was with equal astonishment that both the second line of the American regulars and the troops of the enemy contemplated these men, steadily and without faltering, *advance with shouts and exhortations into the hottest of the enemy's fire,* unaffected by the continued fall of their comrades around them. General Greene, to express his admiration of the firmness exhibited on this occasion *by the militia,* says of them in a letter to General Steuben, '*Such conduct would have graced the veterans of the great King of Prussia.*' But it was impossible that this could endure long, for those men were all this time *receiving the fire of double their number.* Their artillery was dismounted and disabled, and that of the enemy was vomiting destruction in their ranks."*

*Johnson's Life of Greene, vol. 2, p. 225.

Colonel Carrington, in "His Battles of the American Revolution,"* says "the North Carolina militia, however, fired *seventeen rounds* before their retreat, and General Sumner so promptly pushed the battalions of Ashe, Armstrong and Blount into the gap that the first line was restored and the British in turn retreated."

G. W. Greene thus describes the conflict: "Meanwhile, the first line was bearing up against the weight *of the whole English army*. Their blood had been warmed by the skirmish, and their fire now ran from flank to flank throughout the line, neither too high nor too low, but striking with that fearful precision which daily practice gives to the hunter's aim. It was answered by the deep, regular volleys of the British musketry. The fearful sound spread far and wide through the gloomy twilight of the wood. And still the militia held their ground without wavering, and still the unshaken British line kept up its deadly fire."

Stedman, in his History,† says "the pressure of the enemy's fire was such as compelled the third regiment, or 'Buffs,' to give way, the regiment being composed of new troops. The remains of those veteran corps, the 63d and 64th regiments, who had served the whole of the war, lost none of their fame in this action. They rushed with bayonets into the midst of the enemy, nor did they give ground until overpowered by numbers and severe slaughter."

The courage and constancy of the North Carolina

*P. 580.   †Vol. 2, p. 378.

militia are thus avouched by American and English historians. Colonel Malmedy, who commanded them on that day, was a French nobleman, who, like Lafayette, had volunteered his services to the Continental Congress and came to aid the colonies in their struggle for freedom.

If, justly or unjustly, reproach had been cast on the name of the North Carolina militia, for not rallying again to their standard at the battle of Guilford Court-House, after having poured such deadly fires into the advance of the British line, that reproach was blotted out on the sanguinary field of Eutaw Springs. They set thereto their seal of blood, on this bright September day, that, in the language of Erskine, "they were born free and would never die slaves."

This militia was mostly from the strong Whig districts who had early and devotedly espoused the cause of independence, and were ever ready to maintain the liberty for which they declared. Their obstinate and unyielding courage, on this day, was never excelled by any troops, and was equalled only once, in the invasion of the South, by the troops of North Carolina, who fought, at Camden, under "Hal." Dixon, "as long as a cartridge remained in their belts." To these "embattled farmers" be everlasting honor! In war they handled their muskets and bayonets with the skill and gallantry of heroes; in peace, they drove the ploughshare with the industry and constancy of patriot citizens. In both spheres they were Carolinians worthy of their race and their

State, and their memories should be ever enshrined in the hearts of their liberated countrymen.

Overpowered by numbers, these stern men retreated sullenly; but as they fell back in sight of the North Carolina regulars, General Sumner gave the "Forward!" and the battalions of Ashe, Armstrong and Blount, were pushed so promptly into the gap, says Carrington, that the first line was restored and the British in turn retreated.

It was at this crisis in the battle, when the North Carolinians had forced the British to retreat, that General Greene sent the laconic message to Otho Williams, who commanded on the left of the second line, "*Let Williams advance and sweep the field with his bayonets.*" So admirable and soldierly was the forward movement of the North Carolina regulars, made under General Sumner, that General Greene, in a burst of enthusiasm, exclaimed, "*I was at a loss which most to admire, the gallantry of the officers or the good conduct of their men.*"* It is probable that at least one-third of the troops who drove back this charge of the British, with so much impetuosity and intrepidity, were the same men who did such deadly work, with their hunting rifles, at Guilford Court-House.

They had been drilled and disciplined at Halifax, and at the camp on the Santee, and were burning to redeem the reputation which their inexperience had so tarnished in the former conflict. They had bayonets now, instead of squirrel rifles, and had been taught to use them, and their splendid charge

*Johnson, vol. 2, p. 225.

on the advancing line of English veterans, "who had fought through the whole war," was evidence of how well they had learned the military lessons of the camp. Officers and soldiers vied with each other in deeds of daring and heroism, and as the watchful eye of the American commander glanced from one to the other, in this brilliant *coup de main*, his face beamed with joy and admiration; but when the conflict was over, he declared that he did not know on which to bestow the highest praise. Here let history place the wreath of honor, undivided and unfading forever, on the brow of officer and soldier alike.

Colonel Stewart, witnessing the discomfiture of his line, ordered up his reserve, but it was swept away in the torrent of retreat, which was rushing before the bayonets of Williams and Sumner, and all seemed lost to the British army. Majoribanks alone held his position in the black-jacks on the creek, and the whole British line swung around him, like a pivot, on the right. Helter-skelter they fled through the field containing their camp, and on to the brick mansion-house in its rear. Lee's infantry alone was saved from disorder and confusion in the pursuit, and were well nigh entering the house with the enemy, but Major Sheridan was victor in the race, and repelled the infantry, who retreated, holding some prisoners they had taken between them and the garrison to protect themselves from its deadly fire.

Victory, which was now in the American hands, was jeopardized and almost lost by a hitherto unseen and unexpected foe; but one which has so often conquered heroes and patriots before, and destroyed the hopes which fortune had placed in their hands. General Greene had distributed his hogsheads of rum to his troops on the eve of battle; fatigue had whetted their appetites for another potation, and as they entered the British camp they discovered this lurking enemy among the tents. They paused to drink and repeat the toast to their good fortune, when the vigilance of Colonel Stewart detected their indiscretion. His troops were machines of military discipline, and at the word of command, fell into ranks and were soon on the Americans that loitered among the "fleshpots" of the camp. The Americans were driven back. Charge after charge had been made on Majoribanks, but that man, of the lion heart, still stood like a stonewall and resisted every assault. Colonel Henderson had fallen a wounded victim to his fire on the flank; Colonel Washington was a wounded captive in his hands, and a lieutenant and an ensign of this gallant band of cavalry were left alone to lead its shattered columns.

Lee had been ordered to charge on the right, but was not to be found by the messenger. Coffin was advancing unopposed on the American right and the tide was setting fast against the American arms. Some one blundered again by rushing the cannon in the field to bombard the mansion-house, but dragging it too close, the artillerists were shot down by the garrison and the cannons were abandoned.

Greene still held to his prisoners taken in the early part of the action; but seeing that all would be lost if his army were not re-organized, ordered a retreat. Coffin was advancing, Lee could nowhere be found, and Greene called on Colonel Hampton, who had succeeded Henderson in the field, to cover the retreat.

This was gallantly done. Coffin was driven to the field again, but Hampton, in his impetuosity, was exposed to the fire, from the black-jacks, which Colonel Polk declared seemed to him "to kill every man but himself."

The retreat of Coffin gave the Americans time to rally west of the British camp, in the woods, where the first conflict began.

The enemy was too much crippled "to venture beyond the cover of the house."

General Greene halted long enough to collect his wounded, and having made arrangements to bury his dead, left a strong picket under Colonel Hampton on the field; he withdrew his army to Burdells, seven miles distant.

"Both parties," says Johnson, "claimed the victory, but there is no difficulty in deciding the question between them upon the plainest principles. The British army was chased from the field at the point of the bayonet and took refuge in a fortress; the Americans were repulsed from that fortress."

But in my judgment, it was not the fortress that gave the English the victory claimed. It was the camp, with its rum and spoils, that demoralized the pursuit of the enemy and intoxicated the pursuers.

Disorder and indiscretion, weakness and indecision followed, and the victory was lost.

In reading the history of the Revolutionary war, the student of this day is often astonished, and sometimes amused, to read the reports of our officers who state with much glorification that they captured a large quantity of *necessary* supplies, so much wanted in the American camp, and in the enumeration of these "necessary supplies" they begin with "rum" and follow with "bread and hospital stores." It was seldom that "rum" was ever destroyed to lessen the burden of the march. We have seen that Greene sent back his baggage before the battle began, but was careful to retain the "hogsheads of rum and hospital stores."

The British commander did not stay long or consider much "the order of his going."

"McArthur was called up from Fairlawn to cover Colonel Stewart's retreat; and leaving seventy of his wounded to his enemy, and many of his dead unburied; breaking the stocks of one thousand stand of arms and casting them into the spring; destroying his stores and then moving off precipitately, the English commander fell back and retreated to Fairlawn."*

General Greene pursued for one day, on the road to Charleston, but finding that Colonel Stewart still retired before him, and being now left at lib-

---

*Johnson, vol. 2, p. 232.

erty to watch the movements of Cornwallis; and his wounded and prisoners requiring his attention, he resolved again to retire to the High Hills of the Santee.

The last regular army of the Crown had been driven to its seacoast defence, bleeding and dying. Majoribanks, the gallant deliverer of this shattered army, was wounded, and shortly thereafter died. He was buried on the roadside in their flight to the sea. Webster and Majoribanks, it may be said of them, that they offered themselves as willing sacrifices to their king, knowing that only with their lives could be purchased the escape of their commands from destruction. Both survived their battles long enough to be told that the American commander had fled from the field, but both lived to find that commander following the line of their flight. Both died on their way to the sea, and were buried in the land they fought to enslave. To the credit of that land no dishonor has been shown to their last resting-places, and, though foes to American liberty, their names, as soldiers, will ever awaken in every manly breast, a feeling of pity for their misfortune, and a chivalric sentiment of admiration for the heroic spirits which animated them in their discharge of duty to their Crown and kingdom. The brave are never contemned.

The Americans captured and held 500 prisoners as the result of this battle. They lost forty prisoners. They captured one cannon, and by indiscretion lost four. Sixty-one American officers had been killed and wounded. Twenty-one of these had died on the field of battle, and among them Colonel Richard Campbell, of Virginia, who had shared the honors and the toils of the campaign from "Camp Repose," on the Pee Dee, to this last battle in the south. He fell as his victorious troops were driving the enemy before them; he was pierced by a ball through the breast, and only survived a few hours.

The whole American casualties are given by General Greene, as one lieutenant colonel, six captains, five subalterns, and ninety rank and file, killed; two lieutenant colonels, Henderson and Howard, seven captains, twenty lieutenants, twenty-four sergeants and two hundred and nine rank and file, wounded. Colonel Washington fell into the hands of the enemy a wounded prisoner.

The British casualties are given by Colonel Stewart, as three commissioned officers, six sergeants and seventy-six men, killed; sixteen commissioned officers, twenty sergeants, and two hundred and thirty-two men, missing. Total casualties six hundred and ninety-three. These casualties are, however, far below the true figures, for he lost five hundred prisoners, double his admitted loss of missing.

On the 12th day of September, four days after the battle on the 8th, General Greene recrossed the Santee at Nelson's Ferry, and on the 15th was in his old camp at the "High Hills of Santee." His army was soon reduced to less than one thousand effective men, with nearly six hundred wounded, of both armies, in his charge. '

On the 9th of November, General Greene's camp was enlivened by the news of the surrender of Cornwallis at Yorktown.

On the 18th the High Hills were abandoned, and numerous minor operations concluded the Southern campaign; but the armies did not again meet in the field."*

*Carrington's Battles, p. 583.

CHAPTER XI.

Sketches of Charles and Joseph McDowell—Joseph Graham—Major "Hal." Dixon—Brigadier General Jethro Sumner—General Rutherford—General Butler—The End.

IT was not my original purpose to relate all the minor military transactions which occurred during the invasion of the Southern Colonies, nor to record the conflicts between the Whigs and Tories, which were collateral to the general operations of the American and English armies, and, therefore, I shall not further pursue the narrative of those less events which followed the battle of Eutaw Springs.

Here is a pleasant resting-place, for the contemplation of North Carolinians, where her Regular soldiers won such imperishable renown and her Militia were no less gallant and steady than her Regulars. North Carolina furnished half the soldiers who fought the battle of Eutaw Springs and drove the British army of invasion forever from the Southern provinces. The tidings of this victory reached Yorktown and inspired the besiegers with fresh spirit and enterprise, and brought dismay to those within, who were only counting the days when their captivity would begin. Independence was about to burst like a beacon light over the American States.

It is due, however, to some of the heroes of North Carolina, who bore such conspicuous parts in this noble struggle for liberty, that they should be better known to our people, in order that honor may yet be done to their memories.

To the brothers, CHARLES and JOSEPH McDOWELL, of Quaker Meadows, and to their no less gallant cousin, Joseph McDowell, of Pleasant Garden, Burke County, North Carolina, are due more credit and honor for the victory of King's Mountain than to any other leaders who participated in that decisive and wonderful battle. Yet, the name of McDowell does not appear on the granite shaft, raised by patriot hands, on those memorable heights—a reproach to the intelligence of the men who wrote its inscriptions and an indignity to North Carolina which contributed so largely to construct the monument. It was Colonel Charles McDowell, and Major Joseph McDowell, his brother, who originated the idea of organizing a force to capture Ferguson, and in conjunction with their cousin, they were the most prominent in executing the plan which they had conceived.

Major Joseph McDowell was subsequently a General of militia and was known as General McDowell. He also served as a member of Congress from North Carolina during the years of 1787, 1788, 1791 and 1792. In 1788 he was a member of the State Convention which met for the consideration of the Federal Constitution. He was of Scotch-Irish descent; his ancestors came to North Carolina by the way of Virginia. The McDowells of North Carolina, Virginia, Kentucky and Ohio are all of one common stock.

On one of the foot hills of the Blue Ridge, a beautiful round knob, selected for its lovely view, and overhanging the "Quaker Meadows," is the cemetery of the McDowell family. On a slab of marble, erected as a head-stone, is this inscription:

"TO THE MEMORY OF
GENERAL CHARLES McDOWELL,
A WHIG OFFICER IN THE REVOLUTIONARY WAR,
WHO DIED, AS HE HAD LIVED, A PATRIOT,
THE 31ST MARCH, 1815, AGED
ABOUT 70 YEARS."

By his side is the unmarked grave of Major Joseph McDowell, his brother. Not a stone is raised to his memory; not a line is carved to recount his deeds of valor and patriotism; no epitaph tells the story of King's Mountain and Cowpens and Ramsour's Mill, where he was foremost in the fight; no record speaks to the stranger and says, here lies a hero who was victorious in every field, and never turned his back on a foe. The only mark that indicates the grave of this gallant soldier is the letter J rudely carved on a white oak tree that stands at its head.

What a reproach to those who enjoy the liberties that were purchased with his blood! Will the State he loved and served so well suffer this reproach to continue?

Close by his side, the remains of his cousin,

Joseph McDowell, of Pleasant Garden, lie. On a head-stone is this inscription:

"HERE LIES THE BODY OF
CAPTAIN JOSEPH McDOWELL,
BORN 27TH FEBRUARY, 17—5,
(the other figure obliterated)
AGED 60 YEARS."

GENERAL JOSEPH GRAHAM, who was Major of mounted infantry, or dragoons, during the war, has done more to vindicate the truth of North Carolina's Revolutionary history than any citizen she has produced.

The carefully-prepared articles which he wrote in 1821, for Judge Murphey, who was, at that time, collecting material for a history of North Carolina, have been published in the University Magazine, at Chapel Hill. They were designed to correct the misstatements of cotemporary historians, who were blindly following in the footpath of error, which others had trodden, as is so much the custom of this day. They were written by Major Graham, who was an eye-witness and participant in most of the events related, and he appeals to the hundreds of his associates, then living, for the truth of his story.

To these sketches the author again acknowledges his indebtedness for much that has been reproduced in this book.

Perhaps the most brilliant officer, whose services enriched the annals of that memorable invasion, was MAJOR "HAL." DIXON, whose dashing and impetuous courage was so splendidly displayed among the shattered legions of Gates, at Camden. He refused to fly when his comrades had been driven from the field and his devoted band had been left exposed to the bayonet charge on its front and flanks. With a fierce spirit he faced his battalion to the charge, from either side, and fought as "long as a cartridge was in his belt," then, resorting to the bayonet himself, he cut his way through the attacking hosts and made good his retreat. We know from the roster that he died July 17th, 1782, after Independence had been won, but where he closed his eyes in death or where is his unmarked grave, we cannot tell. His letters, in 1781, several times, speak of returning to Caswell County, and it may be that his remains rest there, "in hope again to rise."

Among the militia officers, whose constant labors and services were devoted to their country's cause, two men deserve most honorable mention: BRIGADIER GENERAL GRIFFITH RUTHERFORD, of Rowan County, and BRIGADIER GENERAL JOHN BUTLER, of Orange County. They were seldom out of the military field, and always bore themselves proudly and manfully in battle. General Rutherford was severely wounded at Gates' defeat in August, 1780, and afterwards was a great sufferer in the prison camp of the enemy at St. Augustine. He was exchanged in July, 1781, and in September he was again in the field. He was honored by having a county named for him. He subsequently removed to Tennessee, where a like honor was in store for him.

The greatest soldier of that day, from North Carolina, was BRIGADIER GENERAL JETHRO SUMNER, of Warren County. We know that he passed, without reproach, through the terrible campaigns of Washington, in New Jersey and Pennsylvania, and survived as one of the seven hundred from a brigade of more than five thousand men, and was promoted for gallantry and skill displayed amid those bloody scenes. For his constancy, fidelity and great influence in the State, he was detached to raise the four new regiments of regulars in North Carolina in 1780–'81, and his letters during that period evince such a lofty and unselfish patriotism that they challenge the admiration of every reader. If his patriotic offer to command the militia, assembling for the battle of Guilford Court-House, had been accepted, it is probable, nay, almost certain, that the revolutionary struggle would have ended at that place, instead of Yorktown, and that the lives of thousands of good men would have been spared. Under his eye, and with his discipline and example to prepare and encourage them, the North Carolina regulars and militia were among the foremost in the fight, exciting the wonder and admiration of General Greene, at Eutaw Springs.

In the most distressing condition of public affairs; amidst the jealousies of the smaller men of that day; without arms or equipments for his soldiers when organized; surrounded by doubting patriots and disloyal Tories, he never lowered his crest or trailed his flag in the dust, but with undaunted will and unswerving faith, he struggled manfully against every obstacle and danger, until at last he was able to put in the field three battalions of disciplined soldiers, who gave the final and fatal blow to British prestige and power in the South. He made no parade over his victory, but was as modest in triumph as he was constant and faithful in disaster. One of the earliest military orders preserved in North Carolina is this:

"IN COMMITTEE OF SAFETY, November 28th, 1775.
"HALIFAX.
"Ordered that Major Jethro Sumner raise what minute men and volunteers he can and follow Colonel Long with the utmost despatch.   A copy by order,
"OROND^r. DAVIS, *Clerk.*"

And from that day to the end of the struggle, more than seven years, he was in the active service of his country. It is not recorded of him, that he ever fled from the foe or left his soldiers in the field. He enjoyed the full confidence of Washington, Lafayette and Greene, and was their correspondent while he was in the South.

His letters do not indicate that he was either educated or cultivated, but he possessed that native genius and originality of thought that gave him confidence and power in every emergency. He knew men and things from observation and experience, and was ever ready to profit by the knowledge.

He was not irritable like Greene, and, in his unguarded correspondence, never spoke evil of his enemies. He was hopeful, patient, serene and faithful in the most trying scenes of life, and never faltered in his devotion to the cause of the Colonies.

I have no authentic record of General Sumner's early life. Wheeler says he was born in Virginia, but Wheeler is so often inaccurate that he cannot be relied upon. In the same sketch he says, "General Sumner behaved gallantly at Camden." He was not there. He was appointed Colonel of the third regiment of Regulars the 15th of April, 1776, and Brigadier General the 9th January, 1779.

After the war General Sumner married a wealthy widow, a Mrs. Heiss, of Newbern, by whom he had three children—Thomas Edward, who died without issue; "Jacky," who also left "no continuance;" Mary, his daughter, married Hon. Thomas Blount, a member of Congress, and brother of Major Reading Blount, who fought at Eutaw Springs. She had no children, and the generation of General Sumner ended with her death.

He was buried in Warren County, near the road that runs from Louisburg to Warrenton, and near the old Shocco Chapel. There is a slab over his grave with this inscription:

"TO THE MEMORY
OF
GENERAL JETHRO SUMNER,
ONE OF THE HEROES OF
1776."

Not a county or town in the State bears his name. The day of his death and his birth are alike unknown. No voice has been raised in eulogy of his heroic character; no public recognition of his services has ever been made; modest and unpretentious in life, neglected in his death, this great Carolinian sleeps in the solitude of the forest, where the waste of time will soon obliterate the trace and memory of his grave.

> " Lo! here he lies, who every danger braved;
> Unwept, unhonored, in the land he saved."

Will not some young North Carolinian undertake the honorable task of having these sacred remains removed to the capital of the State, and marked by a monument, worthy of the memory and heroic deeds of this noble soldier?

My task is done. My duty to my State is performed. In reading the histories of the invasion of the Colonies, in 1780–'81, my heart burned with indignation at the many misrepresentations, of the people of North Carolina, which had so long gone unchallenged. I was surprised at the way the State had been robbed of her honors, and unjustly reproached by unworthy men, and astonished that our own authors had repeated these reproaches, rather than take the trouble to investigate the truth of history and repel them. I therefore determined to do what I could to correct these misrepresentations, and resent the reproaches so unjustly cast on my native State, which I so fondly love. This book is the result of that determination.

It was prepared among the busy cares of a lawyer's office, with a full practice on my hands; but if it shall serve to awaken the slumbering pride of our people, who have been more modest than wise, or provoke them to investigate the truth of North Carolina history, or increase their love and devotion to the "good old North State," the object of my book shall have been accomplished.

THE END.

Appendix A.

NORTH CAROLINA TROOPS IN THE CONTINENTAL LINE.

A REGISTER OF OFFICERS, WITH DATES OF COMMIS-
SIONS, MADE UP UNDER DIRECTION OF THE
SECRETARY OF STATE* FROM RECORDS
IN HIS OFFICE, OCTOBER, 1884.

FIRST REGIMENT.

COLONELS.

Moore, James------1 Sept., 1775
  Brigadier General 10 April, 1776

Nash, Francis------10 April, 1776
  Brigadier General -5 Feb., 1777
Clark, Thomas -----5 Feb., 1777

LIEUTENANT COLONELS.

Nash, Francis-------1 Sept., 1775
Clark, Thomas ----10 April, 1776

Davis, William------5 Feb., 1777

MAJORS.

Clark, Thomas------1 Sept., 1775
Davis, William-----10 April, 1776

Williams, William B, 13 June, 1776
Walker, John------20 April, 1777

STAFF.

ADJUTANTS.
Williams, William--1 Sept., 1775
DeKeyser, Lehansyus,
         16 Sept., 1775

SURGEONS.
Guion, Isaac---------1 Sept. 1775
Helmburgh, Fred-15 March, 1778

PAYMASTERS.
Bradley, Richard--5 March, 1777
Lord, William -----11 Dec., 1776

COMMISSARY.
Kennon, William--23 Sept., 1776

CHAPLAIN.
Tate, James---------13 Oct., 1775

JUDGE ADVOCATE.
Boyd, Adam---------— Oct., 1777

*Hon. W. L. Saunders.

CAPTAINS.

Davis, William 1 Sept., 1775	Thompson, Lawrence, 15 Aug., 1776
Picket, William 1 Sept., 1775	Bowman, Joshua 18 Sept., 1776
Dickson, Henry* 1 Sept., 1775	Dixon, Tilghman 5 Feb., 1777
Allen, Thomas 1 Sept., 1775	Rolston, Robert 8 March, 1777
Rice, Hezekiah 1 Sept., 1775	Tatum, Howell 3 April, 1777
Rowan, Robert 1 Sept., 1775	Brown, John† 26 April, 1777
Davidson, George 1 Sept., 1775	Reed, James 8 July, 1777
Moore, Alfred 1 Sept., 1775	Armstrong, Wm 29 Aug., 1777
Walker, John 1 Sept., 1775	Summers, John 10 July, 1778
Green, William 1 Sept., 1775	King, James 1 April, 1780
Grainger, Caleb 1 Sept., 1775	Callender, Thomas ——, 1780
Hogg, Thomas 1 March, 1776	

LIEUTENANTS.

Lillington, John 1 Sept., 1775	Blythe, Samuel 5 Feb., 1777
Berryhill, William 1 Sept., 1775	Baker, Peter 8 Feb., 1777
Rice, Hezekiah 1 Sept., 1775	Hall, Thomas 8 Feb., 1777
Bowman, Joshua 1 Sept., 1775	Varner, Robert 8 March, 1777
McNeill, Hector 1 Sept., 1775	Watters, Samuel 29 March, 1777
Brandon, William 1 Sept., 1775	King, James 3 April, 1777
Thompson, Lawrence, 1 Sept., 1775	Rogers, Patrick 3 April, 1777
Tatum, Absalom 1 Sept., 1775	Rice, John 8 April, 1777
Hill, William 1 Sept., 1775	Marshall, Dixon 26 April, 1777
Hogg, Thomas 1 Sept., 1775	Scull, John 26 April, 1777
Dixon, Tilghman 20 Oct., 1775	Hair, John L 16 Aug., 1777
Reed, James 7 July, 1776	Council, Robert 20 Aug., 1777
Callender, Thomas 1 Jan., 1777	Milligan, James 29 Aug., 1777
Gambelle, Edmund 20 Jan., 1777	Armstrong, William ——, 1777
Walters, William 5 Feb., 1777	Craven, James ——, 1777
Summers, John 5 Feb., 1777	

ENSIGNS.

McAlister, Neil 1 Sept., 1775	Picket, Thomas 20 Oct., 1775
Childs, James 1 Sept., 1775	Brown, John 20 Oct., 1775
Graham, George 1 Sept., 1775	Cheese, John 11 June, 1776
Moore, Maurice, Jr., 1 Sept., 1775	Craven, James 11 June, 1776
Neill, Henry 1 Sept., 1775	Callender, Thomas 11 June, 1776
Rolston, Robert 1 Sept., 1775	Marshall, Dixon 28 March, 1777
Taylor, John 1 Sept., 1775	Crawford, David 10 June, 1777
Turner, Berryman 1 Sept., 1775	Erwin, John ——, 1777
Pope, Henry 1 Sept., 1775	Council, Robert ——, 1777
Tatum, Howell 1 Sept., 1775	Milligan, James ——, ——

SECOND REGIMENT.

COLONELS.

Howe, Robert 1 Sept., 1775	Martin, Alexander 10 April, 1776
Brigadier General 10 April, 1776	Patton, John 22 Nov., 1777

LIEUTENANT COLONELS.

Martin, Alexander 1 Sept., 1775	Harney, Selby 22 Nov., 1777
Patton, John 10 April, 1776	Murfree, Hardy 1 April, 1778

*Afterwards Colonel "Hal" Dickson.
†Afterwards Colonel.

(475)

MAJORS.

Patton, John _____ 1 Sept., 1775
White, John _____ 10 April, 1776
Murfree, Hardy _____ 1 Feb., 1777

STAFF.

ADJUTANTS.
White, John _____ 1 Sept., 1775
Ingles, John _____ 3 May, 1776
Evans, Thomas ____ 22 Nov., 1778

SURGEONS.
Pasteur, William ___ 1 Sept., 1775
McClure, William ___ 7 June, 1776

PAYMASTERS.
Fenner, Richard ____ — ——, 1777
Spicer, John _____ 11 Dec., 1776
Fenner, Robert _____ 1 June, 1778

QUARTERMASTER.
Slade, Stephen _____ 1 Jan., 1778

COMMISSARY.
Salter, Robert _____ 23 April, 1776
Salter, James _____ 19 Dec., 1776

CAPTAINS.

Blount, James _____ 1 Sept., 1775
Armstrong, John*__ 1 Sept., 1775
Crawford, Charles __ 1 Sept., 1775
Murfree, Hardy ___ 1 Sept., 1775
Toole, Henry Irwin_ 1 Sept., 1775
Keais, Nathan _____ 1 Sept., 1775
Bright, Simon _____ 1 Sept., 1775
Payne, Michael ____ 1 Sept., 1775
Walker, John _____ 1 Sept., 1775
Fenner, William ____ 1 May, 1776
Herritage, John _____ 3 May, 1776
Vail, Edward, Jr___ 21 Aug., 1776

Hall, Clement ____ 19 April, 1777
Martin, James _____ 20 April, 1777
Tarrant, Manlove___ 24 Oct., 1777
Ingles, John _____ 12 Nov., 1777
Cradock, John _____ 21 Dec., 1777
Allen, Charles _____ — ——, 1777
Gee, James _____ — ——, 1777
Williams, Benjamin — ——, 1777
Fenner, Robert ____ 4 Oct., 1777
Daves, John _____ 8 Sept., 1781
Evans, Thomas ____ 1 June, 1781
Budd, Samuel _____ — ——, 1782

LIEUTENANTS.

Grainger, John _____ 1 Sept., 1775
Smith, Robert _____ 1 Sept., 1775
Herritage, John _____ 1 Sept., 1775
Hall, Clement _____ 1 Sept., 1775
Vail, Edward, Jr.___ 1 Sept., 1775
Tate, Joseph _____ 1 Sept., 1775
Fenner, William ___ 1 Sept., 1775
Williams, John _____ 1 Sept., 1775
Gee, James _____ 1 Sept., 1775
Williams, Benjamin, 1 Sept., 1775
Gardner, William __ 20 Oct., 1775
Fenner, Robert _____ 1 Jan., 1776
Vance, David _____ 20 April, 1776
Lowe, Philip _____ 3 May, 1776
Worth, Joseph _____ 3 May, 1776
Standing, Thomas__ 3 May, 1776
Martin, James _____ 3 May, 1776
Nash, Clement _____ 3 May, 1776
Ingles, John _____ 3 May, 1776
Graham, Richard __ 8 June, 1776
Martin, Samuel ____ 8 June, 1776

Tarrant, Manlove___ 8 June, 1776
Allen, Charles _____ 8 June, 1776
Evans, Thomas ____ 19 July, 1776
Jacob, John _____ 1 Nov., 1776
Williams, John ____ 21 April, 1777
Buford, William ___ 15 May, 1777
Luton, James _____ 4 Oct., 1777
Daves, John _____ — Oct., 1777
Andrews, Richard__ — ——, 1777
Cradock, John _____ — ——, 1777
Cotgrave, Arthur___ — ——, 1777
McIlwaine, Stringer — ——, 1777
Parkinson, James __ — ——, 1777
Rolstone, Isaac _____ — ——, 1777
Raiford, John _____ — ——, 1777
Sawyer, Levy _____ — ——, 1777
Campen, James ____ — ——, 1777
Budd, Samuel _____ — ——, 1777
Slade, Stephen _____ 11 Jan., 1781
Fenner, Richard ___ 12 May, 1781

*Afterwards Colonel.

(476)

ENSIGNS.

Vipon, Henry .... 1 Sept., 1775	Tochsey, William ... 3 May, 1776
Pugh, Whitmel ...... 1 Sept., 1775	Sawyer, William .... 15 May, 1776
Oliver, John .... 1 Sept., 1775	Evans, Thomas ...... 6 June, 1776
Lowe, Philip .... 1 Sept., 1775	Kilbey, Wm. Tyler .. 6 June, 1776
Gardner, William .. 1 Sept., 1775	Jacobs, John .... 6 June, 1776
Cleveland, Benjamin, 1 Sept., 1775	Bickerstaff, John .... 8 June, 1776
	Rolestone, Isaac ..... 8 June, 1776
Cook, James .... 1 Sept., 1775	Vance, David .... 8 June, 1776
Caswell, William ... 1 Sept., 1775	Campen, James .... 11 Dec., 1776
Clinch, James ...... 1 Sept., 1775	Williams, William . 11 Dec., 1776
Woodhouse, John .. 1 Sept., 1775	Pilley, John .... 11 Dec., 1776
McClammy, Joseph 20 Oct., 1775	Daves, John .... 30 Sept., 1776
Standing, Thomas .. 20 Oct., 1775	Curtis, Reuben ..... — ——, 1777
Allen, Charles ...... 20 Oct., 1775	Luton, James .... — ——, 1777
Worth, Joseph ...... 20 Oct., 1775	Slade, Stephen ..... 5 Sept., 1778
Cradock, John ...... 3 May, 1776	Lacey, John .... 20 May, 1779
Tarrant, Manlove ... 3 May, 1776	Fenner, Richard ... 10 Jan., 1780
Smith, Samuel ..... 3 May, 1776	

THIRD REGIMENT.

COLONEL.

Sumner, Jethro 15 April, 1776.   Brigadier General, 9 Jan., 1779.

LIEUTENANT-COLONELS.

Ashton, William .. 15 April, 1776	Dixon, Henry ...... 12 May, 1778
Brewster, Lott .. 25 Oct., 1777	

MAJORS.

Lockhart, Samuel 15 April, 1776	Eaton, Pinketham 22 Nov., 1777
Dixon, Henry ...... 8 July, 1777	Emmett, James .... 15 Feb., 1778
(From 1st Regiment.)	

STAFF.

ADJUTANTS.
Washington, Robert
　　　　　　　　15 April, 1776
Hodgton, Alvery ... — ——, 1777
Hart, Anthony ..... — ——, 1778

SURGEONS.
Hall, Robert .... 17 April, 1776
Usher, William ..... 4 Dec., 1776
Ridley, William ... 21 April, 1777

PAYMASTERS.
Bradley, Richard ... — ——, 1777
Ballard, Kedar ..... 10 Oct., 1779
Blount, William .... 11 Dec., 1778

QUARTERMASTERS.
Wilson, Whitfield 24 April, 1777
Colman, Charles .... 14 Oct., 1777
Clandennin, John .. 14 Dec., 1779

COMMISSARY.
Webb, John .... 23 April, 1776
Amis, William ..... 6 May, 1776
Amis, Thomas ..... 22 Dec., 1776

(477)

CAPTAINS.

Brinkley, William_16 April, 1776
Eaton, Pinketham_16 April, 1776
Emmet, James _____ 16 April, 1776
Granberry, Thomas,
      16 April, 1776
Gray, John_____16 April, 1776
Barrot, William___16 April, 1776
Granberry, George, 16 April, 1776
Cook, James_____16 April, 1776
Jones, Daniel_____— ——, 1776

Ballard, Kedar_____— Nov., 1777
Wood, Matthew_____ 22 Nov., 1777
Madearis, John _____ 23 Dec., 1777
Edmund, Nicholas _— ——, 1777
Bradley, Gee_____19 Sept., 1778
Montford, Joseph ___9 Jan., 1779
Yarborough, Edward—Jan., 1779
Fawn, William_____— ——, ——

LIEUTENANTS.

Ballard, Kedar_____16 April, 1776
Lytle, Micajah _____3 May, 1776
Wood, Matthew_____24 July, 1776
Linton, William_____24 July, 1776
Bradley, Gee_____— ——, 1776
Madearis, John_____15 April, 1777
Fawn, William_____15 April, 1777
Montford, Joseph__16 April, 1777
Rushworm, Wm___16 April, 1777

Hart, Anthony_____16 April, 1777
Yarborough, Edward,
      16 April, 1777
O'Neal, Charles_____20 July, 1777
Clandennin, John__23 Dec., 1777
Hodgton, Alvery___— ——, 1777
Granberry, John___— ——, 1777
Tillery, John_____— ——, 1777
Lackey, Christopher — ——, 1777

ENSIGNS.

Clandennin, John_15 April, 1776
Yarborough, Edward_8 May, 1776

Morgan, Benjamin__— ——, 1776
O'Neal, Charles___18 April, 1777

FOURTH REGIMENT.

COLONEL.

Polk, Thomas _____15 April, 1776.

LIEUTENANT COLONELS.

Thaxton, James_____15 April, 1776 | Armstrong, John_____17 July, 1782

MAJORS.

Davidson, William__15 April, 1776 | Nelson, John_____3 Feb., 1778

STAFF.

ADJUTANTS.

Williams, William___15 April, 1776
Covington, William_28 March, 1777
Slade, William _____1 June, 1778
Pasteur, Thomas ____26 June, 1779

SURGEONS.

Boyd, Hugh_____17 April, 1776
Usher, William_____24 April, 1777

QUARTERMASTER.

Douglas, William____10 Feb., 1777

PAYMASTERS.

Pasteur, William ____12 Dec., 1776
Duncan, Robert_____— ——, 1777
Pasteur, Thomas_ ___19 Oct., 1782

COMMISSARY.

Southerland, Ransome,
      23 April, 1776
Mallett, Daniel_____16 Dec., 1776

CHAPLAIN.

Atkin, James_____5 April, 1777

CAPTAINS.

Moore, Roger ......16 April, 1776	Nelson, John........16 April, 1776
Ashe, John..........16 April, 1776	Goodman, William....1 Oct., 1776
Maclaine, John .....16 April, 1776	Williams, James .....3 April, 1777
Smith, Robert ......16 April, 1776	Lewis, Micajah ......25 July, 1777
Coles, William T....16 April, 1776	Carter, Benjamin .....1 Jan., 1779
Harris, Thomas.....16 April, 1776	Brevard, Alexander ..20 Oct., 1780
Philips, Joseph .....16 April, 1776	

LIEUTENANTS.

Williams, James......7 June, 1776	Roulledge, William ..25 Jan., 1777
Coots, James........20 Nov., 1776	Jones, David ....3 April, 1777
Whitmel, Blunt.....20 Nov., 1766	Polk, Charles........25 April, 1777
Carter, Benjamin....22 Nov., 1776	Slade, William ....1 May, 1777
Brevard, Alexander ...9 Dec., 1776	Redpeth, John......20 Aug., 1777
McGibbony, Patrick ..9 Dec., 1776	Gillespie, Robert....— Aug., 1777
Williams, William....9 Dec., 1776	Knott, William......— —, 1777
Wilkinson, Reuben...9 Dec., 1776	Hickman, William....— —, 1777
Pollock, Jacob.......— —, 1776	Pasteur, Thomas.....29 Dec., 1778
Alexander, Charles...20 Jan., 1777	Hollingsworth, Charles .—, —
Moslander, Abel.....25 Jan., 1777	

ENSIGNS.

Brevard, Alexander..27 Nov., 1776	McCarthy, Florence...1 May, 1777
McGibbony, Patrick.27 Nov., 1776	Nelson, Alexander ....1 July, 1777
Pasteur, Thomas.....15 July, 1777	Gillespie, Robert.....— —, 1777
Murray, William.....1 April, 1777	Curtis, Joshua........— —, —

FIFTH REGIMENT.

COLONEL.
Buncombe, Edward......................15 April, 1776.

LIEUTENANT COLONELS.
Irwin, Henry........15 April, 1776	Dawson, Levy.......19 Oct., 1777
Davidson, Wm. L ....4 Oct., 1777	

MAJORS.
Dawson, Levy.......15 April, 1776	Blount, Reading .....— —, 1782
Hogg, Thomas ....4 Oct., 1777	

STAFF.

ADJUTANTS.	PAYMASTER.
Darnall, Henry......15 April, 1776	Rogers, John, Jr......11 Dec., 1776
Verrier, James.........1 Oct., 1776	QUARTERMASTER.
Armstrong, Thomas, A. D. C., 28 March, 1782	Swann, Nimrod .....18 June, 1777
SURGEON.	CHAPLAINS.
Cooley, Samuel ......16 April, 1776	Foard, Hezekiah....20 April, 1777
COMMISSARY.	Boyd, Adam..........1 Oct., 1777
Mallett, Peter......23 April, 1776	

(479)

CAPTAINS.

Blount, Reading ---- 16 April, 1776	Coleman, Benjamin -- 30 April, 1777
Enloe, John -------- 16 April, 1776	Groves, William ----- 17 Aug., 1777
Caswell, William ---- 16 April, 1776	Armstrong, Thomas -- 25 Oct., 1777
Alderson, Simon ---- 16 April, 1776	Goodin, Christopher -- -- Jan., 1779
Stedman, Benjamin - 16 April, 1776	Porterfield, Dennis ---- 1 Feb., 1779
Simons, Peter ------- 16 April, 1776	Stewart, Charles ----- 12 May, 1780
Williams, John P ---- 16 April, 1776	Bailey, Benjamin ----- 8 Sept., 1781
Ward, William ------- 16 April, 1776	Reed, Jesse ---------- 1 April, 1782
Darnall, Henry ------- 1 Oct., 1776	McNees, John ------- 2 Nov., 1782

LIEUTENANTS.

Eborne, Thomas ---- 16 April, 1776	Roberts, John ----- 28 March, 1777
Cooper, William ---- 16 April, 1776	Hewell, William --- 28 March, 1777
Armstrong, Thomas - 16 April, 1776	Ewell, William ----- 20 April, 1777
Groves, William ---- 16 April, 1776	Blount, Thomas ---- 28 April, 1777
Lockey, Christopher -- 3 May, 1776	Stewart, Charles ----- 23 July, 1777
Little, Micajah ------- 6 May, 1776	Diggs, Anthony ----- 20 Aug., 1777
Allen, John ---------- 1 Oct., 1776	Smith, Jabez -------- 1 Sept., 1777
Bailey, Benjamin ----- 1 Oct., 1776	Gerald, Charles ------ 19 Dec., 1777
Curtis, John --------- 1 Oct., 1776	Allen, Walter -------- 4 Oct., 1777
Eborne, John -------- 1 Oct., 1776	Ivey, Curtis --------- 10 Oct., 1777
Hodges, John ------- 1 Oct., 1776	Holland, Spier ------ 25 Oct., 1777
Long, Nehemiah ------ 1 Oct., 1776	Allen, Thomas -------- ——, 1777
Reed, Jesse --------- 20 Oct., 1776	Verrier, James ------ — June, 1778
Sugg, George -------- — ——, 1776	Crutches, Anthony --- 18 May, 1781
McNees, John ------- 8 March, 1777	

ENSIGNS.

Holland, Spier ----- 24 March, 1776	Allen, Walter ------ 28 March, 1777
Alderson, Thomas ---- 3 May, 1776	Ivey, Curtis -------- 23 April, 1777
Hodges, John -------- 4 May, 1776	Gerald, Charles ----- 30 April, 1777
McKinne, James ----- 9 May, 1776	Crutches, Henry ---- 20 Aug., 1777
Palmer, Joseph ------- 6 June, 1776	Verrier, James ------ 20 Aug., 1777
Bush, John --------- — ——, 1776	Smith, Jabez ------- — ——, 1777
Wooten, Shadrach ---- — ——, 1776	Crutches, Anthony --- 27 Feb., 1780
Diggs, Anthony ---- 20 March, 1777	

SIXTH REGIMENT.

COLONELS.

Lillington, Alexander - 15 April, 1776 | Lamb, Gideon ------- --- 26 Jan., 1777

LIEUTENANT COLONELS.

Taylor, William ------ 15 April, 1776 | Ashe, John B -------- 2 Nov., 1778
Lytle, Archibald ------ 26 Jan., 1777 |

MAJORS.

Lamb, Gideon ------ 15 April, 1776 | Donoho, Thomas ---- 13 Oct., 1781
Ashe, John B -------- 26 Jan., 1777 | Dougherty, George --- 17 July, 1782
McRee, Griffith J --- 11 Sept., 1781 |

(480)

STAFF.

ADJUTANTS.
Crafton, Bennet ..... 15 April, 1776
Coffield, Benjamin ... 17 May, 1777

SURGEONS.
McClure, William ... 17 April, 1776
Wilson, Robert ...... 8 June, 1776

PAYMASTERS.
Moseley, William .... 11 Dec., 1776
Cheesboro, John ...... 3 July, 1777
Dixon, Charles ...... 19 Jan., 1778

QUARTERMASTERS.
Johnson, James .... 2 April, 1777
Shaw, Daniel .... 2 June, 1778

COMMISSARY.
Hart, Thomas ...... 23 April, 1776

CAPTAINS.

James, John .... 16 April, 1776
Mitchell, George .... 16 April, 1776
Council, Arthur ..... 16 April, 1776
McRee, Griffith J .. 16 April, 1776
Taylor, Philip ...... 16 April, 1776
Lytle, Archibald .... 16 April, 1776
Saunders, Jesse ..... 16 April, 1776
Ashe, John Baptista. 16 April, 1776
Glover, William ...... 7 May, 1776

Donoho, Thomas .... 10 Sept., 1776
Dougherty, George ... 28 Oct., 1776
White, Thomas ...... 20 Jan., 1777
Child, Francis ...... 26 Jan., 1777
Williams, Daniel .... 1 April, 1777
Pike, Benjamin ..... 28 April, 1777
Little, William ..... 28 Jan., 1779
Hadley, Joshua ..... 13 June, 1779
Jones, Samuel .... — ——, 1781

LIEUTENANTS.

Little, William ..... 16 April, 1776
Armstrong, Andrew. 16 April, 1776
Goodin, Christopher. 16 April, 1776
Moore, Dempsey .... 16 April, 1776
Thompson, Samuel .. 16 April, 1776
Glover, William ..... 16 April, 1776
Pike, Benjamin ..... 16 April, 1776
Henderson, Pleasant 16 April, 1776
Williams, Daniel .... 16 April, 1776
Child, Francis ...... 16 April, 1776
Love, Amos .... 16 April, 1776
White, Thomas ..... 16 April, 1776
Armstrong, Thomas. 16 April, 1776
Kennon, John .... 16 April, 1776
Donoho, Thomas .... 16 April; 1776
Dougherty, George .. 16 April, 1776
McCann, John .... 16 April, 1776
Hart, John .... 7 May, 1776
Owens, John .... 7 May, 1776

Martin, Samuel ...... 6 June, 1776
Jones, Maurice ..... 15 June, 1776
Lytle, William ...... 6 June, 1776
Grant, Reuben ...... 6 June, 1776
Pasteur, John .... 2 July, 1776
Parker, Kedar ...... 19 Sept., 1776
Green, William. 28 Oct., 1776
Jones, Samuel .... 1 Jan., 1777
Hadley, Joshua ...... 1 April, 1777
Hilton, William ..... 1 April, 1777
Porterfield, Dennis .. 2 April, 1777
Walker, Solomon .... 20 April, 1777
Handcock, William .. 28 April, 1777
Dickinson, Richard .. 10 Oct., 1777
Shaw, Daniel .... 11 Oct., 1777
White, Matthew ..... — ——, 1777
Dixon, Charles ...... 8 Feb., 1779
Saunders, William ... 8 Feb., 1779

ENSIGNS.

Lytle, William ...... 16 April, 1776
Grant, Thomas ..... 16 April, 1776
Porterfield, Dennis.. 16 April, 1776
Hadley, Joshua ..... 16 April, 1776
Walker, Solomon .... 16 April, 1776
Grant, Reuben ...... 16 April, 1776
Singletary, Richard.. 16 April, 1776
Outlaw, Edward .... 16 April, 1776
Parker, Kedar .... 7 May, 1776
Jones, Samuel .... 6 June, 1776

Green, William .... 6 June, 1776
Dickinson, Richard ... 2 April, 1777
Dixon, Charles .... 2 April, 1777
Williams, Theophilus. 2 April, 1777
Mixon, Charles ...... 2 April, 1777
Saunders, William ... 2 April, 1777
Shaw, Daniel .... 2 April, 1777
Liscombe, John ..... 28 April, 1777
Cheesboro, John .... 25 April, 1779

(481)

SEVENTH REGIMENT.

COLONELS.

Hogun, James _____26 Nov., 1776 | Mebane, Robert _____9 Feb., 1777
Brigadier General __———, .— |

LIEUTENANT COLONEL.

Mebane, Robert_____ _____27 Nov., 1776.

MAJORS.

Brewster, Lott_____27 Nov., 1776 | Fenner, William _____24 Oct., 1777
(To 3d Regiment.) | (From 2d Regiment.)

STAFF.

ADJUTANTS. | QUARTERMASTER.
Dawes, Abraham ____22 Dec., 1776 | Dawes, Josiah _____10 July, 1777
Beeks, William_____— Dec., 1777 | COMMISSARY.
PAYMASTERS. | Bryan, Hardy_____11 Dec., 1776
Harvey, James_____11 Dec., 1776 | SURGEON.
Guion, Isaac_____— ———, 1777 | Hamilton, Hanse ___— April, 1777
Baker, John _____— June, 1778 |

CAPTAINS.

Brickell, Thomas____28 Nov., 1776 | Vaughan, James_____19 Dec., 1776
McGlaughan, John __28 Nov., 1776 | Dawson, Henry _____19 Dec., 1776
Poynter, John_____28 Nov., 1776 | Baker, John_____6 July, 1777
Walker, Joseph _____28 Nov., 1776 | Dayley, Joshua _____12 Oct., 1777
Bell, Green_____28 Nov., 1776 | Ely, Eli_____12 Oct., 1777
Cotten, Josiah _____28 Nov., 1776 | Ferrebee, William ____1 July, 1781
Macon, John_____11 Dec., 1776 | Walton, William_____1 Aug., 1781
Ely, Lemuel _____17 Dec., 1776 |

LIEUTENANTS.

Hays, James_____28 Nov., 1776 | Snowden, William___28 Nov., 1776
Baker, John _____28 Nov., 1776 | Ely, Eli _____11 Dec., 1776
Lynch, John_____28 Nov., 1776 | Myrick, John _____11 Dec., 1776
Powers, James _____28 Nov., 1776 | Moore, John_____17 Dec., 1776
Whedbee, Richard___28 Nov., 1776 | Dayley, Joshua_____19 Dec., 1776
Winborne, John_____28 Nov , 1776 | Harrison, William___19 Dec., 1776
Eason, Seth _____28 Nov., 1776 | Ramsay, Allen _____19 Dec , 1776
Watson, Thomas____28 Nov., 1776 | Barrow, Jacob_____22 Dec., 1776
Ferrebee, William___28 Nov., 1776 | Bailey, Benjamin____22 Dec., 1776
Barrow, Samuel ___ _28 Nov., 1776 | Walton, William____17 April, 1777
Vaughan, James_____28 Nov., 1776 | Jones, Thomas_____15 Aug , 1777
Macon, John_____28 Nov., 1776 | Dillon, Benjamin ___ 12 Oct., 1777
Bryant, John, Jr ____28 Nov., 1776 | Lassiter, Jethro_____12 Oct., 1777
Coleman, Theophilus, 28 Nov., 1776 | Gee, Howell_____— Nov., 1777
Noblen, William ____28 Nov., 1776 |

ENSIGNS.

Mercer, John _____28 Nov., 1776 | Bailey, Benjamin____28 Nov , 1776
Dillon, Benjamin____28 Nov., 1776 | Harrison, William___11 Dec., 1776
Caustauphen, James.28 Nov., 1776 | Sledge, Arthur _____19 Dec , 1776
Lassiter, Jethro_____28 Nov., 1776 | Whitaker, Hudson___22 Dec., 1776
Myrick, John_____28 Nov., 1776 | Gee, Howell_____15 April, 1777
Blanton, Rowland___28 Nov., 1776 | White, William_____17 April, 1777
Lynch, John_____28 Nov , 1770 | Jones, Thomas_____17 April, 1777
Webb, Elisha_____28 Nov., 1776 | Bryan, Benjamin .. 27 April, 1777

31

EIGHTH REGIMENT.

COLONEL.

Armstrong, James ....26 Nov., 1776.

LIEUTENANT COLONELS.

Ingram, James.......27 Nov., 1776	Dawson, Levy........19 Oct., 1777
Lockhart, Samuel...— Sept., 1777	Harney, Selby ......22 Nov., 1777
(From 3d Regiment.)	

MAJOR.

Harney, Selby ....27 Nov., 1776.

STAFF.

ADJUTANTS.	QUARTERMASTER.
Bush, William.........12 May, 1781	Graves, Francis.......1 Sept., 1777
Bush, John ....7 Aug., 1781	COMMISSARY.
SURGEON.	Green, Joseph........11 Dec., 1776
Loomis, Jonathan ...26 Nov., 1776	Blount, Jesse.........11 Dec., 1776
PAYMASTER.	
Taylor, John ....24 July, 1777	

CAPTAINS.

Walsh, John.........28 Nov., 1776	Ward, Edward.......28 Nov., 1776
Raiford, Robert.....28 Nov., 1776	Tartanson, Francis...16 Jan., 1777
Hargett, Frederick ..28 Nov., 1776	Quinn, Michael ......1 Aug., 1777
Pope, Henry........28 Nov., 1776	Dennis, William.....20 Sept., 1777
Gurley, William.....28 Nov., 1776	Chapman, Samuel....5 April, 1779
May, James, Jr......28 Nov., 1776	Pearl, James ....17 July, 1782
Nixon, Thomas .....28 Nov., 1776	

LIEUTENANTS.

Williams, Nathaniel B., 28 Nov., 1776	Godfrey, William....28 Nov., 1776
Quinn, Michael .....28 Nov., 1776	Mills, James.........28 Nov., 1776
Dennis, William ....28 Nov., 1776	Mills, Benjamin.....28 Nov., 1776
Chapman, Samuel...28 Nov., 1776	Carraway, Gideon...28 Nov., 1776
Foreman, Caleb.....28 Nov., 1776	Respess, Richard....28 Nov., 1776
Greer, Robert ......28 Nov., 1776	Bush, John ....8 Feb., 1777
Jones, Philip........28 Nov., 1776	Messick, Jacob......24 April, 1777
Wood, Solomon.....28 Nov., 1776	Langford, Alloway ...1 Aug., 1777
McNaughton, John..28 Nov., 1776	Bush, William ......15 Aug., 1777
Rhodes, Joseph.....28 Nov., 1776	Owen, Stephen......15 Aug., 1777
Singletary, William..28 Nov., 7776	Hollowell, Samuel...20 Sept., 1777
Lewis, Joseph ......28 Nov., 1776	Graves, Francis......26 Oct., 1777
	Pearl, James ....29 Oct., 1777

ENSIGNS.

Lanier, James, Jr ---28 Nov., 1776	Respess, John........28 Nov., 1776
Pearl, James........28 Nov., 1776	Custis, Thomas .....28 Nov., 1776
Messick, Jacob......18 Nov., 1776	Bertie, Thomas .....28 Nov., 1776
Carpenter, Peter ....28 Nov., 1776	Langford, Alloway....8 Feb., 1777
Jones, Samuel ......28 Nov., 1776	Bush, William ......10 April, 1777

(483)

NINTH REGIMENT.

COLONEL.
Williams, John P............................26 Nov., 1776.

LIEUTENANT COLONEL.
Luttrell, John...............................27 Nov., 1776.

MAJOR.
Polk, William................................27 Nov., 1776.

STAFF.

ADJUTANTS.	COMMISSARY.
McSheehy, Miles....12 Feb., 1777	Dent, William......11 Dec., 1776
Nuthall, Nathaniel...26 May, 1777	Guion, Isaac......11 Dec., 1776

SURGEON.
Johnston, Lancelot ..22 Dec., 1776

CAPTAINS.

McCrory, Thomas...28 Nov., 1776	Rice, Hezekiah......28 Nov., 1776
Cook, Richard D....28 Nov., 1776	Brevard, Joel........28 Nov., 1776
Ramsay, Matthew...28 Nov., 1776	Henderson, Michael.28 Nov., 1776
Wade, Joseph J.....28 Nov., 1776	Hall, James..........— May, 1777
Rochell, John.......28 Nov., 1776	Sharp, Anthony.....24 Aug., 1777

LIEUTENANTS.

Brown, Morgan.....28 Nov., 1776	Reese, George......28 Nov., 1776
Bullock, Daniel.....28 Nov., 1776	Harris, West.......28 Nov., 1776
Brevard, John......28 Nov., 1776	Ross, Francis.......28 Nov., 1776
Daniel, James......28 Nov., 1776	Yancey, Charles.....28 Nov., 1776
Johnson, Joshua....28 Nov., 1776	Hart, Samuel.......28 Nov., 1776
Dickerson, Nathaniel,28 Nov., 1776	Stewart, Joseph.....28 Nov., 1776
Neal, William......28 Nov., 1776	Covington, James...28 Nov., 1776
Rochell, Lovick.....28 Nov., 1776	Dobbins, Hugh......— ——, 1777
Sharpe, Anthony....28 Nov., 1776	Lewis, William....— March, 1777
Williams, Ralph.....28 Nov., 1776	Tatum, James.........1 Jan., 1778
Stewart, George.....28 Nov., 1776	Clark, Thomas.......1 Feb., 1779
Spratt, Thomas.....28 Nov., 1776	

ENSIGNS.

Ferrall, Micajah.....28 Nov., 1776	Moore, Robert......28 Nov., 1776
Clark, Thomas......28 Nov., 1776	Johnston, Joseph....28 Nov., 1776
Brice, Peter........28 Nov., 1776	Little, William.......6 Dec., 1776
Pearce, George......28 Nov., 1776	Rice, Jeptha........15 March, 1777
Smith, John........28 Nov., 1776	Nuthall, Nathaniel...20 May, 1777
Coleman, John......28 Nov., 1776	McRory, James.......2 May, 1777
Thomas, John......28 Nov., 1776	Tatum, James......12 Aug., 1777
Hicks, William......28 Nov., 1776	Washington, William,15 Aug., 1777

(484)

TENTH REGIMENT.

COLONEL.

Shepard, Abraham ....17 April, 1777.

LIEUTENANT COLONELS.

MAJORS.

STAFF.

SURGEONS.	QUARTERMASTERS.
Green, James W ...... 7 Dec., 1779	Verrier, James ...... — April, 1779
Forgus, James ...... 20 Aug., 1782	Campbell, James .... 10 Sept., 1779
SURGEON'S MATES.	Graves, Francis ...... 6 Nov., 1778
Moore, William ..... 19 Jan., 1778	Steed, Jesse .... 13 July, 1781
Green, James W .... 10 June, 1778	
Forgus, James .... 21 Feb., 1782	
Bull, Thomas ....— ——, 1782	
Maclaine, William ....1 Jan., 1783	

CAPTAINS.

Herron, Armwell .... 19 April, 1777	Rhodes, Joseph J ...... 1 Aug., 1777
Wilson, James .... 19 April, 1777	Shepard, William .... 20 Jan., 1778
Gregory, Dempsy ... 19 April, 1777	Mills, James .... — June, 1779
Jarvis, John .... 19 April, 1777	Campbell, James .... 14 Dec., 1779
Moore, Isaac .... 19 April, 1777	Bacot, Peter .... 8 Sept., 1781
Vanoy, Andrew ...... 19 April, 1777	Jones, Samuel ...... 11 Sept., 1781
Stevenson, Silas ..... 19 April, 1777	Moore, Elijah .... 13 Oct., 1781

LIEUTENANTS.

Barber, William .... 19 April, 1777	Wright, David ...... 15 Feb., 1778
Cook, George .... 19 April, 1777	Varcaze, James .... 17 March, 1778
Cannon, Lewis ...... 19 April, 1777	Southall, Stephen .... 1 April, 1778
Campbell, James .... 19 April, 1777	Lawrence, Nathaniel ..1 June, 1778
Koen, Caleb .... 19 April, 1777	Snowden, Nathaniel .. 5 June, 1778
Lowe, John .... 19 April, 1777	Wallace, James ..... 30 Nov., 1778
McCauley, Matthew .19 April, 1777	Ferrell, Luke L ...... — ——, 1778
Nicholson, Robert ... 19 April, 1777	Turner, Robert ...... — ——, 1778
Rountree, Reuben ... 19 April, 1777	Dillain, John .... — Feb., 1779
Jones, Timothy ..... 19 April, 1777	Cowan, David ..... 20 March, 1779
Ferebee, Joseph ...... 5 May, 1777	Morehead, James .. 23 March, 1779
Ferrell, William ..... 8 Sept., 1777	Campbell, John ..... 20 April, 1779
Jones, Samuel .... 4 Oct., 1777	Dudley, Thomas ... 20 June, 1779
Hays, Robert .... 9 Oct., 1777	Lord, William .... 1 Aug., 1779
Moore, Elijah .... 12 Oct., 1777	Lewis, Joel .... 1 Aug., 1779
Graves, Francis ..... 26 Oct., 1777	Hargrave, William .30 March, 1780
Cooper, Solomon .... 20 Jan., 1778	Foard, John .... — ——, 1780
Faircloth, William ... 20 Jan., 1778	Ashe, Saml .... 23 Jan., 1781
Gatling, Levy .... 12 Feb., 1778	Pyeatt, Peter ...... 30 March, 1781

(485)

LIEUTENANTS—*Continued.*

Brevard, Joseph........1 Aug., 1781
Dixon, Wynn..........5 July, 1781
Hill, John............5 July, 1781
Scurlock, James.......1 Sept., 1781
Bell, Robert..........8 Sept., 1781

Alexander, William....8 Sept., 1781
Steed, Jesse..........8 Sept., 1781
Holmes, Hardy........— ——, 1781
Williams, Nathaniel..— Jan., 1782

ENSIGNS.

Wright, David........19 April, 1777
Shute, Thomas ....19 April, 1777
McRenolds, Robert ..19 April, 1777
Hays, Robert.........16 Aug., 1777
Richardson, John .....1 Oct., 1777
Cawall, Butler........— ——, ——
Singleton, Robert....— ——, ——
Gatling, Levy........— ——, ——
Hargrave, William....20 Jan., 1778
Orrell, Thomas .....14 March, 1778
Mossom, Richard ....4 Sept., 1778

Foard, John.........30 Nov., 1778
Charlton, William...14 March, 1779
Gibson, Thomas......20 Feb., 1780
Dixon, Wynn.........1 March, 1781
Hill, John ....4 April, 1781
Daves, John ....6 May, 1781
Brevard, Joseph ......9 May, 1781
Alexander, William..10 May, 1781
Bell, Robert ....18 May, 1781
Steed, Jesse..........1 June, 1781

ARTILLERY.

Kingsbury, John, Captain.................................19 July, 1777
Jones, Philip, Captain-Lieutenant ....19 July, 1777
Wall, James, 1st Lieutenant..............................19 July, 1777
Vance, John Curton, 2d Lieutenant........................19 July, 1777
Douglass, Robert, 3d Lieutenant ....19 July, 1777

APPENDIX B.

[Inasmuch as the formation of "The Guilford Battle Ground Company" led to the production of this book, I deem it proper to include the charter and organization of that company. It now owns the battle-field, about 70 acres.]

AN ACT TO INCORPORATE THE "GUILFORD BATTLE GROUND COMPANY."

The General Assembly of North Carolina do enact:

SECTION 1. That for the benevolent purpose of preserving and adorning the grounds on and over which the battle of "Guilford Court-House" was fought on the 15th day of March, 1781, and the erection thereon of monuments, tombstones, or other memorials to commemorate the heroic deeds of the American patriots who participated in this battle for liberty and independence, it is enacted that J. W. Scott, Thomas B. Keogh, Julius A. Gray, Dr. D. W. C. Benbow and David Schenck be and are hereby declared to be a private corporation, until their successors are elected, by the name of the "GUILFORD BATTLE GROUND COMPANY."

SEC. 2. That the capital stock of said company shall not exceed twenty-five thousand dollars, to be divided into shares of twenty-five (25) dollars each. That when ten shares or more of said capital stock are subscribed, and ten per cent. thereof paid in, the stockholders may meet and elect not less than five nor more than nine directors of said company, by a majority vote of said stockholders, who shall succeed the persons hereinbefore named as corporators; and this board of directors, so elected, shall elect one of their number President. The stockholders may also elect any other officers of the company they may deem proper and necessary.

SEC. 3. The "Guilford Battle Ground Company" shall have power to contract, and sue and be sued by its corporate name; may have a common seal, and exercise all the ordinary and general powers of a private corporation of this kind. It shall have power to acquire, by gift, grant, or purchase, the title to all the lands on or over which the said battle of "Guilford Court-House" was fought, or any part thereof or adjacent lands thereto not exceeding one hundred acres, or rights of way or other easements of land, or water necessary or convenient for the proper enjoyment of said land. It may erect houses thereon for use or ornament; erect monuments, tombstones or other memorials; may adorn the grounds and walks; supply the grounds with water; plant trees, flowers and shrubs thereon, and do any other like things for the improvement and beautifying of the property. It may allow the United States, or any State or corporation or individual, to erect any monument, tombstone or other memorial, or any ornament or useful improvement thereon, to carry out the purposes of this act, on such terms as may be agreed upon by the parties. It may receive gifts or aid from the United States, any State, corporation or individual, or agree with them to make any improvement thereon. Any city, town or other municipal corporation or any other corporation may subscribe to the capital stock of the said company, or make donations to the same; it may make all necessary by-laws, rules and regulations, not inconsistent with the constitution and laws of the State, for the proper care, protection and regulation of the property of the company and the monuments, tombstones, memorials, houses and other property and ornaments and adornments thereon, or for the protection of the trees, flowers, shrubbery, walks, lawns, springs, wells or other like property thereon. That the principal office of the company shall be in Greensboro, North Carolina.

SEC. 4. It shall be a misdemeanor, punishable by fine and imprisonment, if any person or corporation shall wilfully destroy, demolish, deface or misuse any monument, tombstone or other memorial, or any fence, enclosure, tree, shrub, flower, spring, well, or any ornament or adornment placed upon the grounds, or any tree growing thereon, or shall wilfully deface, destroy or demolish any house, pavilion or like fixtures thereon, or shall wilfully trespass on the grounds after being notified not to do so, or shall wilfully obstruct the ways and walks of the company leading to or over the grounds.

SEC. 5. This act shall be in force from and after its ratification.
Ratified the 7th day of March, A. D. 1887.

ORGANIZANIZATION.

The first meeting of the Stockholders of the "Guilford Battle Ground Company" was held in Greensboro, N. C., on the 6th day of May, A. D. 1887, in the parlor of the Benbow House.

At that meeting, it appearing that upwards of ten shares of stock had been subscribed and more than ten per cent. paid in, the stockholders were called to order, Hon. D. Schenck elected President, and Thomas B. Keogh requested to act as Secretary.

The President stated the object of the meeting to be to organize a company to raise funds to purchase, reclaim and beautify the ground upon which the battle of Guilford Court-House was fought, March 15, 1781, as recited in the charter of the "Guilford Battle Ground Company."

The charter was read and accepted, and ordered recorded in the report of the proceedings.

After discussion of various details, the election of a Board of Directors was proceeded with, which resulted as follows:

Hon. D. Schenck, Julius A. Gray, Dr. D. W. C. Benbow, J. W. Scott and Thomas B. Keogh.

The Board elected as the officers of the company:

Hon. D. SCHENCK, President, Greensboro, N. C.; THOMAS B. KEOGH, Secretary, Greensboro, N. C.; J. W. SCOTT, Treasurer, Greensboro, N. C.

THOMAS B. KEOGH,
Secretary.

INDEX.

                                                                 PAGE.

ADAIR, JOHN:
   Furnishes twelve thousand dollars for the King's Mountain campaign ----- 133
ALEXANDER, ELIAS, Revolutionary Soldier:
   Humorous anecdote of ----- 151
ANDERSON, MAJOR, of Maryland:
   Brings away only organized force from Gates' defeat ----- 93
   Killed at Guilford Court-House ----- 93
APPENDIX A ----- 473
APPENDIX B ----- 486
ARMSTRONG, MARTIN:
   Letter to Colonel William Campbell ----- 307
ARMSTRONG, MAJOR JOHN:
   Captain in second Continental regiment ----- 21
   Letters to General Sumner ----- 428-429, 434
   Commands battalion at Eutaw Springs ----- 451
ASHE, GENERAL JOHN:
   Defeated at Briar Creek March 3d, 1779 ----- 34
   Betrayed by his servant and captured; died in October, 1781, 34
ASHE, COLONEL JOHN BAPTISTE:
   Captain in Wilmington District ----- 25
   Marches to join Greene July 17th, 1781 ----- 437
   Commands battalion at Eutaw Springs, Sept. 8th, 1781 - 451
AUGUSTA:
   Surrendered to American forces, 5th June, 1781 ----- 419-421
   North Carolina militia storm Fort Grierson ----- 417

BATTLES OF:
   Camden, August 16th, 1780 ----- 88
   Charlotte, defence of, September 26th, 1780 ----- 106
   Cowan's Ford, February 1st, 1780 ----- 240
   Cowpens, January 17th, 1781 ----- 209-210
   Eutaw Springs, September 8th, 1781 ----- 448
   Guilford Court-House, March 15th, 1781 ----- 293
   Hanging Rock, August 5th, 1780 ----- 69
   Hobkirk's Hill, April 25th, 1781 ----- 401-402
   King's Mountain, October 7th, 1780 ----- 156 to 174
   Musgrove's Mill, August 19th, 1780 ----- 79
   Pyle's defeat, February 25th, 1781 ----- 278
   Siege of Charleston, April 2, May, 1780 ----- 32
   Siege of Ninety-Six, June 18th, 1781 ----- 423
   Whitsill's Mill, March 6th, 1781 ----- 289
BLOUNT, MAJOR READING:
   Captain from Newbern District ----- 24
   Command battalion at Eutaw Springs ----- 451
   Letter to General Sumner ----- 438
"BLUE HEN'S CHICKENS" ----- 97

(490)

	PAGE.
BUFORD, COLONEL:	
Command massacred by Tarleton	45
BUTLER, BRIGADIER GENERAL JOHN:	
At Guilford Court-House	304
Mentioned	467
BURKE, THOMAS, GOVERNOR:	
Letter in regard to Colonel Alexander Martin's trial	31
Captured by Fanning	445
CAMPBELL, COLONEL WILLIAM:	
Commands at King's Mountain	141
Joins Greene with 60 men, March, 1781	308
At Guilford Court-House	324
CAMPBELL, COLONEL RICHARD:	
Joins Greene	272
Killed at Eutaw Springs	461
CARRINGTON, COLONEL EDWARD, Q. M. General:	
Surveys the Dan	191
CARUTHERS, DOCTOR OF DIVINITY:	
Quoted	338–339, 350–352–353
CASWELL, GOVERNOR RICHARD:	
At Gates' defeat near Camden	88
Flees with Gates to Charlotte	99
At Halifax, February 23d, 1781	264
Unfriendly to General Sumner	267–268
CHRONICLE, MAJOR WILLIAM:	
Joins the pursuit of Ferguson	151
Commands the men of Lincoln	159
Killed at King's Mountain	167
Romance of his life	175
CLEVELAND, COLONEL BENJAMIN:	
Joins the over-mountain men at Quaker Meadows, October 1st, 1780	139
His speech to his men	145
At King's Mountain	169
Gets Ferguson's charger	175
CORNWALLIS, CHARLES, EARL OF:	
Left in command by Clinton, June 5th, 1780	47
A heartless commander	48
Arrives at Camden 14th August, 1780	87
Marches to North Carolina September 7th, 1780	102
Denounces Charlotte	115
Retreats from Charlotte	180
Sick in the Waxhaws	182
At Turkey Creek January 17th, 1781	226
His fatal delay and tardiness in not following Morgan	230
Reaches Ramsour's Mill 25th January, 1781	232
Leaves Ramsour's Mill 28th January	232
Burns his heavy baggage	233
Deceived by Greene	258
At Hillsboro	261
Narrow escape at Guilford Court-House	376
Retreat of	390
Horse shot under him	376

	PAGE.

COUNCIL EXTRAORDINARY:
  Members of 269
DAVIDSON, BRIGADIER GENERAL WILLIAM LEE:
  Assembles militia after Gates' defeat 100
  Killed at Cowan's Ford, February 1st, 1781 242
  Killed by Frederick Hager, a Tory 242
DAVIE, COLONEL WILLIAM R.:
  At Hanging Rock 69
  Defends Charlotte 106
  Appointed Commissary General 192
  Sketch of his character 64
DECKHARD RIFLE 81
DEKALB, BARON:
  Death of 92
  Gallantry of 92
DIXON, COLONEL "HAL.":
  Captain in First Regiment 21
  Conspicuous bravery at Gates' defeat 89
  Pet of the soldiers 94
  Tribute to 466
DOAK, REV. SAMUEL:
  Prayer before battle of King's Mountain 136
DUNLAP, MAJOR, in British army:
  Wounded 126
  Revengeful attack upon him for his infamous conduct 128
  Killed 129

EATON, MAJOR PINKETHAM:
  Captain in Continental army 23
  Reorganizes the Guilford militia 394
  Joins Greene 16th May, 1781 399
  Killed at Fort Grierson, Augusta 418
EATON, BRIGADIER GENERAL THOMAS:
  At Guilford Court-House 305
  Sketch of 306

FERGUSON, COLONEL PATRICK, of English army:
  Sketch of 117
  Inventor of breech-loading rifle 117
  Famous pistol shot 118
  Killed at King's Mountain 170
FORBIS, CAPTAIN ARTHUR:
  Death at Guilford Court-House 378
  Anecdote of 351
  His gallantry in battle 352
FORD, LIEUTENANT COLONEL, of Maryland:
  Killed at Hobkirk's Hill 406
FRANCISCO, PETER, the Giant:
  Kills eleven men at Guilford Court-House 365
FRANKLIN, JESSE, GOVERNOR:
  At Guilford Court-House 301

	PAGE.
GATES, MAJOR GENERAL HORATIO:	
Defeat at Camden	94
Flight to Charlotte	95
Rides a famous racer	95
Superseded by General Greene	186
GILMER, ENOCH:	
The humorous American spy	155
Anecdote of	158
GRAHAM, MAJOR JOSEPH, of Lincoln County:	
Severely wounded near Charlotte	113
Sketch of	466
Fight at Hart's Mill	275
At Pyle's defeat	278
GREENE, MAJOR GENERAL NATHANAEL:	
Assumes command of the Southern army, Dec. 4th, 1780	186
Sketch of	186–187
At Camp Repose	197
Perilous journey from Camp Repose to join Morgan, January 28th, 1781	232
His cordial relations with Morgan	232
Letter from Sherrill's Ford, February 30th, 1781	249
Narrow escape from capture	251
Mrs. Steele presents him some gold, anecdote of	252
Forms a junction with Huger at Guilford Court-House	254
Crosses the Dan, 14th February, 1781	259
Recrosses the Dan to North Carolina, February 23d, 1781	273
Selection of Guilford Court-House as a battle-field	320
Orders North Carolina militia at Guilford Court-House to fire two rounds and retreat	335
Narrow escape at Guilford Court-House	378
Begins pursuit of Cornwallis	389
Rescues the artillery at Hobkirk's Hill	408
At Eutaw Springs	450
GREGORY, BRIGADIER GENERAL:	
Wounded at Camden	93
And captured	98
GUILFORD COURT-HOUSE:	
Battle of	293
Defence of North Carolina militia at this battle	337 et seq
HAMBRIGHT, COLONEL FREDERICK, of Lincoln:	
Wounded at King's Mountain	168
HESSIANS:	
Desert at Ramsour's Mill	234
Character of	314
Contract for their hire	314–315
HILL, COLONEL:	
Quarrel with General Williams	144
HOGUN, BRIGADIER GENERAL JAMES:	
Colonel of the 7th regiment	29
Appointed Brigadier General	31
Commands at Charleston	42

(493)

	PAGE.
HOWARD, COLONEL, of Maryland:	
Commands regiment at Cowpens	210
Charge at Guilford Court-House	367
HOUSTON, REV. SAMUEL:	
Diary of March, 1781	347
Account of battle of Guilford Court-House	348
His character	347
HOWE, MAJOR GENERAL:	
Duel with Gadsden	33
HUGER, GENERAL:	
Joins Morgan and Greene at Guilford Court-House	254
Commands brigade at that battle	311
JEFFERSON, THOMAS, Governor of Virginia:	
Letter of, in regard to militia at Guilford Court-House	354
KIRKWOOD, CAPTAIN, of Delaware:	
Sketch of	323
KERR:	
The crippled spy	154
KOSCIUSKO:	
Surveys the Catawba	191
LACEY, COLONEL:	
Goes to Campbell's camp on Greene River	153
LEE, LIEUTENANT COLONEL HARRY:	
Joins Greene at Camp Repose	198
Description of his Legion	198
Character of	199
At Guilford Court-House	368
Errors as a historian	358
LESLIE, MAJOR GENERAL, British army:	
Commands the right at Guilford Court-House	330
LINCOLN, MAJOR GENERAL BENJAMIN:	
Succeeds General Howe in the South	33
Commands at Charleston	40
LOCKE, COLONEL, of Rowan County:	
Marches to Ramsour's Mill	55
Commands regiment of infantry under Pickens	262
LYNCH, COLONEL CHARLES:	
Commands battalion at Guilford Court-House	309
Originator of lynch law	310
MACON, NATHANIEL:	
In Greene's army	384
Eulogy on, by Senator Benton	384
MALMEDY, COLONEL, French Nobleman:	
Commands North Carolina militia at Eutaw Springs	450
MARION, GENERAL FRANCIS:	
Joins Greene September, 1781	446
Commands brigade at Eutaw	450

	PAGE.
MAJORIBANKS, MAJOR, in British army:	
Skill and gallantry at Eutaw	457
Death of	460
MARTIN, COLONEL ALEXANDER, of Guilford:	
Appointed Lieutenant Colonel	21
Appointed Colonel	22
Defence of	29
Member of Council Extraordinary	269
MATTOCKS, CAPTAIN:	
Killed at King's Mountain	168
MCARTHUR, COLONEL, in British army:	
Surrender at Cowpens	217
MCCALL, CAPTAIN:	
Joins General Morgan	200
MCDOWELL, COLONEL CHARLES:	
Attacks detachment of Ferguson's corps at Bedford Hill	126
Campaign in 1780 to Musgrove's Mill	76
Sketch of	465
His home	139
MCDOWELL, MAJOR JOSEPH, of Quaker Meadows, Burke County:	
Commands the Burke men at King's Mountain	142–170
At Ramsour's Mill	57
Sketch of	464
At Cowpens	200–210
MCDOWELL, CAPTAIN JOSEPH, of Pleasant Garden, Burke County:	
At Cowpens	220
Grave of	466
MILLS, COLONEL AMBROSE, Tory:	
Captured at King's Mountain	174
Hung at Gilberttown	179
MOORE, BRIGADIER GENERAL JAMES:	
Appointed Colonel	20
Appointed Brigadier General	22
Death of	26
MORGAN, BRIGADIER GENERAL DANIEL:	
Arrives at Hillsboro, North Carolina	184
Gates gives him a separate command	184
Sketch of	196
Morgan detached to separate duty by General Greene	194
At Cowpens	224
Retreat from Cowpens	226
Crosses Sherrill's Ford on Catawba	230
Disabled by rheumatism and retires from the army	257
Letter to Greene about battle at Guilford Court-House	321
NASH, BRIGADIER GENERAL FRANCIS:	
Appointed Colonel of Regulars	22
Appointed Brigadier General	27
Killed at Germantown	28
NASH, GOVERNOR ABNER:	
Patriotic letter of, September 10th, 1780	100
Letter February 23d, 1781	264–265
Sumner's letter to, about Caswell	267

NORTH CAROLINA MILITIA:
   At Cowpens 200
   Johnson's error about 200–201
   Elect General Andrew Pickens to command them after General Davidson's death 263
   Greene orders to fire two rounds, at Guilford Court-House, and then retire 335
   Reorganization of 394
   Under Major Eaton 395
   Assault Fort Grierson 417
   Five hundred of, join Greene on the Santee 441
   Fire seventeen rounds at Eutaw Springs 453
   Commanded by Colonel Malmedy 454
   Tribute to their courage 454

NORTH CAROLINA:
   Furnishes South Carolina regiments 441–442
   Colonel Williams, of South Carolina, recruits his regiment in Rowan County 143

O'HARA, GENERAL, of British army:
   At Trading Ford 253
   Wounded at Guilford Court-House 364

OLIPHANT'S MILL:
   Depot established at 393

ORANGEBURG:
   Captured 415

OVER-MOUNTAIN MEN:
   Assemble at Sycamore Flats 134
   March 26th September, 1780 136
   Reach Quaker Meadows, 30th September, 1780 139

PACOLET:
   Skirmish at 123

PAISLEY, WILLIAM:
   Anecdote of 353

PICKENS, GENERAL ANDREW:
   Joins Morgan 200
   At Cowpens 210
   Selected to command North Carolina militia 263
   Commands at Augusta 416
   At Eutaw Springs 450

PRESTON, COLONEL JOHN, of Virginia:
   Joins Pickens' forces February, 1781 307

PRISONERS:
   Exchange of, May, 1780 43

PYLE, COLONEL:
   Was physician, account of 282

RAMSOUR'S MILL, BATTLE OF:
   Graham's narrative of 51
   Grave of Captain Dodson at 62

	PAGE.
RAWDON, LORD:	
Leaves Camden	414
Relieves Ninety-Six	423
Captured at sea	445
READ, COLONEL JAMES, of North Carolina:	
Commands regiment of horse	391
Remains with Greene	391
Fine character of his troops	298
Sketch of, by Hon. George Davis	299
RIFLE:	
Deckhard	81
Breech-loading, invented by Major Ferguson	82
Against bayonets	161
RUTHERFORD, BRIGADIER GENERAL GRIFFITH:	
At Rees' farm, June 14th, 1780	51
Pursues Tories	68
Wounded at Camden	89
Sketch of	467
RAMSEUR, MAJOR GENERAL STEPHEN D.:	
Mentioned	430
SEVIER, COLONEL JOHN:	
"Nollichucky Jack"	130
At Sycamore Flats	134
At King's Mountain	164
Awarded Ferguson's sash	175
SHELBY, COLONEL ISAAC:	
Campaign	69
Cedar Springs, at	78
Musgrove's Mill, at	79
At King's Mountain	163
Gets Ferguson's large silver whistle	175
SINGLETON, CAPTAIN ANTHONY, of Artillery:	
Commands artillery at Guilford Court-House	311
Says militia behaved "exceedingly well" at Guilford Court-House	355
SMITH, CAPTAIN JOHN, of Maryland:	
Kills Colonel Stuart in personal combat at Guilford Court-House	367
Sketch of	410
SOUTHERN PROVINCES:	
Condition of, in 1779–'80	37
STEELE, MRS.:	
Presents General Greene a small bag of gold	252
STEVENS, GENERAL, of Virginia:	
Surveys the Yadkin	191
Wounded at Guilford Court-House	362
STUART, HON. LIEUTENANT COLONEL, of British army:	
Encounter with Captain Smith	367
His sword exhumed in 1866	367

	PAGE.

STUART, CAPTAIN DUGALD:
  Letter in regard to Guilford Court-House and North Carolina militia 349
STOKES, CAPTAIN JOHN:
  Arm cut off at massacre of Buford's men, sketch of.... 45, note.
SUMNER, BRIGADIER GENERAL JETHRO:
  Collects scattered militia after defeat of Gates 100
  Superseded by General Smallwood 102
  Tenders his services to Caswell, which are not accepted 266
  Refuses to meet Caswell personally 267
  Caswell's error in regard to 268
  Mistakes of historians in regard to 426
  Efforts to raise new brigade of Regulars .... 427 *et. seq*
  Letters 428
  Appeal to the people 430
  Letter to Greene 431
  Letter to Baron Steuben 433
  Order to Colonel Ashe, July, 1781 437
  Letter to Governor Burke, 14th July, 1781 437
  Reaches Hanging Rock August 1st, 1781 438
  Estimate of his brigade of Regulars 439
  Courage and skill at Eutaw Springs 455
  Sketch of 468
SUMTER, GENERAL, of South Carolina:
  Defeats Tarleton at Blackstocks 186
TARLETON, LIEUTENANT COLONEL BANISTRE:
  Massacre of Buford's men by 44, 206
  At Cowpens 213
  Encounter with Colonel William Washington at Cowpens 217
  Character 206
  Wounded in the hand at Guilford Court-House 374
THOMAS, MAJOR:
  Captures Lord Nairne on Pee Dee 82
TORRANCE TAVERN:
  Skirmish at 245
WASHINGTON, COLONEL WILLIAM:
  Captures Claremount 192
  At Hammond's Store 202
  At Cowpens 216-217
  Encounter with Tarleton 217
  At Guilford Court-House 323
  At Hobkirk's Hill 408
  Wounded and captured at Eutaw Springs 457
WEBSTER, LIEUTENANT COLONEL, of British army:
  At Gates' defeat 88
  Wonderful escape at Whitsill's Mill 290
  Wounded at Guilford Court-House in the knee 364
  Account of his death 371
WHITSILL'S MILL:
  Fight at 289

	PAGE.

WILLIAMS, COLONEL OTHO :
   Commands light troops 258
   At Guilford Court-House 327

WILLIAMS, GENERAL JAMES :
   Killed at King's Mountain 169

WILFONG, JOHN :
   Soldier at King's Mountain and Eutaw Springs 430

WINSTON, MAJOR JOSEPH :
   At King's Mountain 164
   Joins Greene February, 1781 300
   At Guilford Court-House 300

FULLNAME PLUS SUBJECT INDEX.

----, Joel 435
ADAIR, John 133
ADAMS, John 412 Robert 310
ALDERSON, Simon 24 479
  Thomas 479
ALEXANDER, 61 152 Charles
  478 Elias 151 Jno Mck 247
  Miss 175 Susannah 113
  William 485 Wm 60
ALLEN, Charles 475-476 John 24
  479 Thomas 21 474 479
  Walter 479
ALSTON, William 22
AMIS, Thomas 476 William 476
ANDERSON, 223 Maj 93 222 327
  354
ANDREWS, Richard 475
APPENDIX, A 473 B 486
ARBUTHNOT, 39 45
ARMAND, Col 87
ARMSTRONG, 35 87 285 440 453
  455 Andrew 25 480 Capt 62
  422 Col 29-30 431 436 James
  25 397 482 John 21 398 418
  425 428-429 434 437 439 451
  475 477 Lieut 438 Maj 300 302
  Martin 307-308 325 Thomas
  25 478-480 William 474 Wm
  474
ARNOLD, 270-271
ASHE, 268 440 453 455 Gen 34
  305 J B 451 John 33 478 John
  B 398 425 437 479 John
  Baptista 480 John Baptiste 25
  John Jr 24 Lieut 438 Lieut
  Col 266 Saml 484 Samuel Jr
  25
ASHTON, William 476
ATKIN, James 477

AUGUSTA, North Carolina
  Militia Storm Fort Grierson
  417 Surrendered To American
  Forces 5th June 1781 419 421
BACOT, Peter 484
BAILEY, Benjamin 479 481
BAILY, Benjamin 23
BAKER, John 481 Peter 474
BALFOUR, Col 115 Nesbett 313
BALLARD, Kedar 23 476-477
BANCROFT, 37 92 102 203 409-
  410 Mr 41 44
BARBER, William 484
BARRETT, Capt 354
BARRINGTON, Shute 189
BARROT, William 477
BARROW, Jacob 481 Samuel 481
BATTLES, Of Camden August
  16th 1780 88 Of Charlotte
  Defence Of September 26th
  1780 106 Of Cowans Ford
  February 1st 1780 240 Of
  Cowpens January 17th 1781
  209-210 Of Eutaw Springs
  September 8th 1781 448 Of
  Guilford Court-house March
  15th 1781 293 Of Hanging
  Rock August 5th 1780 69 Of
  Hobkirks Hill April 25th 1781
  401-402 Of Kings Mountain
  October 7th 1780 156-174 Of
  Musgroves Mill August 19th
  1780 79 Of Pyles Defeat
  February 25th 1781 278 Of
  Siege Of Charleston April 2
  May 1780 32 Of Siege Of
  Ninety-six June 18th 1781 423
  Of Whitsills Mill March 6th
  1781 289

BAYLOR, Col 95
BEARD, Valentine 25
BEASON, 157
BEATTIE, Capt 209
BEATTY, Capt 406
BEATY, Robert 246
BECKS, William 481
BELL, Green 481 Robert 485
BENBOW, D W C 487-488
BENSON, Capt 403
BENTON, 387 Senator 384
BERRYHILL, William 21 474
BERTIE, Thomas 482
BEVILL, 318
BICKERSTAFF, John 476
BIGNAL, Mr 269
BLACK, Col 239
BLAIR, James 139
BLAKENY, William 313
BLANTON, Rowland 481
BLOUNT, 440 453 455 James 21 475 Jesse 482 Maj 437 439 Mary 470 Reading 24 398 425 433 438 451 470 478-479 Thomas 24 470 479 Whitmel 23 William 476
BLUE, Hens Chickens 97
BLYTHE, Samuel 474
BOSE, 315
BOWMAN, Capt 62 Joshua 21 474
BOYD, Adam 473 478 Hugh 477 John 174
BRADDOCK, 196 292
BRADLEY, Gee 477 Jas 23 Richard 473 476 William 175
BRANDON, 109 Capt 52 55 57-58 Col 144 John 107 Maj 152 William 21 474
BRETIGNY, Marquis 301
BREVARD, 435 Alexander 478 Hugh 54 Joel 483 John 248 483 Joseph 485
BREWSTER, Lott 476 481
BRICE, Peter 483
BRICKELL, Thomas 481

BRIGHT, Simon 21 475
BRINKLEY, William 23 477
BROWN, 350 417 Capt 451 Col 70-71 202 416 420-422 John 474 Morgan 483
BROWNFIELD, William 24
BRYAN, 70 73 75 Benjamin 481 Hardy 481 Samuel 68
BRYANT, John Jr 481
BUDD, Samuel 475
BUFORD, 45 68 75 206 285 Col 44 53 184 William 475
BULL, Thomas 484
BULLOCK, Daniel 483
BUNCOMBE, Edward 22 31 478
BURDELL, 446
BURGESS, Zephaniah 23
BURGOYNE, 84 98
BURKE, 53 133 141 Gov 31 42 437-438 445 Thos 30
BUSH, John 24 479 482 William 482
BUTLER, 298 324 349 351 353 360 Gen 89 265 274 305 307 389 395-396 398 John 35 83 304 322 467
CALDWELL, Capt 97 David 322 338 353 Dr 379 William 24
CALLENDER, Thomas 474 474
CALLOWAY, Thomas 310
CAMPBELL, 129 139-140 145 150-151 153-159 164-166 169-170 172 172 293-294 302-303 309 328 351-352 357-358 360-362 364 368-369 Archibald 314 Arthur 131 136 Capt 114 Col 33 133-134 141-142 175 261 339 James 484 John 395 484 Lieut Col 403-404 Richard 272-273 296 451 461 William 131-132 136 272 277 307-308 311 324
CAMPEN, James 475-476
CANNON, Henry 24 Lewis 484
CARDEN, Maj 70
CARPENTER, Peter 482

CARR, James 24
CARRAWAY, Gideon 482
CARRINGTON, 193 346 403 455
    Col 43 253-254 256 331 401
    453 Edward 191
CARTER, Benjamin 478
CARUTH, John 262
CARUTHERS, 301 350 352-353
    356 E W 338
CASSEL, William 24
CASWELL, 50 84 86 88 94 185
    268 426 Brigadier Gen 265
    Gen 99 101 263-264 267 296
    Gov 31 33 80 266 Richard 269
    William 476 479
CAUSTAUPHEN, James 481
CAWALL, Butler 485
CHAMBERS, 146 Samuel 138
CHANDLER, William 151
CHAPMAN, Capt 437 Samuel 482
CHARLTON, William 485
CHEESBORO, John 480
CHEESE, John 474
CHILD, Francis 24 480
CHILDERS, Abraham 25
CHILDS, Francis 397 James 371
    474
CHITTIM, John 175
CHRONICLE, 172 174 Maj 131
    151 155 159 167 175
CLANDENNIN, John 476
CLARK, 211 Col 32 Thomas 20 31
    473 483
CLARKE, 47 125 156 422 Capt 80
    Col 42 78 80-81 124 127 129
    146 150 Elijah 122 Lieut Col
    77 Thos 22
CLAYTON, Joshua 23
CLEMENTS, William 24
CLEVELAND, 136 148 154 164
    168-170 173 Benjamin 131 476
    Col 127 133 139-140 145 159
    175 Larkin 140 171
CLINCH, James 476 Joseph 23
CLINTON, 39 41 44-47 333 387
    Henry 19 32 38 118 124 235

CLINTON (cont.)
    305 312-313 386
CLOVER, William 24
CLYDE, William P 317
COCHRANE, Maj 119
COFFIELD, Benjamin 480
COFFIN, 407-408 451 457-458 Col
    446 Maj 448
COLE, William Temple 24
COLEMAN, Benjamin 24 479
    John 483 Theophilus 481
COLES, William T 478
COLLINS, 179 Abram 147
COLMAN, Charles 476
COLQUHOUN, Adjutant 381
COOK, George 484 James 25 476-
    477 Richard D 483
COOLEY, Samuel 478
COOPER, Solomon 484 William
    479
COOTS, James 25 478
CORNWALLIS, 45 47 52 63 74 92
    96 98 115-116 120-122 149-150
    152 155 159 162 176 178-179
    183 185-186 190 194 199 204
    216 225 227-232 234 239 243
    251-254 256 258-261 263 270
    272-273 283 286-289 292 308
    313 316 328 332-334 344 360-
    361 366 370-372 375-376 378-
    379 381 385-387 389 392 399
    460 462 Charles E 314 Earl
    189 384 Frederick 44 314
    Lieut Gen Earl 380 Lord 18-
    19 43 48 53 67-68 86-88 93 102
    124 147 182 203 224 233 238
    247 250 293 312 321 354 377
    390 431 445
COTGRAVE, Arthur 475
COTTEN, Josiah 481
COUNCIL, Arthur 480 Austin 25
    Extraordinary Members Of
    269 Robert 474
COVINGTON, James 483 William
    477
COWAN, Capt 430 David 484

COXE, Frank 151 158
CRADOCK, John 475-476
CRAFTON, Bennet 480
CRAIG, David 24 James H 270 Maj 432
CRAIGHEAD, Capt 73
CRAVEN, James 474
CRAWFORD, 146 Charles 21 475 David 474 James 138 Maj 64
CRUGER, 448 Col 423
CRUTCHES, Anthony 479 Henry 479
CUMMING, Rev Mr 358
CUMMINGHAM, Col 124
CUNNINGHAM, 211
CURTIS, John 479 Joshua 478 Reuben 476
CUSACK, Adam 124
CUSTIN, John 24
CUSTIS, Thomas 482
DANIEL, James 483
DANSEY, William 314
DARNALL, Henry 478-479
DARNELL, Henry 24
DAUDSON, George 21
DAVES, John 475-476 485 William 21
DAVIDSON, 180 186 205 243 317 438 Col 60 Gen 100 110 112 144 178 195 236 238 240-242 244 246 248 262-263 George 104 474 Thomas 237 239 William 22 477 William L 99 William Lee 200 235 397 Wm L 51 478
DAVIE, 66-68 73 82 96 Col 105-106 108 110-112 181-182 186 193 246 402 Gen 65 Maj 51 60 64 69-70 72 75 Mr 74 William R 104 192 Wm R 95 101 393
DAVIS, George 298 Orond 469 William 473-474 Wm 22
DAWES, Abraham 481 Josiah 481
DAWSON, Henry 481 Levi 22 Levy 478 482
DAYLEY, Joshua 481

DEBUYSSON, Lieut Col 96
DECKHARD, Rifle 81
DEKALB, 84 86 88 93 222 327 Baron 50 62 Gen 96 98 Maj Gen Baron 92
DEKEYSER, Lebansyus 473
DELAFAYETTE, Maj Gen Marquis 436
DENNIS, William 482
DENT, William 483 William Jr 25
DEPEYSTER, 165 168 172 Capt 170
DESPARD, J 381
DETROTT, Ensign 381
DICKERSON, John 25 Nathaniel 483
DICKINSON, Richard 480
DICKSON, Henry 21 474 Joseph 107 167 Maj 108 279
DIEHL, Patricia S 13
DIGGS, Anthony 479
DILLAIN, John 484
DILLON, Benjamin 481
DIXON, 90-92 222 327 Charles 480 Col 89 94 Hal 396 398 454 466 Henry 476 Maj 398-399 428 432 Tilghman 474 Wynn 485
DOAK, Parson 171 Samuel 136
DOBBINS, Hugh 483
DOBSON, Capt 62 64
DOHERTY, Capt 431 436 438 George 433
DONOHO, Thomas 24 479-480
DOUGHERTY, George 25 479-480
DOUGLAS, William 477
DOUGLASS, Capt Lord 381 Robert 3d 485
DRAPER, 127 149 300 Lyman C 120 Mr 121 220
DUBUY, Maj 330
DUBUYSSON, Lieut Col 92
DUDLEY, Thomas 484
DUNCAN, Robert 477
DUNLAP, 129 Maj 126-128

EAGLES, Joseph 299
EARLES, Baylis 147
EASON, Steth 481
EATON, 298 323 376 417 439
   Brigadier Gen 343 Gen 265
   346 389 Maj 396 399 419 431
   434-435 P 395 Pinketham 23
   394 398 416 418 476-477
   Pinkethan 267 Thomas 267
   305 322 William 306
EBORN, John 24
EBORNE, John 479 Thomas 479
EDMONDS, Capt 451
EDMUND, Nicholas 477
EGGLESTON, 285 417 Capt 279
EICHENDROBT, Capt 381
ELY, Eli 481 Lemuel 481
EMMET, James 477 Jas 24
EMMETT, James 476
ENLOE, John 24 479
ERSKINE, 454 Lord 250
ERWIN, John 474
ESPEY, Capt 167 174
ETHERIDGE, William 23
EVANS, Thomas 475-476
EWELL, William 479
FAIRCLOTH, William 484
FALLS, Capt 52 55 57-58 62
FANNING, Col 445 David 122
FARMER, Col 238 244
FARR, James 25
FAUNTLEROY, Capt 354
FAWN, William 477
FEAR, Edmund 221
FENNER, Richard 475-476
   Robert 475 William 22 475
   481
FEREBEE, Joseph 484
FERGUSON, 77 79 81-82 114 116
   118-122 125-128 131-132 135-
   136 138 140-141 146-147 150-
   155 157-166 169-171 173-175
   177-179 183 203 207 212 308
   333 342 464 James 117 Maj 78
   Pat 148 Patrick 48 75 103 117
   149

FERRALL, Micajah 483
FERREBEE, William 481
FERRELL, Luke L 484 William
   484
FINLEY, 402 Lieut 311 368
FLEUCHER, Lieut 73
FOARD, Hezekiah 478 John 484-
   485
FOOTE, 347 365
FORBIS, 302 349 351 360 Arthur
   255 322 378 Capt 339 352-353
   Col 379
FORD, 223 Col 311 327 364 Lieut
   Col 403-406
FOREMAN, Caleb 482
FORGUS, James 484
FORNEY, Abram 304 340
FOX, Adjutant 381
FRANCISCO, Peter 310 365
FRANKLIN, Jesse 301
FRASER, Simon 314
FREEMAN, John 123
GADSDEN, Christopher 33
GAINES, Capt 451
GAMBELLE, Edmund 474
GAMBLE, 434 Capt 429
GARDEN, 337-338 356
GARDNER, William 475-476
GATES, 86 101 185 197 304 311
   325 327 426 466 Gen 74 80-81
   85 87 95-96 99-100 141 145
   178 183-184 186 Horatio 84
GATLING, Levy 484-485
GEE, Howell 481 James 22 475
GEORGE, King 72 158 280-281
GERALD, Charles 479
GERMAIN, 46
GIBSON, Thomas 485
GILBERT, 128 William 127
GILCHRIST, Thomas 394
GILLELAND, 170
GILLESPIE, Capt 128 Robert 478
GILMER, 157-158 Enoch 155
   William 175
GIVENS, 247
GLOVER, William 480

GODFREY, William 482
GOODIN, Christopher 479-480
GOODING, Christopher 25
GOODMAN, Capt 438 William 23 478
GOODRICKE, Capt 381-382
GOODRICKS, Capt 329
GORDON, 310 338 407
GORE, Ensign 381
GRAHAM, 106-109 145 154-155 237 240-241 243-246 274 276 Adjutant 111 Capt 275 279 281 Gen 64 160 181 235 253 263 304 442 George 474 Gov 29 31-32 426 Joseph 51 104 113 165 236 262 278 441 466 Maj 105 Richard 475 William 144 159
GRAIFE, Lieut 381
GRAINGER, Caleb 21 John 22 475
GRANBERRY, George 477 John 477 Thomas 477
GRANDBURY, John 23 Thomas 23
GRANGER, Caleb 474
GRANT, Ensign 381 Reuben 25 480 Thomas 25 480
GRAVES, Francis 482 484 Jesse Franklin 301
GRAY, John 23 477 Julius A 323 487-488
GREEN, 151-152 369 374 Col 199 311 327 James W 484 Joseph 482 William 474 480
GREENE, 127 192 194 198 203-205 223 227-228 231 233 254-261 263 270 272-274 277 289-290 292 296 298-303 310-312 318 322 324 327 332 355 364 367 369-370 373-374 383 385-386 389 393 396 401-404 406-409 422 432 437 439-440 450 459 469-470 G W 453 Gen 20 29 43 187-188 191 193 197 199 232 235 237-238 241 249-251

GREENE (cont.) 253 264-266 268 271 275-276 286 288 294-295 297 304 306-309 313 320-321 326 328 334 336 338 340-342 351-352 354 368 378 384 387-388 391-392 395 397-400 410-416 423-431 433-434 441 444-446 449 452 455 457-458 461-462 468 George Washington 335 337 346 356 Nathanael 84 186 293 335 372 William 21
GREER, Robert 482
GREGORY, Dempsy 484 Gen 84 89 91 93 98 Isaac 83
GRIERSON, 417 Col 419
GROVES, William 24 479
GUILFORD, Court-house Battle Of 293 Court-house Defence Of North Carolina Militia At This Battle 337
GUION, Isaac 473 481 483
GUNBY, 405 409 Col 327 367 403 410
GURLEY, William 482
HADLEY, Joshua 25 480
HAGER, Frederick 240 242
HAINES, Thomas 24
HAIR, John L 474
HALL, Clement 22 475 Col 240-241 246 James 262 483 Robert 476 Thomas 474
HAMBRIGHT, 170 172 Col 131 159 164 167 174 Frederick 144
HAMILTON, 70-72 312-313 Col 53 273-274 318 328 Hanse 481 John 52 306
HAMMOND, George 430 Maj 144
HAMPTON, 148 168 Adam 25 Andrew 123 131 Col 134 392 442 458 Edward 124 Jonathan 146 Noah 123-124 Wade 124 441
HANDCOCK, William 480
HANGER, Maj 106 110-112 114
HARDEN, Capt 59-60

HARDMAN, Maj 451
HARGETT, Frederick 482
HARGRAVE, William 484-485
HARNETT, Cornelius 30 305
HARNEY, Selby 474 482
HARRINGTON, Col 35
HARRIS, Thomas 478 West 483
HARRISON, 354 Col 401-402 404
  William 481
HART, Anthony 476-477 John 480
  Samuel 483 Thomas 480
HARVEY, James 481
HAWES, 363 368 Lieut Col 311
  327 403 405-406
HAWKINS, Maj 266
HAWSEY, Capt 80
HAYNE, Isaac 445
HAYS, James 481 Robert 484-485
HAYWOOD, Richard B 28
HEISS, Mrs 470
HELMBURGH, Fred 473
HENDERSON, 458 461 Col 457
  Michael 483 Pleasant 25 40
  480 William 40 450-451
HENRY, 221 Alexander 147
  Moses 174 Robert 127 174
HERNDON, Col 127 Maj 154
HERRITAGE, John 22 475
HERRON, Armwell 484
HESSIANS, Character Of 314
  Contract For Their Hire 314-
  315 Desert At Ramsours Mill
  234
HEWELL, William 479
HICKMAN, William 478
HICKS, William 483
HIGGINS, Col 64
HIGH, Alsop 23
HILL, 144-145 153-155 Col 69-70
  73 143 152 John 485 William
  21 441 474
HILTON, William 480
HODGES, John 479
HODGTON, Alvery 476-477
HOGAN, James 481
HOGG, Maj 437

HOGG (cont.)
  Thomas 21 474 478
HOGUN, 29 40 Gen 42 James 31-
  32
HOLCOMB, Lieut 365 Philemon
  310
HOLLAND, Spier 479
HOLLINGSWORTH, Charles 24
  478
HOLLOWELL, Samuel 482
HOLMES, Hardy 485
HOOPER, William 394
HOPSON, John 25
HOSKIN, 316
HOSKINS, 350
HOUSTON, Capt 62 Mr 49 348-
  349 362 382 389 Samuel 347
  357
HOWARD, 211 223 238 370 409
  411 461 Brigadier Gen 381
  Col 93 216 237 311 451 Gen
  373 382 John Eager 367 Lieut
  Col 210 256 327 403 405
HOWE, Maj Gen 33 Robert 21-22
  31 474 William 32 313
HUGER, 119 254 405 Brigadier
  Gen 327 Gen 74 233 237 249
  311 403 Isaac 194
HUGHES, Ensign 381
HUNTER, Maj 351
HUSBANDS, Vezey 171
HYRNE, Maj 230
INGLES, John 475
INGRAM, 29 James 482
INMAN, Capt 79-80
INNES, Col 79 123
IREDELL, 407 Mr 394
IRVING, 120
IRWIN, Col 67 69-70 Henry 22
  478
IVEY, Curtis 479
JACKSON, 211 Lieut 262
JACOB, John 475
JACOBS, John 476
JAMES, John 24 480
JARVIS, John 484

JAY, Mr 49
JEFFERSON, 176 353 356 Gov
   295 Th 355
JOHNSON, 127 210 219 250-251
   277 297-298 300 306 308-310
   312 319 324 326 337 342 358
   367 378 382 401 452 458 Capt
   151 167 James 480 James F
   340 Joseph 410 Joshua 483
   Judge 186 200-201 221 275
   318
JOHNSTON, Col 57 James 55
   Joseph 483 Lancelot 483
   Robert 55
JONES, Daniel 23 477 David 24
   478 Dr 365 Gen 428 James 25
   John 123 Maurice 480 Miss
   218 Philip 482 485 Samuel
   480 484 Thomas 481 Timothy
   484 Willie 100 267 306
KEAIS, Nathan 21 475
KELLY, Ensign 381
KENAN, Col 432-433
KENNEDY, Thomas 220
KENNON, John 480 William 473
KENON, John 24
KEOGH, Thomas B 487-488
KERR, Joseph 154
KILBEY, Wm Tyler 476
KING, James 474
KINGSBURY, John 485
KIRKWOOD, 311 359 362 368 377
   403-404 Capt 96 323
KNOTT, William 478 Wm 23
KOEN, Caleb 484
KOSCIUSKO, 191 193-194 264
LACEY, 144-145 153-155 164 Col
   143 169 John 476
LACKEY, Christopher 477
LACY, Col 69
LAFAYETTE, 427 454 469
LAMB, 90 344-348 357 376
   Gideon 22 397 479 Sgt 295
LANGFORD, Alloway 482
LANIER, James Jr 482
LASSITER, Jethro 481

LAWRENCE, Nathaniel 484
LAWSON, 287 310 326 357 359
   362 376-377 Brigadier 309
LEE, 89 199 256 260 274 277-280
   282-283 290 293-294 300 302-
   303 309 311 314 319 324 326
   337 342 351-352 357-358 360-
   361 368-370 383 407 413 416
   418 421 424 451 456-458
   Charles 26 Col 250 272 281
   291 328-329 340 344 389 399
   401 409 414 422 Harry 166
   276 Henry 198 Lieut Col 417
   450 Robert E 198
LENOIR, Gen 160 William 168
LESLIE, 226 231 349-350 Gen 203
   234 382 Maj Gen 315 330
LEWIS, 435 Joel 484 Joseph 482
   Maj 436 Micajah 25 397 478
   William 483
LIGMAN, John 221
LILLINGTON, 31 375 Alexander
   22 479 Col 250 Gen 265 John
   21 474
LINCOLN, 40-41 49 53 201 Gen
   20 39 42 191 Maj Gen 33 38
   Maj-gen 19
LINDSAY, 318 Col 111
LINTON, Col 394 William 23 395
   477
LISCOMBE, John 480
LITTLE, Micajah 479 William 480
   483
LOCKE, Col 54-55 58 262 274 307
   Francis 52 George 111
   Matthew 111
LOCKEY, Christopher 479
LOCKHART, Samuel 22 476 482
LONG, Nehemiah 23 479
   Nicholas 396
LOOMIS, Jonathan 482
LORD, William 473 484
LOVE, Amos 25 480
LOWE, John 484 Philip 475-476
LOWNDES, Gov 33 Rawlins 46
LOWRIE, Judge 175

LUCAS, Mr 247
LUCKEY, Christopher 23
LUTON, James 475-476
LUTTRELL, John 483
LYNCH, 323-324 326 359 362 368
    377 Charles 309 311 John 481
    Judge 310
LYTLE, 35 435 Archibald 24 479-
    480 Micajah 477 William 480
LYTTLE, William 24
MACLAINE, Archibald 299 John
    478 William 484
MACON, John 481 Mr 385-386
    Nathaniel 384
MADACY, Cosimo 25
MADARIS, John 25
MADEARIS, John 477
MAITLAND, Capt 381
MAJORIBANKS, 456-457 460
    Maj 448
MALLETT, Daniel 477 Peter 478
MALMEDY, Col 450 454
MARION, 47 401 413 415 423
    Francis 446 Gen 199 399 412
    414 450
MARSHALL, Dixon 474
MARTIN, Alex 22 Alexander 21
    26 29-30 269 318 474 Capt 51
    168 175 James 255 301 351
    475 Josiah 247 Nathaniel M
    246 Samuel 475 480
MATTOCKS, 168 Capt 167 174
MAY, James Jr 482
MAYNARD, Capt 381
MCAFFERTY, 180-181
MCALISTER, Neil 474
MCARTHUR, 314 459 Col 217
    Maj 82 224
MCCALL, 80 205 211 274 Capt
    275 Col 200-202 Maj 129
MCCAN, John 24
MCCANN, John 480
MCCARTHY, Florence 478
MCCAULEY, Matthew 484
MCCLAMMY, Joseph 476
MCCLURE, Capt 73

MCCLURE (cont.)
    William 475 480
MCCOMB, 107
MCCREE, 435
MCCRORY, Thomas 483
MCDONALD, 29-30 Alexander
    314 Capt 114 Hugh 28
MCDOWELL, 77 81 127-128 133
    135 140 148 164 169-170 177
    205 207 210 228 Capt 57-58
    Charles 75-76 122-124 126 131
    139 141 144-145 175 464-465
    Col 134 136 389 Gen 78 80
    James 464 Joseph 53-54 64
    131 139 142 175 200 211 220
    464-465 Maj 55 201-202 221 T
    D 371
MCDOWLL, Joseph 466
MCFADDEN, Adam 25
MCGIBBONY, Patrick 478
MCGLAUGHAN, John 481
MCILWAINE, Stringer 475
MCKEE, Griffith John 24
MCKENNY, James 24
MCKINNE, James 479
MCKISSICK, Capt 62
MCLAINE, Jerome 23
MCLAINY, Mark 24
MCLEOD, Lieut 316 330 366
MCLINN, Ensign 73
MCLURE, Thomas 24
MCNAUGHTON, John 482
MCNEES, John 479
MCNEIL, Hector 21
MCNEILL, Hector 474
MCREA, Mary 128
MCREE, 299 Griffith J 479-480
MCRENOLDS, Robert 485
MCRORY, James 483
MCSHEEHY, Miles 483
MEBANE, 278 Robert 481
MERCER, John 481
MEREDITH, William 25
MESSICK, Jacob 482
MIDDLETON, 441 Col 442 Henry
    46

MILLIGAN, James 474
MILLS, Ambrose 123 174
   Benjamin 482 Col 83 124 176
   James 482 484
MITCHELL, George 25 480
MIXON, Charles 480
MONTFORD, Joseph 23 477
MONTGOMERY, Miss 379
   William 352 357
MOORE, 28 31 53 426 Alfred 21
   474 Col 54 61 Dempsey 24 480
   Edward 436 Elijah 484 Gen 27
   Isaac 484 James 20 22 26 299
   473 John 52 481 Maurice 26
   Maurice Jr 474 Patrick 77
   Robert 483 Roger 23 478
   William 484
MOREHEAD, James 484
MORGAN, 98 185-186 194 198
   202-205 207-209 212 215-216
   218 224-225 227-233 251 253
   258 270 322 326 335-336 364
   Benjamin 23 477 Capt 403
   Daniel 184 Gen 141 196 200
   210 237 248-249 252 257 321
   340
MORPIS, John 25
MORRIS, Maj 378
MOSELEY, William 480
MOSLANDER, Abel 478
MOSSLANDER, Abel 23
MOSSOM, Richard 485
MOTTE, Rebecca 415
MOULTRIE, Capt 40 Gen 35
MURFREE, 268 Hardy 21 398
   474-475 Maj 266 436-437
MURPHEY, Judge 466
MURPHY, Judge 278
MURRAY, Capt 61 William 478
MYRICK, John 481
NAIRNE, Lord 82
NASH, A 265 Abner 100 178 267
   Clement 475 Francis 20 22 27-
   28 473 Gov 104 143 269 393
NEAL, Capt 154 William 483
NEILL, Henry 474

NELSON, Alex 25 Alexander 478
   John 25 477-478
NEWMARSH, Maj 224
NICHOLSON, Robert 484
NIXON, Thomas 482
NOBLEN, William 481
NORTH, Carolina Colonel
   Williams Of South Carolina
   Recruits His Regiment In
   Rowan County 143 Carolina
   Furnishes South Carolina
   Regiments 441-442 Carolina
   Militia Assault Fort Grierson
   417 Carolina Militia At
   Cowpens 200 Carolina Militia
   Commanded By Colonel
   Malmedy 454 Carolina Militia
   Elect General Andrew
   Pickens To Command Them
   After General Davidsons
   Death 263 Carolina Militia
   Fire Seventeen Rounds At
   Eutaw Springs 453 Carolina
   Militia Five Hundred Of Join
   Greene On The Santee 441
   Carolina Militia Greene
   Orders To Fire Two Rounds
   At Guilford Court-house And
   Then Retire 335 Carolina
   Militia Johnsons Error About
   200-201 Carolina Militia
   Reorganization Of 394
   Carolina Militia Tribute To
   Their Courage 454 Carolina
   Militia Under Major Eaton
   395
NORTON, 368 Col 360 Lieut Col
   315 330
NUTHALL, Nathaniel 483
O'HARA, 116 253 364 366 370 373
   Brigadier Gen 248 315 330
   381 Gen 239 247 249 252 359
   382 Lieut 316 361 381
O'NEAL, 282 Charles 477
OLIPHANTS, Mill Depot
   Established At 393

OLIVER, John 476
ORANGEBURG, Captured 415
ORRELLT, Thomas 485
OUTLAW, Edward 24 480
OVER-MOUNTAIN, Men
　Assemble At Sycamore Flats
　134 Men March 26th
　September 1780 136 Men
　Reach Quaker Meadows 30th
　September 1780 139
OWEN, Stephen 482
OWENS, John 480
PACKETT, William 21
PACOLET, Skirmish At 123
PAISLEY, Samuel 353 William
　353
PALMER, Joseph 479
PARKER, Kedar 480
PARKINSON, James 475
PASTEUR, John 480 Thomas 477-
　478 William 475 477
PATTERSON, Arthur 174
PATTON, Col 42 John 21-22 31
　474-475 Joseph 24 Maj 96
PAYNE, Michael 21 475
PEARCE, George 483
PEARL, James 482
PENDLETON, Edmund 26
PERRY, 218 Sgt Maj 217
PETER, Capt 381
PFIFER, Martin 25
PHIFER, 104 112
PHILIPS, Joseph 478
PHILLIPS, Joseph 25 Samuel 131
PICKENS, 44 205 228-231 273
　276 278 280 283-285 287 300
　303 306 324 340 417 419 421-
　423 Andrew 122 200 210 221
　262 Col 201 211 217 227 288
　Gen 263 274 277 281 297 307-
　308 416 420 450
PICKET, Thomas 474 William 474
PICKETT, Thomas 24
PIERCE, Maj 237 261
PIKE, Benjamin 25 480
PILLEY, John 476

PINCKNEY, Charles 35 46
PITFOUR, Lord 117
PITT, 18
PLUMMER, Daniel 171
POLK, Charles 478 Col 442 458
　Thomas 22 31 116 192 477
　William 28-29 441 483
POLLOCK, Jacob 23 478
PONDER, John 159 162
POPE, Henry 474 482 Willis 25
PORTERFEILD, 87 Lieut Col 96
PORTERFIELD, Col 184 Dennis
　479-480
POTERFEILD, Denny 25
POTTS, Capt 237 247
POWELL, Elias 173
POWERS, James 481
POYNTER, John 481
PRESTON, 285 Col 307-308 324
　John 277 William 311
PREVAT, Isaac 23
PREVOST, Gen 33
PRISONERS, Exchange Of May
　1780 43
PRYOR, J 436
PUGH, Whitmel 476
PULASKI, 118
PYEATT, Peter 484
PYLE, 278-281 284-285 300 306
　344 Col 282 John 283
QUINN, 179 Michael 482 Peter
　147 154
RABB, William 174
RAIFORD, John 475 Robert 482
RAMSAY, 92 302 442 Matthew
　483 Robert 111
RAMSEUR, Stephen D 430
RAMSEY, Allen 481
RAMSOUR, John 125
RAMSOURS, Mill Battle Of
　Grahams Narrative Of 51 Mill
　Battle Of Grave Of Captain
　Dobson At 62
RANKIN, Robert 339
RAWDON, 86 92 401 404-405 414-
　415 423-424 Col Lord 182

RAWDON (cont.)
 Lord 38 48 51-52 87-88 91 116 400 402 411 422 445
READ, 401 Andrew 299 Capt 73 Col 302 389 402 404 407 Dr 252-253 James 298 391 395 429 Sarah 299
REDPETH, John 478
REED, James 474 Jesse 479
REESE, George 483
REINHARDT, Michael 125 W M 125
RESPESS, Richard 482
RHODES, Elisha 23 Joseph 482 Joseph J 484
RICE, Hesekiah 21 Hezekiah 474 483 Jeptha 483 John 474
RICHARDSON, Gen 206 John 485
RIDLEY, William 476
RIFE, Peter 352 357
RIFLE, Against Bayonets 161 Breech-loading Invented By Major Ferguson 82 Deckhard 81
ROBBINS, Wm M 393
ROBERTS, John 479
ROBERTSON, 309 404 Charles 302 Maj 126
ROBINSON, Second Lieut 381
ROCHELL, John 483 Lovick 483
ROGERS, John Jr 478 Patrick 474
ROLESTONE, Isaac 476
ROLSTON, Robert 474
ROLSTONE, Isaac 475
ROSE, Maj 185
ROSS, Francis 483
ROULLEDGE, William 478
ROUNTREE, Reuben 484
ROWAN, Robert 21 474
RUDOLPH, 421 Capt 416 Maj 281
RUGELY, 192
RUSHWORM, Wm 477
RUTHERFORD, 55 91 172 Brigadier Gen 93 Gen 35 52

RUTHERFORD (cont.)
 54 56-57 60 67 83-84 89 92 98 100 102 235 263 Griffith 51 467 James 61
RUTLEGE, Gov 143 269 441
SAINTCLAIR, 323
SALTER, James 475 Robert 475
SALVIN, Lieut 381
SANDERS, 154
SAUNDERS, 435 Jesse 24 480 William 480
SAWYER, Levy 475 William 476
SCARLOCK, James 485
SCHENCK, D 298 488 D R 125 David 487
SCHULTZ, Capt 381
SCHWENER, Lieut 381
SCOTT, 40 Charles 310 J W 487-488 James 246
SCULL, John 474
SEVIER, 126 133 140 164 170-171 173 177 302 309 Col 132 134 136 175 John 75 130 Lieut Col 77 Robert 169
SHARP, Anthony 483
SHARPE, Anthony 483
SHAW, Daniel 480
SHELBY, 125 133 140 148 165-166 169-170 309 Col 77-78 80-81 124 126 131 134 136 141 164 174-175 Evan 172 Isaac 75-76 130 Moses 132
SHEPARD, Abraham 484 William 484
SHEPPERD, James 25
SHERIDAN, Maj 456
SHUTE, Thomas 485
SIMMONS, Capt 51 Richard 275
SIMON, Peter 23
SIMONS, Peter 479
SINGELTON, Robert 485
SINGLETARY, Richard 25 480 William 482
SINGLETON, 323 330 356 361 Anthony 311 322 357 Capt 354-355 393

SITGREAVES, John 24
SLADE, Stephen 475-476 William 477-478
SLAVE, Uncle Mose 318
SLEDGE, Arthur 481
SMALLWOOD, 88 186 Gen 100 102 185 427
SMITH, 223 408 411 Capt 62 412 J Henry 349 Jabez 479 John 222 254 367 407 410 483 Robert 22 24 475 478 Samuel 476
SNEED, Maj 451
SNOWDEN, Lieut 329 Nathaniel 484 William 481
SOUTHALL, Stephen 484
SOUTHERLAND, Ransome 477
SOUTHERN, Provinces Condition Of 1779-80 37
SPICER, John 475
SPRATT, Thomas 483
STANDING, Thomas 475-476
STARRAT, James 25
STEADMAN, 88 91 103 120
STEDMAN, 223 233 343-344 357 383 410 453 Benjamin 24 479 Col 295
STEED, Jesse 484-485
STEPS, James 146
STEUBEN, 432 Baron 272 427 431 433 Gen 452
STEVENS, 88 91 100 287 310 326 348 360 362 Gen 86 191 266 268 273 325 338 347 351 354
STEVENSON, Silas 484
STEWART, 444 Capt 111 Charles 24 479 Col 223 446 448 456-457 459 461 Ensign 381 George 483 Joseph 483 Lieut Col 424
STOKES, Capt 68 John 45 Montford 45
STUART, 3 66 370 374 411 Capt 350 Col 410 Dugald 349 357 Lieut Col 364 367 381 Robert 315

SUGG, George 479
SUGGS, Geo 24
SUMMERS, John 474
SUMNER, 268 429 440 456 Brigadier Gen 396 Gen 100 102 104 267 391 394-395 397-398 418 426-428 430-431 433-434 436-439 453 455 470 Jacky 470 James 25 Jethro 22 31 194 266 425 432 450 468-469 476 Mary 470 Thomas Edward 470
SUMTER, 40 47 81 124 143 415 450-451 Col 67 69-71 186 Gen 97 106 195 413 423 441 443
SWAIN, Gov 75 282
SWANN, Nimrod 478
SWANTON, Capt 381
TALBOT, Ensign 381
TARLETON, 18 44-45 48 51 68 70 73-74 93 106 114-115 119-120 171 181-182 184 186 198 204-205 207-209 212-216 223-224 226-227 230 235 239 245-247 251 275-277 281-286 301 306 315 320 327-329 333 344 357 361-362 368-369 373-374 384 Banistre 203 206 Col 103 112 179 217-218 295 313 343 382 Lieut Col 331
TARRANT, Manlove 475-476
TARTANSON, Francis 482
TATE, 178 209 Capt 329 James 473 Joseph 22 475
TATUM, Abraham 21 Absalom 474 Howell 474 James 483
TAYLOR, John 474 482 Philip 24 480 William 22 479
THACKSTON, James 22 397
THAXTON, James 477
THOMAS, John 483 Maj 82
THOMPSON, Lawrence 21 474 Samuel 480 William 24
TILLERY, John 477
TOCHSEY, William 476
TOOLE, Henry Irwin 21 475

TOOMER, Judge 371
TORRANCE, Tavern Skirmish At 245
TRIPLET, 209
TRYON, 83 Gov 283
TURNER, Benijah 23 Berryman 474 Jacob 23 Robert 24 484
USHER, William 476-477
VAIL, Edward Jr 22 475
VANCE, 221 David 127 220 475-476 John Curton 485 Robert 220 Z B 127 220
VANOY, Andrew 484
VARCAZE, James 484
VARNER, Robert 474
VAUGHN, James 481 Lieut Col 96
VENABLE, Samuel 310
VERRIER, James 478-479 484
VIPON, Henry 476
WADDELL, Mr 371
WADE, Joseph J 483
WALKER, John 21 25 473-475 Joseph 481 Solomon 24 480
WALL, James 485
WALLACE, James 484
WALSH, John 482
WALTERS, William 474
WALTON, William 481
WARD, Edward 482 William 25 479
WASHINGTON, 29 39 42 49 85 89 187 211 217-218 223 256 266 270 274 292 311 326-327 333-334 354 358-359 362 366 369 374 377 386-387 402 405-406 409 411 424 427 469 Col 192 195 202-203 205 215-216 229 237 324 365 368 407-408 457 461 Gen 27 32 41 84 118 186 188 392 Lieut Col 404 President 299 Robert 23 476 William 184 323 451 483
WATKINS, 311 Henry 159 Thomas 303 310 365
WATSON, Col 401 414 John F 28

WATSON (cont.)
Thomas 481
WATTERS, Samuel 474
WEBB, Elisha 481 John 476
WEBSTER, 91 116 315 344 348 350-351 357 362 368 370 373 376 460 Col 115 290 330 345 359 363 371 James 313-314 Lieut Col 87-88 291 308 343 381
WELCH, Maj 61 Nicholas 53
WHEDBEE, Richard 481
WHEELER, 28 69 220 470 Gen 29
WHISTON, Capt 61
WHITAKER, Hudson 481
WHITE, 402 Capt 167 Col 184 John 21-22 475 Joseph 221 Matthew 480 Thomas 25 480 William 481
WHITLEY, John 25
WHITMEL, Blunt 478
WHITSILLS, Mill Fight At 289
WHITTINGDON, 318
WILFONG, John 430
WILKES, 171
WILKINSON, Reuben 478
WILLIAMS, 125 144-145 153-154 164 172 259 289-290 405 456 Benjamin 22 475 Col 78 80-81 124 127 143 152 155 169 247 288 403 451 Daniel 24 480 Gen 143 James 44 142 478 John 22 475 John P 29 479 483 John Pugh 23 Joseph 237 Maj 349 Nathaniel 485 Nathaniel B 482 Otho 95 258 261 274 287 301 311 327 455 Ralph 483 Theophilus 480 William 20 476-478 William B 473
WILLIAMSON, 44
WILMOUSKY, Capt 381
WILSON, 61 248 Col 102 David 52 242 James 484 Maj 55 60 Robert 480 Whitfield 476
WINBORNE, John 481

WINSTON, 136 164 169-170 285
  Joseph 127 302 325 Maj 131
  139 160 300 307
WITHERSPOON, Maj 28 Rev Dr
  28
WITHROW, James 168
WOOD, Matthew 23 477 Samuel
  221 Solomon 482
WOODFORD, 40 Col 35 Lieut Col
  96
WOODHOUSE, John 476
WOOTEN, Shadrach 479
  Shadrack 24
WORTH, Joseph 475-476
WRIGHT, David 484-485
WYLEY, Samuel 48
WYNN, Maj 73
WYNYARD, Lieut 381
YANCEY, Charles 483
YARBOROUGH, Capt 395 419
  Edward 477
YOUNG, Robert 170

www.ingramcontent.com/pod-product-compliance
Lightning Source LLC
Chambersburg PA
CBHW051331230426
43668CB00010B/1234